HORSEMANSHIP

HORSEMANSHIP

A COMPREHENSIVE BOOK ON TRAINING
THE HORSE AND ITS RIDER

by

WALDEMAR SEUNIG

Translated from the German by
LEONARD MINS

COMPLETELY REVISED

DOUBLEDAY & COMPANY, INC.
Garden City, New York

TO MY SONS
WALDEMAR-GEORG
&
GEORG-WALDEMAR

PREFACE TO THE FIRST EDITION

Books do not make a rider good or bad, but they can make him better or worse.

T H E experience gained in forty years spent in the saddle and the repeated requests of friends and fellow riders that I put it down in book form have induced me to publish the present volume.

It is based upon principles that have been proved correct by practical use, and their application within the limits marked out by nature for the individual horse leads most quickly to the desired goal. In this sense, it is a considerably expanded, organically designed, and ordered compilation of ideas and knowledge, some of which I have published in various European technical journals for some years past.

Only in the course of years, as a result of my own experience, have I found confirmation of many truths that I realized in the former Riding Instructors' Institute of Vienna, in the Spanish Riding School, and—to some extent—in Saumur, though as a young rider I was not yet able to realize their interrelationships completely. I was also confronted with dilemmas that seemed to arise from interpretations of the works of masters old and new that were not always correct or stemmed from the fact that an " innovator " employed brilliant dialectics to defend theses that did not stand up under thorough examination.

It is a debt of honour and of gratitude to recall the memory of my revered teacher, General von Josipovich, whose liking for me remained constant through decades. He offered me his help whenever I called upon his clear mind, a mind that grasped all complicated relationships, and showed me the way to maturity and judgment of my own by personal example and the living word. I may, therefore, add that if this book should meet with approval, its success would be chiefly due to the principles and doctrines recognized by Josipovich, for by following them I have been afforded a horseman's pleasures as a Royal Master of the Horse, as the chief riding instructor of a cavalry school, and in the horse shows of our continent, and also led to my selection as a judge in international tournaments.

Horsemanship, which I now hand over to the horseman's world, is not intended to be merely a brief riding manual or textbook—for there are excellent books in this field satisfying all requirements in that they

7

treat the logical structure of training the horse and rider in terse and lucid form. They are not intended, however, to answer the question "Why?" nor can they do so completely. It is left to the riding instructor's judgment to explain the relationship between cause and effect.

Thus the present book is supposed to be more than a riding manual, for it proposes to set forth the component elements of such a manual in their logical sequence by comprehensive analysis of cause and effect, and to provide unambiguous clarification of many problems that are still moot, disputed, and often put aside.

The work of the thoughtful rider not only will prove to be more stimulating but will also approach perfection only if he combines knowledge of the required controls with thorough understanding of the principles and instructions of equestrian doctrine that govern his activity in the saddle.

In this sense, our book is intended chiefly as guide and counsel to the trainer of the young horse coming from the pasture, and we shall accompany horse and rider until the training goal has been reached.

This goal will be limited, of course, by the psychological and physical endowments of the horse and the rider's skill and training objectives. We shall, therefore, discuss both the cavalry and the saddle horse and, on a higher level, the dressage horse. Among tens of thousands of horses, however, one exceptional horse particularly favoured by nature will, in the course of years of work with a master, prove its aptitude for the *haute école*.

Horsemanship is intended to be modern in the best sense of the word, bringing together all that is tried and true in our knowledge of horsemanship. Actually, we know that the relationship between rider and horse is fixed by natural laws that are timeless and belong to no "school", being governed only by physical and mental factors that have remained unchanged since the time of Xenophon. It is equally certain, however, that the rider's skill in making the comparatively great potential force of the horse operate in directions determined by the rider is still undergoing evolution to-day. Whenever a Xenophon, a Grisone, a De la Guérinière, or a Steinbrecht spoke to the horsemen of their age, the art of riding received new impetus; new prospects were opened to it. This evolution is not yet finished, and it will never be, for true art knows no boundaries.

Still, we have made great progress by now. The contributions of animal psychology, dynamics, and kinetography during the last few decades have been supplemented by the literature of hippology (I shall name only Rau and Heydebreck).

The victories in the Berlin Olympics, which were proof of correct training, were the acid test. These victories represent an obligation; they will stay with the younger generation only if the latter continue building on what they inherit from the past.

As may be seen from the Table of Contents, in arranging and organizing the material I have been guided by the fact that the basic training must be the same for every saddle horse, whether it is intended to carry its rider from place to place and over the terrain obstacles of a hunt or in the figures of the *haute école*.

Accordingly, the reader interested in a certain stage of training will find the explanations and instructions he is looking for in the various chapters and their subsections.

WALDEMAR SEUNIG

Stroblhof Castle, Spring 1941.

PREFACE TO THE SECOND EDITION

SEVERAL years have passed since the publication of the first edition of this book, which was written in the shadows of war.

The face of the world, disfigured by deep scars, has changed fundamentally. People are different, too. Friends in whom one believed have disappointed bitterly, while others who were not held in too high regard have proved to be noblemen of the heart. The loss of my home (Stroblhof was destroyed in 1942), the loss of my entire fortune for the third time, and, last but not least, separation from my favourite stallion have devalued things that were sacred to me.

The distress of wartime and the postwar period has again taught us an object lesson that could not be ignored. It concerned everyone and left nothing to be desired in point of plainness. No one could escape it whether he wished to or not.

It sang a dirge of inconstancy, of the evanescence and withering of earthly goods, unprecedented in the past.

And yet! Though irreplaceable cultural values of yesteryear have been depreciated or destroyed, art has not allowed itself to be profaned, it has not fallen victim to irreverent chaos. For art and its teachings are eternal; despite continued creative development, they are not superseded with time, but always emerge victors in their contest with it.

No healthy people, no culture rooted in natural principles, will ever be able to forgo close alliance with the horse and with the happiness it gives us.

In revising the text of the first edition I have not made any material deletions, but I have added much that is new, including matter that I acquired during the war when I directed riding and driving training for armies and army groups.

These comments may therefore serve the purpose outlined in the preface to the first edition. And if the future should want to know the state of horsemanship at the middle of the twentieth century, two hundred years after De la Guérinière, may this book render account honestly, objectively, and *sine ira*. I might speak of the applause with which the critics and friendly readers greeted the first edition of the book, and I might ask that my lifework be received with similar friendliness in its new garb. I do not do so. For, much as I have been honoured and stimulated to new creative activity by the judgment of connoisseurs and virtuosos such as

Josipovich and Rau, the praise of the multitude gives me true satisfaction only if it includes, without flattery, the voices of all those to whom riding and the art of riding are dear for their own sake and for whom the horse —created in an auspicious hour—is the noblest company.

WALDEMAR SEUNIG

Zurich, Summer 1948.

PREFACE TO THE THIRD (AMERICAN) EDITION

I AM delighted that *Horsemanship,* my lifework, which the late Gustav Rau was good enough to call a " gift of Providence to the equestrian world ", is now available in an English edition.

They say, " The rider's education is never finished ", and I have had many opportunities to increase my own experience with horses of all breeds and classes ever since the first edition appeared in 1943.

All of this experience has been drawn upon for the new American edition, and I may be so immodest as to say that the apprentice rider who seeks advice and practical instruction in my *Horsemanship* will find answers to all of his questions—answers that the author has conscientiously tested in the saddle.

As an active participant in past Olympic Games and as the holder of the Golden Cavalry Badge—awarded for victories in international competition—the author hopes that this book may also be of some value to horsemen interested in competition riding.

WALDEMAR SEUNIG

Ansbach, May 1956.

TRANSLATOR'S NOTE

HORSEMANSHIP is the culmination of centuries of tradition and training, teaching and research, on the Continent, where dressage originated and flowered. As the heir to this tradition, Colonel Seunig never took the easy way out in writing his book. Every possible shade of meaning was dealt with in nearly every sentence.

The problems posed by the German original seemed fifty hands high at the outset. There was no equivalent in English for much of the terminology: many of the terms had to be coined anew, such as the differentiation between "unconstraint", "suppleness", and "responsiveness".

One of the pioneer innovations in this translation is the replacement of the antiquated term "aids" (the means of which a horse is controlled) by the simpler and straightforward "controls". (The word "aids" was taken over bodily from the French *aides* at a time when French was the international language of dressage.) Since the rider is supposed to control his horse, this change in ancient terminology will, we trust, make teaching and learning easier for the beginning rider.

I was rescued from the consequences of my rashness in undertaking to do Colonel Seunig's text in English by circumstances fortunately beyond my control: the informed and ready counsel furnished on many occasions by Konrad Fischer of the Kenilworth Riding Club (where the Lipizzan horses were quartered during their visit to this country in 1950) and by Dan Marks, who recently spent several months at the Spanish Riding School in Austria. Nor would the book and I ever have got over the bars without the friendly and untiring assistance of Joseph Marks and his staff at Doubleday & Co.

LEONARD MINS

New York, June 1956.

CONTENTS

CHAPTER THREE

PART THREE: THE *HAUTE ECOLE*

CHAPTER ONE

CHAPTER TWO

CHAPTER THREE

LIST OF ILLUSTRATIONS

Part One

HORSE AND RIDER

THE HORSE

Principles Governing Its Selection

WE shall not discuss the possibility of purchasing an older horse that has seen more or less service from a dealer or from a private owner, since we are concerned in this chapter with ways of approaching the purchase of a foal that may be completely unbroken, perhaps, and of judging such a horse in the light of its future use.

Luckily enough, the three-year-old or four-year-old shown us will not be completely unbroken. In our latitudes it will have spent at least three winters in the stable—the last one on a halter, perhaps, or in a stall of its own. Having its hoof lifted is no longer strange to it, and last year it probably was acquainted with a snaffle, for its farmer breeder used it in light farm work.

Its owner, member of a riding club, has probably already registered and saddled it. This is not objectionable if done properly. Many breeders and growers have acquired such virtuosity in "showing" that the buyer readily tends to consider the gait shown as the horse's natural one. He will then not be spared some disappointment when he finds that his horse will never again travel as well, despite correct training in the saddle, as it did on that bright autumn morning on the imperceptibly rising show track in the castle park.

It is of course a great advantage if the horse is already so accustomed to the saddle that a rider can easily demonstrate its three basic gaits. This can best be done by a friend or a stableman one has brought along, for no power on earth will be able to keep the seller's employees from demonstrating gait and action themselves. In all countries from the Pyrenees to the Vistula I have met with this "passive resistance" against allowing the buyer to show a horse or put it through its paces. Most endeavours to see the horse as God has created it were unsuccessful.

It is a matter of course that one should mount the horse oneself, if at all possible, in order to feel its natural movement. One's own riding is also the test of whether the horse balances under the load as well as its conformation seems to indicate. Your associate will see how the rider and horse fit each other, how the latter is "tailored" to you; and if the horse has

23

been ridden for a few months, the bad habits displayed will offer some indication whether they can be removed during dressage without major difficulty. And at the very outset, when the horse is shown or put through its paces on the snaffle bit, I should like to point out the disagreeable fault of stretching out its tongue. A young horse that puts its tongue over the correctly placed bit at this early date or lets it hang out loosely promises continual mouth difficulties for the trainer, difficulties that always endanger responsiveness to the reins at critical moments even with good horsemanship, especially if this defect has been inherited.

The *size* of the horse is important because it should correspond to that of the rider; that is, when the rider is normally seated in the saddle his knees should be able to lie flat against the side of the horse without projecting beyond the widest point of the chest oval.

Aesthetically, too, it is desirable for a rider with a long trunk to pick a horse with long lines; this also applies to the nearly obsolete side saddle.

A saddle horse can hardly be too small provided it has a deep enough chest and hence is short-legged with low carpal joints. But it can easily be too big, for horses that are more than, say, seventeen hands high are usually not as agile or sure-footed as their fellows of average size. The height of their centre of gravity impairs their ability to balance themselves. And when they fall it is harder for them to get back on their feet, especially if their chests are narrow and their elbows are pressed in. There are weight carriers in Hanover and Ireland, however, up to eighteen hands high that are real life-insurance policies and present a quite harmonious impression. In any event, it is a point in favour of a breed if its bigger, heavier examples make the same typical, sinewy, and swift impression as the lighter horses.

In judging the size of young horses it must not be forgotten that their growth is far from complete at the age of four. Height that exceeds the average does not facilitate training, and big horses require much larger quantities of fodder without being able to do more than smaller horses.

If a horse displays natural mettle and *élan* (which is not the same as high spirits in the stable or excitement produced by general pandemonium), there is every reason to suppose that its erect ears and friendly glance promise willing acceptance of the rider's demands and that it will become a worthy companion without reservation or malice.

If we decide to buy a young horse at an auction, say, at the Trakehnen stud farm, we don't have much time for decision. Still, one did not have to buy a pig in a poke at Trakehnen, for the stud administration made no secret of any defect or blemish, and the horses being auctioned had at least one season of hunting behind them, with the results of this test of constitution and temperament available for inspection. Anyone who bought

Trakehnen horses, preferably at the spring auction where the quality was especially high, did well to bear in mind that their growth would be complete only at the age of six, especially in the case of geldings, and that there would be a change in climate and feeding. Furthermore, because these foals had jumped about like racing horses in the pack during their first easy hunts, their technique would have to be modified, beginning with stepping over bars, in order to turn them into saddle horses and later into show horses.

The greater understanding shown in such retraining and the more time taken with these lovable creatures, confining ourselves to unconstrained saddle riding for a year to a year and a half, the more rapid will later progress be, once they have fully mastered the jump, using their backs, and have completely developed physically. The latter depends often upon their proportion of Arab blood; it is safest, however, not to subject other half-breds to really severe exertion before they have shed their hair in the spring after they are seven years old. This wise self-restraint always pays, for horses treated in this sensible fashion remain fresh and youthful until they are nearly twenty, and sometimes even longer.

We do not intend this to be a comprehensive hippological treatise. We will merely give pointers on conformation, character, and temperament—in so far as these factors can be judged when buying a horse—thus enabling us to predict its subsequent behaviour during dressage.

Let me say at the outset that many a horse that impresses us at rest and when put through its paces, captivating us by a practically perfect exterior, disappoints during training. On the other hand, another horse that was in no way outstanding when purchased, in fact, exhibited many defects of conformation, may later on prove to be far superior to the so-called " model-horse " in the way it uses its " machinery " and in its accommodating spirit, which always adapts to the rider's desires. It is up to the expert to be able to make some sort of prediction during the very first inspection of the horse. This requires knowledge and much experience and still more experience, together with an inborn judgment that cannot be defined but is the one thing that makes the born horseman.[1]

If you are lucky enough to have such an expert at hand (there aren't too many of them), take this prodigy along to the horse sale—you won't regret it.

Hundreds of books have been written on horsemanship ever since

[1] A real horseman must not only be an expert—he must also be able to think and feel like a horse, that is, to realize that a horse is not equipped with *human* understanding. Such a horseman should be both horse and man—a centaur, not only physically, but also psychologically—anthropomorphic and hippomorphic.

Kikulli of Mettani, Mesopotamia, dictated the first rules of hippology (training trotting horses) to priests who took his words down in cuneiform characters on clay tablets around 1400 B.C. They extend from the Greeks Cimon and Xenophon (fifth and fourth centuries B.C.) through Marcus Fugger (1578) and Prizelius (1777)[2] down to the present day. Xenophon is far from obsolete; his remarks on psychology (and on riding uphill and downhill, leading by a nose strap, etc.) have not been superseded by our modern knowledge.

Typical of their period during the past hundred years were Bacsák for Austria-Hungary, Lehndorff, Sr., and Rau for Germany, Gayot for France, Bachofen for Switzerland, and Kozma for Hungary. When we read the classic works of these authors, we feel that they were more than merely qualified. What they did and are still doing for horse breeding will go down in history.

Then it was Dr. Gustav Rau whose counsel was sought and acknowledged as authoritative in all fields of hippology.

The first impression we get as the horse is shown to us should leave us in no doubt that the flat, long, muscular hindquarters are connected with sloping shoulders and a long, well-carried neck through a back that is not too short and through long, pronounced withers. Its steps should be rangy and elastic.

Enough time must be allowed for observation, from *all sides,* that is, in front and behind, during, before, and after movement, in the stable and

---

[2] In his *Complete Hippology*, Prizelius enumerates the titles of 178 basic works already known at that time. Quite a large number when we remember that the riding classes often " had no knowledge of writing because of their high noble birth ".

Here are the most important dates in the history of man's domestication of the horse:

About 2150 B.C. domesticated horses are found as riding and draft animals and as objects of worship in Scandinavia (Scania) and among the civilized peoples of China, India, and Mesopotamia.

About 1850 B.C. horses were introduced into Egypt.

About 1000 B.C. we read that King Solomon is praised as a great horse dealer.

In 677 B.C. the first chariot race (four horses abreast) was held in the twenty-fifth Olympiad.

In 645 B.C. the first galloping race with mounted riders was run in the thirty-third Olympiad.

The Scythians were the first to have an organized cavalry, the Medes (around 630 B.C.) and then the Greeks adopting this military arm. The first races (chariots) were held in Persia in honour of the sun-god Mithra.

Until recently the wild horse, discovered by Przevalsky in Central Asia and named for him, was considered to be the progenitor of our domesticated horse. The latest excavations seem, however, to indicate that our domesticated horse stems from the tarpan, a type of primitive wild horse discovered by the explorer Falz-Fein about the same time in southern Russia. The tarpan itself is the culmination of a long evolution, starting millions of years ago with five-toed animals the size of foxes. The subsequent decrease in the number of toes, reducing contact with the ground when in motion to the absolute minimum, represented an increase in speed and readiness to flee in the unprotected steppes.

in the pasture[3] if at all possible, and in the demonstration ring only if absolutely necessary. This will enable the average judge to make a closer study of the individual parts of the body and their relationship to one another.

A lean, finely chiselled *head*, with strong masseteric muscles, well developed in height and breadth, is an index of great value. Leanness is evidence of mobility and nerve, and divergence of the angles of the lower jaw and adequate space between them testify to good development of the molars, so necessary to digestion.

Concavity of the bridge of the nose, with wide nostrils, is evidence of greater energy of breathing produced by compression and warming up. A slight arch of the line of the forehead between the eyes often indicates a strongly developed wilfulness, which may develop into intractability.

One of the principal attributes of a perfect head is the large *eye,* which should reflect guileless confidence. It should be set low, that is, down towards the nostrils, and should not be sunken. Such an eye will be able to orient itself in the immediate neighbourhood without moving the head, since the large cornea enables much light to enter the eye, and its low position enables the horse to see the ground immediately in front of it without having to lower its head.

The expression of the eye and the set of the ears[4] provide hints of character. An unsteady eye or one that looks "far away" indicates psychological disturbances; a "tranquil ear" indicates inner equilibrium, and short, deeply arched ears are evidence of sensitivity and ability to learn.

But not all breeds can have the heads of Arabs, and we find noble horses of balance and achievement with heavy heads among the Irish and Lipizzan breeds, for example.

The *neck* should be long and free, wide in gullet, that is, thinning down as it approaches the head, with a slightly curved topline and a straight bottom line, the two lines enclosing a broad base that is "set on" the shoulders. Short, heavy necks that are set on low down do not aid equilibrium and hence should be rejected for any usage. But if the set of the neck is good, such a neck can be shaped by stretching it to meet the bit, and its steadiness will make the rider's work much easier. If the neck is thin and set on low, the only thing one can hope for in training is making it steady; one should not try to do violence to nature by demanding that it be held higher as a result of collection.

[3] One should not allow oneself to be deprived of the opportunity of observing a horse at complete ease and in its everyday behaviour. The dealer, however, will not provide this opportunity.

[4] Ears that slant backward are not the same as ears that are laid back. The former are merely an indication of ill-humour or discomfort, whereas the latter are a signal that the horse is ready to kick or bite.

As a balancing rod that promotes motion, the neck plays an extremely important role in the total mechanism of motion. That is why natural carriage of the neck that is altogether too high becomes an obstacle to rapid travel over rough terrain.

Low, short *withers* will never provide a good base for the saddle. The rider's weight thrown too far forward will prevent the horse from achieving balance, the transition to the extended gaits will turn into rushing, and these gaits will never develop smoothly and in correct tempo from freely carrying hindquarters. When we add the danger of pressure owing to the saddle's sliding forward, we can say that blurry "mutton withers" will be a source of perpetual dissatisfaction, no matter how the horse is employed.

If the *shoulder* is long and slopes forward from the withers, we have further guarantee of the formation of a good position for the saddle. A horse with a long neck and withers gives the rider "a lot in front of him," which not only increases his safety but makes it easier for him to have calm nerves in difficult terrain and to maintain the necessary easy control of the reins.

An *arm* of suitable length, connected at approximately a right angle to a shoulder blade covered by well-contoured muscles, guarantees a long-striding step, provided the impulsion and thrust reaching it from the hindquarters are adequate. Without the latter, however, the most splendid pair of shoulders are practically worthless.

Large posterior projections of the ulna in the *elbow joint* are particularly desirable in horses that are destined to do much galloping. If these bony processes (which are important levers) are not "slicked down" and are separated from the side of the chest by at least a finger's width, it may be generally assumed that such an "elbow-free" horse will be able to get out of critical situations skilfully and always remain on its four legs, which will not interfere with one another. Then trotting is done behind the vertical as well as in front of it.

The *forearm* should be long compared to the front cannon and, like the latter, should be broad. Though it cannot be too heavily muscled, the tendons must be well marked on the cannon, and the impression of leanness must not be impaired by any blurredness.

The *front knee* and the *fetlock* will do their job best if they are large enough to provide favourable points of attachment for ligaments and tendons. But both of these joints will not possess much staying power if they are "puffy".

The connection between the cannon and the hoof should be made by a rather long and elastic but strong *pastern*. Too steep a pastern can make an otherwise outstanding horse practically useless. Aside from the fact that the grounding reaction, thudding, is communicated from the hoof to the joints with practically no interruption, thus making premature wear very likely, the inelastic tread also causes premature fatigue of the rider. We might add that horses with upright pasterns take short steps because of the almost vertical, pricking step in their gait, which has little swing to it because it has no phase of suspension; these horses seem to find every little stone in the terrain to stumble over, making one mistake after another.

In conclusion, let me say that if you have to choose between a very soft pastern and one whose angle exceeds 45 degrees, even if only slightly, do not hesitate to choose the "defective" soft one in which the axis of the toe is bent somewhat to the rear; you will not regret it. Owing to its active elasticity, the system of ligaments and tendons that supports and surrounds the treading pastern is much stronger than the bones and joints, which are inevitably damaged if the pastern is too steep. The softer pastern not only ensures a natural mitigation of the impact (landing after a jump) but also promotes the so-called compensating sliding, which allows even hoofs that wear calked horseshoes to slide a bit forward when they land on hard ground. This protects the coffin joint and assists the mechanism of the hoof.

Though catchwords are of little value in judging a horse, where all criticism can be only relative, that is, related to efficiency and kinetics —the way in which a horse makes use of its means of locomotion—I should like to make an exception in this case and repeat the old truism "Without a pastern no horse."

We may suppose that the "necessary evil" of shoeing has not caused any damage in the hoofs of horses that have grown up in the open air. Such horses should be left unshod as long as possible—at most, they should be shod with crescent-shaped shoes on their fore feet. This will greatly promote the circulation of the blood and the breathing of the hoof— gymnastics of the frog. The unshod hoof adheres to smooth ground better, though it cannot be denied that the Mordax antislip calks are very useful on glazed frost or that calked hind horseshoes are necessary for jumping on slippery tournament turf. What one should look for in foals out at pasture is good development of the bars. They act as shock absorbers and protect the joints just as correctly angled pasterns do.

The fore and hind hoofs differ in that the former are somewhat larger and rounder (supporting surface) and the latter are somewhat ovoid (to facilitate thrust). That is why the slope of the hind pasterns (about 60 degrees) should be somewhat steeper than that of the front pasterns.

Backs that are too stiff and straight are passable to-day only for draft animals; but if we intend to ride, we must remember that only a certain length of the back makes possible an unconstrained interaction of the ring of muscles from the croup through the back, the neck, and the belly, and allows the entire mechanism of the horse to swing freely. The length of the back must, of course, be the combined result of long withers, long, straight breastbone (girth furrow!), and a loin of moderate length. Then the loin will be satisfactory, with well-developed lower ribs lying close to the haunches. Such a horse will probably be able to do well on short rations and thus be cheaper to maintain.

A short, "square" horse, in which the distance from the shoulder to the pelvis does not exceed the height at the withers, will always find it hard to keep its balance because of the shortness of its area of support. A long neck—which is a rarity in such horses—may facilitate equilibrium, compensating by its free balancing action.

Much as a pronounced "low point" of the back, in the region of the fifteenth spinal vertebra and at the end of the smoothly sloping withers, is desirable from the standpoint of the rider, extremes should be avoided; unmistakable sway-backs and "hog backs" are causes for rejection. Such backs make extension difficult, imperilling correct dressage as well as the development of speed.

Narrow-chested, long-legged horses will grow tired rapidly, not for want of muscle power, but because the length and curvature[5] of the ribs are too small to provide the heart and the lungs, that is, the breathing apparatus, the necessary room for action. In school training such horses tend to be "cross-legged" in the lateral movements, and since the outer hind foot steps out too far to the side, in the *travers* (also called "*haunches in*"), for example, crossing the line that passes through the centre of gravity, they lose their impulsion and with it their poise and carriage. Moreover legs that are excessively long tend to drag, especially in the collected gaits.

If the *breadth and depth of the chest* are so highly developed that the chest is out of proportion to the rest of the body, we must suppose that such a horse will display a lack of manœuvrability during dressage and insufficient speed.

The *hindquarters* should be long. This is especially true of the distances between the hips and the point of the buttocks, the hip joint and the stifle joint, and the stifle joint and the hock. The latter joint should be as close as possible to the ground, thus providing the desired shortness of the hind cannon. If the angle between the ilium and the thigh bone at the hip joint is just less than a right angle, the stifle joint will lie far in front as a visible sign of this bone structure, and the gluteus maximus muscle will act at a right angle upon the great trochanter of the thigh.

---

[5] The *chest* should be well arched, but, as in all breeds that mature late and are bred for endurance, it should be deep and *long* rather than *round*, with greater curvature in the lower ribs towards the flanks (breathing and fodder-utilizing type). The girth is then six to eight inches more than the height of the horse at the withers.

Stretching and bending then occur under the best circumstances, without any loss of power, and thus promote the gait. If the stifle and hock project to the rear, there is a lack of harmony between the thrust and the ranging action; this results in the ugly " remaining behind " of the hind-quarters and interferes with the harmony of motion, a defect that, like being built too high,[6] is hard to compensate even by perfection of fore-quarters and back.

Broad and strong musculature of the *lower thigh* depends chiefly on the location and size of the most important of the six bones of the *hock*. The longer this bone is and the greater the angle between its axis and that of the tibia, the more room for the development of strong muscles, for then the Achilles tendon is far from the gaskin. And the gaskins are good and wide. This development of the biggest bone in the hock also determines the length and width of the hock itself, to which we must add its depth—the distance between the inner and outer surfaces, the transverse diameter. All three of these dimensions are equally necessary to give this third strongest joint in the horse's body the ability to distribute the pressure of the load of horse and rider (which is often extraordinarily high when striking the ground) and to throw it forward and carry it by means of favourable lever action. The bones and ligaments of this joint must be well defined under a thin skin and must blend imperceptibly into the broad front surface of the hind cannon. These parts of the hind leg, like all the others, must be judged in accordance with the same principles as those used for the forelegs.

If the position of the thigh is correct, steep hocks need not cause too much worry, especially if the hind fetlock is somewhat soft and contributes to absorbing the shock. The forward reach of the hind leg suffers somewhat at the walk, but horses with this conformation can be very useful at the trot and the gallop. The slight extensibility of the angle (which is naturally too wide open in this case) is balanced out by the thrust—the impulsion—which is particularly effective in this case in the suspension phases of these two gaits. But if we try to get from such a horse real flexion and extension, which are required for a correctly ridden middle trot, or an elastic, spirited, springy step in flexion, in complete collection, we will meet the difficulty and realize that nature sets bounds to even the greatest art. However, a hock that is somewhat too sharply angled will certainly not harm a dressage horse if the stifle is at the right location and the thigh is long and sloping. Too open a stifle angle, to be sure, interferes with an otherwise excellent freedom of movement of the hock. It renders

---

[6] The disadvantages of being built too high will be readily seen when the highest points of croup and withers are at the same level. It must be remembered that dorsal processes of the loin and croup vertebrae, as well as an equally long inner angle of the ilium (vertex of the croup), make the croup seem to be higher than it actually is.

long strides in the direction of the centre of gravity impossible, and the hindquarters drag.

Bowlegged horses are susceptible to diseases of the hock, all other circumstances being the same, because of the shocks and load to which that joint is subjected when the angle is unfavourable.

The same holds true of hocks that are too close together or are bowed, the latter defect being more serious, especially when the hindquarters have to execute a turn at the instant they are loaded. As a result, the hind leg evades the correct bending and thus escapes from the rider's control. Whereas the first irregularity, cow hocks, actually assists in overcoming differences in terrain level (as in mountain breeds), and also aids in achieving good performance at the racing trot, bowlegged horses usually lack impulsion and carrying ability. Their hocks provide even worse points of support for the muscles during turns. This impaired machinery often results in diseases of the hock, fetlock, and pastern joints.

Defects of the bone or other leg defects are outside the scope of this discussion. All we need say is that sharply setoff hocks, or even a spavin, a curb, or buck knees that do not result in lameness, are often inborn, like loose knees (though the fetlocks must be normal), and are no reason to reject horses exhibiting these defects.

The more sinewy and highbred the horse, and the tighter and denser the texture of its tendons, muscles, and bones, the less will its efficiency be affected by such defects. The size and location of chestnuts are important—not too near the stifle or too far behind; galls may be the result of infectious diseases, bad stabling and feeding, or too energetic " breaking in " on the lunge. Premature use, especially after gelding, also produces galls. Once the horse has galls, they will return after strenuous exercise, no matter how they have been treated—with heat, plasters, or massage. Once the capsular ligaments and tendon sheaths have been stretched too much, they always fill up with a liquid secretion. As long as the galls are soft, they do not interfere with the elasticity of the gait, but they do betray a certain constitutional weakness. I do not know whether galls can be made to disappear forever by cellular therapy.

Even the horse that is not yet in riding condition should exhibit the contours of distinct *muscles,* which we must look for in front and from the rear. The musculature should reveal a predisposition towards a wide framework, particularly when looked at from behind, for a horse with weakly developed, short rump and thigh muscles which cover the femur and the tibia will be unable to make full use of its motive power.[7]

Although theoretically the bony processes should have spacious and

[7] The rump muscles are well developed naturally in young horses that are destined to become good dressage horses, so that the gap between the thighs seems narrow.

1. Grand Quadrille of the Spanish Riding School. Entrance at the collected walk. Salute.

2. Grand Quadrille of the Spanish Riding School. Reprise at the collected trot.

3. Middle trot. Thoroughbreds frequently become the best dressage horses. Exemplary classical seat. Colonel F. Buerkner on *Caracalla* (Thoroughbred).
4. Traverse (half pass) right in trot. Jessica Newberry on *Forstrat* (Thoroughbred) 1960. VEDEL'S REKLAME-FOTO

5. Collected trot without stirrups. Only by frequent riding without stirrups can a correct seat be attained. Dan Marks on *Sultan* (Trakehnen) 1955.

wide areas for the attachment of the muscles and sliding surfaces, the distance between the two external angles of the iliac crests, the hips, is comparatively small in horses that are often very powerful. On the other hand, the distance between the stifle joints cannot be too large when viewed from the rear; it should be larger than that between the two seat bones (ischia), as Rau has often emphasized.

Once we are behind the horse, we should check whether its hips are the same size or whether it suffers from one-sided dystrophy, an indication of a disease of the leg, usually spavin.

From this position the observer may notice the wobbling swing of a large *belly*. If the horse is young, we need not worry; on the contrary, it is evidence that it was not held on short rations of roughage. It would be a great mistake to try to accelerate the disappearance of this foal belly by withdrawing roughage too suddenly. A tucked-up belly (shad-bellied) is much more dangerous, but if it is due merely to scanty hay rations and too little pasturage, it can be partly corrected by the time the horse is six years old.

The *posture of the legs* should be regular, that is, vertical, with the front legs and hind legs aligned when viewed from the side (also see p. 279). The same holds true for the near and off pairs of legs, which may be checked by having the horse walked or trotted straight ahead to and away from one.

Minor defects of posture may be ignored in high-blooded horses that are not intended for stud uses; these defects will not prevent them from surpassing many a " perfect " model that lacks expression and verve.

Though a book on horses published recently that has had wide circulation states that " the *tail* is of importance only for the *appearance* of the horse," this assertion cannot be allowed to go unchallenged no matter how great our respect for the authors. The tail, by the way in which it is carried, by its silky hair, by the energy with which it resists being lifted, and by the way in which its vertebrae and hair freely swing in the rhythm of motion, may become an important supplement to the patent of nobility constituted by the head. Moreover it furnishes us with information concerning the horse's character, vital energy, verve, constitution, and degree of natural tension, the tone. The various things that an attentive observer can learn from the carriage and movements of the tail of a horse carrying a rider belong in a later chapter. The tail becomes a real barometer that infallibly indicates whether the activity of the back is correct, whether one side of the horse is stiff, whether the horse is pulling or is tired, and whether its rider is misusing his spurs consciously or unconsciously. In short, an expert can read the entire history of the horse and rider from this barometer.

In our case the tail reveals more than pedigree and general vigour. If the horse suddenly stiffens its tail when we inspect it in the stable, it either fears punishment for some stable vice or is excessively timid; it may also be preparing to kick. Trembling of the dock when it is led out of the stable indicates that the seller has "improved" its action by artificial means —pepper.

The first few caudal vertebrae, as a continuation of the sacrum, follow the direction of the croup; when the croup is horizontal the rudiment of the tail is too, being carried in a beautiful arch far from the point of the buttocks. In this case beauty of form is achieved at the expense of efficiency, unless the disadvantages of a horizontal croup—the unfavour-able angle for transmitting impulsion and the diminished carrying capacity—are not partly compensated for by other favourable elements of conformation. If the dock is not a continuation of the sacrum but is clamped between the buttocks, it is an infallible sign of low endurance and low-grade constitution. There are riders who are able to reshape even an unprepossessing exterior by appropriate work, so that we would not re-cognize the unassuming little horse a few months later. They are trainers who actually become sculptors. Together with the muscles of the back, they have activated the levator muscles of the tail and thus produced a quite acceptable carriage of what was formerly a dangling tail. Still, riders who can do this are rare, and you should not count on one's being able to do too much in this respect.

Docking is no longer fashionable, and the new fashion has won the gratitude of everyone but the coachman, whose life is made miserable by tails that catch the reins, and the lovers of the draft horse, who can only imagine the majestic hindquarters of a Percheron decorated with a micro-scopic dock. To be sure, the round or sloping croup of a show horse does not show up well with a long tail. Nevertheless, even hackneys, which tend to this form of croup, have not been docked in England since 1950, as far as we know.

How much short-tailed horses suffer from flies is best illustrated by the custom in certain pasture regions of France of paying much less per day for pasturing docked horses than for long-tailed horses who can polish off large quantities of meadow grass without interruption.

If to-day we have horses that are better jumpers than we had in the past, it is—in addition to the basically changed jumping technique and jump seat—somewhat due to the fact that the primary balancing staff, neck and head, and the more modest complement, the tail, have been given the function for which nature intended them.

As for the *colour* of a horse, one should not insist on a certain colour for sentimental or other reasons unless one is a circus director or under-taker. For the old proverb "A good horse never has a poor colour" may be rephrased as "Not every horse with a good colour is good", and the disappointment we may feel with Apollo may cause us to have an unjustifiable prejudice against its wholly blameless coat.

It would never occur to anyone to select a light-maned sorrel or a light chestnut with " green " legs because of its striking colour unless it had other quite exceptional properties. This is hardly ever the case, however, in animals with a coat of poor, blurry colour.

Sometimes white marks are fashionable, and at other times they are considered " the devil's fingerprints ". The only ones who always dislike them are the stablemen, who have to clean them. It is also a fact that dressage riders dislike crooked blazes or individual white legs, for it is said that there are judges who have fallen victim to optical illusion and spoken of " crooked carriage of the head " or " gaits that are not quite pure " when the horses have gone through their paces like " dolls ".

I shall spare the reader the many proverbs and sayings concerning the colours and markings of a horse. They have been cited repeatedly in the literature, and they seem to me to be of no more than historical value, for they contradict one another, depending on the latitude, the era, and the nation of riders who coined them.

What is most important in a saddle horse is no doubt its *gait,* that is, the way in which it uses its legs in motion. If it engages its legs far forward and easily, and if they spring away from the ground without sticking there too long, the gait is elastic. Elasticity signifies endurance and speed, and that is power. That is why we are justified in saying that if the gaits are good the structure is good.

In the following chapters, dealing with training, we shall discuss gait and the thrust and impulsion developed during gymnastic exercise, because purity and improvement of gait are, together with contact with the bit, proof of the most consistent dressage At this point we shall deal with it only in so far as it is able to give us hints of the natural mechanism of the young horse we are observing and of its capacity for development. In this sense, and framed as a definition, *gait is the natural tendency of a horse to move forward freely when not carrying a load.*

The better the build and the more harmoniously weight and muscle are attuned to each other, the more graceful, the lighter, and the more nearly correct will the gait seem to be.

As long as the untrained horse carries no load, its hind legs will tread the ground either flabbily or with a light springy step, depending on its predisposition and the prevailing circumstances, but they will not provide much thrust because the incentive, load and influence, is lacking.

Though we could not insist strongly enough, when inspecting the horse in its stall, that it be allowed to stand before us completely free of constraint (advancing a front leg is always suspicious), we must also insist that it walk and trot past us freely when it is put through its paces attached to a halter. It must not be incited by music, whip, stablemen "accidentally" located behind corners and bushes, and the other tricks and pyrotechnics customary in that part of the country to produce gaits that one will probably have admired for the first and last time on the day of purchase.

A specialist will not be fooled even by this sort of act, but will be able to judge what part of the display produced in the artificially stimulated state can be reproduced in refined form after months of bending and stretching of the hindquarters and what is nothing but exalted action that is totally unrelated to gait. The average rider, however, will be unable to improve the natural gait by means of gymnastics without assistance and an instructor. Such horsemen should therefore observe the natural gait of the unsaddled horse, because this is the most that it will display later on when saddled, once it has grown accustomed to carrying a load and certain muscles have been strengthened. I am deliberately choosing such a borderline case for the sake of completeness, for as we go along we shall prove that a horse that spends its whole life moving about in "natural posture" will not enjoy life as much as a horse that has learned in dressage to relieve the load on its legs by using a co-operating, springy back; this will keep it young and fresh to a ripe old age.

Thus continued riding in natural posture is justified only by the rider's incompetence or his lack of time to "make" an older horse, or for individual specimens of German, Irish, or French breeds that possess exceptionally favourable structure combined with activity. Such exceptional horses "mounted by a stallion", which are naturally in good *equestrian balance,* so to speak, are rarities, however; they are usually exorbitant in price and in any event not to be discovered upon command.

To those however who do not consider riding merely a healthy form of massage or a means of transportation when the motor car breaks down in the mountains or elsewhere—and the author is concerned only with those for whom association with horses is a vital necessity and the content of their lives—let me say that a walk and a gallop that are inherently bad can be improved only little by dressage, though wrong dressage can make them much worse than they were to begin with. A mediocre trot affords somewhat greater room for development, but only those horses that have inherited the proper build and have strengthened it by pasturage are able to achieve the light, free, and long-striding, springy step of the forehand with engaged haunches, even after dressage by an expert. A good walk is certain evidence of an equally good gallop, but it is by no means evidence of an efficient, ground-covering trot, which is a function not only of a satisfactory mechanism but also of satisfactory verve and impulsion.

We see the most experienced and best riders not trying for the impossible in the improvement of defective gait; in selecting their horses they attach the greatest value to a well-developed mechanism present at birth. This is found in a *rectangular horse* (height at the withers less than length of the trunk) with long shoulders, forearms, thighs, gaskins, and comparatively long back, such as are desired to-day by breeder, farmer, and rider alike. Only such a frame will guarantee the springy co-ordination of all parts in motion without loss of power and contribute best to the impulsion developed subsequently by the rider. It is understandable that a horse of good conformation will also have a pleasant disposition. Its back will vibrate more easily, and hence the pains that are unavoidable during dressage will be much milder, so that there will be less and less occasion for stiffness and cramps.

Now to the showing itself, which must be supplemented by quiet observation in the pasture if it takes on the aspect of a country fair, as described above.

When the horse is shown in free action, the hind hoofs should tread two or more hoof-widths in front of the foreleg hoofprints at a walk. This forward engagement of the hind legs accords with their job of acting as lever and support in the direction of the centre of gravity, which is shifted forward in free, unconstrained action.

We will then see that small, short-legged horses that are deeply built, with long shoulders and gaskins, possess strides that often exceed those of horses that are much larger and have much longer legs, provided, of course, that both display the same angle and impulsion of the hindquarters.

Horses that are too high in the rump will often have their hindquarters step far beyond the tracks of the front hoofs, but their walk is only apparently ground-covering, since the harmony between hind and forequarters is disturbed. The latter take short steps into the ground if the horse does not have exceptionally good development of its neck and shoulders. Measurements made by Perkuhn and Magnus have given us interesting information concerning the expansion of the withers by nearly an inch during three-quarters of a year of dressage. But reshaping such " downhill " horses, which will always have difficulty with the position of their saddles and the equilibrium of their gaits, is a true labour of Sisyphus, and everyone desiring untroubled pleasure in the saddle should be advised against it.

In the *trot* the natural thrust is more sudden than it is at a walk, and it hurls the body forward, so that the length of stride is increased by the distance covered in the suspension phase. Without external inducement the hind hoofs will just about reach the tracks of the front hoofs even when the horse's mechanism is perfect. But if increased thrust and natural swing are added, which should be produced by a touch of the whip *by way of exception in this case only*, remounts that have the right conformation for trotting will repeat the picture of the hind legs' exceeding the front hoofprints by a considerable distance that we described above in our discussion of the walk.

In contrast to the walk, natural thrust and impulsion from the hindquarters at the trot can even compensate for obvious defects of the forequarters, which by themselves afford only mediocre propulsion and ground-covering. Examples of this are the racing trotters, which formerly very often had a steep pair of shoulders.

It is best to observe the *gallop* of remounts at the end of their run. The more freely and smoothly the successive jumps sweep over the ground and the more ground they cover (without harsh repetition), the better the gallop. Further information about the foal's action at the gallop will be provided by observing it in playful competition with its companions in the pasture.

As we are dealing with the purchase of young horses that have been ridden little or not at all, it will not always be possible to try them out in the saddle. This, however, is the most important and decisive factor in choosing horses already accustomed to carry a rider.

The foregoing far from exhausts the topic of gait, but because the way in which the horse uses its legs has the greatest influence upon its training, the gait, its development, and mistakes that may occur, will always be referred to in the following chapters that deal with dressage. Additional information needed for understanding will be given at the proper places.

Let us say at the outset, however, that no branch of equitation has been wrapped in so much mystery or contains so many traditional errors as the theory of motion.

If we have to choose between mare and gelding, and if they are of approximately equal quality, the *gelding* should be preferred. With such a horse we are not only protected against the often rather unpleasant circumstances attendant on heat but usually have a guarantee against excessive sensitivity.

A horse should not develop into a kicker if it is handled correctly, but we must admit that kickers do exist and that about eighty per cent of the horses displaying this vice are mares. Though we do not deny that the great tournament champions include many mares, it is nonetheless true that geldings are superior in dressage and jumping. Generally speaking, it seems that the vital energy of highly bred mares is best employed in distance races and cross-country riding, as the names of many winners of such tests indicate.

It is certain that the psychological equilibrium of the gelding, which is less easily shaken, enables it to undergo a test of considerable difficulty with greater composure, whether in the dressage rectangle or the jumping enclosure.

This sensitivity of mares (which may develop into ticklishness, with squealing and swishes of the tail, if they are not handled correctly) and their tendency to be built somewhat higher in the hindquarters are other factors that make it inadvisable to select a mare if a gelding of equal value is available.

Colts should have been gelded, if possible, in the spring of their second year, that is, as yearlings; then their hindquarters and loins will have developed in full harmony with their backs and forehand, and the general impression will not be disturbed by a stallion's neck.

There are breeds, like the Arabs, Lipizzans, or Barbs, whose males are not subjected to a castration that can be called completely unnecessary in their case. As saddle horses they retain all the charm of careless nature and good disposition, that is, spirit (animation combined with grace), gentleness, mettle, and understanding. When we look at such *stallions* we understand the suffering of many breeders who would prefer not to have any of their beautiful foals gelded, " for then ' he ' isn't a whole horse any more! "[8]

Recently the quadrilles and demonstrations of stallions, young and old, at every time of day and night, in tourneys in the open air and in covered stadiums, have overcome the prejudice against " the stallion, a tempestuous animal ". But this prejudice was not entirely unfounded. Only selected breeding for disposition and character plus the kind and consistent training of the young horses by the stud farm personnel have made it possible for half-bred four-year-old stallions to spin about in the apparently wild figures of a jumping quadrille to the sound of music, under floodlights, and to the thunderous applause of thousands of spectators in the hall, and then to let themselves be used as unruffled jumping horses.

Notwithstanding the stallion's higher intelligence and increased perceptive faculties, which aid in dressage up to and including the *haute école,* the civilian or military rider, no matter how experienced a horseman he may be, would be well advised not to buy a stallion of a Western breed.

The fact that there are some unbearable and difficult Arab and Lipizzan stallions and Anglo-Norman stallions that are as gentle as lambs and can be ridden even by children and young girls on every occasion, provided they are not subjected to erotic temptations, are merely exceptions that prove the rule.

In this connection it should be added that you should get a written guarantee against the failure to remove both testicles in geldings, which is not always readily detectable but can later get you into the most difficult situations. Likewise, before making the sale final, you must insist upon a detailed investigation of the eyes by a specialist equipped with the necessary ophthalmoscope. A predisposition to ticklishness and kicking is

[8] The French characteristically call a stallion a *cheval entier.*

revealed by stroking the back, croup, and hind legs with a riding crop.

Since whistling and the heaves may occur as the consequence of foals' diseases (acclimatization), the possibility of such diseases must also be considered in pasture horses that have never borne the burden of a rider. Observation of the nostrils and the walls of the belly after letting them run for a *long* time at a good pace on the lunge, and of the characteristic noises during this run, provides the expert with the necessary information.

In the foregoing paragraphs we have tried to point out the most important physical properties that must be present in some degree to afford any guarantee that the young horse, the remount, will at least turn into an average saddle horse than can be used in many ways. During its training the skill of the horseman will consist, first, in calling upon parts of the body that are particularly well developed for increased activity by exercises that are appropriate to the individual case; second, in developing the weaker parts gradually by making demands on them that increase imperceptibly; and third, in involving all the forces that the horse does not voluntarily put at the service of correct walking and load-carrying by means of appropriate influence. Art and skill are used to strengthen what is weak and to release what is concealed, so that with patient and understanding labour the *goal of training—harmonious unison of activities of all muscles developed to the limit of their perfectibility and placed at the service of the rider without resistance—*is attained.

But the greatest art and skill cannot replace what is naturally lacking or is highly infirm, such as the hindquarters. To save disappointment later this must be kept in mind when a young horse is purchased.

It is fairly certain that the young horse we are inspecting is better than average provided it has verve, outstanding conformation, and gait. Only after years of work will this be proved, however, for not until then will we have complete information concerning three factors that exert a decisive influence upon the value or worthlessness of a horse, namely, *constitution, disposition,* and *character.* If these three factors are not present in the desired degree, any outstanding achievement is questionable.[9]

To judge the constitution of the young horse, that is, its hereditary power of resistance against influences that damage its organism, such as over-exertion, poor or inadequate feed, and colds, we call upon its pedigree for assistance. We can infer the presence of certain excellent qualities from the relationship of the horse to certain families, especially in the thoroughbred. The leanness and the prominence of the tendon and joint

[9] The capacity for achievement is visible (even to the expert) only to a certain extent in the exterior of the horse.

apparatus are also evidence of the potentialities of the respiratory, circulatory, digestive, and nervous systems, even under the thick layer of fat and flesh of the foals paraded before us in pasture condition. But we will be able to get a final verdict on the constitution of our horse only when we ask it to do hard work within the framework of the purpose for which it was bought and observe its carriage and every stirring of life, including what seems to be the least significant, before, during, and after performance.

Nor will matters go very differently in our judgment of disposition and character. They will be revealed only during work, when greater demands are made of the horse. Only after the remount (which is as yet undeveloped and not in full possession of its strength) has displayed its *activity*—its animation[10]—will we be able to say that our horse has a good, lazy, or too lively disposition.

This is also how we learn whether its character, that is, its nature, is good, refractory, or fearful, the latter characteristic often being coupled with good nature.

If we succeed in finding a horse of good disposition with a bit of liveliness, we have hit the jackpot. Such a horse trusts its own strength and its own bones and will not lose its head nor give up even in critical situations, provided it has the required freedom of the reins; and when it works it will go forward pleasantly on its own.

As disposition and, above all, character can be recognized completely only during the course of training, it is natural that their psychological effects upon the body of the horse can be dealt with from case to case as we discuss training.

When inspecting the untrained horse we must not allow ourselves to be deceived by stable mettle or spirit that is artificially produced. When the dealer shows us a young horse at a cadenced trot, snorting and with its tail fluttering like a banner in the wind, this is no guarantee that we will not find it to be a lazy and obstinate horse in our own stable. On the other hand, a sloth languidly swinging along may turn into an eager, good walker once it has put on muscles and attained full possession of its strength.

The eyes, the set of the ears, and the tail are signs of disposition and character. Horses with fearful, little eyes that have an evil or far-off look promise nothing good—leave them alone! We are often tempted to buy a good-looking two-year-old. We intend to let it run free for a year or two in the little pasture alongside our house in the country and then to begin work with the lunge and riding. Tempting as this may appear, I must advise against it. The low price due to the youth of the foal is

[10] The ancients had the right word for the fiery, active horse, *impatiens otii* (impatient of idleness).

balanced out by the subsequent cost of feeding and care, and we cannot always predict how the young animal that looks so attractive now will grow up. And then one must remember that only a very large pasture, such as that usually found only in stud farms, gives the foal the opportunity of really stretching its legs in long gallops. It has no such opportunity in small pastures. Joints and tendons that have no occasion to do so will not develop adequately, and heart and lungs that can never work at top speed will not enlarge the chest. Instead of the harmonious horse we expected, we will be shocked two years later to see a slab-sided, short-ribbed, long-legged, and narrow-chested hay eater.

CHAPTER TWO

THE RIDER

I. The Rider's Physical and Psychological Qualifications

JUST as we speak of born judges of horseflesh, so there are *born riders*. They really exist and are not the product of the imagination of a romantic poet.

A person who receives certain physical and psychological qualities at birth will make faster progress than his companions when learning to ride; he will more rapidly master the difficulties that every human body must overcome before it adapts to the movements of the horse in the balanced seat. And once such a rider has learned his craft and devotes himself to training young horses or to correcting difficult and spoiled horses, this superiority becomes even more prominent.[1]

Such a gifted rider always possesses *equestrian tact,* which is the special ability to do precisely the right thing, what is called for by the machinery and the psychological state of the horse at any given moment, or to avoid doing the wrong thing.

Anyone who combines a free, and therefore "feeling", seat with love for the horse, industry, endurance, psychological equilibrium, adaptability, and experience will acquire equestrian tact up to a certain degree, but only the born rider, the man with a talent for riding, will display it to perfection, for this man also possesses the gift of diagnosis, a gift that can be developed only if it is inborn, as in a great physician.

As the brilliant Italian Alvisi put it: "A good rider is a psychologist who knows himself and his horse. But he is also his horse's doctor; if his treatment is wrong, he makes matters worse, that is, he intensifies the error. . . ."

There have been talented horsemen who have charted new paths and made positive contributions to horsemanship. The history of cavalry tells

---

[1] Before World War I, and before riding clubs took over pre-military training, the German cavalry looked with disfavour upon the groups who "already knew how to ride". The undeniable advantage of greater familiarity with the horse was out-weighed by the handicap of a faulty seat that had already become habitual. It always took a long time to root out these bad habits before any work of development could be planned (as in the retraining of badly ridden remounts).

of these few outstanding masters who have influenced the development of the art for nearly twenty-five hundred years.

The appearance of these geniuses always marks an auspicious hour for horsemanship: Xenophon (fourth century B.C.), Caracciolo (sixteenth century), Newcastle (died in 1675), De la Guérinière (died 1751), Seeger (died 1865), Seidler (died 1880), Steinbrecht (died 1885), Caprilli (died 1907), Heydebreck (died 1935), Josipovich (died 1945). Their schools signify epochs of horsemanship, milestones on the road to new knowledge.

Our list omits the names of many whose systems and personal horsemanship reveal indisputable traits of genius. When we think of Baucher —not the Baucher of his stormy youth, of course, the object of ridicule and caricature, the scarecrow of grotesque backward riding—or Fillis, who won over even the pedants of horsemanship by the captivating *brio* of his performances, or D'Aure and others, we freely confess that we neither can nor want to resist their dynamics. And why should we? They were all blessed by the genius of horsemanship. Their theories did not endure because their systems contained much that was false, based upon wrong assumptions, as well as much that was good and positive. They lacked the only thing that guaranteed life and permanence: inner truth.

The work of these innovators was fruitful and beneficial, however. Only the rider who was casual, and therefore worthless, could remain indifferent to their amazing skill, which often rose to the level of true art. All those to whom horsemanship was dear were challenged to take a stand; and out of the ferment, the clash of ideas, clear and definite perceptions crystallized—often only after decades.

Baucher's and Fillis's systems are governed by a law whose inexorable rigour controls the development of any art, for every art must go astray, lose its vitality, and degenerate into magic when its principles and forms of expression depart from natural sources. Fillis remained an artist only so long as his Germinal and Markir displayed the apotheosis of pure gaits. When he "invented" new figures, he was nothing but a tremendously skilled necromancer and trickster, and his great art turned into flashy affectation.

The rider whose *figure* facilitates balance and control is at a great advantage. In general a slender figure of medium build (the asthenic-leptosomic figure) is to be desired because such a figure makes it very much easier for the rider to select a horse that fits him well, that is, "tailored" to his figure. If we were to make comparisons with daily life, the figure of a runner or dancer is similar to that of the "rider's figure". The short-legged rider, with an athletically developed upper body, whose knotty wrestler's musculature has a tendency to cramped contraction, will find it hard to keep his balance, and even harder to moderate the control exercised by his hand. The layman, to be sure, considers either the lightweight jockey or the martial guardsman the ideal figure of a rider, though both of these types really find it very hard to control horses that are not "tailored" to their figures.

Since it receives the impulses of the moving horse, on the one hand, and transmits the riding controls originating in the small of the back, on the other, *the base of support* plays a dominant role, together with the legs and the hands. It consists of the *thighs* and *pelvis,* which are connected together in the hip joint.

If the pelvis is low and narrow (that is, if the distance from the ilium to the lower edge of the ischium is small and the distance between the two ilia themselves is relatively small), the centre of gravity is low and more stable, even when the upper body is sitting straight and unconstrained, as in the normal seat. This increases the rider's ability to urge the horse onward, unless the lower end of the spinal column—the pelvic vertebrae—slopes too much to the rear and thus affords only slight support to the ischia when it is thrown forward. And if the buttocks are too fleshy, we get an even greater impression of a base of support slipping to the rear. As a matter of fact, the surplus flesh that sticks out behind interferes greatly with the pushing forward of the buttocks, which can act as an impelling force without the assistance of other parts of the body only if the rider's weight acts upon the dorsal processes of the horse's spinal column (which are vertical in this region) at an angle that is at least 90 degrees.

The principle that only an extended surface of contact affords stability, plus breathing and swinging in time with the mechanism of the horse, is satisfied by a thigh that is flat on its inner surface. Anyone who is not born with this fortunate configuration, which is a great advantage for a solid seat in the saddle—and in this respect we men have an advantage over the fair sex—will have to spend years massaging the disturbing, round fleshy muscles to the rear until he obtains the desired "flat thigh". The best cure is riding without stirrups and often pulling one's body forward.

Well-shaped thighs afford still another advantage. When turned inwards from the hip joint and lying flat with relaxed, opened buttocks, they naturally cause the *knee* to take the right position—"slapped on the saddle like a hunk of raw meat", as a chief riding instructor of the Spanish Riding School of Vienna used to put it.

The proper position of the knee, about which so much has been said and for which so many remedies have been offered, is a result of just placing the base of support correctly and throwing the small of the back forward. This must precede every control, and it will make the rider "grow longer from the hip joints downward" and "grow taller from the hips upward".

Anyone who is master of his seat and his controls will be able to do without the pampering knee pads sewn underneath the saddle flaps.[2]

A good knee position never becomes a problem for the well-set-up rider if he is properly instructed, though it costs the rider not so well favoured by nature considerable sweat. He must undergo wearisome massage, for a steady, absolutely fixed knee is an indispensable prerequisite for success, both for the dressage rider and for the rider who hopes to pluck the laurels that hang somewhat lower over tournament jumps. He will jump his horse satisfactorily only if his knee, now justifiably supported by those beloved pads, constitutes the sole stationary pole for the other parts of the body, some oscillating downward and others upward and forward.

For aesthetic reasons we should like to see everyone born with straight *legs,* though moderate knock-knees have never prevented anyone from sitting a horse well; the other extreme, a flat, closed knee position, is not at all helpful, although the layman often regards bowleggedness as a characteristic feature of a " rider's figure ".

High *shoulders* always give the appearance of constraint or neglect; they also raise the rider's centre of gravity somewhat higher (which does not help balance, if we are to split hairs).

Too short a *neck* gives the impression of squatness, especially as it is usually combined with high, heavy-set shoulders. It is not merely a matter of external appearance when we demand that thrown-back shoulders be set off by a freely rising, well-proportioned neck.

The *spine* is the stem to which head and limbs are attached. It is more flexible at two points: the neck, where the vertebrae of the back are loosely jointed to the cervical vertebrae, and the small of the back, where they are connected to the pelvic vertebrae mentioned above.

The *upper body,* that is, the part of the body above the hips or above the pelvic hinge, anatomically speaking, that is supported and outlined by the spinal vertebrae (except in cases of obesity, which we trust is not the case), should be able to assume the upright posture of the normal seat, in which it can remain longest and most comfortably without growing tired. This posture is promoted by a naturally straight spine, that is, a spine approaching a flat S shape, which facilitates control of the horse in general.[3]

The spinal column itself is buried under masses of tissue, and the length of the approximately horizontal spinous processes varies, so that the out-

---

[2] Pads should be used only for horses that are so narrow-shouldered that the pads must take over the shoulder's role of supporting the saddle and knee; they support the seat and thus indirectly assist the horse's mouth in jump training and in hunting as well.

[3] The nature of the *normal seat* will be discussed in greater detail in the following section, " Seat and Controls ". In this seat the line from the hips to the lower edge of the ischia coincides with the plumb line passing through the rider's centre of gravity, provided the pelvis rests vertically upon its supporting surface: the back of the horse moving in equilibrium.

line of the spine indicated by their ends does not provide reliable information on the course of the vertebrae proper (which is the only thing that
matters). It is difficult, therefore, to fix the actual path of the spinal
column, so important for seat and driving, even when the body is exam-
ined in the nude. Only a driving ability that is naturally favoured by a
comparatively straight spinal column can furnish us with objective information on this point.

Another valuable physical property of a rider is his ability (which is
partly inborn) to contract his muscles elastically rather than convulsively.

Once such a rider has profited by the initial lessons of the balanced seat,
and provided no nervous feelings of fright, that is, psychological cramps,
cause him any physical cramps, he will make rapid progress.

I should like to quote an old proverb: "There is more than one way
to run." Just as classic races are won by thoroughbreds whose configuration is anything but perfect, there are and have been riders who do not
meet the canons set forth above in many respects but still have managed
to achieve an enviable degree of skill and great success as a result of
fanatical zeal, energy, and passion. On the other hand, I know riders
with the figures of an ephebe who barely achieve mediocrity as riders, for
they lack the spirit that conquers stubborn matter and makes it serve its
purpose!

Xenophon, as well as the history and legends of antiquity, proved that
animal psychology is not a recent science, although since its revival by P.
Scheitlin of St. Gall (1840) and its expansion in the last hundred years, it
has become a full-blown science.

When Alexander the Great tamed Bucephalus, he succeeded, not because of the Macedonian prince's firm seat, but because of his mental
attitude, for he had thought his way into the horse's soul. Parenthetically,
Alexander's steed owed its not very pretty name "Oxhead", the literal
meaning of Bucephalus, to the brand that its Pharsalian breeder had
applied to its right shoulder in accordance with the prevailing custom of
the time. Alexander was the first practical animal psychologist, and who-
ever has to handle horses should also be one. The fine sensitivity revealed
in the writings of Xenophon did not survive the period of Hellenic culture.
There were grave throwbacks to barbarism in this respect, owing partly
to the brutalization of the times and partly to a lack of interest in the
emotions of the animal, which was supposed to be destined by the Creator
to be a submissive slave (the Cartesian approach). In the sixteenth century, when the Inquisition and witchcraft trials were in full bloom, the
Italian Grisone gave horsemen the following advice: "If your horse
comes to a halt or goes backwards, place a man behind it, provided with a
vicious cat tied to a long pole in such a way that she lies belly upward
with the free use of her claws and teeth. The man should hold the cat

close to the legs of the disobedient horse so that she can bite or scratch it," and "if a young horse refuses the very first time that it is supposed to be ridden, it is very useful for it to be punished by several men with sticks." Another specimen of equestrian sadism reads: "If your horse refuses to approach the mounting platform because of fear of work or excessive high spirits, hit it with a stick between the ears and elsewhere on its body, except in its eyes [sic!], and then it will do your bidding wonderfully. . . ."

Judging from these examples of the Neapolitan's style, things must have been fairly lively in the riding schools of the cinquecento.

Nor was it altogether safe for a horse with the best disposition in the world if it were too gifted. In 1601, for example, a certain white horse that knew a few remarkable tricks was placed on trial and burned because it was possessed of the devil.[4]

The Duke of Newcastle also handled his horses fairly roughly at times; but it came to be realized more and more that senselessly harsh and unfeeling treatment irrevocably ruin character and create crafty criminals who only wait for the moment when they can repay with interest the injustice done them.

A last vestige of irrational remount dressage is to be found in Sohr's *Riding Manual,* written in 1825, which was drawn up, to be sure, for the wild horses of the Ukrainian, Bessarabian, and Moldavian steppes on which part of the Prussian cavalry was mounted at the time. Sohr gives instructions for an "accelerated method of forcible breaking", which he states "may be useful" at times. Many were the victims left to die on the battlefield of the riding grounds, not only wild horses that were absolutely unwilling to realize what their destiny was in this world but riders and grooms as well.

Ten or twenty years later, Baucher, who doubtless displayed traits of genius, revolutionized part of the riding world by his apparently brilliant successes, even turning the heads of more sensible people like those usually found in ministries of war,[5] but the reaction against his method, which

[4] J. W. Draper, *History of the Conflict between Religion and Science.*

[5] In Prussia, for example, the horses of a regiment of cuirassiers were trained in accordance with Baucher's principles. Monteton, Sr., who was an eyewitness, recounts with his characteristic grim humour how these unfortunate creatures took revenge on their torturers during close-order drill before illustrious guests.

In his old age, however, a miracle occurred. Baucher found the road to Damascus. Saul became Paul. The salutary change in his opinions went so far that he now concentrated on steadying the necks that he had formerly made artificially loose. The only bit he ever used after 1864 was the snaffle, and his previous brutally cruel leg work was based upon knowledge of the decisive significance of the inner leg, now armed with nothing but a blunt spur.

" I used to begin with complicated movements, but to-day six months are not too long to get my horses to go straight," he told L'Hotte, the chief riding instructor at Saumur at the time; and a few days before his death, he said, " Whenever and wherever difficulties occur

either broke a horse's heart or drove it to desperation, was a healthy and enduring one.

Seidler's and Seeger's pamphlets attacking the sham art of the French of that time tell us how deep-rooted by then was the knowledge of the natural training process of the horse, both mental and physical alike, among the leading minds of the riding world. More and more emphasis was laid upon the rider's having to have certain mental qualities if he is to influence the horse.

The foregoing remarks on the evolution of animal psychology and the various detours and blind alleys into which it was led have only apparently diverted us from our actual topic, the *psychological qualities* that a rider must have. Descriptions of methods and practices that were bad because based upon practically no psychological attitude towards the horse or upon an attitude founded on false assumptions at least show us how training should not be done. Rational horsemen sought ways of achieving better results by using new methods, all founded, however, upon tried and true old principles.

As far as the horse was concerned, horsemen endeavoured to supply the stud farms with stallions and brood mares of perfect disposition and character by careful selection, thus breeding colts that would not cause difficulty for less highly skilled riders and grooms.

As for the rider, horsemen endeavoured to combat an estrangement from animals, that is, to awaken an understanding of the horse's inner life, because they grew more and more convinced that *psychological contact between rider and horse* can simplify and shorten training considerably by mitigating many hardships, awakening ready obedience in the horse, and increasing its dependability in critical situations. Another consequence of this friendly relationship, which by no means excludes respect but which must grow out of confidence, is the fact that horses remain useful and fresh for longer time if they are not worn out battling against demands that would produce no resistance at all if approached correctly.

The research done in animal psychology constitutes another great advance in man's endeavour to utilize the animal psyche for greater co-operation.

Psychological contact and the psychological influence exerted by the rider are inconceivable to-day apart from methods of training. The num-

with a horse, they can only be eliminated for good if the horse is bridled with a snaffle." His last words, and the legacy he bequeathed on his death-bed to his favourite pupil L'Hotte, were " Never rein back! " (Also see General l'Hotte's *A Cavalry Officer* and Decarpentry's *Baucher*. Both authors were masters at Saumur, and L'Hotte was also commandant of that school. L'Hotte, a cavalry general, adapted the *French Cavalry Manual* of 1876 to the Austrian one. General Decarpentry is to-day a world-famous international dressage judge.)

ber of resources available to the rider in this respect is limited only by the number of individuals involved.

I should like, however, to classify the rider's psychological states that make utilization of these resources possible under three headings: love of the horse, mental equilibrium, and energy.

Most important is *love of the horse*. It is the leitmotiv that should underlie all our intercourse with this most lovable of creatures. A horse will overcome its inborn shyness and gain *confidence, the fundamental condition for mutual understanding,* with a man whose love it feels. Subsequently, when strictness or punishment becomes necessary, the horse will know that it was deserved, for it has never suffered injustice or arbitrariness. It has been able to judge the rider's good nature by the fact that he was on the lookout, so to speak, for the slightest indication of responsiveness to his controls to find an opportunity to reward his horse, and that he was magnanimous in forgetting to punish when the mistake was due to clumsiness or inadequate understanding.

During gymnastic training the rider's justified demands must display a precision that bounds on pedantry, but he must never be petty.

Affectionate, uniformly calm treatment in the stall aids training very considerably, especially with young horses. The horse should be quiet and ready to learn as it comes out of the stable where it has had time to digest not only its feed but also what it learned yesterday; it should return to the stable quieted, the mental and physical relaxation it requires not being thwarted by the vibration of overstimulated nerves owing to previous careless and rough treatment by the rider.

The classical words of the old Austrian cavalry manual: " The rider who depends on his horse, which he loves and cares for more than himself. . . ." indicate that the only one who can depend upon his horse under all circumstances and be certain that it will be ready to give its very last bit of obedience and endurance is the rider who has made it his friend by affectionate treatment.

Anyone who loves his horse will be patient, and *patience,* inexhaustible patience—especially when psychological and physical defects are present—is necessary to make the horse understand what we want of it. Patience is equally necessary in order not to grow immoderately demanding, which always happens when we do not reward an initial compliance by immediate cessation of the demand, but try to enjoy a victory until the horse becomes cross or confused.

The second psychological quality the rider must have is *mental equilibrium.* This should cover, of course, riding and everything involved in riding, but it should also protect the rider against losing his sense of proportion and his ability to estimate his own achievements and those of

6. The phase of motion at the walk, in which the left hind foot has just been grounded; this directly precedes the transition to the trot or the gallop right. Before entering upon the latter, the left hind foot is grounded somewhat prematurely, along a line passing between the two forefeet. (The left hind leg is sketched in outline.)

7. Work on the longe.

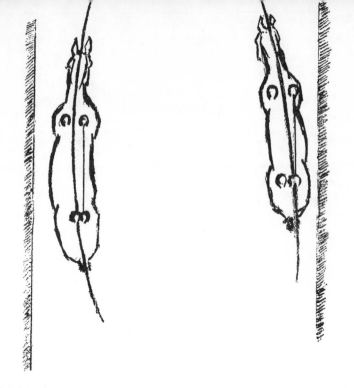

8. Shoulder-fore left (first position). The outer hind hoof tracks the outer forefoot; the inner hind foot is about half a foot width inside the hoofprint of the inner forefoot. Seen from the front, the inner hind hoof is visible between the forefeet.

8a. Position right (second position). The inside hind hoof tracks the inside forefoot; the outside hind foot is about half a foot width inside the hoofprint of the outer forefoot. Seen from the front, the outer hind foot is visible between the forefeet.

9. Lateral movements (reading from left to right): (1) Shoulder-in left. (2) Counter shoulder-in right. (3) *Travers* left (croup-in). (4) *Renvers* right (croup-out).

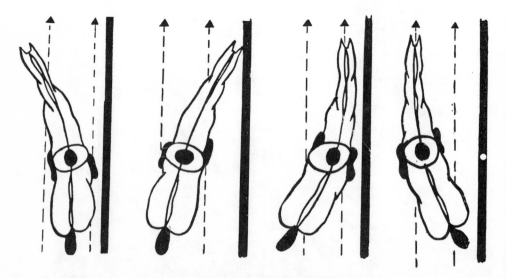

his horse compared to others. "Know thyself", the inscription on the temple of Apollo at Delphi, holds true for the horseman as well as for the philosopher.

To be in psychological equilibrium as a rider, one must have a sure *understanding* of what and how much can be asked of a horse in any period of time and when it can be asked, based upon one's own conscious feelings: the result of experience, hard work, and a study of the anatomical mechanism of the horse. Furthermore the rider must have a sure understanding of the natural limits to what a horse can do, since it can achieve no more than the degree of perfection that is attainable for it even under the best rider. And even though there be no love of one's best companion, this understanding will keep an angry rider from administering excessive punishment and thus destroying by his brutality the confidence that a horse should never lose in his rider. The mental freedom, objectivity, and general superiority that are a result of this mental attitude will tell the rider that a breach of the contact between the two souls produced by disappointed confidence is harder to restore than it is to maintain. Once this contact has been broken, a scar will always remain at that point, because of the horse's tremendous memory, and will break open again on occasion.

Mental equilibrium, or the correct mental attitude towards the horse, is most important in training a remount, that is, in its education, habituation, and dressage. If the rider has the gift of correct and appropriate diagnosis as an ideal complement to understanding, a gift which cannot be acquired by learning and experience alone but with which one must be born, he will be able to handle the hardest job anyone has to do in a saddle—restraining ruined and particularly difficult horses. The ability to diagnose will keep him from doing the wrong thing when only a quick decision can save the situation, and the slightest mistake or false step may mean danger to life.

Now we come to *energy,* another psychological quality that the rider must have at his command constantly.

"Like a woman, a horse does not like the weak; still less does it respect them," Alvisi says in his *Aphorisms,* and a truer word was seldom spoken.

It is always well, if only for the sake of the character and the legs of a young horse, to use diplomacy instead of struggle in reaching our goal. But we must never avoid a struggle if the horse should notice that we were yielding. At such a moment yielding just for the sake of not disturbing the good relationship at any price and maintaining friendship would be quite wrong, for this friendship loses its value if it is not based upon respect, upon the animal's acknowledgment of man's superiority.

No serious struggle need ever arise during the training of young horses, but there are criminals thoroughly spoiled by their previous riders who try to place their rider in a situation where he cannot and must not avoid the struggle for power. At such critical moments it is only the rider's energy that can save the situation, supported by a firm and positive seat and a few lashes with the whip. The truest sort of friendship can bloom later out of such a conflict. But it will always be an uneasy peace until a battle fought with cold energy to a victorious end has cleared the air and proved that the rider's spirit and will are stronger.

Just as each horse is an individual, riders also develop into individuals, even though they were trained by the same instructor. Build, temperament, and character, plus the personal opinion of the relative value of certain lessons, often unconsciously determine the degree as well as the predominance of certain influences in the concert of controls.

Thus horses that are the product of one specialist are remarkable for particularly good carriage, while those "made" by another exhibit a brilliant gait with particularly fine and polished transitions; one rider seems to have a secret remedy for rushing, while another's industry stands out. The individuality of the artist has impressed its stamp upon the horse, which displays the personal signature of its master.

II. Seat and Controls

As we have said, we have no intention of writing a riding manual. There are books like Museler's, the *Swiss Riding Manual* of 1939, the *German Riding Manual* of 1926, and its simplified shorter version of 1937 that fill this need, and I consider it not only presumptuous but highly unnecessary to endeavour to do something paralleling these outstanding works—the "better" would doubtless be an enemy of the good.

The present book has as its objective accompanying the young horse from its first steps on the lunge and under a saddle to the completion of its training by a perfected rider—if we may use the phrase.

A really comprehensive discussion of seat and controls would fill a book by itself; we shall deal with them only in so far as the *seat* and the changes —the *controls*—deliberately exercised by the rider are the instrument by means of which the rider physically influences the horse.

This tool should be made a precision instrument; it should have an appropriate shape and be highly polished so as to achieve the maximum effect without expenditure of excessive energy when correctly applied Our notions of the nature of the seat and of its employment, its action —the controls—must be quite unambiguous, allowing of no doubt whatsoever. That is why we shall discuss them in some detail here, because they are mentioned constantly in the following chapters.

When we leaf through old books on horsemanship or look at pictures of antiquity, the Middle Ages, and modern times, we realize that the rider's *seat* has gone through many changes.

A passage in Xenophon's *Treatise on Horsemanship* (Chapter VII), which is so worded as to leave room for false interpretation, is responsible for the notion that the riders of antiquity, who used no stirrups, rode their horses using a straight crotch seat. This is not so at all. Study of equestrian friezes (Prinias in Crete, 600 B.C.), reliefs on tombs (Athens, 500 B.C.), Alexandrine coins and intaglios, pictures on vases, and other works that have come down from the period before and after Xenophon prove that they did not use a crotch seat supported by neither saddle nor stirrups; this would have produced too great fatigue if the rider stayed on his horse for any length of time. Even though the trot was employed very little at that time, not even an Assyrian cavalryman could have long endured a crotch seat at the walk and the gallop without the support of stirrups.

Only after the introduction of the Italian school saddle and the jousting saddle do we see men in armour and, later on, manège riders standing in their stirrups, with their crotch merely touching the saddle, a straight upper body leaning backwards, and stiff legs stretched out straight ahead (the standing seat).[6]

De la Guérinière is mistakenly regarded as the "inventor" of the present seat on the ischia instead of the crotch. A German, the equerry Pinter von der Au, preached this seat in the saddle in his *Horse Treasury,* published in Frankfurt in 1688, or half a century earlier, but as a star of the second magnitude, Von der Au was unable to have his views prevail at a time when the Duke of Newcastle and Pluvinel dominated horsemanship.

De la Guérinière, however, was the first to introduce, together with his seat (what we to-day call the balanced seat), the saddle *à la française,* the light French saddle, which had a smaller seating area with mere hints of

---

[6] Though stirrups were used in the Far East, in China and Japan, more than two thousand years ago, they came into common use in the Holy Roman Empire only in the tenth century under Otto I.

In Europe the Frankish chieftain Childeric I (fifth century), the father of Clovis, is supposed to have "invented" stirrups as well as horseshoes. As for nailed horseshoes, recent explorations have proved that they were known to the Celts as early as the pre-Christian era (sixth century B.C.).

The Arabs, who became a people of horsemen and horse breeders only after they had subjugated Persia, so rich in horses (536), made the acquaintance of the saddle fitted with Scythian iron stirrups that had come to Persia via Chinese Turkestan. It was only the horse and these accessories that enabled the Arabs to set out on conquests without precedent, until they were stopped for the first time by Charles Martel's Franks at Poitiers in 732.

front and rear pads, in contrast to the Italian saddle and the less important
Pluvinel saddle, also known as the saddle *à la royale*. In this saddle, also
known as the English hunting saddle, the rider was no longer squeezed
into an artificial standing saddle seat, with stiff legs; there was enough
room in the saddle for his buttocks, and his legs could assume a natural
position.

Only towards the middle and the end of the nineteenth century did
Anglomania, the new technology, and the spread of cross-country riding
and easy trotting loosen the excessively rigid framework of the regulation
seat. Such concepts as "natural suppleness of the spine" and "natural
balanced seat in harmony with the movements of the horse", which Seeger
and Steinbrecht made the foundation of their doctrine of the saddle seat,[7]
became common knowledge among horsemen. This seat took the place of
an "academic seat under all circumstances", which had hardened into a
wrongly understood formula that made no allowance for individual differences and ignored the laws of balance, with the rider's weight following
the horse's movements in jumping and at rapid gaits. Around the turn
of the century Caprilli and the *modern racing seat* extended the frame of
action of the seat from the original position of the normal seat, and recon-
ciled it with the extremely extended framework of the racing and jumping
horse, a tendency, moreover, whose advantages had been set forth forcefully and convincingly by Steinbrecht.

Aside from marginal cases, like the racing and jumping seats just mentioned or a specially effective seat that might be required at times for an
unbroken or intractable horse, the "repertory" of the seat is confined to
the *basic form—the normal seat*—and two other forms based on it, which
need be used only temporarily, that is, until the control has achieved its
purpose.

There are numerous intermediate stages between these two extreme
forms of seat, the *crotch seat* (see p. 60) and the *seat that exercises
increased driving force*, and although barely perceptible to the eye, they
provide just as many nuances for the sensitive and understanding rider,
enabling him to increase the precision of his controls, as circumstances may
require, to an unprecedented degree of fineness. First let us take up the
normal seat. This is a seat in which (1) it is easiest for the rider to keep
the distribution of his own weight in balance with the equilibrium of the
horse, which is determined by the energy and direction of motion that
often change with lightning speed; (2) the rider can continue riding for the
longest time without appreciable effort, that is, without fatigue, and with
the horse exhibiting correct motion and posture.

---

[7] The seat must be flexible, adapting to the state of equilibrium of the horse at any instant
instead of acting as a so-called *candelabra seat*, which makes the rider look like a tin
soldier, a foreign body on the horse.

These two requirements, first, ability to adapt and second, minimum expenditure of energy, are satisfied by the normal seat in a practically ideal fashion—provided, of course, we have a horse that moves in equilibrium on nearly flat ground, i.e., is poised, without hastening or holding back.

Since in the normal seat the upper body rests chiefly upon the two seat bones (the ischia, which are shaped like sled runners), that is, their lowest point, located at about the fifteenth spinal vertebra of the horse, the load may be shifted to their front edge (the crotch seat) by tilting the hips slightly forward. Similarly the load can be shifted to their rear edge (the seat that provides increased drive) by a similar tilt of the hips backward. If we are using the normal seat, we occupy the "interior line", tactically speaking, and are protected against any occurrence, as we can take the shortest path to the most effective position whenever the necessity should arise.

This sled-runner shape of the base of support affords the flexibility required for rapid shifts of the centre of gravity. Together with other factors, it enables the rider to "go along" with the horse. In turn, the position of the seat bones, as the base of support, vertically underneath the hips and the straight but supple spinal column, enables the rider to protect himself against continual contraction of the muscles in the small of his back and his buttocks. It also protects him against fatigue, because the point of support lies in the same vertical line as the rider's centre of gravity, and he requires no effort to maintain his equilibrium.

This indicates almost automatically how the rider's hips and legs must be placed in the normal seat in order to provide the most favourable conditions for the carriage and gait of the horse and for the carrying of the rider.

When the saddle is designed correctly and placed in the correct position, the buttocks rest in the middle of the saddle, with their muscles relaxed, supported chiefly by the lower edge of the two seat bones. These bones must be as close to the surface of the saddle as possible; wrong contraction and tension should not force the buttock muscles between the bones and the saddle. The hips are vertically above the seat bones. To the extent that the buttocks, with their full width resting in the saddle, allow, the flat inner surface of the thighs, turned outwards from the hips and hanging down freely, must embrace the side of the horse and thus give the knee a firm, low position that increases the base of support and thus facilitates balance and the ability to feel motion.[8]

[8] We might add that when the legs are stretched too far because the stirrups are too long, the basis of support is increased in the vertical direction (the gripping of the horse's sides), but at the same time the horizontal basis of support is narrowed so much that the seat become too unstable and loose and imperils balance.

The upper body is kept straight and naturally upright above the vertical line from the seat bones to the hips, so that the spinal column, which has the shape of a rather flat S, is not impeded by cramped tension and can follow or sustain movement as required and swing with it. This swing serves the purpose of absorbing the shocks of the gait that cannot be taken up by the knee, the shoulders, and the elbows alone, so as to guarantee a deep seat that does not leave the saddle.

By means of very minute oscillations of his spine, hardly perceptible to the eye, the rider who has a " soft" seat is able to " sit out " the movements of his horse, that is, to stick to the saddle. Practically speaking, the secret of this soft seat can be solved only by persistent riding on a spirited horse, without stirrups, of course. When the horse " jogs ", the small of the back allows the pelvis to go forward in the saddle (pushing the pelvis forward, " going along "). The upper body becomes longer and relatively heavier at the moment the pelvis is pushed forward, so that the buttocks, which follow the oscillations of the back faithfully, can remain *in* the saddle. This presupposes, of course, that the rider is seated at the lowest point of the horse's back—at about the fifteenth vertebra in a horse of normal build. At this point motion is felt least, as in the middle of a motor-car or bus.

The soft seat, as we understand it, differs fundamentally from a " doughy " seat, where the small of the back is flabby. It evades the movements of the horse and thus loses any ability to control it. It also differs from a seat that absorbs and paralyses the reactions by means of rhythmic swings of the legs. Though we observe these two wrong variations of the soft seat in natural riders in rural areas and in horse markets, there is still another variation, worst of all because it readily confuses the layman. This is the rider who pulls himself into the saddle artificially. He first evades the " jog " with the small of his back and then uses his buttocks to push the horse up against the restraining rein. Neither the soft seat nor the " action " of the forelegs is genuine with such riders, who may even be found in horse shows.

The head and the neck should rise freely from the slightly squared shoulders, which are allowed to carry their natural weight. (Any stiffness in the neck is inevitably transmitted to all the rest of the body!) The rider's appearance should bear the stamp of self-confident and calm superiority. A neglected carriage of the head, which is so common, gives the impression (and is also the expression) of a careless or cramped seat. It is not a mere blemish, as so many inveterate " nodders " claim, for it may have quite unpleasant consequences in the open country—a Buddha lost in the contemplation of his navel is more likely to fall off his horse in the event of sudden capers than a rider accustomed to carrying his head high.

The fact that the rider's head is comparatively heavy and has a not inconsiderable effect upon the rider's centre of gravity because of its high position is another reason for not carrying it so as to produce a false distribution of weight. Every shift of weight, produced by a deliberate or unintentional movement of the rider, finds a desired or undesired "echo" in the well-tuned instrument of the horse's body. I have ridden Lipizzans of the Spanish Riding School in Vienna that were so sensitive that the change in balance produced by the rider's inclining his head to one side was enough to have them depart from a walk to a gallop towards that side. Another example that is no less convincing is the jockey who looks behind him in the home stretch and loses the race.

If the shoulders are squared back, it is quite unnecessary to command "Chest out". This results in hollowing of the back, the worst error of all, in riders who are not yet supple. Pulling the chin in slightly or making the back of the neck touch the collar will cause the sternum to come forward. This will produce a slight arching of the chest with the deep breathing that promotes posture and relaxation without a bad effect on the position of the other parts of the body.

A long trunk, which does not make balancing easier, any more than a high pelvis does, also has this disadvantage: when the arms are a bit short it is difficult to keep them in the right position. The upper arms should hang down vertically, the inner surface of the forearms touching the body at their mid-point, and the horse's mouth, the reins, and the hands should then form a straight line.

The action of the hand is correct when the back of the hand is in the same plane as the outer surface of the forearm. Hands that are bent in at the wrist necessarily allow their sustaining and receiving controls to take place from the arms, while hands that are bent out at the wrist allow their yielding controls to take place in the same way. Both impair precision of control and looseness of the arms and of the seat as a whole. Whether the hand is held higher or lower should depend solely upon the position of the horse's mouth, which in turn depends on whether it carries its head higher or lower; in other words, it is a function of the degree of collection of the horse. It follows, therefore, that any binding instruction, say, to hold the hands about one handbreath above the pommel, is quite wrong. Regulations of that sort were drawn up for military needs, the full-pack cavalry saddle.

If the saddle and the girth are correctly placed for a horse that moves freely, that is, without stiffness, the girth will be vertically underneath the lowest point of the saddle and one to one and a half handbreaths behind the olecranon. The leg, which is slightly bent back from the knee, will hang down alongside the body of the horse just behind the girth, which will be visible in front of the leg. Then the leg will easily be able to maintain contact with the horse's sides in natural, elastic tension without deliberate pressure. Having the leg over the girth would make it impossible to secure continuous soft contact with the horse's flanks in that narrow area. The low heel,[9] feathering with every step, will then lie in approximately the same vertical line as the shoulders and the hips if the legs are of normal length. When the thigh is flat and the knee and heel are low, this contact will continue all the way to just above the ankle. When the spur is used, this contact will even extend to the heel, which is raised for this purpose. But continuing in this position for any length of time would make the horse insensitive to the action of the legs or make it feel that it was being squeezed, thus producing convulsive cramps. Master Stensbeck described the condition of a leg that exerts correct influence as " active suppleness ". It must be emphasized that the build of the horse and of the rider affects the position of the legs, and *nothing is more harmful than to try to press all riders into one mould of seat*. All other things being equal, a short-legged rider will have a firmer seat on a short-ribbed and flat-ribbed horse than the long-legged rider. The latter would have to place his leg so far to the rear in order to be able to exert control that his knees would necessarily open.

Many riding instructors demand that the rider's feet be perfectly parallel to the longitudinal axis of the horse. If the pupil follows this advice conscientiously, either he will have to open his knees so that the inner side of his leg can remain in contact with the horse's flanks, or he will have to abandon the latter objective in order to keep the knee in contact with the saddle. But if the pupil wants to retain a fixed knee *and* contact and still tries to follow that instruction literally, he has to turn his foot inwards at the ankle.

But turning in at the ankle is just as bad as turning it out. In both cases the foot loses its springiness. This stiffness is communicated to the muscles of the calf and interferes with their unconstrained contraction and relaxation (elastic springiness), thus rendering delicate control more difficult. Turning the toes out affects the whole leg below the knee, so that the muscles of the calf begin to pinch the horse.

The position of the foot should be the same as it is in walking, the toes turned somewhat away from the horse, as is the natural consequence of the position astride the saddle. This makes the inner edge of the sole lie a fraction of an inch lower than the outer edge, as may be easily seen by an observer in front of the horse or at the side.

[9] As will be shown in greater detail when we discuss controls, the heel is depressed most when the rider pushes his pelvis forward to give signals to the horse.

The widest part of the sole, from the little toe to the ball of the big toe, rests on the stirrup bar. If the latter is wide enough, only the outer parts of the foot, the toes, touch the outer side of the stirrup. When the toes are held parallel to the horse or turned towards it, the ankle is turned and hence stiffened, so that the ball of the foot no longer touches the stirrup bar.

The heels should lie lower than the toes even when riding without stirrups. Letting the toes hang down completely relaxes the *biceps femoris,* which must contract and relax elastically like the extensor muscles on the outside of the leg in order for the seat to be firm and the controls precise. If the toes hang down, we can squeeze until we are out of breath, but we make no impression upon the horse, and the " control " does not come through.

While we are discussing riding without stirrups, we might add that the favourite and comfortable habit of turning up the stirrup should be abandoned. It is better to take the slight amount of trouble required to pull out the stirrup leathers, for when the stirrups are turned up, these straps squeeze the thigh, and the seat, which is supposed to be forward in the saddle, involuntarily moves to the rear.

The stirrups must be long enough to enable the heels to lie lower than the toes when the buttocks fill the saddle, the thighs are closed, and the legs rest with the ball of the foot against the stirrup bar. Their length varies according to the gait of the horse, the length of its ribs, and the length of the rider's legs.

They should be shortened by two to four holes for jumping and for supporting the relieved crotch seat in rough terrain, since the horse becomes thinner as its framework is lengthened and in the extended gallop, thus narrowing the horizontal area of support of the seat and making the latter less stable. This also enables the rider's knee and hip joints to absorb the more severe movements of the horse, while the buttocks, which are now supported rather more by the crotch and are *on* rather than *in* the saddle, facilitate suppleness of the back and " going along " with the horse.

Generally speaking, I might add that in case of doubt it is better to have the stirrups one hole too short than one hole too long. If they are a bit too short, your legs will not grip the horse as well, but your control will be steadier because of your firmer seat. If they are too long, you are making a sacrifice for the sake of alleged good form that must be paid for dearly, for every inch of excessive stirrup length loosens the seat and deprives the rider of control. If you feel that your seat needs freshening and ironing out, which is the case at least once a year even for the best riders, ride without stirrups on the lunge for a few weeks if possible. After this sort of treatment you will be astonished that your feeling has grown finer. Your seat has stretched out and grown deeper, so that you feel cramped by the shorter stirrups and you buckle them longer than before.

The first type of seat evolved out of the basic form of normal seat just described is the crotch seat (also known as the forward seat), with all its modifications and nuances, such as the racing seat, the hunting seat, the jumping seat, the cross-country seat, and the relieving, correction, and remount seat. All these seats have one thing in common: they are intended to ease the load and facilitate the activity of the back. *Like the second type of seat based on the normal seat, the seat that provides increased drive, the crotch seat is one of the controls helping to achieve a definite purpose for a short time. The rider returns to the normal seat as soon as this purpose is achieved.* It is used to lighten the hindquarters for jumping, for young horses, for horses with weak or sensitive backs, for accelerating the gaits, and for horses moving freely, as at the full gallop, racing, etc.[10]

The crotch seat that acts as an aid has nothing in common with the false type of seat bearing the same name, which is produced by stirrups that are too long or by saddles of poor design.

The correct crotch seat arises from the normal seat when the rider, with the small of the back strongly braced, carries the upper part of his body farther forward " going with the movement ", and shifting his weight from the bottom of his ischia, his seat bones, to the front edges of these bones and his thighs. *The crotch seat cannot be maintained by balance alone, like the normal seat;* it requires the muscular force of the knee, which presses against the saddle somewhat more, though not tensely. The increased forward push of the pelvis forces the knees and the heels downward. Generally speaking, the knee is the most important factor when shortened stirrups are used for faster gaits and for jumping. Fixed in position, it becomes a shock absorber and acts like a hinge for all the parts of the body above the knee, since the rider is supposed to stand from his knees and not in his stirrups.

The second type of seat arising from the basic form of the normal seat is the seat that provides increased drive. I say "increased drive" because the normal seat itself, without any contribution on the part of the rider, sustains motion and thus acts like a driver as the result of the correct action of the rider's weight upon the motion of the horse.

[10] As the front and hind pairs of legs are extended particularly far apart and almost simultaneously at a free extended gallop, and especially at a racing gallop, the part of the horse's body between its forehand and hindquarters grows longer and therefore thinner and narrower (like a stretched rubber band), so that the stirrups must be shortened to correspond with the pace (as in hunting).

Now if the pelvis is pushed forward by a greater elastic contraction of the small of the back, the rear edges of the seat bones carry a greater load than in the crotch seat. The hips slant backwards more or less, depending upon the degree to which the small of the back is contracted, and the normal seat's vertical line from the ischium to the hip slopes to the rear like the pelvis. The increased tightening of the small of the back when the pelvis is pushed forward and the upper body is carried upright— the characteristic feature of the seat that provides increased drive—pushes the horse forward to the hand, puts it "in hand". It begins to chew and grow supple, stretching or bending the joints of its legs more fully as the reins give or are kept elastically taut.

We shall often have occasion to speak of suppleness when we discuss the gymnastic training of the horse. Since suppleness is often confused with absence of constraint, these two concepts, which are practically synonymous in ordinary language, must be clearly differentiated in so far as riding is concerned.

Every horse should and can move unconstrainedly, i.e., elastically contracting and relaxing its muscles more or less energetically, no matter how it is ridden, from the first time it is mounted to the end of its training, that is, at every stage of dressage. It is a matter of course that the horse can move without constraint only when all psychological cramps and anxiety states (which are immediately reflected in the horse's body, of course) have given way to trusting surrender to the saddle. Moreover its nerves, which communicate orders to the muscles, must spare the latter all unnecessary labour as a result of their correct "co-ordination".

An unconstrained gait, however, must not be confused with sloppy running. In the latter state the horse is under the "compulsion" of the added weight it is carrying, which compels it to seek a supporting "fifth foot" in the rider's hand to keep it from hurrying.

The state of suppleness sets in only when the horse, previously walking, trotting, or galloping underneath the rider in the unconstraint of natural poise, stretches its body to reach the bit as the result of drive. Drive produces impulsion and gait and then the horse grows supple in consequence of further drive, chewing the bit as a sign of gratitude.

It carries its unconstraint along with it into the state of suppleness, which, like all the other stages of training up to and including the complete responsiveness to all influences that we have set as our final goal, is inconceivable without an easy, elastic contraction and relaxation of the muscles unimpeded by any cramps or stiffness.

Except for the first weeks of training, when the action of the legs and the hand must be separately "explained" to the young horse in order to win over its will so that moving forward or standing still becomes more and more of a reflex action in response to a touch of the riding crop and later of the legs or to a restraining action of the hand, all the controls must always work together, must affect the whole horse.

This means that individual controls, exercised separately without co-ordination, will never achieve their purpose. All three instruments, weight, legs, and hands, the entire seat, must always co-operate in the concert of controls. Only the purpose in mind and the individual case as determined by configuration, disposition, and degree of dressage can say which of these three instruments will predominate or whether all three will be of the same importance and intensity.

If we are to continue with our comparison of the controls to instruments playing in concert, we must look for a conductor who decides when the voices enter and how loud they should be, who is in command. Nature has made wonderful provision for such a conductor by furnishing the rider with the small of his back, located somewhat above his centre of gravity and a little to the rear. Like the painter's brush on the maulstick, the parts of the body that execute orders find support at this central point, this " first and last argument of a rider's influence ", whose elastic contraction (tightening) initiates all controls and lends emphasis to their " getting through " when needed, so as to harmonize their actions.

By means of the seat bones associated with it, the small of the back sets up the weight control as well as all others. Hence whenever the rider encounters resistance, he must fix the small of his back, i.e., he must throw it forward; only in rare cases of serious insubordination need he arch his back to exert greater force.

If we compare training a young horse with learning to read and write, the controls are the ABCs, the multiplication table, which it has to learn before making further progress.

In our discussion of this training we shall show how the controls are constantly refined, corresponding to the growing understanding and responsiveness of the horse, so that once training is completed, a horse of good configuration, whose obedience is not impeded by any physical handicaps and whose will parallels that of the rider's, requires only the merest of hints. The only reason why these hints are not insubstantial signs is that the bodily controls must govern their degree and intensity or, in a word, regulate them.

Before dealing with the controls separately and then considering their co-ordination, we shall confine ourselves here to the general principles governing their use, as displayed in a horse that is ideally mounted.

There will be departures from this ideal in all other cases, depending upon the degree of dressage, the will, and the verve of the horse, so that they cannot all be encompassed in one lapidary rule. Each deviation demands the individual attention of the rider to that special case. These deviations will be taken up in the chapters on training, for, as we have said, the principles of horsemanship cannot be employed like the mathematical formulas of engineering.

The *leg* is the control that produces the motion of the horse, setting it in motion and maintaining it. Neither the hand nor the rider's weight can take its place.

Only after the horse is in motion, unresistingly using its muscles to move forward and carry the rider, can the rider drive it forward, slow it down, or make it change direction by distributing his weight. But these weight controls will achieve their purpose only when supported by leg and hand, that is, when all three controls work together.

Application of the legs just behind the girth, as discussed in the section on the normal seat, may be of two kinds, squeezing and stimulating.

The result will be a change in pace or of carriage or of both, depending on how the rest of the seat—weight and hands—behaves. This result can likewise merely maintain pace and carriage, if they are about to be lost (half halt).

Leg pressure may be brief or prolonged; when prolonged, it pushes the horse forward. It must cease as soon as obedience is secured, and the legs should then resume their previous state of "active suppleness", resting gently against the flanks of the horse.

If one leg lies somewhat behind the position prescribed for the normal seat, i.e., well behind the girth, it exerts pressure either to prevent the horse from leaving the track or to cause it to do so. In the first case the leg acts as a *guard*, while in the second it provides *lateral drive*.

Whereas the leg located just behind the girth always acts as a forward impeller, whether as pressure or as stimulus, except in the shoulder-in figures, *the lateral action*[11] *of the leg located more to the rear of the girth is merely indirect.* The drive required must then be supplied principally by the other leg, which retains its position just behind the girth. Here, too, the shoulder-in exercises constitute the sole exception.

Even when the guarding leg assumes the threatening position farther back of the girth, any driving force that may be necessary to maintain the gait must be exerted principally by the other leg.

As we have indicated in our discussion of the seat (position of the leg), every control, including leg control, is supported by the increased forward push of the pelvis.[12] This stretches the entire seat and therefore forces the

[11] The lateral-driving leg control, which is supported by the rein on the same side (indirect flexion), is one of the few controls that acts directly upon the body without the mediation of the horse's brain, almost a purely mechanical compulsion which can be used to force the horse to execute a sort of turn on the forehand, though the form will be poor, or to force its legs to move when it seems to be rooted to the spot.

[12] When no control signal is given, the small of the back should be thrown forward only enough to keep the hips vertical.

knee and heel down, thus stretching the calf muscles that are like elastic springs in motion, which itself is an aid to well-ridden horses.

The *equal pressure of both legs,* graduated to conform with the sensitivity of the horse, makes the horse go forward, that is, commence its gait, accelerate it, or make it more pronounced, so that it is essentially always a driving force. In the course of training, the horse learns that this pressure may also mean collection (increased bending of the hindquarters' joints), if the weight and the reins are in agreement; it also learns the meaning of the lateral-driving leg placed farther behind the girth.

The leg is used to stimulate, activate, and accelerate the gait whenever the hind legs drag or move dully, so that the horse's steps are not as vigorous and do not cover as much ground as should be expected from the horse's configuration and machinery and the rider's will. Therefore when the position of the leg is correct, a stimulating leg will act just like a pressing, driving leg.

Now how do the stimulating leg controls arise?

The legs of a supple-seated rider, which are in soft contact with the horse, receive impulses from the oscillations of the barrel, the latter swinging with every step to maintain balance and moving in the direction of the hind leg that is about to alight in order to provide vertical support. In so doing, the legs "breathe" with these movements of the horse and in unison with the oscillations of the sides of the horse's barrel.

These impulses are different, depending upon the frame and gait of the horse. They are especially visible and perceptible at a free walk or gallop and in horses with broad movements of their hindquarters. They are barely perceptible, but very clearly felt by a sensitive rider, at the trot and in a collected horse.[13]

Now by elastically tensing his calves as the result of lowering his heels, the rider supplies an *actively stimulating, emphasized leg control* in time with these alternating impulses. This control may range from the merest hint to a vigorous threat, depending upon the sensitivity of the horse and the stage of dressage it has reached. But here too, as with every other control, the rider must endeavour to secure the desired effect with a minimum of effort. As stated above, the stimulating leg control, like the pressing control, always acts as a drive and may be exerted as vibrations, independent of the rhythm of the horse's motion, or as light taps, to call attention to the controls even with horses that are not completely trained.

---

[13] In *collection,* one of whose characteristic features is the close proximity of the hind hoofprints, these oscillations are not pronounced, as the hind feet track upon nearly the same line—a very narrow base line—so that the weight compensation required is a minimum.

At the trot the simultaneous beats of the diagonal pairs of legs and the highly stable centre of gravity of the horse, which is located quite close to the point where the straight lines connecting these pairs of legs intersect, and therefore is subjected to practically no lateral displacement, reduce to a minimum the oscillations required to balance the weight.

If the leg controls do not come through, that is, if not enough attention is paid to them, although the stage of training of the horse should make it able to follow them, their action is intensified by brief *pricks of the spurs,* on one side or both as needed, or by application of the spurs. Strong spurring, with yielding reins, should emphasize the controls persuasively only in case of serious disobedience and malicious resistance; it also acts as punishment. To spur a horse, the rider holds the knee fixed, turns the heel inward towards the horse's flank, and raises it, depending on the length of his legs. That is why spurs that are buckled on high are an advantage for long-legged riders. Spurring is done from the ankle, with the stirrups at the heel (see also p. 227).

The *riding crop* is just as much a part of the rider's equipment as his spurs. Not only is it an indispensable accessory in training young horses —because most natural in its action—but it is needed even by *haute école* riders. It is best to use the crop instead of the spur with sulking, reserved horses and ticklish mares.

The crop should be shaped so as to grow thicker towards the end in order that the hand need not close tight to hold it. It must be long enough to reach behind the rider's leg when normally employed.

Many riders have the unconscious habit—which is the essence of every bad habit, unfortunately—of letting their legs swing back and forth or constantly hit against the horse. Then they wonder why their controls are not effective, forgetting that swinging legs cannot halt the horse and are powerless against a backward creeping of the hindquarters as well as against the dragging of one hind foot.

Habitually tapping legs prevent the horse from staying in contact with the " leg ", for they deprive the horse of the very control that it is supposed to have when in motion.

The natural pulsations of the barrel provide a simple answer to the question of the instant at which the stimulating leg control should be exercised. A supple seat, smoothly yielding to the rhythm of movement, automatically finds the correct moment, just before the hind leg leaves the ground,[14] when the wall of the belly wobbles on the side of the hind leg that is still resting on the ground. It should utilize the impulses received as a reflex emphatically if it wishes to exercise conscious and intensified stimulation. But if a horse responds vigorously to the controls, the rider secures impetus as well as gait by virtue of his normal seat alone, without conscious driving.

If we place too much stress on the times when stimulation can be exerted automatically when speaking to young riders, they endeavour to seize these moments deliberately; they become stiff, and their controls are applied too early or too late.

[14] Compare the driving whip of the racing jockey in the home-stretch.

The laconic statement in the riding textbooks that "the leg has the job of acting on the hind leg on the same side" is an answer to a second question—Upon which hind foot does a single, impelling leg control act?—that is neither clear nor complete.

I should like to replace that statement, which can be found in one form or another in practically all contemporary riding manuals and textbooks, with a rule that puts the matter in a basically different light.

The horse is able to respond to any summons only with the leg that is about to leave the ground, no matter how the acceleration of the gait is elicited in a horse in motion.

The correctness of this proposition may be readily established.

Hardly any influences (controls) can be transmitted directly to the parts of the body for which they are intended; this transmission must pass through the horse's brain and nerves.

Here is a practical example by way of explanation.

Say, a horse is trotting on the lunge. The trainer cracks his whip to make its movements more lively, because its hindquarters are too un-wieldy. Which hind leg will accelerate the gait when the whip is cracked, if we assume that the horse reacts without being frightened? You can try this out on yourself. Walk a few steps at a calm, easy speed, and imagine that you suddenly want to accelerate your gait. What leg will you use for that purpose? Most certainly the leg that happens to be in contact with the ground at that moment! One of the many optical illusions that underlie riding concepts is responsible for our not having realized this in the case of the horse. Let us go further. Whether we use ourselves or a horse as the experimental subject, we will find that the leg that happens to be in mid-air literally springs forward at the instant the impulse to accelerate the pace (due to one's own will or to the crack of the whip) is received. But when we make the test on our own body, we will notice that the foot that happens to be in contact with the ground at that very instant and provides us with support leaves the ground with greater force. This is what accelerates the gait, the leg that happens to be off the ground merely having to step out farther to provide room for the stronger push-off. And that is the optical illusion which leads us to con-clude that the foot that is already in motion is the one responsible for the acceleration.

Hence statements like the ones found in the *German Riding Manual* of 1926 are not entirely correct: "In motion, the leg drives the horse's hind foot on the same side correctly only at the instant that foot is off the ground. The action that stimulates the hind foot in question is based upon the influence of the leg at this moment."

The answer to the preceding question of which hind leg is acted upon by a single driving leg control yields the following useful application: If

I simply want to drive a horse forward without affecting its carriage or direction in any way, it makes no difference, essentially, whether I do so with one leg or another, with a riding crop, the lungeing whip, or by clicking my tongue—the horse will accelerate only with the foot that happens to be touching the ground. But if I want to affect a single hind leg in order to influence the body of the horse with respect to direction of motion, carriage, balance, collection, straightening, etc., it is always done with the leg on the same side. In this action the controls of weight, reins, and the other leg must always co-operate, however.

In any forward and lateral movement of the horse's body (two tracks) the oscillations of its trunk will not be of equal magnitude, but they still permit of a rhythmic increased pressure of the leg that provides the lateral impulse at the instant the hind leg that is to be impelled sideways is off the ground. The instant when the hind leg on the same side does not act as a support is the most favourable one for getting it to yield.

In the trot, which also includes a phase of suspension, the sideways-impelling leg can act only from the instant when the hind leg on the same side leaves the ground to the instant when the other leg leaves the ground so that all four legs are in the air. Even with the best intentions in the world, the horse is unable to make its hind foot follow the impelling leg on the same side because it has no base of support during the phase of suspension.[15]

The same considerations hold good for the phase of suspension in galloping. It follows from what we have said that driving leg controls are unable to effect any acceleration during the suspension phases at the gallop and the trot.

The horse sometimes tightens up as a result of cramplike tensions and does not fill out the rider's seat. Then the trunk's oscillations, which are regular only in an unconstrained pure gait, are not uniform, owing to stiffness on one side or both (crookedness). These cases are outside the scope of this discussion and will be taken up when we discuss the training of the young horse.

The seat, by its very nature, is a control in a certain sense, as has been pointed out above.

The forward-tilted crotch seat, which makes the rider's centre of gravity harmonize with the forward-shifted centre of gravity of the horse, becomes a *weight control*. Likewise, when the small of the back is pushed forward without the rider's upper body leaning backwards perceptibly, the increased forward-driving seat enables the horse to bend its hindquarters more be-

[15] This is merely theoretical, however, because of the brief duration of this phase of suspension in trotting (see footnote on p. 193).

cause of their increased load and to adapt its own centre of gravity to that of the rider's, as is done when weight control is used to halt the horse. If the loading and driving weight control is not supported by any accepting rein control, the driving action predominates, and the horse improves its carriage and gait (half halt) if the reins merely sustain or moves faster if the reins yield.

The rider also uses a weight control to initiate turns and bends; this control consists in a flexing of the muscles of the small of the back on the side on which the turn is made, a resultant pushing forward of the respective seat bone (which fixes the weight control), a lengthening of the inner leg, and a slight advance of the outer shoulder. As the horse's area of support from left to right—its transverse axis—is much shorter than its longitudinal axis, it is particularly sensitive and receptive to lateral shifts of the rider's weight. Long before it has learned to respond to shifts of weight forward or back, it readily follows the mechanical persuasion of an increased load on the inner side as soon as it has commenced unconstrained, natural trotting.

But all excessive shifts in weight, which are usually due to mistakes the rider makes in his seat and to his lack of balance, result in exactly the opposite of what we desire.

Whereas the leg control is a driving control, the *rein control* produced by the action of the hands is essentially a restraining one. It follows, therefore, that when used *alone*, it can bring the horse to a standstill in one way or another, but it can never fulfil its real purpose of *leading*, that is, determining gait, pace, carriage, and direction.

Leading presupposes positive contact with the bit, the elastic contact with the rider's hand sought by the horse as it stretches out to reach the bit as a result of driving. Contact with the bit sets in with the beginning of suppleness; it is assured in a responsive horse.

The rein controls required for good guidance may be *yielding, sustaining, and receiving;* they comprise a whole gamut of hand influences, ranging from the mere opening of the fingers[16] to an extension of the entire arm, from a tighter closing of the fingers (as if one wished to squeeze only a few drops from a sopping wet sponge), when the small of the back

---

[16] This really involves the same kind of sensitive fingering that a piano virtuoso develops. The reins are hardly ever narrow and flexible enough, and a glove is hardly ever thin enough, for a rider with sensitive controls. This rider's horses will all have " gentle mouths " or their mouths will become gentle, as may be proved by the long wear got out of the gloves. Parenthetically, the tailor's bills for riding breeches will be low despite extensive riding if the seat is soft and follows the action of the horse with feeling.

While we are talking about reins, let us point out that braided reins are fully justified in cross-country riding and can be very useful because they do not slip and thus are less of a temptation to pulling, but they make it harder for the reins to slip through the fingers, and control becomes coarser during training.

is flexed, to the turning in of the completely closed hands and the slight withdrawal of the arms.[17]

Though there may be times at which more energetic control is unavoidable, guidance must never become rigid and unfeeling. The completely closed hand used when the reins are tightened must never become hard and fixed, and even with this increased sustaining action, the elasticity residing in the fingers rather than in an artificially turned-in wrist must keep the contact with the bit elastic. Whenever it is necessary to use the reins, it should start as a mere hint; it must never degenerate into continuous pulling. It must cease at the slightest sign of yielding, since otherwise it will produce resistance that interferes with the gait.

When the hand is not exerting influence, it should constitute a straight line with the outside surface of the forearm, the fingers bent only at the middle joints and lightly closed to form a hollow fist. It should be kept passively in a straight line from the horse's mouth to the rider's elbow. The thumb lies flat, without pressing, in the same direction as the bone of the forearm. (The wrist should not be rounded or bent outwards, as this produces an artificial, hard control.) Thus the hand must be steady, as if it were holding a glass of water, and it must never turn into a cramped fist even when strong action is employed, which requires a fixed hand with firmly closed fingers. The fist makes the rider lose his " feel " for the horse's mouth and kills " feel " in the horse's mouth.

The hand can be steady only if it finds support in the small of the back, which is flexed more or less for this purpose. But the small of the back can provide the support at all times only if the seat is firm and independent. This is also a prerequisite for a soft hand, which promotes mouth activity and follows motion elastically. The mysterious " good " or " poor " hand is, therefore, nothing but an immediate consequence of the seat, standing as a rule in direct ratio to the good or bad qualities of the latter. We say " as a rule " only because a rider with a good seat may be able to do without psychological balance and healthy nerves, which affect control directly. To be sure, a really good seat can be achieved only upon a horse with a correct gait, that is, a horse that also responds correctly to the reins, which can never be entirely true in the case just mentioned.

In a well-made, and hence responsive horse, a slight displacement of both hands to one side suffices to bring about the desired change of direction in unison with the other controls, though the two hands should never be brought to the same side of the horse's neck. The reason for this is that

[17] The yielding rein control achieves its greatest effect when the hand advances from the upper arm, as is the case in racing, jumping, etc., and when the horse chews the bit. The frame of the horse is extended forward, controlled by the rider; the horse stretches with the sliding reins and follows them to the limit of its extension without changing gait. Even after the horse chews the bit, it is still controlled by the leg and the loose reins (see also pp. 158-159).

the rider's shoulders must always be aligned with those of the horse, so that the hands, which are connected to the shoulders through the loosely hanging arms, participate in the shoulders' movements. The outer hand advances together with the outer shoulder somewhat, exercising a *restraining rein control* by limiting the bending of the horse's head and neck. This is the fourth rein control. The rider's outer shoulder is advanced and his inner shoulder is drawn back, thus automatically providing the active control of the inner rein. This may be reinforced as necessary by closing the fingers further and turning the hand.

The *opening rein* is of considerable use with young horses which are not yet able to follow the active rein control, as well as in work to even the load on all four legs later on. The movement of one hand somewhat to one side, with the fingernails turned upwards, makes it easier for the horse to begin its turn and diminishes the danger of its falling upon its outer shoulder.

This disturbance of lateral equilibrium, which endangers even loading on all four legs and thus equilibrium as a whole, may reoccur in later stages of training and will be exploited by the horse when it disobeys the rider. We must therefore be careful never to carry the reins " over the neck ".

If the horse succeeds in " binding " the rider's hand, so that the latter feels the horse's mouth as a dead, leathery pressure, the hand loses its freedom of action and is soon utilized by the horse as a prop and a " fifth foot ".

When the horse achieves suppleness by stretching out to reach the bit, it comes up to the bit and *chews,*[18] which is its acknowledgment of

---

[18] There is a *right way of chewing and a wrong one.* In the right way the lower jaw is hardly open, and the lips are closed. The lower jaw follows the bit like a coupling. These movements of a relaxed masseter muscle that carries the bit, which are independent of the timing of the gait and are produced only by the controls, resemble a murmuring. They convert the saliva into foam, which is visible at the horse's mouth. The necessary flexing of the neck ligament, the ligamentum nuchae, is also a result of this chewing.

This chewing is directly produced by a swallowing (rather than chewing) action of the tongue. This movement also increases the secretion of the parathyroid glands, which become more prominent.

Chewing that coincides with the gait's rhythm is wrong. The cramped masseter muscles make the horse's teeth gnash, producing sounds that resemble the cracking of nuts.

Equally wrong and an indication of incomplete suppleness is rattling of the bit, in which the snaffle is rhythmically rattled against the bar mouthpiece as a result of a movement of the tongue like that occurring when fodder is masticated.

In contrast to the noisy gnashing and rattling that occur in time with the gait, the low clicking of the bit, on the other hand, is not a fault but rather music that is welcome to the rider's ear. It is manifested as a nearly inaudible, non-rhythmic clicking, produced by the tongue falling back into its channel after the swallowing motion that occurs in correct chewing. As it does so, it lets the mouthpieces that it had lifted up drop back again, causing the snaffle mouthpiece to click against the curb mouthpiece.

False gnashing and rattling of the bit are indication of psychological and physical tensions and are totally unrelated to the chewing that testifies to true, complete suppleness. Since the correct action of the reins and of the concert of all the controls and proof that the horse carries itself.

Most riders are uncertain about the point inside the mouth at which the bit acts directly. If the tongue and its channel are normally shaped, the one-piece bar mouthpiece acts only upon the tongue, unless the liberty of the tongue is too great. The jointed snaffle mouthpiece does not act upon tongue and bars, as we are often told, but normally acts only upon the former and the edges of the lower lip that cover the bars.[19] As these edges are thin and can be pushed aside when the hand is hard and unstable, thus exposing the bars, the latter are sometimes subject to pressure.

Essentially the same principles apply to *riding with one hand* as to riding with divided reins.

Everything we have said concerning steadiness, softness, lightness, position, and carriage of the hand applies to riding with divided reins as well as to riding with one hand, whether a snaffle or a bit and bridoon is used, the differences being slight. Riding with divided *snaffle reins* is standard practice in the riding hall because, when we are riding horses that have not had much training, it often happens in the turns that the outer hand must yield to the mouth and advance fairly far forward, or that the inner hand must move laterally away from the horse's body in order to act with an " opening " rein. Holding one or both of the snaffle reins lower down for a while, as well as raising one hand or the other on occasion, likewise requires riding with two hands.

The reins have to be divided for jumping and climbing no matter what bridling is used in order to be able to yield fully in the direction of the mouth on both sides of the neck.

Lastly, only riding with divided reins assures us broader control. The hands, sometimes separating by more than a handbreadth, support the restraining legs in controlling the hindquarters in order to limit their turning out, to prevent refractoriness, or to control them by stronger use of the small of the back with the upper body leaning back.

If the curb bit is used with divided reins, the left rein should be separated by the little finger and the right rein by the ring finger so that they can be quickly combined if necessary in the left hand.

When divided snaffle and curb are used, especially when riding over obstacles and rough terrain, the curb reins should be imperceptibly relaxed whenever possible, the snaffle reins passing under the little finger

we have compared correct chewing to a murmuring, these vices may be compared to blabbering.

Nosebands that are buckled too tight prevent the horse from chewing and cause a dead mouth.

[19] The fact that horses stick out their tongues proves that the tongue is more sensitive at this point, and that many horses prefer pressure *solely* upon the bars as the lesser evil.

of the left hand and the ring of the right hand maintaining the necessary contact with the bit. This helps to keep the mouth fresh.

If the snaffle rein is held taut (all four reins equally held tight in the left hand), the right arm hangs down naturally from the shoulder. Then the hand lies behind the right thigh, and its slightly opened palm must be turned towards the body of the horse. This appears to be a pedantic requirement that is taken from military regulations, but it possesses a deeper meaning and significance for all riders. Experienced riding instructors know only too well that any other position of the right arm usually produces unconscious stiffness and distortions in the rider.

There are many occasions when *riding with the snaffle reins in one hand* can actually work miracles even in a young horse. Temporarily riding with one hand offers great advantages not only with remounts, however, but also with horses that are already well ridden and with riders in all stages of training. These advantages have a favourable effect upon the gait of the horse as well as the suppleness of the rider's seat.

Two examples will prove this.

If we take a young rider whose seat is not yet flexible enough and whose stiffness is communicated to his horse as long as he rides with divided reins, and make him gather the reins in one hand, we will see that the horse immediately works with much less constraint and greater satisfaction.

But we can go still further.

If we take a rider who is otherwise quite good, whose horse is already able to take a few piaffe steps, and advise him to gather the reins in one hand whenever the horse becomes difficult in the piaffe, we notice that the horse discovers the rhythm of the piaffe.

Why did the difficulties in our two examples cease as soon as the reins were taken up in one hand?

The young rider on an old horse is unable to sit properly as yet; he disturbs his seat either by holding fast convulsively with both hands or by trying to manipulate the stiff horse with his reins. Once he gathers the reins in one hand, he tires more quickly and releases the horse more, so that the latter abandons its cramped tension and allows its back to swing. Then the rider, too, can sit better and more softly.

In the second instance, the rider who is otherwise skilled and has a good seat is as yet unable to handle a young horse that is still being trained; he endeavours to treat it in circus-like fashion by means of alternating rein controls, right-left and left-right, as is often advocated in riding textbooks; his success may be imagined. But as soon as he gathers the reins in one hand, and the horse accepts the milder and quieter guidance by stretching out to reach the bit and begins to let its back swing, it suddenly discovers the transition to the piaffe without difficulty.

It is quite certain that most horses stretch out to make contact with the bit more readily when guided with one hand.

Anyone who participated in cavalry exercises before 1914 knows that the dragoon, hussar, and uhlan horses performed best during these exercises when they had to be managed with one hand. The resulting free gaits, the light trot, the freedom from the worry of having to keep the horse in a certain form, and finally the rider's attention, which was distracted from the horse and focused on keeping direction, etc., also contributed to make the horse less constrained and to keep it from tightening up, so that we can really say that these horses owed a large part of their easy riding qualities to the more vigorous rates employed in the exercises. In hunting, too, many a puller would move much more calmly and pleasantly if its rider could be prevailed upon to ride with one hand.

In concluding this section on rein controls we should like to point out that the remedy for *powerful reactions of the horse against the hand,* such as an attempt to bolt, is not hanging on to the reins without the support of the seat. On the contrary, we often see that strong men are "carried away" by their horses even at a walk, whereas riders who are by no means any stronger can do whatever they please with the same horse. The former are immediately pulled forward out of their loose seat at the critical instant, and their legs are thrown aside. The latter hold the horse by means of their closed, deep seat and let its strength be expended against their pelvis, which finds its support and fixes the weight control in the seat bones, now drilled into the saddle, so to speak. Thus they allow any bucking against the hand to be controlled by the supporting pressure of the buttocks—they know how to use the small of their backs. It is not the strength of the arms that matters! Our Hercules would lose out in a tug of war against a much weaker opponent if the latter were able to use a rock or a small trench as a point of support.

III. Riding Manners and Customs

There are written and unwritten laws for the cavalryman, the hunter, the tournament rider, and for anyone riding horses or enjoying their company, laws that differ in their externals but reflect the same psychological state, the same mental attitude in essence.

This international attitude, international in the best sense of the word, regards the horse as a true and devoted friend, comrade, and servant and considers the rider as privileged in every way by his domination of this masterpiece of creation.

The written laws are based upon experience and the result of scientific research and are justified by reasons of pure utility—the maintenance and care of costly, often irreplaceable horses. The unwritten laws have an altogether different origin.

The written laws alone could fill volumes. Every good riding manual and textbook of hippology contain their essential features. If a rider drives his horse at a murderous trot on hard pavement up to the stable door, then throws the rein to the stable boy and quickly vanishes in order to freshen up after these exertions and does not see his horse again until the next time he goes out riding—provided it is not raining or too hot or too cold—then hoists himself into a saddle that has been put on the horse in slapdash fashion, his saddle horse will not last very long.

Weakness, thy name is Man. Even the conscientious groom of such a " fancier " will find his eagerness beginning to slacken. He will modify the feeding schedule to suit his own convenience, tie up the horse for the night to spare himself the bothersome job of grooming, clean the saddle and harness in a niggardly manner, and put it on the horse carelessly. For he knows that his employer stays away from the stable and is not interested in the grooming and turnout of his horse so long as it is fairly fat and isn't lame.

In time such a horse, treated like a bicycle, will grow restless as soon as it sees its heavily spurred rider, even if it has been raised with the milk of human kindness. Associated ideas—the appearance of the man equipped for riding—painful drilling of the toes into the ribs, and heavy plumping in the saddle when mounting—powerful grip of the paw on the curb reins—have, with constant repetition, been impressed upon the excellent memory of a horse as a cause-and-effect series of ideas. No wonder, therefore, that the horse thinks of flight as soon as the coarse rider who produces the feeling of discomfort (pain) appears, and actually tries to bolt as soon as it is in the open and the stableboy has released its head.

Anyone who is uninterested in the care, maintenance, feeding, horse-shoeing, and stall of his horse, who lets it stand for days without getting any exercise, who neither sees nor feels nosebands and girths that do not fit or twisted curb chains and stirrup leathers that are tucked under, who does not avoid ground that is too soft or too hard when he could reach his objective by a path that is not as hard on the horse's legs if he were only less lazy mentally and a little more attentive, who lets the horse trot or gallop always on the same lead, usually straightaway from the stable, who does not give his horse an opportunity to drink its fill during long rides, who makes new demands on the horse whenever it prepares to dung, who forgets to loosen the girth on occasion, and lastly, who utilizes his temporary power over the tied-up animal to take revenge and to inflict "reprisals" for misbehaviour that he was not strong enough in the saddle to suppress (reprisals, moreover, that the horse will repay with usury when the rider is powerless), sins against laws that should be known to every young rider. Not only is he not acting like a horseman, but his violation of riding manners and riding customs will also result in direct injury to the health and usefulness of the horse, and the incorrigible rider will be taught a lesson in the only way he understands—by suffering a loss.

Though respect for these "written moral laws" can be secured by more or less energetic insistence of the instructor and older companions or by fear of material loss, there are also offences against *equestrian tact*—used here in the sense of correct behaviour towards one's fellow horsemen. These can be avoided, like indiscretions in social intercourse, by the naturally healthy social sensitivity and the innate feeling for decorum that exist in every rider whose mental balance is not upset.

It is hard to lay down binding rules for equestrian tact; it is largely a matter of feeling; furthermore, what is called for and the only possible thing to do to-day may seem pedantic and pompous to-morrow under different circumstances. These are situations in which a true horseman will find the unmistakably correct attitude purely instinctively and as a matter of feeling.

First of all, there is one's behaviour towards older riders and the fair sex, which lends true charm to our riding pleasures in the hunting field and across country. Though proper behaviour at the hunt in order to avoid annoying others and oneself will be discussed in more detail in the section on "Hunting", I should like to take up a few instances here that recur frequently in daily rides.

One instance of bad manners that cannot be censured too much is the disagreeable practice of passing. Not everybody is as firm in the saddle as you are, and when you rapidly pass an older gentleman who comfortably jogs along merely for the sake of his health or a young lady on a thorough-bred that recalls its youth on the turf (racing ground) only too often, you will not make many friends. If you are really in a hurry, and making a wide detour is impracticable, you must always find time to stop, once you have caught up with the other rider, and to ask politely, hat in hand, whether you may be permitted to ride ahead.

A young rider often has the privilege of riding cross country with an older one. It may happen that the latter's inexperienced horse slows up at obstacles or the like. Without an expressed invitation to do so it would be quite wrong to seize the opportunity of showing off and exhibiting the cross-country and jumping ability of your own horse.

When riding as part of a group, wait until the last rider has got into the saddle.

The rider who first notices holes, bits of glass and wire during the ride calls them to the attention of those behind him so that they can protect their horses from injury. One should not clatter at a fast pace over wooden bridges, which are often in a state of decay. If your neighbour's horse has a stone in its hoof, or if something is out of order in its saddle, you are expected to come to its assistance readily. Each rider must keep the place he has once chosen for himself in the troop; he must not come too close to the horse ahead of him, and in general he should ride " for the open hole ". While in the saddle it is wise not to try to catch a runaway horse that has thrown its rider. It will find its way back to the dismounted group by itself.

Maximum care should be exercised if you know that one of the horses is a kicker. The owner of such a horse is *ipso facto* highly unpopular, even if he were otherwise the most charming of persons. But if your horse happens to be a kicker, remain modestly in the background or at a safe distance off to a side. You'll be vastly more popular. It might be added that it is customary to braid a brilliant red ribbon into the tail of kicking horses as a danger signal.

Praiseworthy and instructive though it may be for famous tournament riders to participate in minor tourneys with their exceptionally well-trained and well-made horses, the objective of this participation is not entirely achieved if these riders, exploiting tourney regulations down to the last detail, allow their top-notch horses to compete in the elementary classes. They take the prizes away from the local talent who are unable to compete with them either in ability and experience or in the opportunity for training their horses, which can't measure up on other counts as well.

It is much more tactful for such a celebrity to exhibit his stable " out in the sticks " without competing for prizes. The tourney will be a bigger drawing card, and will doubtless reimburse the host riding club for any expenses for transportation and board.

It is false ambition and cruelty to animals to insist on completing a course with an inadequately trained horse that is obviously unequal to it. You merely provide a spectacle for the gallery and give the man who sets up the obstacles a nervous breakdown. The only correct thing to do is to break off the circuit and to take one or another of the easier obstacles near the start before returning to the stable.

It may happen that you do not agree with the judges. But this difference of opinion must not be expressed aloud on the tourney grounds. One must and should ride to win, to be sure, but one does not take part in tourneys only to win. This should be especially borne in mind when your opponent is victorious after a hard fight. Be the first one to congratulate him. You must be able to lose with dignity.

An old proverb says: "Another man's horse and your own spurs are matters of confidence"; and another rider can give you no greater evidence of his confidence in you that to let you have his own horse which he has "made" over the course of years, employing all his mental and physical talents.

In the riding hall everyone who is riding at a walk should keep the track free, mounting and dismounting in the middle out of consideration for the others. Moreover unthinking clicking of the tongue, to which one's own horse rapidly becomes insensitive, should be avoided because it irritates the other horses.

The Spanish Riding School of Vienna is not only the *haute école* of equitation proper but a high school of *riding-hall manners in their most highly developed form*. If one has the good fortune of observing how the trainers there play with their horses in all the gaits, on both hands, in the saddle and dismounted, without disturbing the others or uttering a loud word, he realizes what distinguished riding manners, in their purest state and sanctified by ancient tradition, signify.

The outfitting of horse and rider is a topic by itself. It is poor taste to deck the horse with as much leather as possible and to "liven" the picture with bandages and blankets in brilliant colours; it smacks of the commercial stable and the circus and belongs (with certain restrictions) only in historical quadrilles and the like.

The appearance of the horse is most beautiful and most impressive when it is appropriately groomed and in the pink of condition, displaying the form given it by the Creator, not concealing it by coloured harness. The expert will not be deceived by such frippery anyhow. The best way of making a horse look more beautiful than it is at rest will always be to ride it well.

Indispensable saddle and bridle tack, which should be strictly utilitarian, should not be conspicuously new, as if it came right out of the shopwindow; on the contrary, it should produce its effect by unpretentious simplicity and a certain patina of use, though it should be of superior workmanship and design and bear the unmistakable stamp of expert and careful maintenance. It is a matter of course that the saddle must be so constructed and fitted that the rider does not find it hard to "feel" and "think" the swinging back of the horse from the lowest point of the saddle, located in the centre of the seat area.

The getup of horse and rider often provides fairly clear indications of the latter's character. It is a visiting card that often yields rather profound insight into the innate qualities of the rider.

Moreover the provisions of tourney regulations concerning bridling and saddling in the various competitions are the best guide to what is appropriate and good style.

The same holds true, *mutatis mutandis,* of the riding habit. If it is simple, of superior quality, and strictly appropriate to the purpose in hand, the rider will harmonize externally with his horse, saddled and bridled in accordance with the same principles.

The rider, who should attract attention solely by his good riding, must banish from his wardrobe everything ostentatious or eye-catching, such as wide, ballooning riding breeches, excessively large spurs (which are best eliminated entirely), patent-leather boots (except on certain occasions), or inappropriate, ornamented riding crops that remind one of a toyshop. Likewise, it is best to leave cuirassier curb bits, sharp snaffles, patent bits,[20] martingales, and similar auxiliary equipment in the locked showcases of the tack room.

One can go too far in this respect, however. A red coat, for example, must start on its career as a red coat, and you will have to wait patiently until weather and perhaps more or less voluntary contact with Mother Earth have given it the desired patina. In our latitudes, where it rains much more than we should like during the hunting season, a diligent hunter will not have to wait too long for his riding jacket to show the welcome marks of wind and weather. But an occasional hunter would do better to shine in fresh, brilliant red rather than have his habit bleached by a chemical process.

What the rider wears should be left to his own judgment. If his habit fits the occasion and is modern in the best sense of the term, it is correctly chosen. He should follow the prevailing fashion of course, for otherwise he would be conspicuous. The true rider rejects everything that is excessively modern as an eccentric exaggeration.

Breeches and boots are most important for the rider. The breeches should fit well around the knee and the seat. The boots should fit tightly about the heels, leaving play for the toes and ankles, but not too tightly around the calves. They should have one-piece soles, that is, no " step " as they pass over the stirrup and no high heels to catch in the stirrup. It is advisable for the breeches to be of lighter colour than the coat, except for the black formal habit of the civilian rider and the uniform, which are subject to special regulations. This harmless contrast stresses the appearance and harmony of the rider's seat and figure without being in any way obtrusive or ostentatious.

A glove of even the finest workmanship diminishes somewhat the

---

[20] A horse often takes to such a highly praised patent bit very well for the first time, and seems to have abandoned any idea of resistance to the reins. The rider's disappointment will be all the greater when the annoying vices return as soon as the horse has recovered from its initial astonishment.

" feel " that should connect the hand to the horse's mouth. That is why many riders prefer to ride without gloves when working their horses, unless etiquette or other circumstances such as cold or rain make a protective covering for the hands a necessity.

One thing more. There are many kinds of headgear and salutes. Each has its own justification and is appropriate to the circumstances and to the habit that one is wearing. But a salute on horseback should always be the expression of self-confident, calm dignity, which should always characterize the over-all appearance of the rider; hence it should never be hasty and careless. The proud gracefulness with which the riders of the Spanish Riding School doff their two-cornered hats to the picture of Charles VI may serve as a model because it is in complete harmony with the surroundings.

One of the worst offences against good riding manners is to enter another man's stable without the knowledge and express invitation of the owner. If one does so, he is suspected of wanting to learn more or less harmless stable secrets unfairly. Another bad habit is discussing in company the good and not so good features of other men's horses. Such discussions can reach the owner's ears only too readily distorted. " Women and horses that are not talked about are best ", as a robust horseman's saying puts it, and anyone who has witnessed the painful consequences for all concerned of a remark that was intended to be quite harmless will readily understand that all topics but two were permitted in my old regimental mess.

Hunters and yachtsmen, fencers and tennis players, in fact, all sportsmen have their technical terminology with its figurative meanings a d foreign derivations, which are riddles to the outsider.

The beginner should avoid entering into the conversations of experts, and this is especially true of the horseman and the racing world. His effort to sound like an " insider " produces exactly the opposite effect and merely makes him look ridiculous.

Part Two

TRAINING THE YOUNG HORSE

CHAPTER ONE

FROM THE PASTURE TO THE STALL AND THE LUNGE

I. Getting Accustomed to New Surroundings and Getting Acquainted

THE preceding sections dealt with the physical and psychological qualities that equip the rider to be the respected friend rather than the rigorous teacher of his horse. We now return to the real hero of this book, the young horse, accompanying it through the various stages of its training and bidding it good-bye only after its training is complete.

Let us assume that our young pupil has safely reached our stable unharmed after many dangers and dramatic scenes during loading, rail transport, and the final march through suburban streets. The last visible and smellable trace of home has vanished with the farm hand who accompanied it and was responsible for it, for Johnny got away as soon as he received his princely wage and the last stalk of familiar pasture hay ran out in the freight car. It finds plenty of straw in the spacious stall in our stable, as well as more hay than it had at home, but the young horse must gradually get used to this, to the drinking water, and to the entirely different surroundings before it decides to yield to its feelings of hunger and thirst, often after hours of fasting. That is what usually happens to young horses that are transported to their future homes from a wholly different rural environment without the proper transition, such as is offered the young cavalry horse by the remount depot.

We must make allowances for these changes if we do not want to see the young animal—tossed about from the very start—become refractory in its further training or perhaps suffer serious impairment of health as a result of the change of feed and climate.

The horse has probably seen little if any oats since the time it was a yearling. The change in feeding must proceed very slowly, a foal fresh from the pasture being given, say, only one quarter of its oats ration at first. The ration is increased from week to week, so that it gets the ten to fifteen pounds of *hard feed* it requires only after one or two months, depending on how soon the so-called " change of flesh " takes place. The interim ration should be supplemented by a larger quantity of hay—

fifteen to twenty pounds—plus such refreshing supplementary feeds as grass, carrots, bran mash, salt, lime, and the like, and the transition to stable feeding should be made as imperceptible as possible. The recommended hay is timothy mixed with some clover.

The horse should be accustomed to *chaff*, preferably rye straw, from the very start, as this enables it to make much better use of its oats. It would be quite wrong to crush the oats, since they lose much of their nerve-stimulant action. This was proved by the zoo-technician Sanson (A. Sanson, *Traité de Zootechnie*, Paris, 1910).

Enough *straw* should be fed as chaff and forage litter—say ten to twelve pounds daily—to fill the intestines, especially in horses with grass bellies which must not be allowed to disappear rapidly, and to stimulate the digestive glands. The horse should not be allowed to eat it *ad lib.* because of the danger of colic (use muzzle). It is better to *feed* and *water* four times daily instead of three because of the small digestive capacity of the horse's stomach, thus making for better utilization of feed and more rapid acquaintance with the stable hand. Frequent feeding is also advisable because it breaks the monotony of the twenty-two hours spent in the stable, employs the horse in a pleasant occupation, and keeps it from acquiring stable vices, such as crib biting, weaving, and licking.

The horse should be watered a full half hour before oats are fed. In summer, say, at 5.30 a.m., 11 a.m., 3 p.m., and 6 p.m.; watering again one half hour after the hay ration has been eaten is especially important at this season as well as when the coat of hair is shed in the spring and autumn. Then rations of salt are also indicated for older horses. The oats ration of, say, 11 pounds (for horses that are already acclimatized) should be fed as follows: 1 pound at 6 a.m.; 2 pounds at 11.30 a.m.; 3½ pounds at 3.30 p.m.; and 4½ pounds at 7 p.m. The ration increases after the forenoon's work, with most of the hard feed eaten before night-time, so that digestion will not be disturbed.

Mixing the oats with chaff, say in a 3 to 1 ratio, is desirable because the increased and prolonged mastication makes for better utilization of the starch in the oats. When the horse is fed a straight oats ration, ten times as many undigested grains are found in the manure as when the rations contain chaff. The mixture should be moderately moistened to prevent the chaff from being blown out of the feed bag. If the chaff is cut finer than one inch in length, the horse does not chew it, and it may cause constipation colic.

We are greatly tempted, of course, to show the horse at the next riding-hall tournament in winter. It may have a chance of winning a prize in the preliminary tests, especially as riding qualities do not count as yet. A blanket is therefore placed on the horse during the cooler August evenings to prevent the growth of coarse hair during the autumnal shedding period.

Good as this system is, it may become dangerous if we are not absolutely certain that the temperature of the stable is uniform and that the horse, once accustomed to them, is kept under blankets constantly. A horse that does not sweat excessively is in less danger of catching cold in winter when led out of the warm riding hall (well covered with blankets, of course). For my part, I prefer a winter coat that is less silky and short, but it must not lose its healthy lustre which shows off horses excellently. When kept in this condition, they feel quite comfortable at temperatures of about 50 degrees F. in the stable and are also able to stand a considerable drop in temperature provided the stable is dry and well ventilated. The respiratory diseases that are especially dangerous to young horses occur in much milder form or not at all if the horses are sensibly hardened, and we no longer need worry that the blanket may slide off or may not be replaced after the horse is groomed. To be sure, the horse must be walked or led about for a longer time after work in the riding hall before being led through the draughty yard to the stable, for the icy north wind blows through every chink and space between the blanket and the body of the horse.

Clipping is advisable if the winter coat is too long, though the horse must then be more thoroughly blanketed. We might add that if clipping is decided upon, the very thin belly skin and the lower leg should retain their natural coat. The excessive heat is not produced in these parts of the body, and, having very little muscle, they feel cold as quickly as hands and feet in a human being.

Frequent, unforced *lifting of the legs* is very useful. A daily check should be made of the horse's progress in this respect. The occasion should also be employed to check the groom's *care of the hoofs*. After the daily washing a very thin coat of unsalted animal fat should be rubbed into the sole and frog as well as into the region of the strip at the edge of the coronet where the growth of the hoof originates. The hoof should be somewhat moist when this is done because then the fat is absorbed, and thus the hoof is protected against drying out. No fat should be rubbed into the hoof walls, which are covered with a glaze and hence are not porous; they should be polished with a cloth and an onion until they shine with the dull lustre of a well-groomed fingernail.

The bulbs and the frogs should be disinfected once or twice a month by painting them with wood tar, but this is effective only if tar-soaped oakum is pressed deep into the two commissures and the cleft with a thin stick. It is also advisable to bandage the hoofs in clay or moist bran during the hot season of the year.

There need be no haste about *shoeing,* though the height of the walls of the hoofs should be adjusted every six to eight weeks and the bearing edges, which wear away irregularly, should be rounded off with a file. The blacksmith must also remove horny pieces of the frog that are half loose, under which dirt and decay can often find lodging.

No shoeing of any kind is required if the owner of the horse is lucky enough to be able to exercise it outside the riding hall on soft, springy forest paths or fine, sandy meadow land. Such terrain causes very little wear of the hoof. Pebbly ground should be avoided.

Crossing macadam roads to reach bridle paths does not harm the hoofs at all, and footing is more certain[1] without shoes than with ordinary summer horseshoes. The only thing that increases wear on the edges of the hoofs and frays them is sharp-edged gravel, especially when the transition from the bottom edge to the hoof wall is not rounded off with a file.

Light crescent horseshoes are all that is needed if the front hoofs wear away faster at the toe than elsewhere.

There are numerous advantages in delaying the shoeing of young horses. During the period of growth, which is far from complete when the corner incisors begin to articulate after the end of the horse's fifth year, the mechanism of the hoof[2] can function more freely when unencumbered by the " necessary evil " of the horseshoe. The hoofs " breathe " better when they are in direct contact with the ground.

Uncontrolled capering when the horse is led or worked on the lunge— bandaged or not—is also less dangerous, for a hoof weighted and armoured with shoe and nails is much more destructive than one in its natural state, even though some savants may claim that the clash of shoed hoofs never causes bony excrescences.

At the beginning the hindquarters may swing out to a side, especially on the lunge. When that happens, a shoed hoof can cause all sorts of damage, producing coronet or pastern bruises in spite of hoof pads and guards; these bruises may become chronic all too readily and remain with the horse as " enlarged fetlocks " for the rest of its life.

If you let your horses go unshod, you must be prepared to encounter much shaking of heads (especially by the blacksmith and his friends). Nor are all horses equally adapted to this. Congenital hardness and consistency of the hoof horn, which vary with breed and country of origin, play an important part. Horses that have grown up in rocky mountain terrain, as well as horses that have a high percentage of oriental blood, almost

---

[1] The frog increases friction. Shorten the horse's steps when the ground is icy.

[2] The hoof mechanism is best defined as the expansion of the hoof when grounded, owing to the pressure of the weight of the body. This expansion increases from front to back and is followed by the corresponding contraction when the hoof leaves the ground. This phenomenon also acts as a blood pump within the hoof.

always have highly resistant, ringing hoofs that resemble hard rubber. But here, too, there are exceptions that prove the rule.

I can remember thoroughbreds, Trakehnens, Anglo-Arabs from southwest France, and horses from the regions of Lublin and Kisbér, all of whom had gone unshod for years; I rode them only cross country and in the riding hall, to be sure, and when I had to take a road, I carefully selected only asphalt roads, making sure to avoid rubble-stone.

The real saddle horse that is ridden on all sorts of terrain and the horse that is expected to do precision jumping over difficult obstacles on smooth grass naturally require protection and support in the form of horseshoes appropriately shaped, and they need screw calks at the heels of all four shoes. These calks recently proved their worth with the German military team at the 1952 Olympics at Helsinki. According to the head of the team, General Viebig, the Hestal hardened steel screw calks deserve part of the credit for the fact that the German team was the only one that completed the cross-country test on the second day of the competition without a fault. Not only do these screw calks give horse and rider a feeling of safety when jumping and landing in broken forest and meadow terrain, but they are also indispensable for military gallops on stony roads and slippery turf, once the chips are down. Hestal calks are also indispensable in dressage rings, where grass has grown smooth because of frequent clipping, unless it happens to be fluted red fescue (*Festuca rubra*) which prevents slipping. This is particularly true in turns if the horse is not to lose all desire to develop its machinery.

A spacious *stall* or box resembling a pen, with the top of the door opening directly to the outside air, is the ideal stand for a horse.

The horse, untied in its stall and appropriately blanketed if the weather is cold or if it is bothered by flies, can look out into the open, with its organs of respiration and sight in constant contact with the hardening fresh air. Occupied in observing the outside world, it never feels boredom, the cause of most stable vices. (The lower half of the door should be fitted with two bars and hinges to prevent any squeezing of the horse's legs when it is lying down.)

The worst thing that could happen to all veterinarians would be for all horses to have open-air stalls of this type, for diseases of the respiratory organs, the eyes, and the legs would be reduced to a minimum.

Care of the physical well-being of the horse, which thus effects a transition to its new surroundings that differ so much from what it had known before, goes hand in hand with its growing accustomed to its groom and rider.

To-day strictly selective breeding for disposition, character, and conformation, plus treatment that allows for psychological factors and even familiarizes a weanling with the halter and contact with human beings, enables us to accustom the horse to snaffle, saddle, lunge, and lastly, the rider.

This represents considerable progress when we realize that only a little more than a century ago the light cavalry remounts coming from half-savage studs, which had known humans only as devils equipped with branding irons and lassos, had to be tamed by forcible treatment, though their obedience was far from final even after the horse had been tamed.

Horsebreaking was the custom at the time and even later. "The beast has to give in", and if it did not want to, it was lunged with bags of sand on its back and on three legs. The American Rarey and his "whispering method" had many followers, and Major Balassa had a wide field for his activities. Moreover, both of them (like Spohr later on) based their work on principles that were psychologically unimpeachable, employing force only as a last resort. Prior to that time superstition was an important factor. Ropes that had been used in hanging were worth their weight in gold. Florinus (1750) asserted that, covered with a woollen cloth and wrapped around the legs of refractory horses, they turned the worst criminals into lambs.

Too great rigidity in describing how the young horse is accustomed to objects that are strange and therefore excite fear and suspicion, such as saddle, bridle, blankets, and girths, as well as lungeing, the rider, mounting, and carrying the load of the rider, would be a mistake.

External circumstances, individuality, disposition, character, sensitivity, and familiarity with the corresponding impressions may make it necessary to devote no more than a few days to accustoming the horse to the objects and occurrences of daily riding, or else as many weeks.

We can, however, lay down the following principle that is generally true and it applies to every individual case: *The trainer must begin by trying to influence the senses of the horse, to awaken feelings of pleasure, and then to make use of the horse's highly developed memory in order to set up associations of ideas that produce direct connections in its brain between something that is very agreeable and something that is somewhat disagreeable.*

The approach of the groom, who provides the horse with feed several times a day, elicits the first direct association of ideas; a human being signifies the satisfying of hunger. With this initial confidence as a basis it will tolerate more and more contacts that are essentially unpleasant to it. At first saddle, blankets, etc., are brought to the horse together with its feed and are hung up on the wall of the stall near the horse during feeding time. Later on, these objects which look so sinister at first gradually lose their terror and can be brought closer and closer to the horse so that it can sniff them while it is offered such titbits as bread and carrots.[3] Once this is accomplished, much, if not all, has been gained, and the time soon comes when the saddle without stirrups or girth can be slid down the neck in the direction of the hair growth and put on so as to cover half of the withers. The horse should be rewarded during this procedure and afterwards, of course, in order to divert it from the unaccustomed feeling and to establish the association of ideas: saddle-feed.

The same procedure is followed for the other riding and lungeing equipment. We might add that many remounts are in great terror of the blanket, so that twice as much care should be employed when putting it on for the first time. A horse quickly loses all fear, however, if it is given its oats in the blanket which, after the blanket has been eaten clean, is then brought close to the upper edge of the neck and slowly opened out and drawn backwards. The more time taken for these things, the sooner will fearful and shy horses lose their distrust and begin to realize that they need expect no pain from human beings.

Practically all young horses will already be accustomed to the snaffle. If they still cause difficulty when bridled, however, twist some hay or grass around the bit, which may be disconnected at the left end, then turn the horse around in its stall and slip the bridle over its head while its neck is stretched out forward and downward. If the left hand holds the tasty bit in front of the horse, half yielding and half withdrawing it, its initial resistance will soon disappear.

What was said above concerning *accustoming the horse to the saddle* can be employed in the riding hall equally well after the horse has been exercised at the lunge until it is tired. Here again it is well to establish an association between the first placing of the saddle on the horse and gifts of food. It should be stressed that the saddle (without stirrups at first) should lie well up front at the withers, with its girth located where it produces the least discomfort for the present, i.e., just behind the elbows. The girth is tightened just enough to keep the saddle from sliding off to one side.

It is evidently best for the horse, rider, and groom that the remount never hit upon the idea that it can offer highly successful resistance to the buckling on of the girth by wind sucking. Once a horse has learned this

---

[3] At this stage a bit of bread is the best lure and reward. Many young horses have to learn to like bread, to be sure. In such cases the bread should be offered together with a handful of grass, which all horses like to be fed in their stalls, or together with carrots. They soon get to like the taste. Gaining a horse's confidence by rewarding him with bits of sugar is not recommended for all young horses; it accustoms them to licking, playing with the lips and tongue, and the like. Licking and gnawing of parts of the stall as a result of previous gifts of sugar, together with boredom and imitation, are often the original causes of the vice of crib biting.

vice as a natural preventive against rough or sudden constriction, it develops unexpected virtuosity, often making the groom despair of ever buckling on the girth, and the rider despair when tightening the girth en route.

In addition to wind sucking, which is fairly harmless, other dangerous vices, such as resenting saddle pressure with its sequels of throwing the rider and somersaulting, which have cost many a horse and rider their lives, may develop from mistakes made the first time the horse is saddled.

If we have a trained windsucker in our stable, time-consuming rituals have to be performed before we can go out riding. In many cases leading the horse around at a walk and trot for some time suffices; then it can be resaddled correctly and is ready for the ride. Others make things more difficult and have to be lunged with a long snaffle rein before they yield. This is not much fun if time is short. Still others yield after they are moved forward and back a few times dismounted and are then saddled. If the girth is then loosened one hole before mounting, everyone is satisfied.

It is also useful to wet the saddle pads with cold water. The feeling of wetness and cold on its back causes the horse to bend its back downwards so that it cannot suck the wind.

But all these devices take time and improve no one's temper because they have little to do with riding and could easily have been avoided if the initial training of the young horse had been done with more care.

We are dealing, luckily enough, with an unspoiled horse. The next day, after it has completed its work with the lunge, we place the saddle on its back again, and we do this for a few days until it tolerates the saddle in the correct position without any sign of dislike.[4] The girth is then tightened imperceptibly and brought closer to its proper position, where the ribs are fuller. It is now time to let the stirrups, which were attached to the saddle during the past few days but were run up and secured, swing freely after the horse has been tired by work on the lunge, first at the walk and then trotting. This is also the best sort of preparation for accustoming the horse to the rider's legs.

If the horse is advanced in its training, the time has come when one can mount in the saddle, letting the remount, which has already learned to move on the lunge, do the same work as before but this time carrying the weight of the rider. The additional weight must, of course, be taken into consideration in fixing the amount of work to be done by the horse.

---

[4] The elastic surcingle made of braided latex linen, which fits the horse without squeezing and interferes with breathing and blood circulation less than the usual rigid girth, is especially recommended for sensitive horses.

II. Lungeing

Lungeing is an excellent way of strengthening the confidence of the young horse in man—even outside the stable—and quieting it down. It also provides the unconstrained movement it requires to keep healthy. Sensible lungeing also gives the horse its first notions of driving and restraining controls, thus paving the way for the first time it is mounted. Untroubled by the muscular aches that the rider's weight would cause it at first, it will reach forward for the bit more easily under the mild urging of the whip, rediscovering in this suppleness the balanced long strides characteristic of its machinery. In this sense lungeing is also the best corrective method of restoring unconstraint and natural carriage to horses that are psychologically and physically cramped. Such horses will have faulty gaits, and lungeing will make it possible to begin their retraining.

The period of lungeing must be prolonged if the horse is still so young and undeveloped—say, three and a half to four years old—that having to carry the rider's weight would cause damage to the tendons, bones, and joints that are still too weak.

The *equipment* required for lungeing includes the lunge, the cavesson, the side reins, the whip, and the surcingle. The *surcingle* is buckled either over the saddle or over a folded blanket, depending on whether the horse, wearing a snaffle bit but no bridle, enters the ring saddled or unsaddled.

If the horse is saddled, the surcingle must not be buckled any tighter than the well-tightened saddle girth to keep the latter from wrinkling. If the horse is lunged without a surcingle, for one reason or another, the narrow belt that used to be quite fashionable proves useful at the beginning. It connects the two saddle flaps beneath the belly of the horse to keep them from flapping as it moves. This lungeing girth, as it is called, should be well padded and six to twelve inches in width. It should have a ring or a loop in the middle for attaching the snaffle reins in addition to the upper rings attached at various heights for the side reins. Work on the lunge loses some of its value if the horse manages to pull the surcingle forward. That is why care must always be taken that the surcingle runs across the lowest point of the saddle seat, bearing against the rising front of the saddle, and that it can also be supported by the saddle girth itself.

I do this by buckling it somewhat behind the saddle girth rather than entirely on top of it.

The surcingle receives even better support, to be sure, if its bottom consists of a narrower belt with a buckle.

But if the horse is lunged for any reason at all without a saddle, which keeps the surcingle fixed in its correct position, a buckled crupper may spare the trainer considerable annoyance in some cases, since it helps to keep the surcingle in position. The bottom surface of the crupper must be kept particularly soft (possibly padded), however, to keep it from causing a bald spot at the croup.

The *lunge* must be at least twenty-five feet long, though it is better to have it over thirty feet, so that we are rarely compelled to pay out the last loop to the very end, and a somewhat larger circle can be laid out to allow a young horse to caper about, releasing its tensions if necessary. The hemp of which the lungeing tape is made must not be too smooth but must allow the tape to slide through the hand fairly smoothly.

The *cavesson* should be provided with a heavily padded noseband which fits so snugly over the bony portion of the bridge of the nose as to leave no free play. If it is too loose, the person holding the lunge will cause the horse unintentional pain. The lunge is snapped onto a single ring in the middle, which must not be attached to a projecting lug; this is a barbarous device whose lever action ruins the horse's joints. The tongue of the buckle must be on top. If the horse tends to go off at a tangent, the lunge should be fastened to one of the rings alongside the middle lungeing ring, intended for working on the right and left hand, in order to prevent shifting of the cavesson. If the cavesson's cheek strap is too long, the noseband will lie too low, causing troublesome pressure upon the sensitive cartilaginous end of the bridge of the nose, interfering with breathing, and also pinching the corner of the mouth.

To give the snaffle the free play required for its eventual use by the rider and to keep the leather parts of the cavesson that lie underneath it from exerting any troublesome pressure, the noseband, the throatlatch, and the front strap of the cavesson are fastened underneath the cheek straps and the throatlatch of the snaffle, which is placed on the horse without a head halter, the middle straps being drawn tight to keep the outer cheek-piece of the cavesson from injuring the eye on that side.[5] The head stall and front of the cavesson lie above the corresponding parts of the snaffle.

For the time being, the two *side reins* are made long enough to keep from disturbing the horse in its natural carriage when walking freely, being buckled or snapped to the rings high up on the side of the sur-cingle and to the rings of the snaffle (which is provided with a thick bit) underneath the snaffle reins. Check to see that they are both of the same length by stepping in front of the horse, putting a finger of each hand in the corresponding snaffle ring, and drawing the horse to you.

[5] Care should be taking in fitting the cavesson to have the point where its middle strap (jowl strap) is sewed to the cheekpiece be at the same height as the outer corner of the horse's eye.

The so-called Holleuffer loop reins[6] can be advantageously substituted for the two side reins, especially on horses that tighten their backs, have too high a carriage, and are unable to stretch out and lower their heads. As these loop reins invite it to slide forward and down to the reins, so to speak, the horse finds it particularly pleasant to stretch out to reach the bit.

The *whip* should be long enough for the trainer standing at the centre of the circle (he takes over the job of holding the whip after a few hours) to reach the horse with the tip of the lash. The handle of the whip and the first third of its shaft should be rigid and so heavy as to counterbalance the remainder of the shaft, which tapers down to the end and grows more flexible, plus the cord. The over-all length of whip plus cord should be twelve to sixteen feet. Only a balanced whip handles easily.

For the initial lessons it is good to have a small riding hall in which at least three sides close off the circle or a hedged-in ring like those used in circuses. Otherwise we can take our stand somewhat off to the side of the longitudinal axis of the hall, so that the lungeing circle has the support of at least the two walls that form the corner of the building.

The horse is brought out to the riding school for its first lungeing lesson with light bandages and, if at all possible, without shoes, at least on the hind feet. The side reins and lunge are not attached as yet. First the side reins are snapped on at the right length, and then the lunge[7], which is folded in the hands in superimposed loops, is attached to the cavesson ring.

The horse is first led around the whole riding hall on the left hand a few times to familiarize it; the assistant, who takes over the whip later, walks on the off side with his hand on the cheek strap of the snaffle while talking quietly to the animal. The horse is accompanied on the near side by the trainer who does not use the lunge in any way. The trainer's right hand is kept free for patting the horse. The horse is walked around on

[6] Two reins, each twice as long as a snaffle rein, run from the *bottom outside* of the girth (because of the fact that the shoulders are broader than the neck and in order not to cramp their freedom of movement) through the snaffle rings to the upper inside of the girth; when the horse is saddled, they are fastened to the rings attached at either side of the pommel.

A trainer wishing to make the side reins and hence the horse's mouth completely independent of shoulder motion, which cannot help being a disturbing factor, can combine the two ends of the reins that are otherwise attached right and left to the girth, slip them through a sleeve (to keep them from abrading the front legs), and buckle them to the bottom of the saddle girth. But now they must run from the *bottom inside* through the snaffle rings to the *top outside*.

[7] The trainer must fold the lunge correctly before attaching it to the cavesson. He does this by grasping the loop at the end of the lunge with his left hand and stretching out the untwisted lunge with his right hand as far as his right arm will reach. Then the right hand returns the stretched-out portion of the lunge to the left hand, reaching out again to the right and so on until the entire lunge lies in uniform superimposed loops in the left hand, leaving about two feet at the snap-on end free.

the left hand because most horses turn on the left hand rather than the right. After a few circuits the rectangular track becomes an ellipse and finally a circle, on which the rest of the exercising takes place. The lunge-ing trainer approaches the centre of the circle gradually, paying out the loops in the lunge until he turns slowly at that spot. Since he is still without a whip in his right hand, he uses that hand to hold the end of the lunge with any remaining loops and leads the lunge with the left hand, which is farther from the horse. The part of the lunge between the two hands must not hang down too low. The trainer's right (outer) shoulder is turned towards the shoulder of the horse, his left, leading, arm is slightly bent, and his hand is closed over the lunge, which runs over the second joint of the index finger with the thumb pointing to the head of the horse. The position of the trainer's body enables him to offer success-ful resistance if the horse suddenly starts moving too fast by bracing his right (outer) foot against the ground and bending his upper body back-wards with a hollow back, seeking further support, if necessary, with the leading hand braced against the left hip.

This normal position of the lungeing trainer is one in which his pull on the lunge acts forward as well as sideways. This prevents serious injury to the horse's legs, such as shoulder lameness, interference wounds on the inside of the hind fetlock joint, etc., which may easily occur if the pull acts to the rear when the horse jumps around aimlessly.

Another point that cannot be emphasized too much it this: The lunge-ing trainer *must* turn about a fixed point which lies beneath his inner heel or between his two legs.

No one would think of questioning the importance of a steady hand when riding. And yet we see many thoughtless trainers describing irregular, more or less concentric little circles when lungeing; they do not realize that it is impossible for the horse to find steady support in the necessarily unsteady leading hand, so that the lunge cannot be kept in even, light tension. Cases that require the lungeing trainer to leave his place, especially with horses that have not been lunged sufficiently, will be taken up later.

The young horse is now moving to the left around a circle, led by the assistant, the future whip bearer, who accompanies it on its off side. The lungeing trainer at the centre of the circle seeks to maintain contact with the slightly sagging lunge. As soon as the horse (which prefers moving along straight lines when at liberty) has grown familiar with the unaccus-tomed curved line of the circle and has calmed down, the assistant begins to trot and then leaves the horse free, imperceptibly lowering his left arm, though he continues to run alongside the horse; only later, when the horse trots along with sureness by itself, does he fall back more and more.

If the horse tends to slow down, he drives it forward from behind by urging it on and swinging his arm. If the horse understands what is wanted of it and keeps up its pace, the assistant moves towards the lungeing trainer inside the circle and accompanies the horse halfway between trainer and horse, following behind the lunge. If it comes to a stop, the assistant leads it again, but this time at the inner cheek strap. As work at the trot is continued, allowances are made for the fact that at this gait (and at the gallop) the horse's head is naturally carried somewhat higher and the neck and its muscles also swing in a narrower frame than at a free walk. The side reins must be adjusted (shortened) accordingly.

To bring the horse to a stop, the lungeing trainer shortens the lunge as he moves sideways in the direction of his inner shoulder (the shoulder away from the horse) until he is on the circumference of the circle in front of the horse. While he rewards the already somewhat tired horse with bread or oats, the time may perhaps have come when he can stroke its neck, shoulder, back, and hindquarters with the folded whip. If the horse shows no fright, the assistant can take over the whip. As training continues, he carries it folded for the time being under the armpit that is away from the horse, pulling it out behind his back in a threatening raised position in his outside hand only after he has released the horse, which does not want to go forward once the assistant is left behind.

After the horse has trotted around the circle several times again, it is stopped once more; if it shows any tendency to turn off to the outside, the trainer again adjusts his movement to the side so as to get the horse between the wall and himself.

We then take up the *change of hand.* If the horse is quiet, it can be turned on the forehand in a volte, the trainer drawing the horse forward and to the left by the snaffle reins, which he grips underneath the chin, at the same time using the folded whip, held horizontally, to exert light pressure against its ribs every time it lifts its near hind foot. If the horse readily obeys, letting itself be pulled forward willingly, the occasion should be seized to reward it. It should forget that the whip was the terror instrument of inspection by buyers, and it should establish this association of ideas: "If I yield to the pressure of the whip shaft (which I should really prefer to evade), I'll get oats!" This obedience is facilitated by the mechanically compelling pull forward and to the side and by the lateral control applied at the moment that helps the horse to yield to the pressure.

After the turn has been made, the exercises previously described are repeated in the same sequence on the right hand. Having stepped perhaps over *cavalletti* lying on the ground on the way to the exit, with the side reins unfastened, the pupil, burdened with no unpleasant impressions, may be allowed to go back to the stable with a good conscience.

It is not likely that everything will actually go so smoothly, and we should *avoid trying to teach the young horse too much during the first few lessons.* It must digest all its new impressions in peace and be able to reflect on them in the stable. The transition from what is easy to what is more difficult should be made only when it has understood the simpler tasks, and new demands should be made in such a way that there can be no misunderstanding or confusion on the part of the horse. One of the many proofs that a horse requires a certain time to familiarize itself with new requirements, to grow accustomed to them, even though it may be physically able to comply with them at once without mistake, is the fact that a horse that performed an exercise very badly only yesterday, for example, manages to accomplish it to-day without any difficulty.

Elementary lungeing has as its purpose merely this: to enable the horse to recover on the lunge the same free, natural gait that it used to have in the pasture, to get it to understand the driving and restraining controls, and, later on, by getting it to move faster than it really wants to, to lay the foundations for initial obedience. Unconstrained movements on the lunge strengthen the health of the horse, which is always somewhat uncertain in periods of transition, and during the next few weeks, together with the "change of flesh," its general condition is improved so much that bearing the burden of a rider does not produce phenomena of fatigue, such as excessively cramped arching or sagging of the back.

The whip controls used in lungeing are a preparation for the riding crop, the leg, and the spur, the hand control being transmitted by the lunge, the cavesson, and the side reins. The weight controls that complete the whole are provided only by the rider's weight, however, and it is his feeling that brings leg, weight, and hand in tune with one another as training progresses.

In lungeing all that the trainer has at his command is the feel of his hand and his sense of sight; these, however, are too little to advance the horse beyond a certain point, for dead instruments can never take the place of the supple, sensitive seat.

Lungeing without the assistance of the cavesson has certain disadvantages. No matter whether the lunge is fastened to one snaffle ring or both or to the chin strap, the mouth suffers because of the often unavoidable, more powerful, hand controls, the use of which is very poor preparation for guidance by the rider. On the contrary, tongue difficulties, which arise very easily when the snaffle is too low, deviation of the lower jaw backward or to the side, and other vices and defects are often attributable to battles that were waged against a lunge attached to the bit. The vibrations of the lunge when stopping or getting the horse to move out, which will be discussed later, do not create a favourable atmosphere for the stretching of the horse's body to reach the bit, which is attempted only shyly at first.

The cavesson may be left off, however, and replaced by a head stall fitted with a ring and reinforcing hoops if the bridge of a horse's nose is very sensitive to the firm pressure of the cavesson or if the trainer does not feel he has the necessary skill and delicacy.

The *voice* is another indispensable aid in lungeing. It is used to calm the horse and also to explain the various controls to the horse, so to speak, when they are employed. If these are always repeated with the same call and the same tone of voice, an attentive horse will do what is demanded of it in a surprisingly short time, almost without any influence of the lunge and whip. Except at the outset, when the leading assistant (usually the groom, whose voice and smell the horse already knows) calms the horse down by speaking to it, it is important that the lungeing trainer begin to raise his voice so that the horse's attention will be attracted to his calls from then on.

As soon as leading is no longer required, the assistant takes over the whip and walks behind the lunge as the whip bearer, accompanying the horse on a smaller circle between the lungeing trainer and the horse. He lets the cord drag while pointing the whip with his outstretched off arm against the horse's croup. As the horse gains more confidence, he aims it at the hocks.

To *drive the horse forward,* the man carrying the whip lowers it, drops behind somewhat, and swings it upwards against the hindquarters, so that the control acts unmistakably from the rear to the front; later on, merely swinging the whip suffices or, if necessary, touching the horse in the direction of the ribs behind the girth.

The lungeing trainer always calls out the command to start and the kind of movement required with the same word and the same intonation for each individual case.

When the horse slows down, which becomes a classical half halt or full halt only later when the driving controls are also applied, the man carrying the whip remains in place, as he does later on when the horse speeds up or tends to run away. It would be wrong for him to remove the whip from its position pointing against the croup or hocks, to conceal it behind him, and to move away from the lunge towards the centre of the circle, as is seen so often. The horse must and will get used to the sight of the whip. If the man carrying the whip conceals it and moves away as soon as the horse shows any sign of disturbance, it will quickly exploit this compliance and work itself up into artificial excitement whenever it wants to keep the annoying warning of the whip away from its body.

The appropriate call of the trainer, combined with a gentle taking up[8] and relaxing of the lunge or merely shaking it, will be enough to make the horse slow down or come to a stop.

If the horse is not yet certain in its movements, a few steps sideways towards the circumference of the circle (the lunge trainer shortening the lunge as he approaches to keep it taut) will make the call and the lunge controls clear to the horse.

At the beginning many horses try to break out of the circle, usually in the direction of the exit. When this occurs the lungeing trainer must not move away from his fixed position, but the man carrying the whip quickly gets behind the horse and drives it forward decisively; in this case motion as rapid as possible is not only permissible but absolutely necessary. Once the horse resumes its travel on the circle, the man carrying the whip returns to his position behind the lunge.

As long as this bad habit of breaking away is merely an instinctive urge to return to the stable, a man standing outside the circle and raising his arms threateningly can be of service. Later on, to be sure, the horse must be framed between the two controls, lunge and whip, in such a way that the lungeing trainer (who now carries the whip as well) is able to choke off any misbehaviour in the seed. But even now, whenever the horse shows any sign of wanting to break out, the trainer must anticipate this misbehaviour and prevent its occurring by having the man carrying the whip make a threatening movement as if he were going to get behind the horse.

This procedure should also be followed if the horse holds back. As a rule even a slight dropping back of the man carrying the whip will result in more energetic motion forward.

If a horse turns inwards and loosens the lunge, the man carrying the whip raises it and swings it downwards on the lunge, letting the whipcord touch the horse's shoulder or neck; later on, a slight gesture of the whip carrier in this direction will suffice to make the horse get back on the circle.

Soon the trainer will be able to achieve the same effect with sensitive horses by shaking the hand holding the lunge a little more vigorously. The wriggling of the lunge produced by this shaking affects the near eye of the horse, and makes it move outwards onto the circle. To explain this control, or if shaking the line is not enough by itself, the raised leading (inner) hand is moved to the outer shoulder, with the arm bent, and then the entire arm makes a rapid swing in a semi-circle towards the horse's head. The strong impulse that this imparts to the drooping lunge acts as a menacing threat to the horse's eyes, at the same time throwing the snap

---

[8] In taking up the lunge one should try to make the pull effective at the moment when the inner hind leg touches the ground. This keeps the hindquarters from falling out of step when the lunge is taken up repeatedly, which would entail loss of the horse's free gait.

end of the lunge attached to the cavesson ring outwards; this constitutes an additional warning to get back to the circle and thus on the lunge.

There are horses that always pull on the lunge and try to turn out. The lunge trainer tries to make these horses contact their bits more easily by alternately raising his hand up to his shoulder and letting it down again. These are the cases when it is advisable to attach the lunge to one of the rings of the cavesson on the side corresponding to the leading hand in order to prevent the cavesson from slipping.

Many horses shy and run away at the slightest provocation, out of fear or high spirits. The same thing will happen in many horses that are high-bred, whose natural muscle tone is particularly marked as a constitutional racial quality.[9] Such horses should be allowed to run until they tire themselves out, the trainer remaining quite passive. Any attempt to slow down the pace by exerting painful lunge controls would only be pouring oil on the fire, and it would only further excite horses that are not in complete possession of their psychological equilibrium because of anxiety states. Painful tugs at the cavesson merely intensify the feeling of discomfort that is produced by the fear-inspiring object, from which the horse will try to escape by even more rapid flight—its natural defence. It is just as senseless to prevent the horse from cavorting about when it wants to release its muscle tension by livelier movement.

When the footing is poor and it is feared that the horse may fall, and if calming calls and alternately taking up and loosening the lunge to moderate the horse's contacts with its control fail, the lesser evil should be chosen, and the lunge should be shortened to make the circle narrower; this diminishes the forward thrust and produces a quieter pace. If possible, such heroic measures should be avoided with horses that are not fully developed, for such horses can suffer serious injury to tendons, joints, and bones when forced to travel on a narrow circle.

When excessive rushing is due to nothing but stable mettle and high spirits, the horse has had too little exercise or is overfed. Its treatment should not be confined simply to quieting it every day. The trouble should be attacked at the roots by appropriate workouts and eliminating the surplus feed.

The childish cavorting of a young horse is a natural phenomenon and does not hurt it if the circle is large enough (up to sixty feet in diameter) and the ground underfoot is soft and springy without presenting any danger of slipping. The side reins are adjusted so as not to restrict the natural movements of its neck; the instinctive sense of equilibrium produces all the regulating movements that protect the foal in pasture from damaging its legs even in its wildest leaps.

What we have said about the voice also applies to the *whip controls,*

[9] The other extreme is the flabby tone of horses with grass bellies.

driving and repelling. If the controls are always exercised from the same initial position, differing merely in degree, from the bottom upwards and from the rear to the front as driving controls, and from top to bottom and along the lunge as controls returning the horse to the circle or enlarging the circle, the horse will very soon learn to distinguish between them and follow them correctly.

If the whip and lunge controls described above are not effective, although the horse ought to be physically and psychologically able to follow them, they are reinforced and intensified to the point of *punishment* if the horse is definitely malicious.

Punishment with the whip is dealt out with the same swings and at the same places as the controls. They are merely intensified. They must be vigorous and follow disobedience instantly. Indecisiveness when administering punishment incites to disobedience even more than when riding. A well-deserved stroke of the whip, applied at the right time and at the right place, works wonders and can break incipient refractoriness once and for all.

If the horse tugs at the lunge at excessive speed and cannot be brought to a half halt or a full halt, initiated by repeated and increasing pulls inwards on the lunge[10] and by the voice, the leading hand releases contact for an instant and then tugs rapidly and forcefully on the lunge. This control, called a saccade, may be repeated, if necessary, until the horse obeys. The trainer may also be compelled to employ these saccades in a milder form as a control to slow down the pace.

Suddenly pulling in on the lunge or letting it sag in order to make the lunge punishment particularly severe is no longer punishment but butchery, like hitting the horse's croup from above, and unworthy of a horseman.

We need not add that whip and lunge punishment can be effectively supplemented by the voice, so that calling out sharply will suffice later on to stifle disobedience in the bud and to make actual punishment unnecessary.

A man who has succeeded in getting all the forces of a horse to serve him unresistingly with little or no punishment possesses equestrian tact in the highest degree—he will have the willing obedience of his companion and friend as an ally and will be able to master many a critical situation that he would be unable to cope with if mounted upon an intimidated slave deprived of any will of its own.

The main objective of this preliminary work on the lunge, which may last several days or as many weeks depending upon the strength and

---

[10] These tugs are most effective while the near front foot is in the air (see also the footnote on p. 102 and the first paragraph on p. 194).

10. Extended walk. Jessica Newberry on *Forstrat* (Thoroughbred) 1960.
VEDEL'S REKLAME-FOTO
11. Regular or middle walk. Captain O. Frank on *Giessvogel* (Hungarian) 1947.

12. Middle trot. Note the light yet positive rein contact. Jessica Newberry on *Forstrat* (Thoroughbred) 1959. H. STING, CELLE

13. Working trot in acquired poise. Colonel Alfred Mylius on *Cottstown* (Irish) 1940.

14. Fluid long-striding middle trot. Note the extreme forward impulsion. Colonel M. Thommen on *Directeur* (Irish) 1945.

intelligence of the pupil, has been to accustom the horse to its surroundings and to everything that goes on in the riding hall and to acquaint it with what is demanded of it. The horse has learned to keep on a circle and to move along at a natural trot (which it is allowed to discover for itself), its legs moving at an even rate, neither slowing down nor hurrying.

This is the foundation for actual work on the lunge, which has as its objective driving the horse to achieve suppleness on the lunge and a development of the gait and flexibility that correspond to the horse's conformation.

This work on the lunge is done in the following order: The horse is driven at first to develop its impulsion, while retaining its uniform gait and hence its poise. As a result its hindquarters will engage farther forward and provide greater impulsion, thus causing the entire horse to stretch out on the lunge.[11] Once a horse has attained suppleness by stretching to reach the bit, the first step has been taken towards dependable contact with the bit, in our case dependable response to the lunge. The horse becomes increasingly conscious of the vigorous oscillations of its back, which are a result of the increased flexion and extension of the hind legs in order to participate more fully in forward motion and in carrying the load. The joints of the hindquarters become more supple, resulting in a springy, lively, expressive step.

Changes of gait and of rate or halts cause as little difficulty to a well-lunged horse that has progressed in this sequence as the two-track figures or close turns with a rider later on. All we will have to do is to get the horse to understand the new requirements, to habituate it, so to speak. The gymnastic preparation that makes all physical accomplishment possible has already been done.

In the preliminary lessons on the lunge the side reins were buckled so as to allow the horse a wholly natural, extended carriage. For only if a young horse can stretch out forward and downward when appropriately driven will it reach for the bit itself. But using too long reins would be a mistake, for then the horse would be unable to come up to the bit no matter how much it tried.

[11] In order to avoid repetition, brief explanations and definitions of the principal horsemanship terms that repeatedly occur in this book, such as unconstraint, suppleness, gait, impulsion, thrust, timing, action, expression, natural and acquired balance, carriage, flexion, position, crookedness, straightening out, even loading on all legs, responsiveness, obedience, collection, forward engagement, dragging, tensed (i.e., floating), prancing, etc., steps and right and wrong arched and sagging back, are set forth in Part Two, Chapter Two, Section 1.

Clear and unmistakable definitions of these concepts, with the major distinctions involved —in other words, a purification of the terminology—seemed highly necessary since such confusions as those of responsiveness with suppleness, or of gait and thrust with impulsion, etc., are common. One often hears experts discussing some equestrian concept with each participant using a different meaning for the term.

In actual lungeing the length of the side reins depends upon the progress of the horse, so that these reins can be shortened as the horse becomes increasingly able to carry itself on its more highly bent hindquarters while maintaining its pure, lively gait. But the horse must always be able to yield somewhat, even when the side reins are shortened considerably. Corresponding to the horse's flexion on the circle, the outside rein must be made somewhat longer than the inner one.[12]

The side reins should be made somewhat longer when beginning work, to relax the horse until it has been well exercised.

The trainer now takes the whip as well, holding the folded lunge in his leading hand and the whip in his off hand, handling it in the same way as set forth above for the man holding the whip. Now that the driving and restraining controls are exercised by the same person, we can be sure that they will harmonize, with a favourable effect upon the precision and delicacy of the work. Only the man holding the lunge feels in his hand the exact time and degree of whip control required. The horse is also more attentive, since all controls issue from a single point—a central station, so to speak—and it is no longer distracted by anything else. It requires a certain talent and uninterrupted attentiveness to fasten the near eye of the horse to the movements of the whip. Just as an unsteady leg position results in an uneven movement of the horse's leg when riding, the same thing occurs when the horse's eye is diverted from the whip during lungeing.

The work will consist principally of developing and maintaining an

---

[12] The time-consuming adjustment of the side reins, which often is done too late, can be avoided by eliminating them and the cavesson and fastening a round, flexible line to the respective outside snaffle-ring. From this ring the line is passed through a ring at the bottom end of a buckle strap about six inches long, which is sewed to the top of the surcingle and enables that ring to move. The line is then passed through the inner snaffle ring, from there passing to the hand of the lungeing trainer.

Like the two other procedures mentioned below, this type has the altogether inestimable advantage of enabling the hand to yield more effectively and maintaining an even pace (half halt) despite more vigorous forward drive. In other words, the hand can be active, which is never completely possible when it is restricted by the rigid side reins.

This work bears fruit when the young horse already has positive contact with the bit as a result of its preparation on the lunge with side reins, and longitudinal flexion is wanted.

Increased collection is obtained by attaching the lunge to the inner snaffle ring, then passing it through the surcingle ring and leading it through both snaffle rings from the outside inward to the hands.

If a horse displays a tendency to turn its off shoulder out and to pull its neck and head in more than longitudinal flexion requires, a third method of connecting the lunge—inner snaffle ring, surcingle ring, outer snaffle ring, and then directly to the hand underneath the horse's head—is particularly useful. This arrangement straightens the horse (as it leads and supervises the off shoulder) and collects it to the same degree.

The three kinds of lungeing described above should be attempted only by lungeing trainers who are exceptionally sensitive. But they achieve extraordinary progress when used by an expert after preparatory work with cavesson and side reins to reinforce contact with the bit.

extended, lively gait, of changes of rate,[13] and halts, which are achieved by the controls described above, made as delicate as possible. The driving whip control will assist the half and full halts, depending on the horse's understanding and the increasing flexing ability of the hindquarters.

Once the initial natural poise approaches closer to an acquired characteristic, the time has come to begin with *gallop departs* from the trot. The trainer brings the horse somewhat inside the circle by pulling slightly on the lunge, yielding as soon as it has responded to this pull and at the same time applying a driving whip control. The horse's complying with this release by moving outwards creates the most favourable position for a gallop depart, and an unconstrained and supple trotting horse will involuntarily change into the gallop. Later on, the hand and whip controls will be reduced to mere symbols, the command, always given with the same intonation, sufficing.

The gallop makes increased demands upon the horse's posture and therefore should not be allowed for too long a time; the circle used for galloping should also be as large as possible.

If we want the horse to change from the *gallop to the trot,* we break the sequence of steps in the gallop by tugging on the lunge; soothing calls make the horse understand that it should decrease its gait. This voice will soon be able to take the place of the other controls in this transition as well.

Young horses are often unable to maintain a gallop for a long time and therefore fall into a loose trot. It would be a mistake to try to hustle them from this hurried gait into another gallop again, by way of punishment, so to speak. The gallop would start without balance and would turn out worse than the previous one. When this happens the best thing to do is to let the horse first find calm timing and carriage at the trot, then apply the controls for a renewed gallop depart once it is fully relaxed.

If deliberate laziness is the reason for the horse's failure to gallop correctly, rather than clumsiness, its dormant animation must be awakened by vigorous, "inflammatory" whip controls. The posture that we have given the horse during its work at the trot and gallop by increased forward drive from the hindquarters to the shortened side reins would be too confining for the walk, which lacks the impulsion of the other gaits.

If there is no time to lengthen the reins,[14] simply disconnect them and throw them crosswise over the horse's neck. This is an excellent oppor-

[13] The trotting rate should be speeded up at those parts of the circle that approach the walls of the riding ring.

[14] It is very useful to have a second and longer pair of side reins for the " intermission " walks; they are attached to the spare rings of the surcingle and cross over the horse's neck; after the side reins employed for trotting and galloping have been unfastened and crossed over the neck, the " walk " reins are attached instead.

tunity to reward the horse, to exercise the "free walk on a loose rein", and to undertake occasional walks over *cavalletti* and other objects.

It is too soon to undertake *walking on the lunge, the hardest thing to accomplish in all horsemanship*.[15] As the side reins that assist the lunge are a dead instrument and cannot yield at the right moment like the rider's hand, which is a part of the supple seat, this sort of walking would be a direct invitation to the horse to "lean on the bit" or to play with its tongue behind it, to turn its neck, lower jaw, and hindquarters in all directions, to tighten its back, and to lose its free, pure walk. In other words, *do not think of collection at the walk* so long as you have to employ dead instruments.

Collection while dismounted, which can be of great use at times, will be taken up in a later chapter.

It will be very useful for the trainer to have his work observed and checked from time to time by an expert standing outside the circle. Mistakes in longitudinal flexion, such as the hindquarters turning out (especially upon the left lead), increased load on the outside shoulder, and the neck bending in front of the withers, will be more obvious to the outside observer than to the man at the centre of the circle. He can call the trainer's attention to wrong bends and mistakes before they become so deep-rooted that they are hard to eliminate and make subsequent work in the saddle difficult.

[15] That is why the old masters used to say, "Trotting develops the gallop and prepares for walking."

CHAPTER TWO

BASIC INSTRUCTION IN THE ORDINARY OR ELEMENTARY FIELD (CROSS-COUNTRY) SCHOOL

I. The Evolution of Horsemanship.
Definition and Explanation of Some of the
Principal Concepts of Horsemanship

NOWADAYS the value of a book on riding cannot be measured by whether it offers something new at any price, something based on totally new principles. Any such attempt would be pure humbug and would harm horsemanship. As far as horsemanship and method are concerned, there still are many notions to be corrected, but in our search for new laws of a physical-mechanical and psychological nature we must not touch the body of underlying principles. It has stood the acid test and will remain the basis for all future progress.

Riders and thinkers must contribute to the progress of the art now more than ever. This is done, not by undermining its foundations, but rather by continuing to build upon them. Then riders are restorers and innovators in the best sense of those terms, for they guard against stagnation and *rigor mortis.*

When we speak of perfecting the art, we believe this can be done in two ways: in practice and in theory. As for the first, it is the practical, creative artist, the equestrian genius, who is fused with his horse into one unit, who makes its will his own, and who proves that there are no limits to art. Otherwise it would be formalistic mathematics, and its perfection would simply be a matter of physical dexterity and the application of scientific data.

In the field of theory it is the thinker and the scientist who place new knowledge at the service of practice, which has the last word concerning the constructive value of this knowledge.[1] Closely related to this con-

---

[1] The healthy relationship between theory and practice is such that fragments of knowledge secured by observation and experience in the saddle are fitted together into *theses*; these in turn are confirmed by further comparative experimental observation and conclusions based upon logical thinking, resulting in conclusive *theorems.*

structive labour is the endeavour to improve certain horsemanship definitions so that they are clear and finally unmistakable to everyone.

In discussions with experts in the field one finds that they often fail to agree on the nomenclature of horsemanship simply because each has a different interpretation of any given definition or technical term. Differences of this sort are also at the bottom of much misunderstanding, especially on the judges' bench in international dressage competitions.

I therefore think that I am filling a gap in the literature of horsemanship by trying to describe the essence and content of a few definitions in dictionary form and as briefly as possible, definitions that are subject to various interpretations and conceptions, although they are the daily bread of all equestrian activity and discussion.

A. TRAINING

There are some advocates of so-called natural training methods who think that *training* and *familiarization* in open country are enough to prepare the future saddle horse in its natural poise for the job it has to do.

They will succeed up to a certain point, provided the rider has a soft, supple seat, and the horse has good conformation and a good disposition.

Lack of *gymnastic training*,[2] the third decisive factor that complements training and familiarization, will do great harm, for the following reasons:

1. The horse's legs will be worn out prematurely because they are not relieved of their burden by a co-operating, elastic back, which can be developed only by sensible training in the ring regularly alternated with work in the open country.

2. The horse that has not learned how to move forward in correct posture,[3] with all the groups of muscles required for motion and for carrying a load evenly stressed, and taking the long strides that correspond to its articulation, will move forward more slowly—though at the same timing—than another horse that may be less favoured by nature but whose gaits have been developed and improved by horsemanship.

3. Not only will its steps cover less ground, but they will be less springy and hence will tire both horse and rider much sooner.

4. Unless the horse is endowed with rare mettle and possesses the quite unusual build of a balanced horse, it will overload its forehand during any performances that go beyond everyday demands, seeking a "fifth

---

[2] Gymnastic training, or dressage in the narrow sense, is *natural horsemanship*, because the means employed to exercise the horse are adapted to its build and to the mechanism of its natural gait.

[3] It is easiest to carry a load that is correctly distributed and balanced!

foot" in the reins and thus squandering its own strength and that of its rider.

5. The obedience required in open country will then be merely a matter of more or less satisfactory concord with the horse, which is not responding to controls. This obedience always breaks down in moments of excitement and produces dissension in which the rider may have a hard time; matters may even go so far that horse and rider exchange roles.

Therefore if equestrian balance is not sought through gymnastic training based upon the natural laws of motion, all initiative is left to the horse.

B. THE COMPLEX: GAIT, THRUST, IMPULSION, ACTION

Gait is the natural predisposition of the horse, when free and carrying no load, to move forward at three different gaits: the walk, the trot, and the gallop. The trot is the least frequent of the three. The more harmonious its conformation and the more perfectly its weight and muscular forces are attuned to each other, the more nearly correct, the lighter, the more fluid, and the more graceful will the gait appear to be.

As long as the horse carries no load, its hind legs will move either limply or with a slight springiness, depending upon its predisposition, but they will not exercise much thrust as they have no need to.

In the more general sense of the term, the gait of a horse, no matter what stage of training it may be in and no matter whether it carries a rider or not, is taken to mean the more or less satisfactory and appropriate manner in which it employs its legs. In this sense we speak of "pure" or "impure", "lively" or "dragging", "free" or "confined" gait, etc.

Thrust is the engagement of the hind legs towards the base of the plumb line through the common centre of gravity of rider and horse, the hind legs powerfully pushing off the ground in order to play an increased part in forward motion and in carrying the aggregate load of horse and rider.

Thrust is the first stage in developing locomotion and the preliminary stage of impulsion.

As the development of thrust requires human influence, it is no longer a purely natural effect, but an improvement of the gait made visible and tangible by dressage.

In this stage of development of gait horses engage their hindquarters more fully in the direction of the centre of gravity, but they do this on a wide track, so that impulsion is out of the question.

Impulsion originates in the powerful thrust and the suppleness of the joints of the hindquarters acquired in the course of further systematic work, so that the hind legs push off from the ground with a springy step. This also involves an elastic swing even before backward extension is complete.

Such exercises as riding on curved lines, turns, two tracks, halts, backing etc., are employed in achieving suppleness. Work on two tracks is of prime importance in getting the hind legs to track closer together. This is decisive for developing the ability to carry a load elastically and to perfect manœuvrability, which culminates in the pirouette.

Horses that tread far apart are not very light in hand, as we know, and exhibit little impulsion. It should be stressed that the elastic swinging of the back is required for the full development of impulsion; it will be discussed in greater detail when we take up the activity of the back.

Action signifies the degree and nature of the movements of the horse's legs in the various gaits and figures. The term " action " as a characteristic feature for the movement, the actions of the legs, may refer to untrained, unspoiled horses in their natural movements or to horses that have either improved their gait—giving it increased expressiveness—or have had it spoiled. The term is also employed for the activity of the front or rear pair of legs as opposed to one another or separately.

Although " action " is frequently used colloquially instead of " gait ", these two concepts are not wholly identical. We can say " extended ", " flat ", " high ", " impure " action and the like, thus unmistakably defining the gait—the way in which the horse uses its legs, how it puts them down. But the two concepts, " gait " and " action ", begin to differ when we say of a hackney, for instance, that it has " a lot of action ", because it raises its knees extremely high as a result of its special conformation, bred for this purpose and aided by auxiliary reins. If we were to judge the movements of such a horse from the standpoint of gait, we would have to say that its gait is inharmonious and defective because it is close-coupled, with unbent hind joints.[4]

The *natural action* of a horse is affected by whether its forearm is longer or shorter than its cannon, not to mention the effect of its shoulders. Where the forearm is long, so that the knee is low, the action will be flat and cover considerable ground provided the other factors are favourable, while if it is short, the action will be naturally high (Lipizzans).

In riding over broken, rocky terrain, *a grasping (a rather high) action* with free carriage is the best life insurance. This carriage is halfway between the flat action of the race horse and the stepping-in-place of the

---

[4] The high-stepping action of the forehand, obtained by academic methods, which can be increased to the horizontal extension of the forearm (as in the piaffe and passage), is feasible only if the upper and lower points of attachment of the head-neck-humerus muscles lies in the same vertical plane, and the poll is fully pliant.

hackney, which does not gain much ground. The raised front legs, which avoid stumbling over minor irregularities of the terrain, are advanced from this raised position in a fairly high arch, "reaching out", so to speak, and alighting again at a rather steep angle of incidence.

As we have said, the notion that high carriage of the neck by itself, without suppleness of the cervical vertebrae, is enough to achieve the high, fluid steps of the forehand is erroneous. If the poll is stiff (for want of " a few drops of oil ") and the rear edges of the masseteric region press upon the head-neck-humerus muscle that is attached there, the muscle is partially paralysed and can produce nothing but cramped steps.

C. RATE—TIMING

Rate is the time measure of locomotion—the velocity at which the horse covers a certain distance in a certain time.

If the diagonal pairs of legs are light and advance evenly and simultaneously at the trot, if the leaps follow at uniform intervals of time at the gallop and the four hoofbeats do so at the walk, the horse is moving in *time*.

Timing may be regulated in accordance with the rider's will and the horse's stage of dressage, that is, when the timing is correct. But it may also be too slow if the steps follow one another at intervals that are uniform but too long. Again it may be too fast if the uniform time intervals for the steps follow each other too rapidly. As we have said, however, *it remains timing as long as the steps, paces, and leaps remain uniform,* i.e., *are of the same length at a certain rate.*

The horse loses its rhythm as soon as this uniformity is lost; the locomotion is no longer uniform in the physical sense, and the horse begins either to hurry or to hold back.

Colloquially speaking, a horse moving along in time is understood to be a horse whose steps, paces, and leaps are appropriately regulated.

The difference between rate and timing is as follows: Say, two horses travel a certain distance at the gallop, saddle to saddle, in the same time, at the same velocity. Thus their rate is the same. But since one of them requires five hundred equal leaps to travel this distance, while the other requires only four hundred, they are not galloping with the same timing, though they are travelling at the same rate and at a uniform rate.

(*Regulated*) *timing, together with unconstraint, is the foundation of balance and carriage and the first step in all training.*

D. EXPRESSION—CADENCE

Expression is the increased energy imparted to the well-timed gait by the addition of thrust and impulsion. The engaged haunches[5]—the hip and stifle joints—carry more of the load, thus allowing the relieved forehands to reach out higher and more freely, with the front legs alighting very lightly and producing the impression of hardly any support.

These movements are elastic, neither choppy and exaggeratedly extended nor pawing, but fluidly round and smoothly graceful.

But the natural gait of a foal possessing particularly favourable articulation and mettle can also be considered expressive, enabling it to display at moments of excitement the outlines of what the rider may be able to achieve by planned gymnastic training.

Cadence refers to well-timed, lofty, and yet fluid stepping at the collected and schooled gaits.

In the narrower sense, therefore, it may denote increased expression in collection. True cadence has nothing in common with a false floating or the purely external pathos confined merely to the wooden gesture of a pretended passage that is not nourished and supported by the inner mettle of true animation.

The concepts "expression" and "cadence" are synonymous in colloquial equestrian usage in so far as both presuppose a regular timing, whose pronounced rhythm (scanned, so to speak) conveys the impression of expressive or cadenced stepping.

Whereas the word "expressive" refers to the observer's eye, the word "cadence", which is taken from musical theory, refers to a rhythmic regularity in the repetition of well-timed steps within a phase sequence that reaches us through the sense of hearing. But this latter term does not refer to the intensity of the beat, since we know that the more lightly the hoofs touch the ground, owing to elastic thrust by the lowered hindquarters, the less audible the gait will be.

The term "cadencing" is used colloquially to denote the transformation of a too hurried trot, say, into a correct one by the action of the rider, or the transition from the timing of a trot to the sustained timing of the passage, which is also a transformation.

---

[5] Whenever engagement of the haunches is referred to henceforth, it is a matter of course that this also includes the simultaneous bending of the hock in the *phase of support*. This follows from the anatomical interaction of these three most important joints of the hind legs.

Now that we have defined and differentiated the concepts "expression" and "cadence", we should like to emphasize that the widespread notion that the timing at collected gaits must be somewhat slower than at the middle gaits because of the loftier action, with the legs having to cover more ground because of the greater bending of the knee during suspension, rests upon a logical error. The time that the legs lose in collection as the result of loftier stepping, in their suspension phase they gain as the result of the shorter length of the less extended steps. The foregoing notion of slower timing is actually true only of a defective gait (prancing front legs).

If timing is not exactly the same in the middle and collected gaits, the horse's suppleness and responsiveness are not yet fully in order.

The piaffe and passage, in which the rhythm of the timing is slowed down by the rider's deliberately sustaining the rise (and the extension as well in the latter case), constitute an exception to this rule.

E. BALANCE—POISE

Balance in motion is the state in which the horse can maintain itself at the uniform timing it desires, supported only by its own four legs. Balance is present only when the plumb line passing through the horse's centre of gravity lies inside the most advanced point of support for its mass or will lie within that area after the end of the phase of suspension that is present in every trot and gallop sequence.

Since we presuppose a rider sitting in the saddle correctly and attuned to his horse, with the plumb line through his centre of gravity coinciding with that of the horse[6] so that his own weight produces no change in the *proportion* of the load on the various legs of the horse, the word "combined" will be taken for granted henceforth in our subsequent discussions of the horse carrying the rider's load whenever the combined centre of gravity or the plumb line through the combined centre of gravity is involved.

The concept of "equilibrium", in the sense of a quantitatively equal distribution of weight upon all four legs, is incorrect and can be applied only to some of the figures of the secondary field school, which are performed at a higher degree of collection, with the base of the vertical line through the centre of gravity shifted to the centre of the base of support.

[6] The only exceptions to the equestrian rule that the centres of gravity of horse and rider must always coincide are standing in free posture and the free walk. Apart from obvious reasons of a technical equestrian nature, this principle could not be applied to the free walk because the rider would have to lean forward in order to bring his own centre of gravity into coincidence with that of the horse, and such balancing could be achieved only by the exertion of some effort in view of the slow rate of travel of the horse at the walk.

In the lessons of the *haute école* most of the weight is placed upon the hindquarters, so that in some figures (such as the *levade*) the rear point of support carries the entire load.

If the equally distributed load on the two forelegs is greater than that on the hindquarters—say, 55 to 45—the rider will have the feeling of complete balance on a horse moving at the correct ordinary posture. He will have this feeling because he will find that he can maintain his steady seat without any effort and with his upper body erect.

This added load upon the forehand in the elementary field school (the ordinary school) is in accord with the natural laws that have allocated support *and* thrust to the hindquarters, for which purpose they require a certain degree of freedom and relief from load.

The centre of gravity will move forward or back along an equilibrium line, depending upon the share of the load carried by the hindquarters during locomotion.

Once the horse leaves the straight line and turns, the centre of gravity is shifted to one side, along a lateral equilibrium line that is perpendicular to the longitudinal equilibrium line.

In a horse of good conformation that is moving in free posture the centre of gravity is located about fourteen inches behind and above the point of the elbow. The centre of gravity shifts to the rear as coupling and the relative lift of the forehand are increased as a result of the increased load on the hindlegs.

This should be pronounced enough in the riding horse for the horse to be able to exert all its forces and be easily controlled by the rider.

The balance achieved by equestrian means is called an *acquired* or *equestrian balance* to distinguish it from the natural balance of a horse moving without the influence of a rider.

As we have said, the distribution of weight in ordinary riding will never be such as to shift the base of the plumb line through the centre of gravity to the centre of the area of support.

It can be shifted so far forward, however, as to lie ahead of the front edge of the base of support. The horse then loses its balance and hurries, its steps growing faster and faster in its effort to regain its equilibrium.

That is why we may also say that a horse is moving in (natural or acquired) equilibrium, from the equestrian standpoint, if it maintains its timing with the reins loose.

Maintaining balance while moving on a straight line requires that the load be distributed correctly between the lateral pairs of legs as well as between the fore and hind legs. If the right and left pairs of legs (right foreleg and right hind leg, left foreleg and left hind leg) do not share equally in carrying the load, lateral equilibrium is imperilled; the horse grows crooked or its gait is impure or it turns independently of the rider.

A crooked horse can move in natural balance, true enough, but it cannot fully satisfy the requirements of equestrian balance.

In conclusion it should be emphasized that the problem of balance involves more than mere physical formulas. It is no problem at all to the unaffected foal in the pasture, which has solved it to perfection.

We who wish to apply the laws of balance to the horse in motion must not forget that rules applying to stationary bodies are applicable to living beings endowed with a will of their own only with considerable reservations and certain restrictions resulting from the introduction of dynamic forces. We must remember that the advancing legs contribute to the maintenance of balance, i.e., equilibrium, just as much as the supporting legs. These are phases of motion in which the *static equilibrium* (centre of gravity vertically above the area of support) is replaced by a *dynamic equilibrium* without the body's losing its stability (falling).

The better the haunches taking over the load have bent, and the more the hindquarters are lowered, the more will the line of the back, which naturally drops somewhat from back to front, approach the horizontal, relieving the forehand, and the more effortlessly will the horse secure command of its own weight, thus achieving maximum suppleness. Such pronounced bending of the haunches, which would correspond to a maximum concession to control by the rider, is not a working posture that should be aimed at with all horses as the basis for further special training because only few horses can attain it; it is fatiguing, and it restricts the extension of gait in return for making the gait loftier.

Poise is the state of a horse in motion in which it can maintain itself in the uniform timing it desires, supported only by its four legs. It is a result of balance and is impossible without it.

As we see from the two definitions of balance and poise, they are practically identical, except for the added explanatory sentence above. The different degrees of balance in the physical-anatomical sense and of poise in the equestrian sense are two groups of concepts that coincide and are interrelated in so far as poise—ranging from natural, innate poise through all the intermediate stages to that of the schooled horse, acquired by higher dressage—is a function of balance and inconceivable without it.

Impulsion must be added at the trot and the gallop here, just as in maintaining balance. Although this impulsion is not produced by the action of the rider in the preliminary riding lessons, it suffices as natural impulsion to prevent motion from degenerating into hurrying, which would involve loss of forward equilibrium.

The greater the share of the load carried by the hindquarters, the more will the initial natural poise, in which the forehand carries a much heavier load than the hindquarters, with the horse incapable of peak performance for any length of time, turn into an *equestrian* or *acquired poise* that is more useful to the rider. Then the carrying and balancing of the load is effected with the least expenditure of energy, and the freedom of movement increases.

Since the same natural laws apply to balance and poise, nothing more need be said about them here.

F. UNCONSTRAINT—SUPPLENESS—TENSION—RELAXATION— ACTION OF THE BACK—RESPONSIVENESS—ADVANCE— LETTING ITSELF BE DRIVEN

Unconstraint is the psychological and physical state of the horse in which it flexes and relaxes its muscles elastically only as much as is required for uniform locomotion under its own weight increased by that of the rider, thus avoiding all unnecessary expenditure of energy.

In contrast to suppleness, unconstraint alone, without the addition of other factors, such as driving and the resultant increased thrust and stretching of the entire spinal column towards the horse's head, is, one might say, a purely passive matter in which the horse's legs swing back and forth expressionlessly.

A horse that is psychologically and bodily cramped will find it hard to flex and relax its muscles elastically and in a relaxed state.

On the contrary, it will flex and relax them convulsively (tighten up) in order to resist the unpleasant, painful constraint of the load, thus losing the freedom of its gait and its natural ability to balance itself. Or the constraint of an inner tightness (fear, excitement) will be manifested in the same way and will become perceptible to the rider.

External and internal causes (pain, fear) often act in concert to produce a tensed, cramped motion. It is up to equestrian tact and feeling to make the correct diagnosis and to act accordingly.

A third type of constraint that arises neither from feelings of pain nor from those of fear is the muscle tension, the so-called " muscle tone " that is habitual in many highbred horses, which they must be allowed to work off on the lunge or, even better, in freedom before they are mounted until the tension in the horse's muscles is dissolved so that the tightness in its joints disappears.

Unconstraint is attained when the horse allows the rider to take his place in the saddle without tightening its back and begins its natural, well-timed trot without any action of the reins. The correct (i.e., springy, although still not pronounced enough) oscillation of all its body muscles is also apparent to the observer in the relaxed, satisfied expression on the horse's face, its ears half erect, attentive only to the path and the rider, and the natural carriage of the tail, which swings from base to tip in time with the hind leg that happens to be grounded.

As unconstrained and well-timed ground-covering strides are the basis of all equestrian work, it is obvious that these two interdependent prerequisites must exist before further gymnastic training can be undertaken.

Even during subsequent training the rider must always be able to return to this, one might say, primitive, original form of striding in time at the unconstrained, natural trot whenever difficulties arise—the trot that is the foundation for the dressage of the tournament jumper as well as for the *haute école.*

Suppleness is an advanced stage of unconstraint.

It develops out of the latter and out of the energy of the gait awakened by active equestrian action (driving). The rider's leg controls produce swings of the horse's legs, to the front and to the rear, that are as long as the configuration of the horse permits. Corresponding to the greater amount of ground covered because of thrust, these oscillations of the leg will be communicated to the elongating back and neck musculature in waves that are more energetic and longer than those during unconstraint. As a result of this greater energy they will travel as far as the back of the horse's head and result in extension of the poll. This initial extension is a forward stretching of the body to reach the passively awaiting hand, which elastically accepts the weight laid in it by the horse. This constitutes the beginning of the horse's *contact with the bit,* which later becomes a positive "response to the reins".

When a driving seat is used, the horse's contact with the bit will cause it to come forward to the rider's hands, its mouth, poll, and neck yielding and becoming supple while chewing on the bit.

This brief description of the *origin of suppleness,* which will be accorded the space it merits as the *most important and decisive stage of training* in a later chapter, indicates the differences between unconstraint and suppleness.

A horse can move without constraint though it has not found the bit; but it is supple only when the driving controls cause it to flex and relax its muscles (which it has been using at the natural trot without constraint, but only languidly) and extend itself, seeking contact with the bit in order to obtain release there and at the seat.

The suppleness that is initially latent in the lack of constraint of the natural trot, in which the horse flexes no muscles against the rider's weight, is converted by "its willingness to let itself be driven" into an energetic placing of all these muscles at the service of the movement called for by the controls. This involves energetic flexing and relaxing—springiness—combined with a willing acceptance of the load.

Since unconstraint is a preliminary stage of the suppleness that arises out of it, the latter cannot be achieved without the former, though a horse swinging along unconstrainedly with its rider without equestrian suppleness is quite conceivable.

"Unconstrained" is often equated with "relaxed". This leads to blurry concepts. In contrast to the muscles that are stretched statically the horse should always *flex* and *relax* the muscles that are employed for motion in time with its steps and leaps more or less intensively but always elastically and regularly, depending upon the stage of its dressage and the energy that the gait actually requires, which is greatest in the accelerated gaits and those of the *haute école*. It may flex its muscles excessively and relax them hardly at all, so that they are held upwards, that is, they are "tense" as we speak of it colloquially, such as a convulsively arched, tightened back. But the horse can also flex them too little, so that there is practically nothing to relax, as in an inactive, dead, sway-back. In both of these boundary cases the muscles pulsate too little, irregularly, and therefore wrongly. In both cases, therefore, the *action of the tightened back is wrong,* since the latter does not obey the rider's demands without constraint; it is not compliant because it does not swing correctly.

A *locomotion muscle* can never be rendered completely still, in the state of permanent absolute tension or relaxation—dissected out, as it were—if it is fitted into a plan of locomotion and fulfils more or less successfully a definite task in that plan.[7]

We often hear a correctly swinging back referred to as "arched".[8] Since this term may give rise to false conceptions, as if the back had to assume a convex position to be able to "carry" better, it is more nearly accurate to denote its unconstrained docility as "compliance".

Responsiveness is the horse's ability and readiness to respond to driving, restraining, and lateral controls and to allow them to pass through its body from back to front and vice versa as well as laterally. It culminates in the waiving of all resistance to the rider's influence.

Just as suppleness develops almost imperceptibly from unconstraint, its antecedent stage and prerequisite, responsiveness arises from supple-

[7] This is given by way of explanation simply to avoid misinterpretation of the term " tension ", which is continually used colloquially for tightened locomotion muscles, i.e., muscles that pulsate convulsively and thus incorrectly.

[8] Arching of the back is relative: a back that sags under unusual load arches to return to its natural position before it carried a rider, when it was able to swing freely. This arching is nothing but a stretching; anything more would be convulsive tension with all its harmful consequences for gait and carriage.

ness as the result of impulsion and the lateral flexion used to produce even loading on all four legs. It cannot be achieved without the impulsion originating in the hindquarters and flowing forward to the masseter muscles.

A horse may be supple, but that does not mean that it is completely responsive, though if it is responsive it must also be supple. The horse must be just as supple at the highest stage of collection, in which maximum demands are made of the muscular tension, as it is in a freer carriage.

The saddle horse already possesses a certain degree of responsiveness. But if we were to call upon it for a collected walk, for example, such as that employed by a specialized horse prepared for advanced dressage tests, its responsiveness would be inadequate.

The higher the stage of training, the more nearly complete the responsiveness and the more delicate the controls required.

If the horse is responsive, it *goes forward,* for it responds to the driving control, as manifested by its acceptance of the bit, stretching to reach it and accepting it with gentle chewing.

The forward motion of a horse has nothing in common with a disorderly rushing or with speed in general. It is entirely related, however, to the property, promoted by gymnastic training, of responsively *allowing itself to be driven,* that is, to maintain gait or rate as determined by the seat and the regulating hand without evading or hurrying.

A mettlesome horse, with its natural forward drive arising from its diligent disposition and willing character, can be driven more readily than a horse of contrary disposition.

G. FIRST POSITION (SHOULDER-FORE)—SECOND POSITION ("POSITION" AS SUCH)—LATERAL DISTANCE ON TWO TRACKS—EVEN LOADING ON ALL FOUR LEGS—STRAIGHTENING OUT—FIRST DEGREE FLEXIONS (INDIRECT) AND SECOND-DEGREE FLEXIONS (DIRECT)—CROOKEDNESS—CONSTRAINED SIDE—DIFFICULT SIDE

Responsiveness can exist only if the thrust and impulsion of the hindquarters are fully active against the forehand, while the loading and flexing rein controls act fully upon the hind legs on the same side. This requires that the forehand and the hindquarters be so attuned to each other that the horse moving on a single track always has its *longitudinal axis aligned with the straight or curved track* to be followed, so that the hind legs follow the trace.

The principle of following in trace in single-track exercises suffers only one limitation: the hind legs must track very closely together, both laterally and in their advance, in order to secure more nearly complete longitudinal flexion and collection. Consequently the inside hind hoof is visible between the forelegs in the shoulder-fore[9] and the outside hind hoof is visible when riding in " position ".

When the horse moves along a straight track, it may assume a completely straight posture, as is the case in the saddle horse. When moving along curved lines and in the training exercises of shoulder-fore or " position ", however, its posture becomes a slightly flexed-straight position that involves uniform longitudinal flexion.

Lateral distance on two tracks is the distance through which the forehand or the hindquarters are moved from the tracks of the outside hind or front hoof in two-track exercises. The maximum lateral distance on two tracks achieved in military and ordinary riding, that is, in the ordinary or elementary field (cross-country) school, is one step (also see " Two tracks ").

The flexed-straight position (called " position " for short) is required for riding through corners, two tracks, and other exercises because it causes the hind legs to move alongside and past each other, thus achieving better flexion. But it is also an indispensable aid to the rider because it makes it easier for him to prevent resistance or *crookedness,* thus compelling the hindquarters to act directly against the forehand. The only way a rider can control a horse that is not completely responsive and obedient, with the hindquarters and the forehand in harmony, is to employ a pure " position " that involves uniform longitudinal flexion.

It would be unnecessary to demand longitudinal flexion of an ideally trained horse, for it would endeavour to take that position itself in order

---

[9] The shoulder-fore position is called the first position because it precedes the second position, called " position " for short, in the dressage programme. Both of these are training exercises, though the latter is also preparation for certain movements that should be carried out in equestrian posture. They require a uniform, imperceptible flexion towards the inside that traverses the entire horse.

In the *first position, shoulder-fore*, the outside pair of legs moves along the outside trace so that the outside hind hoof tracks the corresponding front hoof. The inside hind leg alights slightly (no more than half a hoof width) inside the hoofprint of the inside foreleg, so that the inside hind hoof is visible between the forelegs when the horse is viewed from the front.

In the *second position*, which is no longer mere gymnastics but also serves as a preparatory position for certain figures, the inside pair of legs moves along the inside trace in such a way that the inside hind hoof tracks the corresponding front hoof. The outside hind leg alights slightly (no more than half a hoof width) inside the hoofprint of the outside foreleg, so that the outside hoof becomes visible between the forelegs when we look at the horse from in front, the inside line of the horse appearing to be entirely straight when moving along straight lines.

Along a curved path the *flexion of the ribs*, i.e., the uniform longitudinal flexion of the spine that causes the ribs of the side in question to be pushed somewhat closer together, must correspond to the trace on a curved track, though the sequence of footfalls must be the same as it is when moving on straight lines. The only difference is that the inside legs must come closer together, depending upon the curvature of the track.

15. Collected trot. Note the animation. Major J. Handler on *Conversano Benvenuta I* (Lipizzan).

16. Extended trot. The rider must be able to sit in the saddle, taking the powerful but regular and springy oscillations of the horse's back. Captain O. Frank on *Cyprian* (Irish).

17. Extended trot. Jessica Newberry on *Forstrat* (Thoroughbred). JUNE FALLAW

to ensure the most favourable conditions for the development of impulsion from a supple hock.

Hence we should not be satisfied with mere following in trace when working in the ring on a single track but should employ the " position " whenever necessary along straight lines and always in riding serpentines and galloping.

" Position " is always required for two-track work as well.

In " position ", even on two tracks, the forefeet should lead the hind feet, which in turn must always follow the forefeet in the direction of motion, never stepping off to a side, just as in the straight-ahead position. This causes the hindquarters' impulsion to act in the direction of the plumb line through the centre of gravity, so that the ratio of the lateral load on the near and off legs, and hence the lateral equilibrium, remains unchanged. Gait and contact with the bit do not suffer. Even loading on the near and off legs,[10] no matter whether the forehand is more or less stressed than the hindquarters, is the distinguishing feature of correct longitudinal flexion.

Any horse that satisfies this condition of even loading on the near and off legs, whether its body is actually a straight line or exhibits a certain flexion of the ribs, is straight.

Straightening, therefore, is the sum total of all the actions employed by the rider to achieve the state of *even loading on all four legs.* When the horse is in this condition, it is able to develop the power and harmony of both halves of its body equally.

Straightening has nothing to do with the linear straightness of the spinal column longitudinally, though it is totally related to the spine's suppleness.

Straightening out means bringing the horse from longitudinal flexion to a linearly straight position.

Without even loading on all four legs, which is the key to complete

---

[10] The false notion that the flexion and load on the two hind legs are not entirely alike when two-tracking on a straight line has persisted down to the present time. General von Josipovich has demonstrated the error of this assumption in Koch's *Reitkunst Im Bilde* (*Horsemanship in Pictures*). Impulsion and purity of gait can be maintained, even on two tracks, only if the off hind hoof carries the same share of the load as the near one.

The only exception to this rule is work on a circle, where the natural tendency of the horse's body (centre of gravity) to lean inward, obeying the law of centrifugal force on curved lines, places additional load on the inner pair of legs and thus causes greater bending of the inside hind leg. But this phenomenon is the result of nothing but centrifugal force alone rather than the lateral flexion of the horse.

Moreover the closer the longitudinal axis of the horse comes to the circumference of the circle, in other words, the more perfect its longitudinal flexion, other conditions (rate and circle diameter) remaining the same, the less will be the action of centrifugal force and the less does its centre of gravity have to be shifted inward. The more defective its longitudinal flexion, on the other hand, the more will an untrained horse have to lean into the circle in order to resist centrifugal force (what the French masters call *coucher dans sa volte*).

balance and hence to certain poise, there can be no impulsion flowing without hindrance through the body from the croup forward, and thus no true responsiveness or collection.

Moreover only the work of flexion to achieve even loading, which must be adapted to each individual case, as will be discussed in subsequent sections, finally loosens the back.

Two other definitions, though minor in themselves, still shed some light on the essential factors in the origin of flexion and the evolution from easy flexion to greater flexion.

The term *flexion of the first degree or indirect flexion* is readily understandable once we realize that every longitudinal flexion must originate in the extension of the off side.

Flexions of the first degree are the first step in all flexion work and are employed until the horse is familiar with yielding to the inner side. Thus they are the easier flexions, because it is only the inside leg and reins, in support of each other, that count, there being no appreciable opposing action of the outside controls.

When flexion of the first degree, whose only purpose has been to loosen up the horse and promote balance by evening out the distribution of weight on the two halves of its body, is intensified, we get *flexion of the second degree,* which is direct in so far as it is produced by the direct action of the outside leg and rein about the inside leg as a fulcrum, though without the employment of any force. This resembles bending a stick about one's knee. If we were to try to flex an untrained horse in this manner at the beginning of its training, it would literally break in two.

Flexions of the second degree are therefore more difficult because the near and outside controls must operate together. The shoulder-in and the *travers* positions, which require direct flexion, also require collection.

Steinbrecht placed the words "Ride your horse forward and hold it straight" at the top of the best book ever written on horsemanship, and the famous French General L'Hotte used the motto "Calm, Forward, Straight" for his book *Questions Equestres.*

The horse can try to evade the demands made upon it by its load, flexion, and obedience in general in various ways. These evasions will be apparent to the casual observer in such symptoms as stiffness, false bends, dropping the lower jaw or moving it to one side, and other vices; but the *evasion of the hindquarters* is the primary cause of all these errors. If the horse evades to the rear with its hind legs, its steps are either too short and hurrying or they seem to be stuck to the ground and are languid and dragging. How it evades depends upon its disposition. In both cases it does not engage its hindquarters as far forward as its conformation would allow. If it evades to one side, the hind legs no longer follow the trace—the horse is crooked.

Crookedness is produced by one hind leg's evading the uncomfortable job of even loading by not advancing straight ahead under the horse's body but somewhat to one side. One result of this evasion is a bending of the horse's body that departs from the direction of motion. This is manifested to the rider by the horse moving against the leg on the side of the evading hind hoof and against the rein on the other side and falling heavily on the corresponding shoulder.

The horse employs this natural weapon of defence, making itself crooked, either from outside rear to the inside front or from the inside rear to the outside front. It will do so almost always in the former direction.

The reason for a horse's one-sidedness is interpreted variously. No entirely conclusive explanation has been found as yet. Many attribute crookedness to the position of the foal in the womb, bent over to the right, but forgot that multiparous animals, such as dogs, are also crooked. In any event it is a fact that asymmetrical conformation is a factor that greatly favours the tendency to execute certain primitive movements chiefly with the stronger and nimbler half of the body even during the period of growth, and this is true of the horse as of all other living creatures. It has also been proved that so-called " left-handed " riders, the left halves of whose bodies are much better developed than the right, unconsciously " make " a horse that turns out from right to left, but when mounted by all right-handed riders it does exactly the opposite, so that it becomes stiff on the right side. This seems to indicate that the horse's defence against the unconscious use of greater force by one half of the rider's body is a factor in the development of crookedness.

The occurrence of crookedness is also considered by many to be connected with the fact that the horse, which is narrower in the shoulders than in the hips, moves far enough away from the wall of the riding school to make the line from the outside shoulder to the outside hip parallel to the wall so as not to rub against it. Though this makes the angle between the inside shoulder-inside hip line and the wall that much larger, it favours an evasion of the inside hind leg and with it crookedness.

This argument does not stand up, however, for then the horse would have to be crooked to the right when riding on the right hand in the riding hall and crooked to the left when riding on the left hand. Its crookedness would change direction at every change of hand, as it would always have to worry about its outside hip. We know from experience, however, that it does not change the direction of its crookedness—remember the greater frequency with which the near stirrup hits the wall.

Further proof that this assumption is fantastic[11] is the fact that if the wall of the riding hall were the sole cause of crookedness, the horse would have no reason to be crooked out in the open, where there are no walls. But we know that crookedness also occurs in open country, almost always to the same side. That is why the work of straightening must be done differently on each hand during gymnastic training (see also pp. 63, 183ff.).

To sum up, we are convinced that crookedness is due to a hereditary disposition of right-footedness. Just as man[12] has always favoured the use of his right arm (which gained in strength and dexterity thereby), the wild horse, when defending itself and following its instinct of protecting its more sensitive left side where the heart is located, turned to the left by kicking off with its outside hind foot, which thus gradually became stronger and nimbler than the inside one. There are enough arguments to support this: pushing off with the outside hind foot when breaking away to the left, which occurs most often; especial strength and nimbleness when turning to the left; preference for the gallop at the inside leads at take-offs for difficult jumps, the outside hind leg doing most of the work in the take-off.

The straightening methods available to the rider to eliminate one-sidedness or crookedness will be taken up later. Since it is the purpose of this section to define our terms as unequivocally as possible, I should like to clarify the difference between the *difficult side* and the *constrained side*, using the crooked horse as an example.

If the horse is crooked from right to left, the outside hind leg, which evades flexion by moving to one side, puts a greater load on the left shoulder and hence the left rein. Hence the inner side is the constrained side, as the throat muscles on that side are tightened, excessively tense, and not entirely compliant. But the really *difficult side*[13] is the hollow off side, where the horse is moving not with but against the leg and is not responding to the reins. Once the rider succeeds in getting the hind legs on the difficult (wrongly hollowed) side to engage forward in a straight line under the load and to have that side of the body come up to the bit, the constraint on the constrained side disappears by itself.[14] Now the impulsion of the

[11] Anyone who thinks that the horse worries about its hips will soon learn otherwise to his sorrow. The horse does not think of what is behind it; this is proved not only by bruised riders' knees but, above all, by the many horses that have one hip larger than the other.

[12] The muscles of the right half of the human body receive their nerve impulses directly from the *left* half of the brain, which gets a better and direct blood supply from the heart.

[13] Resistance and evasion always originate in the hindquarters, except when the conformation of the back is very bad. That is why it is correct to designate the side on which the hind leg is defective as the difficult side.

[14] In this case, therefore, the diagonal leg has indirectly released the horse from the reins on the constrained side, which it loaded more heavily and held fast. This indirect method is the only correct one for remounts; it produces the quickest results although it takes considerable time (also see footnote 70 on p. 224).

two hind legs, which are reaching forward equally, reaches the corresponding reins uniformly.

The uniform pulsations of this sort are changed somewhat when working on two tracks; the wave length of the flexing and relaxing of the back and neck muscles of the inner, hollowed side is shorter than that of the arched and stretched outside, where there is more room for wider oscillations.[15] But the even loading and engagement of the two hind legs always remains the same as the prerequisite condition for impulsion and purity of gait, with the exception of work on curved lines.

There is probably no subject in the whole realm of horsemanship about which there has been so much mysticism as crookedness, and I am inclined to believe that more has been written about this subject than about the same problem in human beings. The importance attributed to natural crookedness was so great that many authors made it the crux of their entire theory of dressage, which was a woeful exaggeration.

It is a fact, however, that it exists and that we have to deal with it as best we can.

Even after we think we have eliminated it once and for all, it often reappears unexpectedly as a means of defence—frequently in the opposite direction—as soon as we make increased demands upon the horse which it cannot or will not satisfy.

One must be either a very bad rider or a very good one not to be disturbed by crookedness. The former rides around the terrain unconcernedly upon his lopsided little horse, seeming to agree with the philosopher Voltaire that " All is for the best in this best of all possible worlds."

Nor does the very good rider worry too much. With his seat symmetrically distributed upon both halves of the horse's body, all he thinks of is riding forward (which has nothing to do with hurrying or riding fast). He develops impulsion and allows any resistances to escape forward, straightening the horse by driving the hind leg of the difficult side underneath the load without tightening up and letting this forward drive spoil neither his temper nor that of his horse.

H. ADAPTING TO THE BIT (CORRECT HEAD CARRIAGE)— THE WRONG BEND—CONTACT WITH THE BIT— LIFTING THE FOREHAND—COLLECTION

Correct head carriage is a consequence of thrust and impulsion, as a result of which the supple horse reaches for the sustaining hand and

[15] The rider's outside hand clearly feels a stronger tug during two-track work.

adapts to the bit. Correct head carriage is inconceivable without previously making sure that the horse is in *contact with the bit.*

If the horse shortens its neck downward in trying to escape from the contact with the bit produced when it stretches its neck forward, we get a so-called *wrong bend* between the second and third cervical vertebrae. The joint surfaces between the two vertebrae are no longer in complete contact, so that there is a gap in the connecting links between the mouth and the hindquarters, interrupting the pulls of the hand and the impulsion coming from the hindquarters.

A horse with a false bend is not responsive, since it uses this as a valve, enabling the controls that should be allowed to pass through the entire spine to escape. We lose correct contact with the bit, that is, the stretching of the entire spinal column, including the vertebrae of the neck, to reach the bit, which is produced by the uniform engagement of both hind legs.

The horse should never abandon correct contact with the bit by getting above or behind the bit or leaning on it. Should it do so, it can interrupt propulsion or arbitrarily change direction. It also has the other extreme of faulty contact with the bit available for " breaking away "; it bores on the bit, thus binding the rider's hands and freeing itself of their influence.

In the past I believe too much was said about correct head carriage, with the sole result of confusing cause and effect. It is a matter of course that the head of a horse possessing correct head carriage should be in a position that approaches the vertical, and, depending on the conformation of the horse, its mouth should be approximately at the level of the hips. Then the action of the reins can traverse the entire spinal column through the pelvis down to the hind pastern joints under the most favourable conditions, i.e., directly, without being stopped or deflected at any point by stiffness or bends. This requires that the horse " come to the bit " by itself, with a supple poll and extended neck and with positive contact with the bit due to driving action. Parenthetically, this expression " come to the bit " might well be employed instead of " producing correct head carriage ", which always sounds like active influence of the hands. The phrase " producing correct head carriage " and the disastrous picture it may well present to the imagination suggest a hardening or tightening of the hands that may be wholly unconscious but is nonetheless harmful. This is like the rider who thinks of the word " jump " when going over obstacles and interferes with the horse, so that it makes mistakes. Another example is the rider who worries too much about some stiffness or other of his horse and begins to pull it to the constraining side without meaning to do so.

Lifting the forehand is a consequence of the lowering of the hindquarters produced by their greater engagement. It is an indication and a consequence of collection. In a correctly collected horse the croup and buttock muscles of the engaged hindquarters exert a powerful tug downwards and backwards upon the muscles of the back connected to them, thus lifting the chest and neck vertebrae of the spine and taking some of the load off the forehand. The more the neck is stretched forwards and *upwards,* the easier contact with the bit becomes. As the absolute length of the neck remains the same and the elongation of its upper edge becomes even greater (see pp. 262-3), the neck must rise if the horse's nose is held vertical, so that the distance from mouth to hand and hence the length of the reins becomes shorter. The steps of the front legs become loftier, corresponding to the reduction of the load on the forehand.

Lifting the forehand is relative so long as it is merely a consequence of the lowered hindquarters and of the passively holding reins; it becomes direct or active when the hands improve the carriage[16] by means of slight tugs on the reins or flex the back by powerful pulls for brief instants whenever the horse is disobedient.

In dressage lifting the forehand must go no farther than having the neck, acting as a lever, lower the back at the loins, but not behind the withers. This faulty lowering of the back behind the withers is clearly felt by the rider as a hollow between his legs, an indication that the hind legs are no longer engaging correctly under the bent back and that the ultimate lifting of the forehand attainable by equestrian means has been exceeded. The ability of the hindquarters to carry the load and to engage is no longer equal to the excessive load put upon them, and the hind legs escape this load by dragging behind.

In conclusion, let us again emphasize that no faultless head carriage is possible without correct contact with the bit and that no correct lifting of the forehand is possible without this correct head carriage.

Correct head carriage and lifting of the forehand are not major goals of dressage but rather accompaniments and consequences of proper work. As such, like the hands of a clock keeping correct time, they tell the expert that the timing and the locomotion of the horse are in order.

But one who does not possess very unusual experience and a trained eye should never try to concentrate upon head and neck alone in judging head carriage and the lift of the forehand. Only observation of the entire horse, of its carriage and especially its gait, this incorruptible evidence of honest work, will be able to prove unmistakably that they are correct.

---

[16] *Direct* or (as it is also called) *absolute lifting of the forehand* will drop into our laps like a ripe apple only in an especially sensitive horse which comes to the bit itself in full responsiveness to controls.

In most horses this requires light tugs on the reins by way of indication for the simple reason that they themselves have no reason to proceed beyond a relative lifting of the forehand.

But if head carriage and the lift of the forehand are faulty, one should not try to cure matters by curing the symptoms, say, by employing direct rein action upon the mouth. The cause lies elsewhere, as we have seen; it should be sought in the prerequisites that make possible correct adaptation to the bridle and lifting of the forehand.

Collection, as the term is used in dressage, is the state of the horse in which it relieves its forehand by increasing the load on the engaged hindquarters in order to concentrate all its forces for a given purpose. Carriage and responsiveness can be raised to their highest peaks, depending upon the degree of collection.

Correct collection requires that the back be stretched considerably. This increased elastic tension is produced by having the croup and buttock muscles of the engaged hindquarters exert a stronger pull downwards and backwards upon the muscles of the back connected to them (as explained above in connection with lifting the forehand). Another contributing factor is the tension of the back muscles in the opposite direction produced via the ligamentum nuchae owing to the extension of the head and neck forward and upward. This elastic tension, which is produced by the lively, energetic gait, and is wholly unrelated to convulsive tightness (see " Action of the Back "), then makes it possible for the lifted neck and head to act as levers upon the hindquarters. Their impulsion is then converted from a forward drive to a supporting force, depending upon the degree and direction in which the rider releases the impulsion and applies it.

Collection in some degree is indispensable in the gymnastic training of the saddle horse; it is also an excellent method of improving the action of horses with poor conformation, though not everyone can do such training.

In judging collection as a whole, one should be careful about taking a few external symptoms for the essentials, saying, " The horse is collected *because* it yields its head and carries its neck high." The following description of a truly collected horse would be more nearly correct, " This horse, collected as a result of correct action upon it, *cannot avoid* coming to the bit with a lifted forehand ".

Not all horses can achieve the same degree of collection as the term is used in dressage. What constitutes the maximum attainable physical and psychological collection for sluggish horses of poor conformation may be merely ordinary posture for born riding horses.

I. RIGHT AND WRONG GAIT—FORWARD REACH OF HIND
LEGS—MISTAKES THAT INTERFERE WITH ENGAGEMENT
OF THE HINDQUARTERS: STIFFNESS OF HIND LEGS,
DRAGGING, TENSED (EXAGGERATED AND HOVERING)
STEPS, FUMBLING, AND STEP-DANCING

There is seldom   riding lesson or classroom lecture in which *forward reach of hind legs,* that is, the engagement of the hindquarters in the direction of the base of the plumb line through the centre of gravity of rider and horse, is not mentioned. The instructor is quite right in emphasizing this fundamental condition for correct locomotion, for without long strides of the hind legs and hence of the forehand (to which the impulse is communicated by the muscles of the back) no extension is conceivable, and hence no yielding and stretching of the back and of its continuation, the neck.

Neither the young horse nor the young rider will make any progress, the former in its dressage, the latter in seat and influence, unless all training is based upon the elastically pulsating activity of the horse's back, which in turn depends directly upon the pure, ground-covering strides of the hind legs.

Many thousands of people have admired the white Lipizzans of the Spanish Riding School of Vienna or top horses being prepared for the Olympics. The spectators include many beginners who are eager to learn. They see that the hindquarters of these horses do not always reach "far" forward and yet their locomotion is correct, as seat and carriage incontestably prove. Why is this?

The regular engagement of the hindquarters is produced by muscular pulsations that are elicited by the controls via the central nervous system, and in turn they produce pulsation of the extensor and flexor muscles that extend along the spinal column through the neck, returning along the belly to the pelvis. These wavelike movements will be shorter or longer depending upon the framework, that is, the degree of collection—provided the necessary impulsion is present. They will be longer when impulsion predominates over support, as in the racing gallop or the free walk. They will be shorter if the motive power of the forward thrust is partially converted into support in advanced dressage, as in bending the haunches, the collected trot, and the collected walk.[17]

[17] The intensity of these pulsations depends, of course, on the intensity of the thrust and of the resultant impulsion. If all other factors are equal, the framework of the horse determines the extension in space, while the impulsion determines the force and the springy elasticity of the muscular activity and hence of the gait, the forward reach.

In the last exercises the centre of gravity of the horse-rider system has been shifted to the rear as the result of the engaged hindquarters, which bear more of the load.[18]

Thus there is no reason for the hind legs to advance beyond the trace of the front hoof in order to provide support, as at the free gaits.

Although the steps become shorter in the collected gaits, the hindquarters do reach forward as much as is possible with the carriage desired and the corresponding rate. If this were not so, the back would cease pulsating correctly, and the most beautiful acquired Olympic figure would be worthless, even harmful.

Let us repeat that the two groups of muscles lying on either side of the spinal column, which pulsate elastically rather than convulsively, must work quite uniformly along a straight line and on a single track. If they do not do so, the horse becomes crooked, with its legs not carrying an equal load on both sides, and we get the *impure* gait with all its variants.

Lastly, if the back is not compliant, owing to the incorrect action of the rider, that is, if the back is held tight in wrong, convulsive tension because of convulsive, inelastic pulsation (for absolute immobility is impossible for locomotion muscles while in motion), we get the "tensed steps" that will be taken up in the next section.

Summarizing, the only decisive factor influencing the degree of forward reach of the hind legs of a horse moving correctly is the plumb line through the common centre of gravity of horse and rider.

In the free, extended gaits, when the common centre of gravity is shifted forward, the instructor's command "Engage the hindquarters" can be fulfilled only if the hind hoof of a normally built horse alights a few hoof-breadths in front of the trace of the corresponding front hoof. The highly collected horse "reaches forward" equally well, however, if its hind leg (which is bent and bearing the load) alights a few hoof-breadths behind the front hoof trace after pushing off vigorously from the ground in time, provided the back is extended and can pulsate as far as the bit.

The back will not function correctly, however, if the hind legs remain far to the rear when they alight and drag sluggishly because they are grounded too long.

Now that we have learned the nature and degree of the forward reach of the hindquarters, we should add a few words about how this can be achieved.

Only the rider's leg can elicit the movement of the hind legs, their reaching forward, once the riding crop has made the horse understand this leg control. Only later is the forward-driving control of the seat as

[18] This refers to the haunches, the hip joint, and the stifle, the former bending throughout the entire reach forward and the latter bending until the vertical is passed.

a whole added, which closes the angle of the unbent forward-reaching hindquarters by temporarily increasing the load it bears. This develops the ground-covering, vigorous, springy strides, the *impulsion* that is the alpha and omega of all dressage.

If the horse moves at a lively gait with the posture desired by the rider, no deliberate and emphasized leg controls are required unless direction or rate is to be changed. The buttocks are in contact with the horse, held at the lowest point of the saddle by the rider's spine, which continually swings with the horse, and the lower leg remains in contact with the barrel of the horse, actively supple and elastically pressing the heel downwards. Together they promote the flexion and extension of the hind legs and thus maintain impulsion and back activity.

The lateral pulsations of the horse's body automatically provide the stimulus for far-reaching and lively engagement.

The young rider grasps these " alternating " leg controls best if he freely follows the movements of the horse, sitting upright and supple.

The rider's " feel " paves the way for theoretical understanding of cause and effect even with these wholly unconscious controls, which are a matter of pure feeling and are reached very rapidly when a relaxed balanced seat is employed on a riding horse.

If the two centres of gravity do not lie on the same vertical line, more effort is required and locomotion is poorer. All riding manuals prescribe that the rider be in harmony with his horse, for full development and improvement of the locomotion machinery is possible only when the rider's seat is right.

Since the seat must give the horse's back more freedom for engagement forward so that the back muscles can pulsate in long waves with unrestricted development of thrust, the seat is permitted—in fact, it endeavours—to assist the increased flexion of the hindquarters in collection by keeping the rider's spine upright. This is sometimes done even by leaning backwards (figures of the *haute école*).

In both of these boundary cases, as well as in the intermediate nuances of posture, the centres of gravity of horse and rider must always lie on the same plumb line. The load that is correctly distributed and balanced is easiest to carry.

Mistakes that interfere with engagement of the hindquarters.

There are skulking, deceitful horses that are unwilling to reach forward with their *stiffened hind legs*. If they were to do so, they would have to surrender their tensed, tightened backs and hence their entire muscular system to the rider's action, and proceed via unconstrained flexion and extension to suppleness, i.e., to unresisting response to the controls. But such horses do not want to do so; they avoid it at any price—until they have found their master.

If an inexperienced rider desires to reinforce his leg control by using the spur, expecting it to exert a "forward-driving" action, he will be disappointed to find that such a tight, deceitful horse resists even more. The stimulus of the spur causes its muscles to become even more convulsed.

In such cases a stroke of the riding crop and riding forward without using the rein as a "fifth foot" will compel the horse to balance itself on its own four legs and will make it, willy-nilly, reach forward honestly with its stiffened hind legs. Otherwise it would lose its natural balance, since the rider is no longer kind (or simple-minded?) enough to do this work for it.

The situation is quite different with horses that *drag* their hindquarters and seem to be stuck to the ground. Such horses avoid even the effort of growing stiff. They could hardly be called tensed; they merely creep around lazily and seem to be begging to be awakened from their sleep. Fairly light touches of the spur on alternate sides, just behind the girth[19] and in time with the gait, make such horses prick up their ears. This results in lively, fresh advancing, and in a few minutes can convert a sluggard into a riding horse with springy, energetic strides.

Lastly, the most frequently observed fault that interferes with the hindquarters' reaching forward, and thus disturbs the gait, is an unsteady hand or an active hand that acts wrongly—*the sawing hand*.

The hands act right-left in time with the gait in an effort to produce a misunderstood head carriage in the horse as quickly as possible. This is the purest kind of sawing, and horses are unfortunately only too ready to comply with this demand that they get behind the bit. The rider is satisfied with himself because he has given the horse an external form that may please the layman's eye, but only too late does he realize that he has also destroyed its gait.

How did that misfortune happen?

The abdominal muscles that swing the hindquarters forward have their contraction basis, their points of support and attachment, at the sternum and the first few ribs. The farther forward these are held, the more freely can the abdominal muscles do their job. This job is done in part by the

---

[19] Applying the leg farther to the rear in the region of the short ribs to drive the horse forward cannot aid the engagement of the hindquarters. On the contrary, it will cause them to drag, since it strikes the belly muscles that swing the hind thigh forward at a point that is too far removed from their basis of contraction at the sternum. On the other hand, at this point the walls of the belly are supported only by the short ribs, which have no supporting connection with the fixed sternum. If the rider's leg action is at all powerful, the belly walls and their surrounding muscles are then pressed inwards, so to speak, and give way to the rear.

scalenus muscle, which begins at the lower cervical vertebrae and connects them with the front of the sternum and the first few ribs. They are visible as a powerfully developed muscular layer that fills out part of the hollow between shoulder and neck (wide base of neck), especially in a well-made horse, and are evidence of consistent dressage.

The unsteady or sawing hand, which pulls the neck to the right and to the left from its base (the part that should be steadiest), thus weakens the scalenus muscle, interfering with it to such an extent that it grows limp and is unable to do one of its jobs, holding the ribs and sternum up to the front.

But without ribs held at the front it is impossible to get the abdominal muscles to swing forward fully; without this swinging we cannot get energetic, sure-footed, and ground-covering engagement of the hind-quarters; and without this engagement there is no gait.

One of the greatest writers on horsemanship of all time says somewhere, " In equitation, in a certain sense, everything is right and everything is wrong."

He is only too right. Even the golden rule: "Work your horse by riding forward" may be fundamentally misunderstood. For it is not so much a matter of *what* you do in the saddle as of *how* you do it. Even a control correctly applied will deaden the horse if it lasts too long, ending up by achieving the opposite of what you intended.

A convulsively tightened, tensed back produces artificially exalted and *exaggerated steps* (also called the floating trot or the extended *passage*), whenever the rate is increased. Similarly, a diminution of the rate that is forcibly achieved by the reins produces hovering.

Horses that display a preference for shortened gaits commit this fault very readily, especially when their tight back facilitates these *hovering steps*. They are either over or behind the bit and move at a shortened trot with *fumbling steps* to avoid taking the industrious, released strides that require honest work.

If the back is excessively relaxed, which is manifest to the eye as an unnatural sway-back and to the rider's touch as lack of springiness and lack of activity, the movements become dull and dragging.

Incorrect guidance also plays a major part in all these faulty states of tension. The hand must lie on the straight line from elbow to mouth. The degree of collection automatically indicates how high it should be above the withers. If you ride with the hand too high, so that the above-mentioned line is no longer straight, the position of the hands interferes with the pulsation of the horse's back, no matter whether the back is too tight, fixed in an arched position that increases its tension, or is a sway-back, for this makes it impossible for the back to assume its natural arch, halfway between excessively tensed and excessively released.

In all these cases the back is unable to do its job of providing a dependable transmission line between forehand and hindquarters, interrupted by no resistances, that ensures a springy co-operation and opposition of forehand and hindquarters and thus responsiveness.[20] The long back muscle, simply called the "back" by horsemen, is connected to the front of the hind legs via two other groups of muscles coupled to it, so that it is part of the rhythm of motion.

When the back is tight and does not pulsate, every stride will be unpleasantly felt by the bones and joints of the horse. That is why it alternates its supporting leg as quickly as possible, taking shorter strides or leaps than in a natural, comfortable, and painless stride. It wears itself out prematurely because of the greater number of strides and leaps it has to take to cover a certain distance, altogether apart from the fact that the joints, which are not supple enough in flexion and extension, are damaged by being permanently held fast at a stiff gait.

The more we acknowledge, after years of experience, that the groups of muscles in the back serve chiefly for locomotion and connection (the work of support is done by the neck muscles, which hold the spinal column of the back in their natural arch when the horse's neck stretches out to reach the bit), the more clearly we realize that only a back that pulsates elastically and unconstrainedly can produce an elastically free and lively gait.

J. "NERVES" AND NERVE—ANIMATION, METTLE, RESTLESSNESS

A nervous horse that has "nerves", which may play it and us tricks, *seems* to be animated and *is* restless because of fear, for it has lost its psychological equilibrium and endeavours to work off this convulsiveness, which has also been communicated to its body, by fleeing forward.

A horse that has "nerve" *is* eager to move and only *appears* restless at times because of an inner feeling of strength, which is manifested in liveliness. It is in complete possession of its psychological equilibrium, the actual basic tone of which is an assurance that handles all critical situations with confidence.

All that a horse possessing nerve (as all riding horses should in more or less degree) requires, together with its necessary dependence upon its

[20] As Schwyter and Zschoake have convincingly demonstrated (*Further Investigations of the Relationship of Bone Formation to the Statics and Mechanics of the Vertebral Skeleton*), the traditional comparison of a horse's back to an arch is completely false. It resembles a bridge truss much more in its combination of tensile elements (muscles and ligaments) and compression elements (spinal processes). Also see p. 263ff.

rider, is a certain independence in broken ground (see "Obedience"), which evokes in the horse a feeling of shared responsibility and allows all the positive qualities mentioned above to be fully effective. Its ready obedience will only be increased by the participation, physical and psychological (horses behind hounds!), that results from the independence it has been accorded.

K. FULL AND HALF HALTS

The *full halt* brings to a stop a horse that is in motion.

The *half halt* is a signal given the horse to decrease its rate, or merely to improve its carriage, or to make the horse easier on the reins, when it bores on the bit and presses on the reins. In both of the latter cases the rate may be the same as before.

Opinions probably do not differ about how to effect a full halt. It is a long road from initially allowing the half-raw remount to run until it comes to a stop, when only the reins are effective because it does not understand the other controls, to the full halt that is perfect from the equestrian standpoint, in which the trained horse gently and fluidly accepts the concerted controls. This road will be described in the appropriate passages of the following sections.

Here we shall merely sketch the origin of a correctly executed full halt, where the *co-operation of all the controls* is most clearly manifested:

Stimulating forward reach of the hindquarters, followed by halting them by leg pressure on both sides of the horse. Loading action of the seat by pushing the small of the back farther forward, keeping the upper body upright and sustaining action of the hands. More or less accepting pull on the reins, as necessary, with unchanged posture of the rider's upper body and passive legs. After the horse is halted: slight relaxation and imperceptible backward motion of the upper body, which reduces the driving action of the small of the back to a mere holding of the reins, while the hindquarters are loaded and held fast. At the same time a slight advance of the hands, so that it is easier for the horse to stand still in hand, as the impulsion that promotes contact with the bit has vanished with the interruption of motion.

If the controls do not co-operate in the sequence given—say, the accepting pull on the reins is made too early or the weight action becomes too much of a driving action because the upper body leans backwards excessively—the stop cannot be soft and fluid but is abrupt.

The controls employed for the half halt are similar, the sole difference being that the hands allow motion to continue accordingly. Driving controls persist and outweigh the restraining ones. Stretching in one's seat and closing one's fingers will suffice for sensitive horses.

L. OBEDIENCE

The horse must meet psychological and physical requirements to be able to obey the rider.

First of all, it must want to obey the rider, and that can happen only if the horse's will is subordinated to that of the rider. Second, it must also by physically able to convert this will into action, in order to be able to perform what is desired correctly.

In training the young horse, *direct action upon its will by physical compulsion should be avoided as much as possible. The rider should substitute for it a far-reaching influence on the animal's psyche.* If the rider possesses the ability to enter into the mind of a horse, which differs from the human mind, he will find hundreds of ways of establishing mental contact with his pupil, and he can use this contact to consolidate his own position of power as well as to gain the confidence of the horse.

The basic mistakes made in handling horses are due to the erroneous opinion that the brain of a horse operates like that of a man or a dog, in other words, that it operates deductively. For example, a horse shies away from an automobile and is beaten by its rider. We assume that next time it knows (deduce = draw the conclusion from the punishment) it will be punished if it shies off again; therefore it will cease being shy. But it is entirely wrong to attribute such powers of deduction to the mind of a horse. Its mind is capable only of *direct association of ideas,* and the next time it encounters an automobile it will shy even more, for it will already have established the direct association of ideas—frightening unknown object (motor car) = blows received when this object appears. Because of its excellent memory, repeated punishment will anchor the association—automobile = beating—as cause and effect so firmly as to turn into an obession or an " auto-suggestion ". When such a ruined horse is sent to a real horseman for retraining, usually much too late, after it has already become an outlaw, it may take months of extraordinary patience to blot out that deep-rooted obsession and substitute other impressions.

The discerning rider will utilize the fact that *associations of ideas sink in as obsessions* (which may rapidly ruin a horse) for his own purpose—to train the horse correctly—and thus he will never have to use physical constraint, which damages the character and the still undeveloped body of the young horse.

Realizing that the horse's will is governed principally by feelings of pleasure or discomfort, he will influence that will by evoking pleasurable feelings, which he associates with certain actions of the horse as a chain of cause-and-effect ideas. In brief, he will richly reward the horse at the slightest indication of clumsy willingness to comply with any new demands, thus making his own work easier on the morrow. The horse will be sure to note that jumping some obstacle or other, for example, is followed by a reward in the shape of oats or even dismounting and being led back to the stable.

The association of ideas—overcoming the obstacle = oats or the end of work—will be established, and the insignificant feeling of discomfort produced at the outset by the unaccustomed effort of the jump will be largely outweighed by the feeling of pleasure occasioned by eating oats.

The way in which the driving leg control, which is the starting point and fundamental prerequisite for all other controls, is made understandable to the horse also comes under this heading.

Actually, there is no reason why the untrained horse should move forward under the pressure of the rider's leg. The spurs, because of the physiological nature of the irritation of skin and muscles they produce, would even cause contraction and hence slowing down.

The horse will try to escape from the feeling of discomfort produced by contact with the riding crop, however, by resorting to its natural means of defence, fleeing forwards. If such forward motion is consistently followed by the cessation of contact with the riding crop, it will soon require only the merest indication of the crop, and later on of the leg that replaces it, to produce a depart or an acceleration of the gait. Thus the horse has learned to interpret correctly the stimulating sensation produced in its brain by the forward-driving leg pressure, which originally left it baffled.

As the horse grows accustomed to following the same impressions in the same manner, the basis is laid for the notion of the rider's superior power, which is really fictitious, over the body of the horse, which has much greater power, so that it never occurs to the horse to attempt a showdown.

The "driving controls" chain of ideas must become an obsession (wholly imperceptible to the horse) that ensures obedience, and in this sense we may call it "mechanical discipline". It has learned to interpret contact with the rider's leg correctly, and as soon as it feels this contact, its brain will transmit the command "Forward!" through the motor nerves to the appropriate muscles of the hindquarters, so that the depart becomes a reflex, so to speak, of the control.

The muscular movements are elicited by nerves whose impulses origin-

ate in the cerebellum. But the reaction time for the roundabout path:
contact with the leg—transmission of this sensation to the brain—transmission of the motor command through the nerve to the muscles, the
organs of execution, is of no practical significance, as the activity of the
nerves coincides with that of the muscles as far as human powers of
observation are concerned.

The horse's brain, the seat of its understanding and will, cannot be
ignored as its central organ, which sets its muscles in motion in response
to our controls.[21] If we cut the brain out of the circuit by anaesthesia,
the horse loses its capacity for motion.

There are cases where the sensations of pleasure evoked by the rider
in the horse are not enough to keep it from misbehaving. Then the rider
must take the opposite road. He influences the establishment of obedience
by producing sensations of discomfort, which the horse then associates
with its misbehaviour as the direct consequence and effect of the latter.
A case in point would be the punishment that immediately follows a
refractory about-face by the horse.

We needn't add that the horse should be rewarded after it has overcome
its impulse to misbehave (which usually occurs at certain places along the
road). This establishes a new association of ideas in the horse: " If I do
not turn around here, I will be rewarded. So it is less painful and more
pleasant not to turn around and to get oats than to make an unsuccessful
effort to do so and get a beating in addition."

The horse does not have a dog's consciousness of guilt for having done
something wrong. It is incapable of thinking logically: " Because I have
misbehaved in turning around I am being punished." But if the rider
is at all consistent, the direct association of ideas—turning around =
punishment—will automatically be impressed upon its brain as an obsession. In this sense we may say that the horse has the " memory of an
automaton ".

Current books on riding are accused, not entirely without justification,
of representing horses as nothing but angels, which appear to wish
for nothing than to please their riders if the latter only allow them to
do so.

No matter how sensitive and skilful the rider may be, no matter how
expertly he rides his spirited young horse, he cannot avoid the remount's
failing to evaluate the well-intentioned efforts of its master correctly or
paying more attention to its surroundings than to its rider and plotting
childish misbehaviour. Likewise at the beginning of training he will be
unable to prevent the lively horse from resorting to methods of getting

---

[21] The only exceptions are the controls that act as mere displacements of weight. These
controls directly affect the mass of the horse, and thus the muscles that displace the centre
of gravity of this mass as if the mass were a lifeless object.

18. *Renvers* left.

19. Shoulder-in to the left and right of the center line. Grand Quadrille of the Spanish Riding School, Wels, Austria, 1955.

20. Traverse (half pass) to the right. Colonel A. Podhajsky on *Maestoso Alea* (Lipizzan) 1955.

21. Traverse left (half pass). Exemplary seat and longitudinal flexion of the horse. R. Waetjen on *Flinker Kerl* (Hanover) 1941.

rid of the load (which it feels is a superfluous burden despite the suppleness of the seat) that make it difficult, to say the least, for the rider to exert his controls in accordance with the manual.

Most young horses are often refractory; they usually desire something other than that desired by the rider at that very moment, even though obedience causes them no pain or perceptible discomfort.

It would be a mistake, therefore, to come to a halt at every fear-inspiring object with a horse that is only partially in hand to allow it to make a detailed inspection. The horse would soon seek out such opportunities and become altogether shy, though a less complaisant rider would never allow that to happen. At the first indications of shying, the most important thing to do is to maintain contact between hand and mouth and to pass by rapidly, detouring if necessary.

In such cases the rider will demonstrate his skill, based upon feel, tact, and a good seat, by succeeding in getting his horse into such a physical state and position, without struggle and in a fully relaxed manner, as to leave it no alternative but to obey willingly. It will always be a triumph of the finest tact for the rider to have realized all his objectives without encountering open opposition.

One should not spare the riding crop or legs on older horses once their maliciousness is clearly realized. A brief prick of the spurs clears the air, for it unmistakably reminds the horse of the contrasting positions of power. After such a conflict that ends successfully for the rider, he is, of course, obliged as the victor to take the initial steps to restore a friendly relationship with his "comrade". It is a matter of course that conflicts of this sort should not be settled on slippery pavements.

An attempt to conciliate the horse when it is in open revolt would be regarded as cowardly bribery, and at the next best opportunity the horse would become a calculating blackmailer exploiting the weakness of its "master".

All indications of inopportune complaisance before the horse has at least manifested a readiness to obey gravely undermine respect and belief in the rider's superior powers, if they do not destroy it for ever.

Another important task of the rider is to develop the horse's confidence in him.

In one of the examples cited above, dealing with the initial training over obstacles, we had the opportunity of making this exercise a pleasant occurrence for the horse by consistently rewarding it after every willing jump. This not only will help to develop a sure, obedient jumper but will also reinforce the horse's confidence in the possessor of superior power. It will respect and obey the rider, who also is a friend and comrade, and it will like him as the donor of pleasurable sensations. Such horses will display eagerness to comply with the rider's will—they will be *willingly obedient*.

Horses that are psychologically cramped, shying out of fear, and those of generally oversensitive disposition, with ruined nerves, can be made responsive to the controls only after their confidence has been won. For their psychological equilibrium is disturbed as long as their nerves quiver and jump, and no contact with them is possible other than kind, relaxed, and patient treatment.

When everything else fails, quiet stroking and the sound of the familiar voice, whose even intonation reminds the horse of previous rewards, are often the only way of maintaining contact. Once this contact is broken in pathologically excitable horses, it may lead to headlong bolting as if they were possessed of a demon, somersaulting or throwing the rider.[22]

Once the rider has succeeded in winning the confidence of his horse, he must, of course, not put this confidence to too hard a test at the beginning. At the start it is always better to be a diplomat and a tactician, avoiding occasions that might produce anxiety states.

But the establishment of confidence begun under the most favourable conditions will be subjected to the gravest crises if something is demanded of the horse that it has not yet understood or that exceeds its physical ability and causes pain. Then the association of ideas—rider = cause of feelings of discomfort—may be established, and once such a chain of ideas has taken root, all progress will be hampered.

In our discussion of obedience training up to now we have considered winning over the horse's will and subordinating it to and synchronizing it with the rider's by means of the direct association of ideas and the gaining of its confidence. We need not add that despite all our efforts to master the horse, we do not want to make it a mere tool without a will of its own. Obedience training goes hand in hand with education, principally by cross-country exercise, the object of which is to keep the horse from losing its sense of self-reliance.

This cross-country training has as its objective letting the horse that is responding to leg control find its own balance without being disturbed by the reins. It employs its neck as the natural regulator of equilibrium and as the chief balancing rod (a subordinate balancing rod being the tail) for this purpose, just as it instinctively used to do as a foal in the pasture. A horse whose will has been broken by brute force and is now in a state of passive tolerance because of its faulty complaisance has lost all self-

[22] The apparently inexplicable falls of suddenly frightened horses on completely flat ground are also attributable to the disordered functioning of their motor nerves (faulty accord of the muscular and nervous forces involved). The propensity to sudden bolting is a psychological vestige dating from life on the steppes.

reliance as well as its spirit and now expects to have its rider prescribe its every step. We can readily imagine how miserably such an animal, debased to a mechanical automaton, would perform in the hunting field and what embarrassing situations its rider, who has perhaps no responsibility at all for its "training", may encounter.

Obedience, in the sense of mastery of the horse's body by the controls and of more or less advanced gymnastic training and responsiveness, is a function of the posture, in so far as the more the horse's own centre of gravity moves towards the centre of its area of support, the more it becomes master of its own mass and its balancing ability. If too much of the load it carries is borne by the forehand, it cannot lift its front legs off the ground as lightly and effortlessly as required for perfect suppleness, no matter how much it wishes to obey. Examples of this are the incredibly willing and obedient polo ponies, specially bred for suppleness but not fully trained in our sense, whose physical obedience must be "facilitated" by bridles and auxiliary reins that are far from simple. The author does not speak of this as a layman, as he has played polo abroad.

Only consistent, systematic gymnastic training in the riding hall (on a flat track) enables the horse to convert the rider's will, expressed through symbolic controls, into action and to perform as desired with ease.[23]

This satisfies the second condition, the physical one, which must be the prerequisite for psychological readiness, as was stated at the outset of this discussion of obedience.

At the risk of repeating myself, I should like to emphasize once more that calm is an extremely important factor in establishing obedience. "Calm, Forward, Straight" was the motto adopted by one of the greatest horsemen of all times. He deliberately put "calm" first; he does not mean calm as a sign of fatigue, but the strong, superior assurance resulting from physical well-being and mental composure. In this state the horse is most attentive to his trainer and is most independent of all disturbing phenomena, which are often due to its extremely sharp senses of hearing and smell.

[23] In many high-bred horses the readiness to obey and meet the rider half-way is more highly developed than the bodily organs, especially the legs. Such horses whose ability cannot match their willingness because their physical strength is not equal to the requirements of their truly big heart are cases of "diamond cut diamond". They require intelligent moderation on the part of the rider to dampen their excessive spirit, which may go as far as self-sacrifice.

II. Riding the Horse for the First Time.
Attaining Unconstraint and Suppleness

A. THE YOUNG HORSE REDISCOVERING THE EASY
NATURALNESS OF POSTURE AND THE NATURAL FREEDOM
AND ASSURANCE OF ITS MOVEMENTS BEFORE IT CARRIED
A RIDER

We now return to the real hero of this book, the young horse. We shall follow it in its training: the gymnastic exercises in the riding hall, followed by consistent, serious education that is always done in the spirit of kindness and understanding and ending with familiarization with the increasing demands made upon its physique.

It has already been introduced to wearing the saddle during its work on the lunge. Once it has been tired out on the lunge, a rider may have been allowed to mount it, and it may have been allowed to carry him back to the stable in order to associate the concept of "rider" with the end of work. This certainly establishes a favourable atmosphere and by no means signifies training the horse to rush to get home.

But let us assume that we want to introduce a horse that has never carried a rider to this new situation, so that it learns to be at ease from the very outset.

Even the best-intentioned horse may experience a panicky fear if it is suddenly mounted. The sudden load and the appearance of a dark shadow high above its back are its initial sensations upon the contact with a rider sitting in the saddle. Even if the rider is not thrown off, the horse will acquire a dislike for mounting, and we will soon have a horse that patters around as soon as it spies the rider, grows tense, and causes difficulty at the very beginning of the workout. This difficulty need never have occurred, however, if the initial mounting had been done with some care.

During the period of lungeing, which should be done for a minimum of several weeks before the first time the horse is mounted, the horse has learned how to run in a circle easily, and it may even have advanced to the point where it can be driven and will stretch to reach the bit.

But even if the latter achievement has not yet become second nature to it—perhaps the time was too short—it has regained its "natural trot" during unhurried lungeing, at a rate chosen by itself, and at strides of equal length, with a posture that is self-chosen.

It is first lunged at this natural trot on the left hand, then on the right, and finally on the left again for a somewhat longer time than on the preceding days, so that it grows tired, and halting and standing still becomes a highly welcome rest.

That is the most favourable moment for the rider to approach the horse from its front, while the lungeing trainer, who has laid aside his whip, shortens the lunge and also comes up to the horse's head. Its groom gives it oats or bread to keep it from noticing these tactical movements, if possible.[24] These rewards should be combined with patting the neck, shoulders, and saddle, the noises gradually getting louder. The less attention the horse pays to these contacts, the more opportune it is to combine them with the rider's leaning against the horse's left shoulder, touching the pommel, putting right hand over the saddle, and the like. But each new movement and contact must be consistently combined with an immediate reward in the form of a delicacy.

Thus the rider ingratiates himself more and more with the horse, which no longer pays any attention to his contacts, and then swings himself up, holding onto the mane and the pommel, without, however, entirely abandoning his support on his toes for the present.

Prepared and distracted in this manner, no horse that is not spoiled or frightened resents finding the rider's left foot suddenly resting in the stirrup, with the toes turned away from the horse. On the contrary, it will merely welcome this harmless movement, for it implies oats again! The rider then lifts himself up in the stirrup a few inches at a time, using his right foot to push off the ground, then touching the ground again and keeping the left foot in the stirrup, rising again and returning to earth again. Each time he rises the thrust of the right leg is stronger, so that the rider can soon lie for a few seconds like a sack of flour with his belly over the saddle. The horse, which is busy feeding and thus distracted, does not mind this kind of load, which increases only inch by inch and ounce by ounce, so to speak.

While the rider's left arm, laid over the right front side of the saddle, maintains the body in the position described above, the free right arm begins very slowly to make movements that resemble those of the right leg when it will subsequently swing over the saddle. Once the horse has also grown accustomed to these movements, the rider lifts his right leg over the horse and fits into the saddle, gently seating himself forward, the assistant fitting the previously adjusted stirrup to his right foot.

Standing under this new load is more unpleasant to a sensitive horse than moving. That is why the assistant standing in front of the horse's

[24] With shy horses, which are the exception nowadays, it is best to have the groom ride the horse for the first time, as it knows his voice and odour. Another relaxed man then takes over the role of assistant, who rewards the horse and holds the off stirrup leather or stirrup during mounting in order to prevent any shift of the saddle, the girth of which is only loosely fastened. The assistant also has the job of slipping the stirrup, which has previously been adjusted to the rider's leg length, over the rider's right foot.

head moves a few steps backwards, the horse following him in order to reach the oats offered and being fed while moving.

The trainer brings the horse, which he leads by the shortened lunge, to the circular track it already knows, where he lets the horse go into a natural trot on the left hand, employing the *accustomed* controls. The rider, completely passive, endeavours to follow the movement of the horse with suppleness, using a crotch seat.

As the trainer takes over the lead, the rider need not and should not do anything about it. He holds onto the mane or, if the horse's mane is cut short, to a wide throat or stirrup strap, and all that he should worry about is going along easily with the horse without overloading the hind-quarters by sitting heavily in the saddle. The trainer sees to it that any capers cut by the horse do not take place in one spot but always forward, and he also prevents the horse from slowing down or stopping by threatening it with the whip, which the horse already knows.

Not only must the rider maintain a supple seat, in order not to disturb the rhythmic motion of the horse by any stiffness of his own body, but he must also be able to keep a firm seat if needed, for he must not allow himself to be thrown. Though this would be no catastrophe for the rider, it would almost amount to one in so far as the further training of the horse is concerned. Once it becomes conscious of its own strength as a result of so easy a victory, it will repeat the endeavour to get rid of the uncomfortable load at the next opportunity. When things have reached such a pass, another rider who is firmer in the saddle will simply have to take over. But this resort to drastic measures should not be necessary at all, and it need not be if preparation is correct and the initial rider possesses the required dexterity and fixity in the saddle. These measures should be avoided if only because the use of force does nothing to improve the disposition of the young horse or its physical development.

If the horse should remain standing despite the threat of the whip, the trainer should place the whip under his right armpit and approach the horse, shortening the lunge as he comes nearer, in order to "unscrew" it from the ground by turning it slightly to the right or the left and getting it going again by leading it a few steps forward. The horse is again rewarded for doing this, of course.

The rider now departs from his passivity to this extent: he strokes the horse's neck, talks to it, and leans forward during halts to offer the horse delicacies in order to accustom it more and more to this previously unknown load and to elicit the conviction that this load constitutes no menace but, on the contrary, only something good.

Once the horse has trotted around the hall a few times, its gait is reduced to a walk, and it is brought to a stop. Here again it is given oats. This is followed by a brief period of trotting again, the rider dismounting after the horse comes to a stop. In dismounting, the rider must again obey the principle already observed when mounting: he should not frighten the horse by any sudden movements. Before withdrawing the left foot from the stirrup the rider should swing himself up into the saddle a few more times, for the horse has now grown tired and quiet and in this state will let itself be mounted with ease and will grow more and more accustomed to mounting by frequent repetition.

Then, as the best reward of all, work is stopped, and the horse is allowed to go back to the stable.

If this principle is followed, the horse will quietly allow itself to be mounted and later will stand still while mounted, both matters of the greatest importance, and they will become matters of course.

There are simpler methods of mounting a horse for the first time than the one described above. For example, one can readily lift one's self upon a horse standing near the wall if the groom puts his right hand under the lifted left leg of the rider. Not many horses will take offence at that, if the rider sits down lightly rather than plopping heavily into the saddle. A similar method is employed in racing paddocks for yearlings, which are often rather difficult to handle.

Sooner or later every horse should be accustomed to the procedure of the rider being given a "leg-up". This is the tidiest way of mounting one's horse because the saddle cannot shift, and climbing is avoided. However climbing cannot be avoided if a very short man has to get up on a very high horse and has no breastplate available, as may sometimes happen.

Lungeing is done only on the left hand the first day the horse works with a rider, as turning to the left is most natural to the horse under these new conditions. The change of hand takes place as necessary on the following days.

Although training should last two hours daily, the initial work with a rider, which takes place chiefly at a natural trot, should not exceed ten to twenty minutes (depending upon the strength of the horse, as manifested by its high spirits or fatigue). If the load were carried any longer, muscles not accustomed to these new demands, aside from other factors that we will take up later, would try to get rid of the pain caused by excessively long strain by an increased convulsive flexing or a similar relaxing. That is another reason for practising mounting and dismounting frequently in the next few lessons. The intermissions can be used for correcting the position of the saddle, lifting the horse's legs, leading it over bars, and the like. The saddle, which was initially placed on the horse with its front covering the shoulder blades somewhat in order to spare the hindquarters and back and not to irritate the horses hind back, is now shoved back to its proper place during these intermissions and buckled down farther back. Then the lowest point of a correctly built riding saddle, which is located at the middle of the seating surface, rests above the point where the withers end and the back begins (fifteenth vertebra). The girth is placed along the plumb line from the lowest point of the saddle to the ground (about nine inches behind the point of the horse's elbow).

I recommend that a back cinch be used for young horses whose saddle position is not yet fully developed and whose withers are indistinct. It can generally be used for "grass-bellied", top-heavy horses or those that are narrow-chested, as well as those that move with an inactive back that does not swing and does not keep saddle and rider in place.

Such a girth, which rests only lightly against the abdominal wall, provides the saddle, which would otherwise slide forward, with the necessary support. It hasn't the disadvantages of the crupper, which irritates the back when attached to a saddle that slips forward and may result in cramps, or the front cinch, which slides forward to the elbow, abrading the latter and making the horse dislike freely advancing its front legs.

When the saddle is laid on the horse in the region of the loins, the back cinch, which is attached to the hindmost billet strap (sewed in for this purpose with a backward slant), is tightened around the belly only enough so that it does not hang loose. Then the saddle is slid against the hair to its normal position. Only then are the saddle girths fastened in the usual manner in the two front billet straps that are still free. The back cinch must be thirty to forty inches longer than other girths, depending upon the size of the horse's belly.

Every horse that is accustomed to correct saddling tolerates the back cinch. Moreover it is supposed to be only a temporary aid. It is not a thing of beauty—but every rider who cannot attain his objective otherwise and who is unable to spend an hour saddling and unsaddling will like it very much.

The better the subsequent gait of the horse, from an equestrian standpoint, and the more its "grass belly" disappears, the less necessity will there be for resaddling to "obtain a good saddle position". Resaddling will then be necessary only to relieve the horse during a rest or to reward it, since the horse regards the loosening of the girth as a reward. The back cinch was known to jousting knights in the twelfth century; it served principally to give the saddle greater firmness when they clashed in combat. It was used until the end of tournaments about the time of the unfortunate death of Henry II of France (1559).

In the stock saddle to-day it still serves as a back support for the tension of the lasso, and we gymnastic riders consider the back cinch "the only way of keeping our saddles in place (in horses whose gait is not yet correct)," as Krane says.

The saddle slides forward even in horses of quite harmonious conform- ation and with a perfectly shaped back if they are ridden with a cramped neck and correspondingly extended nose. They are then using a "lifted forehand" that is not the result of equestrian action upon the *entire* horse from the rear end to the front (say, in the deceptive hope of coaxing elevated steps from the forehand).

In this faulty "star-gazer" carriage the four last cervical vertebrae are pressed downwards, and with them the connecting spinal column of the back, as may be seen by glancing at a picture of the skeleton. For the spinal column is not attached to the shoulder blades and supported thereon through the collarbone, as it is in man, but is merely elastically suspended from them together with the thorax.

The withers, which constitute the front end of the spinal column, are naturally affected by this sagging and are no longer able to offer sufficient resistance to the forward sliding of the saddle.

Another factor contributing to the formation of such an artificially de- formed "downhill" horse that no longer fills out its saddle is the position of the hind legs. They support the resistance in the neck by remaining unengaged and stiff (high croup) and drag behind, resisting the reins.

Let us add right here that there are simpler methods of riding a horse for the first time just as there are for mounting it for the first time, or, putting it better, there is a procedure that apparently saves time. This procedure may be used without danger for good-natured horses that are not very sensitive. But the cases are incomparably more frequent where mistakes made by too hasty handling of the horse when first ridden and by ignoring the remount's individuality have allowed vices and bad habits to take root which the horse will never be able to get rid of entirely in later life.

The procedure of familiarizing the horse for the first few weeks with the driving and restraining controls that are effective in lungeing, of lungeing it prior to the first time it is mounted, of effecting this mounting itself and subsequent riding with the greatest calm and relaxation and concern for its sensitivity may seem pedantic to many people. But it is the way that leads most certainly to our goal, although it is not the most rapid way in every case.

A horse that has regained its natural gait on the lunge and follows the controls, framed between lunge and whip, will not require the rider to intervene with his reins in any way, but will enable him to concentrate his attention on securing a supple seat that does not interfere with its gait.

This preliminary work will make it possible to reduce to a minimum the difficulties that are unavoidable after the initial mounting and those that every back will produce because of the unaccustomed load.

A few days later, after the horse has already grown accustomed to the rider's weight, it will be time for the rider to depart from his passive attitude and to familiarize the horse first with the driving and then with the restraining controls. This is also preparation for free riding, the beginning of which must be left to the insight and feel of the rider.

The rider effects the initial driving forward by touching his riding crop to the horse's shoulder and later just behind the leg. If the horse increases its rate, the control should be removed at once. Once understanding develops, the driving control is increasingly transferred from the lungeing trainer to the rider, the latter gradually substituting leg pressure for the riding crop (the leg wearing no spurs, of course).

This explains the leg control to the horse, which does not know how to interpret it at the beginning (as we stated in the section on obedience), but it grows accustomed to following such control even without the supporting co-operation of whip and riding crop.

The horse must now be acquainted with the action of the reins, which up to now have lain knotted across the neck.

They are fitted so as to establish contact between the hand and the horse's mouth. This connection must be so light that the bit exerts no disturbing effect at all upon the mouth. The length of the reins must be entirely governed by the head and neck carriage chosen by the horse, which is only slightly limited by the side reins; hence they may be either long or short. In brief, the reins must "fit". The rider must not think of guiding his horse; this continues to be the job of the lungeing trainer. The side reins, which are still useful, are buckled or snapped into the rings of the bit *underneath* the snaffle reins, of course. This will prevent the horse's head and neck from turning too much and thus keep it from being distracted by outside events. They must be long enough for the horse to be able to reach them by fully stretching its neck and head forward, but only during training can their final length be determined. If lungeing is done for a considerable time, they will be shortened as the horse grows collected, as stated above in our discussion of lungeing. But when the horse is ridden for the first time, they must again be left as long as they were when it was first lunged.

The rider cannot increase the load on the horse's back as yet to make it change from the trot to a walk. On the contrary, he temporarily increases the pressure of his knees, thus increasing the effect of his weight which has already been shifted to the two sides of the horse by his relieving crotch seat. At the same time he allows the motion at the trot to run its course, using a fixed hand or, if necessary, a hand that alternately accepts and yields, until the horse has made the transition to the walk. These initial rein controls are explained and supported by the lunge controls of his trainer, with which the horse is already familiar. The legs are still inactive. As soon as the horse has fallen to a walk, the rider assumes the normal seat with his legs in gentle contact, giving the horse enough freedom of the reins to prevent any interfering effects of the bit upon its mouth.[25]

At the beginning the transition from the walk to the halt is effected in accordance with the same principles that effected the transition from the trot to the walk, so that the horse comes to a standstill almost by itself.

If it begins to seek contact with the bit as training progresses, the rider's weight, corresponding to the normal seat he then employs, will follow the horse's movement less (not so much), thus putting a load on the hind legs which have been engaged as a result of forward-driving leg controls. Letting the horse run its course until it "comes to a stop", as at the outset, has then become a slowing down, which in turn becomes a halt in the fully ridden horse (see full halt and half halt).

Determining when the horse should be ridden without the lunge is a matter of feeling alone. Once the horse understands the first concepts of the rider's forward-driving and restraining controls and has learned how to follow them without the assistance of the lungeing trainer, once it stands still by itself and exhibits no restlessness during mounting or dismounting, the time has come when the lunge and the side reins can be dispensed with.

Nothing now prevents our letting the young horse, accompanied by a quieter, older horse as a teacher, saunter around a large open area, or in the forest and meadow if local conditions permit, under our load.

Riding at liberty should not be delayed too long, for the movement of a young horse carrying a rider on a curved line, no matter how large the diameter, is not desirable. The time for flexion work on a single track, such as is involved in moving around a circle because of the increased load on the near hind leg, is still far off, and we should endeavour to

---

[25] As soon as the side reins can be left off as training progresses and the horse is ridden freely without a lunge, the reins should be released completely at the walk, so that the horse does not come up against them no matter how much it stretches. This riding with surrendered reins makes the horse's strides long and calm. Only after some four months of training should slight contact with the bit be striven for at the walk. All other influences, with the exception of those that are indispensable to allow the horse to run its course, to prevent excessively lively manifestations of frolicsomeness, and to change direction, would only restrict the natural extension of the walk, since at this gait thrust and impulsion are only slightly effective in assisting pure locomotion.

establish the foundations for natural gait and natural carriage as soon as possible on lines that are as long as possible and interrupted by no change of direction. This has already been done by work on the lunge for the unburdened horse, thus doing valuable preliminary work for us.

As we have said, the rider can take his horse out riding for the first time in a large riding hall or out in the open air. This often depends upon local conditions. What is important is that the horse abandons the false tensing or loosening of the back which it exhibited more or less as soon as it was mounted during lungeing. No matter whether the back is tensed or loose in a cramped fashion because of the disturbing burden, we must always seek to secure compliance of the back by sitting very lightly in the saddle.

Experience has shown that this objective is best achieved at a natural trot, a gait that the horse chooses itself and at which it is allowed to move with very loose contact with the bit. The reins must never be allowed to become a crutch, for then the muscles of the back would not abandon their false tension; they would find support in the rider's hand, and the horse would be spared the trouble of seeking its balance upon its own four legs alone. Since the rider refuses to provide any support for it, the horse is compelled to carry itself in natural posture and must, willy-nilly, utilize all the previously tightened muscles for the jobs they have to do in correct locomotion—it must "uncramp" them.

As soon as this has happened and the horse carries itself without hurrying, the feeling of constraint, which was both cause and effect of a convulsive swinging of the muscles, disappears, and our first objective, absence of constraint, has been achieved. As quiet a trot as possible, at which the horse is in no danger of losing its forward balance and with it its uniform locomotion, its timing, is best suited for these preliminary exercises. It would be harder for the horse to carry itself at a faster trot or at a gallop. Either it would start hurrying, or, in order to maintain the rate without losing its forward balance, it would have to plant its front legs down hard instead of springily for fear of painful tugs on the reins. Thus it would suffer damage to its ligaments and joints.

Once the horse has acquired the necessary suppleness and power in its hindquarters and back, it will commence to gallop by itself. The rider can accept this gait without concern, rounding the corners possibly even more than at the trot. At such a voluntary gait, which is merely the manifestation of an animation that cannot be overesteemed, the horse will be able to carry itself without difficulty, since it is merely doing what it likes to do and what offers no difficulty, except at moments of excitement and convulsiveness which we are able to avoid in the present case. That is why we allow it to gallop along until it returns to the trot by itself. This trot will have gained in flow and impulsion after a few galloping leaps, which are then transformed into trotting forward.

In this first stage of training, which may be called the *period of the natural trot* with calm and absence of constraint as its sole interdependent prerequisites, outward form is of no importance whatsoever.

If its gait is naturally long-striding, the horse should not be held back, whereas if the horse is definitely lazy, the riding crop should be used only enough to keep it from holding back.

As the horse grows somewhat tired—and it will after a few turns around the hall—the last trace of false tension disappears and its timing becomes uniform. The horse supports itself only upon its own legs, has found its natural balance, and therefore moves with natural poise.

The energy of the gait is low, the horse doing only as much as is needed to maintain the gait.

A few circuits of the riding hall at the trot are made in each direction, interrupted by pauses for walking and stopping. Using a light crotch seat, we make it as comfortable for the remount as possible. But once the state of unconstraint has been reached, earlier in some horses and later in others, there is no reason not to assume the soft, elastic normal seat.

The time for this has come when the back neither arches nor sags in a cramp and thus is active to a certain extent though not yet compliant in the equestrian sense.

Since the back is no longer held tight in a cramped position, we shall not be thrown if we now begin a sitting trot.[26] The seat is not yet moved forward, so to speak, as this requires the energetic thrust and engagement of the hindquarters, which are communicated to the back muscles, and that can only be elicited by driving.

After a few weeks the muscles, principally those of the hindquarters, the back, and the neck, will be so strengthened by the natural trot, which forces them to be active without overexertion, that the rider can increase the demands he makes upon the horse. The muscles of the hindquarters and those of the back coupled to them have had no occasion to pulsate

[26] If the rider does not have a really soft and supple seat, it is better to use the sitting trot only after the horse's contact with the bit is assured, and the elastically swinging active back invites one to sit down. Then the contact between the rider's seat and the horse's body, which is not interrupted because he is riding at a sitting trot, has a favourable effect upon the rider's ability to feel and drive his horse. A sitting trot at too early a stage disturbs the movements and back activity of the horse and communicates its roughness to the reins, so that the freedom and extension of the horse's strides suffer and the horse is " held up ", so to speak, by the impact of the rider's weight. (If the seat does not follow the pulsations of the back that run from croup to head, it interferes with these pulsations and produces a cramp of the muscles of the back, and since these muscles are connected to the locomotive muscles of the leg, it results in tightness, that is, loss of the free gait.)

vigorously and at long wave-length owing to the slight energy developed in the hindquarters up to now. All that we have done has been to restore the same freedom and sureness to the gait that the horse possessed when it moved about easily in the pasture without being excited by outside events.

Though this kind of locomotion is the natural one for a horse in freedom, this mere absence of constraint hardly satisfies the requirements of riding. The rider would be unable to lengthen the stride and the leap to the limits of the mechanism provided by the horse's conformation, thus making full use of its machinery.

Nor would he be able to prevent premature wearing out of the horse, because only when the hind legs develop energetic thrust and engage far forward—an additional effort that the horse makes only when induced to do so by the external driving controls—do the muscles of the back swing with the energy required for relieving the legs.

Active, driving influences must compel the horse that now saunters along wholly unconstrained, no longer tightened up and in natural posture, with its hind legs dragging, to make full use of its muscles, which are now freely extended but working at only half their power. They must make it actively come up to the controls, especially the hands, and become supple.

B. SUPPLENESS AS AN EVOLUTION FROM UNCONSTRAINT INVOLVING THE ADDITION OF THRUST

Up to now we have managed to restore the gait and posture of the horse in its unconstrained, easy naturalness.

Our next task will be to get the dragging hind legs to engage farther forward and to stretch out more vigorously, thus causing the muscles of the back to flex and extend more powerfully, more expressively. This is accompanied by greater extension of the entire spinal column forward to the bit, as outlined in the preceding section.

The horse does not yet comprehend combined leg and weight controls, so that all we can use is our leg, which acts to produce more powerful thrusts by the hind legs and their engagement farther forward. If the horse allows itself to be driven, that is, if it lengthens its stride while retaining its timing, the leg control ceases, to be reapplied whenever the energy of the horse's movements diminishes and the hind legs again begin to drag.

The action of the purely driving leg controls, which are the only influence that can cause engagement of the hindquarters, is manifested by increasing the impulsion of the hindquarters, which begins to carry more of the load and thus relieves the forehand, which now steps out more freely, with longer strides, in harmony with the hindquarters. The neck stretches out forwards and down more and more, corresponding to the extension of the back.[27] This extension is felt in the horse's reaching out for the bit.

It is important that we do not provide the horse with any " crutch " in its mouth, that we ride it with reins that are entirely loose, existing only to limit expressions of exuberance or to indicate changes of direction. This has compelled the horse to move with an extended neck and to find its balance by itself.

In this already extended posture, in which it has found its balance, it will be all the easier for the horse, obeying the driving controls, to come to the bit by stretching its body some more. The hands, which formerly yielded at such instants of maximum extension forwards or perhaps downwards, do so no longer. On the contrary, they accept the weight laid upon them by the horse's mouth because of the greater swinging of the hindquarters and the additional extension of the neck. The rider endeavours to hold his hands as steady and as passive as possible, always ready to yield elastically and forward to the pulsations of the rider-horse system rather than to scare the horse away from the bit it has sought so trustingly. The sensitive, "thinking" hand will know how to make contact with the bit as pleasant as possible for the horse. It should be so soft and elastic as to "breathe together" with the rhythmic motions of the horse and the vibrations of its contact with the bit, though imperceptible to the naked eye. To be sure, it will succeed in this only if it is "fastened" to an independent and supple seat, which conveys to it all the pulsations of the horse's body without ever being stiff or tight.

The passive following of the hands, which may later turn into temporary sustaining, once thrust is assured and impulsion has been added, overcomes the resistance of the masseter muscles, stretches the ligamentum nuchae and the previously inactive poll, which allows the head to hang naturally, and brings them into supple co-operation.

The *addition of thrust*, deliberately brought about by our active driving, results in the transition from the first stage of training, *absence of constraint*, to the next one, *suppleness* (see pp. 114-115), whose effects upon the poll and mouth we have just described. This later develops into a correct carriage of the head and flexing of the poll without any conscious effort to achieve this, such as having the hands trying in any way to compel the muscles to obey. All these external indications of a horse undergoing correct gymnastic training are not an end in themselves,

[27] The nose should be extended first forward and then down. Movement down and backwards would signify withdrawal and general discomfort.

however; they are nothing but side effects that are automatically manifested when gait and carriage are correct.

The effect of suppleness and of the resultant stretching to reach the bit is not only manifested in the hands, however. It is paralleled by a change taking place throughout the body of the horse, which helps the seat as a whole.[28]

The elastically pulsating, compliant back becomes more active and carries the rider's buttocks forwards without jouncing them. The horse's ribs, which have been allowed to drop, come closer to the inner side of the rider's calf as a result of its freer breathing (snorting) and the forward reach of its hindquarters. This facilitates a firmer leg position and the supple contact of the legs with the horse's body. The hindquarters, which now carry more of the load, are already engaging somewhat, so the rider has the feeling of being somewhat higher in front. The neck (which has been extended forwards up to now) rises, though retaining all its extension (see " Lifting of the Forehand "). The rider has more of the horse " in front of him ", and his horse, which completely fills the space between his legs, gives him the sensation of being wholly unable to sit otherwise than in the normal position specified, so to speak, by the horse.

The rider's work is far from over, however, once the horse is supple and chews. His active leg and his hands, which flatter the mouth and ask for further confidence by elastically and imperceptibly opening and closing the fingers, must be able to maintain the newly won contact with the bit.

The development of the gait effected by the driving leg controls is paralleled by a transition from the natural balance in natural poise to the beginnings of *equestrian balance in equestrian poise.*

Now the time has come to explain the driving seat control to the horse, which is now ready for it.

As we know, the driving leg control, the only control that is able by itself to make the hindquarters engage, enables us to set the horse in motion and keep it going.

The horse learned to follow the lightly sustaining tugs of the reins in its initial running until it came to a stop. This was converted into slowing down as soon as we were able to hold back the engaged hindquarters with the co-operation of the leg controls, once suppleness set in.

The only thing left for us to do is to combine the forward-driving action of the seat with the action of the legs in the horse's brain. It is

---

[28] Readers who wish to explore the scientific aspect of the effect of load and controls upon the movements of a young horse will find these actions outlined in the section on " Relationship of the Rider's Weight and Controls to the Anatomical Mechanism of the Horse ", pp. 259-266. From the purely equestrian standpoint, the text above should suffice.

easy to do this because the pressure of the seat bones from back to front that is exerted when we push our pelvis forward also exerts a forward thrust upon the horse's back.

Let us say here that in the further gymnastic training of horses of good conformation, which welcome dressage, the driving seat control, which is now exerted more clearly, consists in nothing more than a stretching of the seat.

This stretching is effected solely by pushing the small of the back forward. The upper body, which is then lifted off the hips somewhat, provides the necessary support for the hands to enable them to sustain the legs' contribution to impulsion. This action of the legs is produced by pushing the small of the back forward, thus tensing (bracing) the calf muscles and reinforcing the leg action.

Let us add a few words on the action of the driving seat control, since it must be understood by the horse and employed by the rider in the following period of training in which suppleness has already been achieved.

Pushing the small of the back forward shifts the weight of the upper body backwards, so that the hindquarters, which are engaged under the horse's body because of the driving leg control, are bent even more at their joints, thus stretching out more elastically and rapidly, like tensed springs. As soon as the rider feels that the weight control has had the effect of temporarily increasing the burden on the hindquarters, he must immediately resume the normal seat, which follows the movements of the horse, in order not to prolong the burden and achieve the opposite of what he desires. If he did not do so, the horse would escape the uninterrupted pressure by ceasing to engage its hindquarters. This falling behind of the hind legs would overload the front legs. In equestrian terms the horse would fall upon its shoulders and have a sway-back, which would disturb the harmony of forehand and hindquarters and thus interfere with the gait.

The driving seat control, with all its infinite nuances, is essentially the same, whether used to accelerate the rate or to interrupt it. The end result is determined by the co-operating rein control.

Our ability to make vigorously engaged hind legs bend even more during the few instants they are grounded results in an alternately increased extension and flexion of the hindquarters.

This gradually converts the natural trot into the working trot. The difference between the working trot and the former is, first of all, the longer stride, though the feet must alight with the same timing and must not hurry. *The horse must allow itself to be driven at the working trot.* This does not mean that uninterrupted driving controls should force or pressure it into an ever faster or hastier running. All it means is that seat and controls must make sure that the rate is always a bit faster than the natural trotting rate spontaneously offered by the horse. There is no definite rate for the working trot any more than there is for the working gallop, for different horses have strides of different length. Thus the rate of the working trot must be adapted to the individual case, allowing for the horse's machinery and state of dressage. Horses of good conformation average about 275 steps per minute (1 step = 180 cms.). This figure may also be employed as a standard for the ordinary trot of the well-ridden horse.

At this working trot, which also produces a lifting of the neck, which is now extended not only forwards but upwards as well, thus shortening the reins as the horse responds increasingly to the driving and loading controls, we observe the first indications of impulsion produced by the influence of the rider. This impulsion combines with the natural mechanism of the horse and the thrust evoked by the rider's legs, manifesting itself in elastic, springy thrusts of the horse's legs off the ground and their vigorous though fluid sure-footedness when alighting.

III. Developing and Improving the Gait by Use of the Working Trot and the Middle Trot—Impulsion— Flexion—Evening the Load on All Four Legs—Collection

A. THE WORKING TROT—TRANSITIONS—LATERAL FLEXION BY RIDING ON CURVED LINES

The *working trot* is the gait at which most of our future training of the horse occurs. This gait and the middle and collected trot evolved from it prepare for the gallop and guarantee that the walk, the gait at which most faults creep in, will also present no difficulties later on, even in its collected form.

The working trot is the principal gait employed in subsequent gymnastic training of the young horse, as the natural trot has been up to now, because it compels the muscles to be appropriately active without over-exerting them. Since the trotting horse has only two legs grounded at one time, and these legs are grounded for a shorter period than at the walk, say, it is harder for the horse to use them in resisting the rider's influences. Nor is it easier for the horse to hold back arbitrarily, because the inherent thrust of the trot, which is increasingly associated with impulsion, makes it hard to do so.

22. Shoulder-in right. Dan Marks on *Neapolitano Brezovica* (Lipizzan) 1955.

23. Collected gallop. Karen McIntosh on *Scipio* (Thoroughbred) 1958.
FREUDY PHOTOS

THESE THREE PICTURES
SHOW CLOSELY RELATED
STAGES IN THE COLLECTED
GALLOP

24. Collected gallop right. Dan
Marks on *Sultan* (Trakehnen) 1955.

25. Correct seat of the rider
at the collected gallop. Captain O. Frank on *Cyprian*
(Irish) 1947.

26. Collected gallop. Major J. Handler on *Conversano Benvenuta I*
(Lipizzan) 1955.

Short gallops, which promote impulsion and contact with the bit, should not be neglected during this period of training, especially when the horse spontaneously starts galloping cross country. But it is not yet suitable as a schooling gait, because most horses are as yet unable to carry themselves correctly at the gallop. Their joints, which are not strong enough, would suffer, especially at the corners of the riding hall. Moreover the sequence of steps employed in a gallop is such that the two sides of the horse are not equally stretched. However, these gallops may be used for horses that are able to carry themselves at this gait and thus can be made supple after fewer circuits of the riding hall than at the trot.

Like gait in general, the working trot must be regular, i.e., well-timed, long-striding, and lively. If the horse's timing is faulty, its feet not alighting at uniform intervals of time, its irregular gait will imperil equilibrium and hence carriage.

The gait must be long-striding because only a horse that fully utilizes the capacities of its conformation and its mechanism and takes vigorous strides will be compelled to place its correctly pulsating muscles unreservedly at the rider's service, with its elastic back co-operating and its legs thus being relieved of load.

Moreover a horse whose long stride is developed to the limit of its physical capabilities will travel faster than another horse of equally good conformation that has "lost" its gait because of faulty riding. Long, advancing strides are a relative concept, however, since their length depends upon the posture of the horse at the time and its corresponding rate (see "Engagement").

Finally, liveliness is required, with the horse briskly swinging its hind legs—the third requisite of a correct equestrian gait. Only vigorously and smoothly engaging hindquarters have no opportunity of resisting the load. Muscles that are vigorously active cannot contract convulsively, thus producing stiffness and tightness.

Liveliness of the gait is naturally limited by timing and length of stride. Once the horse advances as far forward as its conformation allows in order to take as long a stride as possible, it can take only a certain number of steps per time interval. If it takes more, it begins to hurry, or it must make them shorter than they should be; if it takes fewer, it is holding back. No matter which it does, it is violating regularity and timing.

The *transitions* from the natural trot, which is always employed at the beginning of the lesson until unconstrained movement is achieved, to the working rate must be made gradually, with increasing controls that are adapted to the sensitivity of the horse. If this involves loss of uniform timing, mere increase in speed is valueless, and damages the progress of dressage. In this work one should always remember that raising the natural trot to the working trot must be achieved by lengthening the stride of the hind legs, which thrust off more powerfully and engage farther forward, the number of strides remaining the same.

Sometimes the gait becomes irregular, and the horse hurries or tries to bolt because of discomfort and pain. This may also be due to high spirits and stable mettle when the lesson is not preceded by some relaxing exercise at the natural trot. Then elastic resistance exercised by the hands, which gently seek support in shortened reins on both sides of the neck, will absorb the excess and moderate the gait. The legs remain passive and the seat is light.

In such cases we must correctly understand the requirement of a long rein. It would be better to substitute the concept of the "fitting" rein for the slogan of the "long" rein.

A remount that often makes the wildest jumps out of flightiness, high spirits, or fright can hardly be brought to order with a long rein.

If we leave the reins long on such a horse before it has been exercised to the point of relaxation, we will have it so little under control that the hands lose all steadiness and softness and pull up high, tugging backwards, whenever the horse is startled.

But if the rider holds the reins comparatively short, so that the hands, held low but not pressing down, can remain in contact with the mouth in every situation, he is no longer in danger of having the hands rise and become hard (because they are unsure) whenever the horse is suddenly startled. This may occur when the reins are too long, even when the rider is highly skilled and experienced, as every honest horseman will readily admit.

Once the horse has calmed down and is no longer tense, it will regain its timing and stretch to reach the readily advancing hands, which then proceed to lengthen the reins. It will again fill out the seat and yield itself unresistingly to the influences of the rider. With this suppleness the horse has given the rider a blank cheque, so to speak, upon its body. Since the last vestiges of concealed tensions have disappeared, the hands will be able to return to their position in front of the rider's body. That is how we make the transition from the "short" to the "long" (but in every case "fitting") reins, without violating the spirit of horsemanship, when riding young horses that tighten up and grow tense during exercise.

There are horses—and these are more difficult to deal with—whose false tensions cause them not to hurry and bolt, but to hold back. In both cases what has to be done is to get the tightened muscles to swing elastically in the correct manner.

Whereas a calming procedure promises the best results for excitable horses, so long as they are not fully developed and trained, a blow of the riding crop or application of the spurs at the right place will really work miracles with horses that are lazy because of disposition and character rather than weakness.

If they then readily advance, no matter how, the punishment must cease at once, and they must be given complete freedom of the reins for a few strides and praised by voice and hand.

After suppleness has been achieved, the transition to the walk and then to the halt will no longer be the result of letting the horse come to a stop, but rather a slowing down of the horse with a seat that does not follow the movement as much (as described in the previous section), the hand absorbing the impulsion and avoiding any backward action if at all possible.

The horse's need for extending its neck forward and down during the pauses, thus resting its tired neck muscles, must also be allowed for in this stage of training. The horse must move at a free, long-striding, but by no means hasty or hurried walk, with surrendered reins. No matter how energetic it may be, this gait must remain relaxed; else the true phase sequence suffers and stiffnesses appear.

In changes from the walk to the trot the reins are gradually shortened so that the purity of the walk does not suffer; the trot starts from this position, which corresponds to the carriage of the head and neck at the trot.

Exercise at the walk in the real sense of the term should begin only after the horse is able to carry itself at all trotting rates and remain responsive, or, in other words, in about a year's time.

There are riders who are not satisfied with the ready and trusting compliance of a horse, but wish to taste the fruits of victory to the dregs because of their lack of understanding and their completely false ambition to be able to show a "completely made" horse in as short a time as possible. In order to imitate the picture of a horse moving at a high degree of collection, they force the neck, "caught" by suppleness, into a position that does not correspond to the capacity of the hind legs, which are not yet supple enough to carry the load.

A horse whose confidence and good will are misused in such a fashion will soon find a way of evading these requirements for which it is not yet ready. It will no longer follow correctly with one or both of its hind legs. When both hind legs evade, it will bore on the bit in order to find a substitute support for the hindquarters, which no longer engage far enough forward, or it will evade the excessive action of the hands on its mouth by shortening and curving it. When only one hind leg evades, it resorts to another weapon of defence that is natural to it and becomes crooked.

It is extremely important for us not to allow this natural crookedness to express itself before we are able to produce even loading on all four legs by *lateral flexion*. And in this effort the less we think of it the more successful we will be. We must concentrate all the more on preventing any stiffness from setting in by continuing to ride the horse forward with even loading on both sides of the horse.

If a horse finds no support in the " forming " and compressing reins and has to balance itself on its own four legs to be able to carry its own weight, it will not have much opportunity to grow crooked in this stage of training.

There is no doubt that we must combat crookedness. But, as clever diplomats, we avoid coming to grips with it for the present in order to be able to combat it that much more successfully once the horse has learned lateral flexion, and we are able to develop the requisite impulsion at any time. Thus our efforts are reinforced by these two allies.

The rider should also avoid excessive influence of the hands or endeavours to " shape " the horse when it is at a standstill after being halted. Rather, the hands·must relax to keep the engaged hind legs from moving backwards. Though they could engage forward in the direction of the plumb line through the centre of gravity even with the somewhat closer framework[29] occasioned by the working trot, this framework must not be retained after the horse has halted. At the present stage of training the horse it will be able to maintain contact with the bit even when halted and to keep its hind legs under the burden they are carrying without placing them behind the perpendicular through the hip joint and the centre of the hoof, but only if it is allowed a freer carriage of the head and neck.

If the horse still evades sideways or backwards, it must be straightened out by means of a slightly stimulating action of the rider's tapping or vibrating legs, allowing it to move forward somewhat.

It is important that the horse now be taught to stand calmly at ease after being halted. This is best achieved if the reins are completely loosened after the advance of the hands that occurs immediately after each halt called for by the rider, though the hands do not immediately give up their contact with the bit.[30]

A horse thus quickly learns to stand still for a long time with reins thrown across the neck. Patting it and praising it, as well as feeding it from the saddle, help in this training.

Relaxing the reins after the horse is halted and after it has changed from the trot to the walk presents a good opportunity to get the horse to

[29] " A closer framework " always signifies a shortening of the line from the mouth to the point of the buttocks, never a shortening of the topline (crest of the neck—back—croup), which occurs only in horses whose movements are wrong (also see p. 263).

[30] At this stage of training the immediate advance of the hands must occur in such a way that they move forward somewhat more than they were drawn back, no matter whether complete loosening occurs after a few seconds or the horse remains for some time in a somewhat lengthened framework, in slight contact with the bit.

chew on the yielding bit offered it by the rider's hands, so to speak, without losing contact with the hands. Lengthening the neck until it is stretched as much as it can in contact with the bit is produced in this way: the rider utilizes the natural endeavour of the horse to stretch its tired neck muscles by letting the reins slide through his open fingers as a continuation of the relieving advance of the hands necessary after every decrease of gait or every stop. The horse must not seek to free itself of the reins either by jerking or by suddenly making the reins long. Its chewing movements induced by the loosening and stretching of the muscles of the neck and back accompany the stretching of the nose, aimed forward and downward, and lengthen the reins by a gentle, alternating pressure in rhythm with the oscillations of the head—as much as the gradually opening fingers allow.

If the horse begins to chew, the walk becomes a free walk with loosened reins;[31] the horse remains in contact with the driving legs and is thus enclosed by the controls despite the complete freedom of its neck.

At the stage of training that our young horse now has reached we are satisfied with a few steps in contact with the bit. Then we throw the reins on its neck, holding them merely by the buckle, so that the walk with loosened reins becomes a walk with surrendered reins.

At the end of its training, and after the horse has achieved the necessary responsiveness by work at the trot and gallop, it will also be worked at the walk in three degrees of gait: the collected, medium (working) and extended walk.

The extended walk with loosened reins is nothing but the free walk with loosened reins described above, the sole difference being that the movements have become smoother and cover more ground, thanks to the advance in gymnastic training. The gait and direction of motion can be changed at any time, as the contact with the horse's mouth remains.

Letting the horse chew the bit is an indispensable aid of training, for it makes the horse's trusting contact with the bit while stretching its back and neck as comfortable as possible for the horse and turns it into a habit. It is also an infallible indication of correct dressage of riding horses, besides being very important in evaluating previous training. Horses that have been forcibly "bolted together" with rough controls will not wait for the reins to slide through the fingers, but will endeavour to free themselves from the artificially compressed form by throwing their head about and stretching jerkily. Others, in turn, which hold back and have got behind the bit, have lost all desire to seek contact with it because of false dressage. Such horses will not obey the summons to stretch out despite driving legs and opening fingers; they are so accus-

---

[31] See Table of Basic Gaits and Their Gradations, p. 323.

tomed to this unnatural, faulty posture, which always enables them to hold back, that the endeavour to reach out for the bit (which must be manifested in every stage of dressage) has been stifled.

If, in subsequent training, the seat drives the horse farther forward to the fixed, unyielding hands, the neck is stretched forward and upward (relative lift of the forehand), as in the half halt.

If the hands slowly give in the direction of the horse's mouth while remaining in contact with it during this increased forward drive, the neck stretches forward. Then the strides or leaps must grow longer, though the timing remains the same, that is, they cover more ground and are somewhat flatter.

This stretching of the horse in hand—whether it involves a fraction of an inch or more—is a by-product of all correct increases in rate. When made the subject of special exercises and faultlessly performed, it can also show the rider that his horse, carrying itself in equestrian balance, was and is responsive to the driving controls.

The difference between letting the horse stretch in hand and letting it chew the bit is that the distance from hand to mouth remains the same in the first case. The yielding hand follows the mouth, which advances in accord with the forward stretch of the neck, and the rate of gait is changed in the direction of longer strides and leaps.

Once the horse has advanced to the stage where contact with the bit at the working trot becomes more and more certain and positive as a result of careful driving, and it does not try to escape the bit, we can say that the horse is in hand, which means that it responds to the controls.

Now for a short time we shorten the reins as much as we can without impairing the gait or the activity of the back. If this demands too much of the horse, the gait loses its free advance, and tensions in the hind-quarters and the back will make themselves felt unpleasantly in the seat. The stiffening or " star-gazing " neck will produce too hard a contact with the bit or creep behind it.

If these faults are manifested, the only remedy is riding forward to improve the gait until the horse correctly comes up to the bit again without evading it. Once that happens, the seat will again be carried along and filled out by the elastically swinging body of the horse.

The difficulties just described occur because we have made excessive demands upon the hindquarters, which are not yet strong enough, and upon the back, which is still flabby and cannot provide the extension and tension (see " Action of the Back ") that are required for all degrees of collection. The horse defends itself by failing to answer the summons and by false tensions, which affect the gait directly.

It has clearly told us that the increased weight of the forehand that is shifted to the hindquarters by shortening the reins has encountered hind legs that cannot bear it because they are not yet able to bend.

One result of such premature attempts at collection will be the opposite of our objective, for the horse, which has bent its hindquarters in a freer framework up to now and engaged them forward in accordance with the stage of its training and degree of development, will lose confidence and learn how to stiffen the joints of its hind legs to defend itself against the burden that it cannot as yet carry. It will grow thinner and thinner in the flanks, so that the rider wanting to do further collection will have to move more and more to the rear with his upper body and legs in order to reach the evading hind legs and the tightened ribs. It is obvious that this lack of understanding on the part of the rider will merely confirm the horse in its false carriage and faulty gait.

Up to the present time we have ridden the turns that are necessarily encountered around the rectangular riding hall or the elliptical track laid out in the open air without any longitudinal flexion, with which the horse is totally unacquainted as yet from the equestrian standpoint.[32] All we were trying to do was to make the curve as flat as possible so that the thrust could act against the forehand undiminished and the timing could be maintained. Because of the longer path that has to be travelled by the outside legs in every turn, driving control must be exerted to keep the outside hind leg from lagging behind. This is also made easier for us by the rein controls.

For the present these controls are merely as follows: the outside rein comes forward, but the inside hand is carried to the side, indicating the direction of the turn to the horse without exerting any tension to the rear (opening rein). At the same time the rider exerts the " explanatory " weight control by pushing the small of his back forward on one side. This results in a forward pressure of the inner seat bone and a lowering of the respective knee and heel. As another factor in this " explanatory " weight control, he advances his outside shoulder. This weight control is also mechanically effective because it induces a natural, unconstrained horse to follow the centre of gravity of the load. The centre of gravity is now shifted to the side of the turn, and the horse follows quite mechanically and involuntarily, changing direction in order to make carrying the load and movement most comfortable. The advance of the rider's outside shoulder results from the seat control and is based on the principle that the shoulders of the rider must be parallel to those of the horse. At the same time the change of his seat makes it easier for the rider to yield with

[32] The modified controls adopted to the individual case employed in turns for horses that are crooked will be discussed in detail in the next section on evening out the load by flexion.

the outside hand, which follows the horse's mouth passively, merely maintaining contact, since an advance of the outside shoulder also involves a corresponding advance of the outside arm.

The seat control ceases after the horse has turned the corner, and the yielding inner rein causes the horse to accept the outside one again, which had been confined to a purely negative role during the turn. Once the young horse responds positively to the driving controls and understands the primitive nature of rein action employed up to now in turns, the outer rein is used to support the inner one by a slight inward pressure upon the outside of the neck and shoulder during the turn. At the outset it should be reinforced by touching the outside of the horse's neck and shoulder with the riding crop, whereas the inner hand should lie, so to speak, upon the chord of the circular arc formed by the horse's body.

Let us re-emphasize that the restraining outer hand must never cross the withers, even when it is laid against the neck, for then its action is no longer felt by the hind leg on that side. Each hand must always remain on its own side of the neck.

Once the horse has learned how to carry itself and respond positively to the controls, an imperceptible shift of both hands towards the side of the turn will be all the rein control required.

The rider should be warned categorically against *riding through the corners* too closely in this stage of training. Turns and therefore corners can be ridden out on the arc of a circle with a radius of three steps only after the horse has become accustomed to the necessary equestrian longitudinal flexion by riding on a circle and, later on, by performing the volte. If we begin to turn corners that closely before the horse has learned to associate the inner controls with the outer ones as a result of work on the circle and before it has learned to obey the outer controls, such forcing of the horse into the corner would harm gait and contact with the bit.

Another reason for not starting to ride out the corners too soon is that the horse does not yet fully respond to the half halt required in this figure before it reaches the corner. It begins to drag its hindquarters in the corner or to stiffen them, and persists in this faulty gait along the short wall that follows, where it tends to move less energetically anyhow.

Even later, when the corners are turned at a working trot, there is always the danger that the horse anticipates this half halt, which does not always imply a diminution of rate, and begins to drag, slowing down its gait arbitrarily.

Corners should therefore be turned sharply only after the horse responds quite positively to the driving controls and has acquired the requisite suppleness and equestrian poise by work on the circle and in the volte.[33]

Later on, this poise can always be checked by the stroking test, which also calms the horse. In this test the hand holding the reins gives up contact with the bit temporarily and slowly moves up and down along the crest of the mane as far as the outstretched arms permit, after which it resumes contact with the horse's mouth. While this is done the driving seat controls, in so far as they may be necessary, should not be interrupted. During the stroking test the nose of the horse should advance somewhat without affecting its carriage. The rate and timing remain unchanged.

Before we begin *work on the circle at the working trot*, the horse must learn to obey the leg and rein controls on one side, having already become acquainted with these controls in the turns through the corners.

The best way to inculcate obedience to leg and rein controls on one side in the horse, while providing a loosening exercise that fills in the inter- missions, is *turning on the forehand*. At the start this is done by having the hindquarters describe a partial circle or, later on, a full circle, about the inner foreleg, which must *move* on the spot. Once the horse accepts the lateral controls and thus becomes responsive to the outside leg and rein, i.e., once the beginnings of a certain degree of longitudinal flexion are present, turning about the forehand in place should be abandoned for turning about the forehand in motion. Then the whole horse is moving forward, no matter how little, and the alighting of all four legs in the foot- fall sequence of the walk affords it less opportunity to grow stiff than when it turns about the forehand in place.

To explain the former exercise to a young horse, we stop in the middle of the riding hall, place additional load on the inner seat bone, shorten the rein on the side opposite the one towards which we want the hind- quarters to move (the inner side) and hold it until the horse releases it. Then the leg, pressing or tapping sideways behind the girth, acts until the inner and outer hind legs have each taken one step to the side. If the laterally driving control is not yet understood, we can aid the horse by tapping its body with the riding crop just behind the leg and by tugging a few times on the rein to turn the head and neck inwards. Once the horse has taken a double step it is allowed to rest. The outside rein, which is completely passive at the beginning, later prevents the shoulder from turn- ing out and the horse from advancing. Actually it keeps the shoulder straight together with the absorbing and restraining outside leg that acts at every second step (that is, the step of the outside hind leg, as a rule, in a horse free of constraint). The burden on the inside hind leg, which

[33] Let us add that the closer the turn, the more exactingly accurate must be the even loading on all four legs and the more impulsion (forward drive) must be present if this turn on the reins is to be clean and precise.

advances and engages under the body, and the amount of its bending are increased by the rider's pushing his pelvis forward on the side corresponding to the concave side of the horse.[34]

Turning about the forehand in place is not a school figure, but it is hard to do without it as an aid in acquainting the horse with one-sided control and making it respond to the outside control. Moreover it is well adapted for teaching a horse that no longer feels the leg to pay attention to it again, because the neck, acting like a lever upon the rest of the body, helps to compel a mechanical yielding to leg action. In this sense turning about the forehand will re-establish obedience even in horses that shy at jumps and are refractory.

As we have said, turning about the forehand in place is supplanted after a few weeks of training by turning about the forehand in motion. This might also be called a volte while swinging if the term did not have the connotation that it might involve a throwing—a turning out—of the hindquarters, but this need not be the case at all.

The volte while swinging constitutes an improvement of yielding to the leg, because it enables us to avoid the disadvantages of the latter. Chief among them are the following: When the figure is exercised in the *form* of a shoulder-in at a smooth gait, the hind legs that advance in the direction of the plumb line through the centre of gravity outside the trace of the front hoofs, and are not yet bent, no longer provide sufficient support. Consequently the horse, stepping to the side rather than forward and to the side, falls upon its shoulders, especially its outside shoulder, which then turns out. It is hard to prevent this, for it occurs in the direction of motion; this turning out is paralleled by a loosening of the base of the neck. Moreover, in such a figure, where the forehand does not precede the hindquarters, the inside forefoot strikes against the outside foot.

---

[34] Until the horse has been made to understand what we want it to do, the weight of the rider may also be shifted to the outside—the direction in which the turn is made—in order that the horse will step to this side in its natural endeavour to support the excess weight.

Once the horse has received training, conditions apparently change in so far as we are able to prevent its evasion to the side by loading one hind leg vertically. This hind leg is kept fixed by the burden. But the contradiction is more apparent than real, for a supporting leg or a leg that is just about to alight to provide support will be grounded off to one side, in compliance with the endeavour to maintain equilibrium, only if the load no longer acts vertically but is felt as an excess of weight.

Aside from controls that act almost mechanically, all theories of weight controls are turned upside down if the horse opposes a change in equilibrium, deliberately or instinctively, which it would comply with at once in a supple state. This reaction is manifested as active or passive resistance in a direction opposite to that signalled by the control. It also occurs in trained horses, whose obedience has already been ensured by the mere hint of controls, when the shift in the rider's weight persists for more than a certain period or exceeds a certain degree of intensity (also see p. 205).

On the other hand, turning about the forehand in motion, with the driving outside leg forcing the forehand to tread on a smaller, volte-like circle, combines the advantages of a turn about the forehand in place (greater effectiveness of the inside rein) with those of yielding to the leg (advancing and alighting of all four legs in the phase sequence of the walk) without any of their disadvantages. The hindquarters tread on an eccentric and somewhat larger circle, with only so many steps forward and to the side being called for (with intermissions) to press the horse up against the bit.

Once the horse responds to the outside controls after preparation in place, with absorption by the outside leg and rein after every two steps taken by the hindquarters, we can begin the turn about the forehand in motion described above.

We can begin work on two tracks about a year after the horse was first mounted. Its longitudinal flexion and the carrying capacity of its hindquarters' joints will be improved by work on the circle and other exercises, and the eagerness, carriage, and gait of the horse will not have suffered by our employing leg-yielding.

We might add that if the volte while swinging is executed, not like a shoulder-in as described above, but like a *renvers* (also called " *haunches out* "), after the horse has been familiarized with work on two tracks (that is, with its head and longitudinal flexion turned in the direction of motion), it is easier for the inside hind leg to evade control. In most cases, especially in horses that grow stiff from the right rear hindquarters to the front left and when motion takes place from left to right, this leg will endeavour to speed up in the direction of motion—that is, towards the right in our case—without honestly engaging under the horse's body.

Renvers work from left to right would therefore merely confirm such horses in their faulty gait (natural crookedness).

If the horse responds to the inside controls when turning about its forehand, we can begin riding serpentines along the long wall of the riding hall.

The first few times we ride at the walk in order to show the horse the new exercise, and then at the working trot. Only one bend is ridden to begin with, as flat as possible.

As the horse's collection improves, the serpentines may be ridden as double and triple serpentines, depending on the length of the wall. They should be ridden at a distance of three strides from the track, using a shortened working trot and a collected trot.

What is most important in riding serpentines, which are later exercised in several successive curves throughout the length of the riding hall, is starting to make the turns smoothly and supply, with correct seat controls complementing and facilitating the turning action of the reins. This turning action always deprives the young horse of some of its impulsion. Horses learn this best at a rising trot, which stimulates their forward eagerness. The driving legs, pulsating with the horse, and with heels down, must be in constant contact with the horse, and the rider must enter into each new concave flexion with his inside heel especially depressed at each change for seat and lead.

The horse must be straightened for an instant prior to every turn. This also applies to changes from or through the circle and for riding figures of eight. However, with the exception of the single serpentine along the wall, these figures (which can also be ridden without change of position) are too advanced for the present stage of training of our young horse.

A few words concerning the technique of the rising trot: every time the rider slips back into the saddle, he should pay special attention to pulling his base of support forward and to his driving leg, because the buttocks, which are continuously in the saddle at the sitting trot, transmitting the driving action of the small of the back to the horse, are fully in the saddle only at every second step at the rising trot. Buttocks that are pushed out to the rear and a rise at the trot that is higher than that required by the impulse of motion destroy impulsion.

If circumstances require that the normal seat, employed in this stage of dressage just as much as at the sitting trot, be abandoned in favour of the relieving crotch seat, the rider's ability to drive with the small of his back pushed forward must be exceptionally well developed. The crotch seat is characterized by an upper body that enters into the movement to a greater extent, with the small of the back pushed forward more and the weight shifted to the inside of the thigh and knee.

It cannot be repeated too often that the rider's knee and ankle joints must be supple at the rising trot. If they are stiff, they make it harder for the legs to lie close to the horse's body, and imperil a precise gradation of their action as well as the firmness of the seat, which then will seek support in the stirrups even when the normal seat is used. Every rider can readily convince himself that pressing the heels down hard during posting also contributes largely to keeping the rider's base of support close to the saddle.

The buttocks should be pushed forwards from the pelvis even more at the instant the horse alternates its diagonals, when the buttocks are pressed forward in the saddle. While this is done the fingers should be open and the heels pressed well down.

And now for much disputed question: *On which hind leg should the rider post?*

The only answer that can be given here is a quite general one. Special cases, such as weakness of individual legs or the refractoriness of ruined horses, must be left to the tact and feeling of the rider in question.

The following is recommended in the riding hall for working a raw remount or a horse that is not responsive enough, is ignorant of the restraining leg control, or does not fully accept it: rising on the outside hind leg. This leg, which carries the heavier load, will advance in the direction of the plumb line through the centre of gravity in accordance with the horse's instinctive effort to find its lateral balance (unless it is disturbed by a rider who provokes crookedness). That is, this leg will engage under the burden in the direction of the traces of the diagonally opposite front legs instead of falling out (also see Decarpentry, *Equitation Académique*, p. 131). That is why the expediment of departing, say, at the gallop right from the trot, when the horse is trotting on the first (outside) hind foot, almost always succeeds without previous " positioning " with equestrian longitudinal flexion (which the horse in question could not assume). Owing to its load this leg will find the position appropriate to the future outside hind leg at the gallop more readily than its unburdened partner. Another reason for preferring the burden placed on the outside hind leg when the young horse is worked at the rising trot in the riding hall is that this spares the inside hind leg, which does more of the work on the unavoidable curved lines anyhow. With the trained horse, which trots on the inside hind leg in the riding hall, as we shall see, the bending gymnastics to which this leg is subjected deliberately on curved tracks are reinforced by this method of loading.

In working in the open with healthy, harmoniously built horses the hind leg should be changed every time the horse takes off at the trot in order to strengthen and supple the muscles, ligaments, and joints of both sides of the body, and thus prevent the horse from becoming crooked.

The following is our reply to the question of which hind leg we should post on in the highly advanced horse, which can already move " in position " and whose lateral responsiveness has consequently been so far developed that it can be ridden in circles no more than six steps in diameter without losing its impulsion, that is, without growing stiff or dragging its feet: in the riding hall it should be on the inside hind leg. The reason is that the rider's seat, adapted to the longitudinal flexion of the horse on the curved lines that frequently occur in the riding hall, which also include close turns, provides the natural position for the inner leg just behind the girth.

Following the natural rhythm of motion of the rising trot on the inside hind leg, the rider's inner leg swings from the position that is best for driving when the inner hind leg has entered its phase of support after advancing. This is the case the moment of the foot alights. This control, which makes the grounded inner hind leg, the supporting leg, thrust away from the ground with increased force, stimulates the outer hind leg to reach forward vigorously in its swinging phase in order to provide room for the stronger thrust of the inner hind leg.

This greater engagement of the outer hind leg is necessary because, as we have said, it has to travel a longer distance than the inner hind leg on the stretched side of the horse's body and the outer edge of the curved track (also see p. 65ff.). The rider's outside leg, with its natural position further behind the girth, acts in a supporting role, for the inside hind leg (which it would have to drive forward in time with the swings of the horse's body) requires less forward drive. It has to travel a shorter distance on the concave side of the horse's body despite the heavier load placed upon it in the turns.

Summing up, the rising trot on the inside leg achieves two objectives on curved tracks: first, the flexing gymnastics of the inside hind leg are deliberately aided. Second, the job of the outside hind leg, which has to travel the greater distance, is made much easier by relieving it of some of its load and by the leg control that is applied at the correct moment when the rider sits down on the inside hind leg, thus assisting in the further reach and engagement of the outside hind leg.

On long rides—cross-country and marches—use the rising trot on the hind leg "offered" to us by the horse. Pedantic dressage and constraint would be a waste of energy that might be costly later on. In general avoid burdening a diagonal pair of legs if one of the legs needs to be spared. With horses that are harmoniously developed on both sides, change the diagonals every time the trot is resumed.

As soon as horses have learned to understand the inner controls as the result of turning corners and making turns on the forehand, we can begin work on the circle at the working trot. This should be possible four to six months after the horse was first mounted.

Another guide to the time when a young horse can be placed on the circle: impetuous horses and horses with much animation should be ridden on curved lines at an earlier date, whereas sluggish and lazy horses should be started later. The latent locomotor instinct must first be awakened in such horses by frequent riding in the open air along straight lines.

Since our young horse was trained on the lunge before it was mounted and, later, carrying the rider, it will find no difficulty in keeping to the curved track. Since the inside legs have a shorter distance to travel than the outside legs, the horse, moving along easily, will take on a certain longitudinal flexion naturally,[35] as this will be less tiring than moving around the circle like a tangential polygon, with a linearly straight spinal column.

In this natural longitudinal flexion, which is reinforced by the rider's inside controls, the horse approaches the outside controls more and more; they exert an increased opposing effect, especially along the open sides. If the tension on both reins is approximately the same when travelling around the circle, it is proof that the horse is responding to the flexing controls.[36]

The longitudinal flexion makes the horse adapt its whole body to the circumference of the circle, so that its inner side becomes concave and its outer side convex. *As on all curved lines, its centre of gravity moves inwards somewhat, depending upon the rate and the diameter of the circle.* The rider's seat must make allowance for this flexion, as was described above in our discussion of turns.

The increased burden on the inside hind leg and the resultant increased bending of that leg's joints, which make work on a circle so excellently suited for the rhythmic-gymnastic exercise of a single hind leg, are a result of this displacement of the centre of gravity to the inside, though the displacement is due to the law of centrifugal force rather than, as is often erroneously supposed, to the flexion.

The hindquarters must be guided and controlled by the legs, the fore-hand by the reins, in order to keep the horse exactly on the circle.

The more supple the flexion of the horse longitudinally, the more easily will the rider's inside leg maintain this concave bending. It must quietly and freely cling to the horse's body just behind the girth and not be pushed away by the movement of the horse as when the ribs are insufficiently flexed. It will then be able to prevent the horse from moving towards the

[35] An observer stationed outside the lungeing circle can obtain convincing proof of this natural longitudinal flexion by observing a raw remount trotting without side reins on the lunge. He will find that the hind legs trace a narrower track than the forelegs even when the lunge is not tight, and the inner hind leg, which carries a bigger load, will engage farther forward than the outer hind leg. As a result of this forward engagement of the inner hind leg, the horse has to take on a *lateral flexion*, that is, a flexion of its ribs. The neck and head also participate in this longitudinal flexion, provided no rapid gait requires that the neck be stretched outside this flexion to act as a balancing rod against the centrifugal force impelling the horse towards the outside. This is a balancing position that can also be observed in circus dressage or in a race horse galloping at top speed around a turn in the track. All experienced tournament jumpers also follow this principle; when they take corners at rapid speed, they give their horse support on the outside rein, with the horse's head towards the outside, in order to keep the inside hind leg from slipping.

[36] Later on, in practising flexion on one or two tracks, the corresponding exercises, especially shoulder-fore and shoulder-in as well as the *travers* flexions, can be developed from this pure longitudinal flexion. It also exists when turning corners and is retained after the corner is turned along the long side for that very purpose.

centre of the circle, acting, if necessary together with the outside rein, which then becomes an opening rein to lead the horse to the side.

On the opposite side to the concave flexion, the outside leg automatically finds its place somewhat further behind the girth, corresponding to the position of the rider's pelvis and parallel to the horse's hips and to the convex bending of the ribs of the horse. Back there, it is able to act as a restraining and driving agent if the croup turns out, thus maintaining the concave flexion in combination with the inner rein, which takes care of the position of the horse's head, turned slightly inwards in harmony with the longitudinal flexion of the entire horse.

The combined action of inside leg and outside rein (and vice versa) described here is called a *diagonal control*, as distinct from a control on the same side of the horse—a *lateral control*.[37]

As the training of the horse progresses, the more the inside controls bring it in contact with the outside controls. The two then supplement and reinforce each other diagonally, so that after gymnastic training is complete, the centre of gravity can be effortlessly balanced along its longitudinal axis (contraction or extension of the horse's frame, change in posture) as well as along its transverse axis (flexion), all precisely measured and controlled by the rider's will and influence.

Displacement of the centre of gravity along the vertical axis, that is, upwards or downwards, as required by exercises over obstacles, makes certain demands on the horse, chiefly on its strength and dexterity but also on its self-reliance and training. In these vertical displacements of the centre of gravity (jumping), which usually occur in combination with longitudinal shifts of the centre of gravity, it is the principal concern of the rider not to disturb the horse but to follow its motions correctly in order that it may automatically effect a distribution of weight that favours overcoming the obstacle.

This will be discussed in detail in the sections on jumping and cross-country riding.

If the hindquarters evade towards the centre when working on the circle (if the horse assumes a faulty *travers* position, which is usually the case on the right hand, especially when the inside reins exerts a tug), we begin by *restoring even loading on all four legs*, i.e., the correct longitudinal flexion for the circumference of the circle, by using forward-driving leg action on both sides with the slightest of rein influence.

If impulsion and obedience to leg control are not yet positive, the work to secure even loading will have to be not so brief. The even-loading controls will then have to be adapted to the individual case, with reference

[37] Also see " direct and indirect flexions ", p. 120.

to the difficult and the constrained sides, no matter on what lead the horse happens to be travelling. What was said earlier in this chapter on evening out the load by flexion should then be applied.

Whenever the liveliness and freedom of the gait begin to suffer during work on the circle, the horse should be taken off the circle and exercised at an increased rate on a straight line in order to awaken its impulsion and eagerness to go forward.

Once the horse responds to the outside controls as a result of work on the circle, we can begin to ride through the corners more closely. If the horse's timing grows worse and the gait becomes hurried and less expressive it is a sign that the horse cannot carry itself as yet, and the corner curve should not be taken as closely.

B. IMPROVING THE GAIT BY USE OF THE MIDDLE TROT—WORK-
ING AT THE GALLOP—EVENING OUT THE LOAD BY FLEXION—
TWO TRACKS—TURNS ABOUT THE HINDQUARTERS—BACKING—
STEPPING UP COLLECTION AT THE TROT AND AT THE GALLOP
—ORDINARY POSTURE AS THE BASIS OF DRESSAGE POSTURE—
WORKING AT THE WALK

The *middle trot* is not a working gait. It is indispensable as an aid to dressage, however, as well as a test of whether or not previous gymnastic training was correct.

The distinguishing features of the middle trot are its extended, vigorous movements. They do not increase the burden on the forehand, however, because they arise from alternately flexing and extending hindquarters' joints; thus they promote thrust and ground-covering as much as they assist in promoting carriage.

The increased extension and flexion of the two biggest motor joints in the body of the horse, the hip joint and the stifle, also results in better development of impulsion. The springy steps of the hind legs pass quite close to each other and swing the readily assumed burden forward and upward elastically. The powerful thrust of the hind legs takes place *before* the joints are fully extended; this elastic thrust and powerful leaving of the ground takes place *from the already bent position*.

Since the middle trot is executed with engaged haunches in equestrian balance when correctly performed, the forehand is able to raise its legs freely. The forelegs alight at the spot to which the front hoof edges point at the top of their travel. If the action of the forelegs is not smooth and rounded but choppy and cramped, in spite of the positiveness and sure-footedness of their easy alighting, it is an indication of faulty tension. The better the horse accepts the bit, the line from its forehead to nose being slightly ahead of the vertical, the better it flexes its poll and allows the impulsion flowing forward to pass through its body. This impulsion is controlled and limited by the hands, which are supported by the small of the rider's back, and is redirected to the joints of the hindquarters as a burden that tenses the hindquarters' springs.

The outward sign of the relative lifting of the forehand is higher carriage of the neck and head as a result of the lowering of the hindquarters. It goes hand in hand with the evolution of impulsion, without which the middle trot is inconceivable. Then the horse always responds better and more positively to the controls, permitting them to pass along its longitudinal and transverse axes.

The horse should carry the impulsion and back activity employed in the intensified gymnastics of the medium trot into the less expressive ordinary trot, where less collection is employed. Only if its back cooperates by pulsating in time and its motion is elastic, will an average horse be able to trot for hours at this working gait without prematurely tiring itself and its rider.

Length of stride and impulsion at the middle trot indicate how far we can go in flexion and collection. If these two are in order, we can increase the load on the hindquarters by resorting to light half halts and limit the ground covered while the forehand steps become loftier. If this causes the horse to lose its timing, and stiffnesses are felt in the seat and the hands, the horse is not yet ready for the increased demands of a collected gait.

But we have not yet got that far with our young horse.

We will be satisfied if after a few days we can increase the working trot on the long sides or the diagonals to a few longer strides; we will step up our demands only when, after weeks have gone by, we can ride the middle trot once or twice around the hall, using generously rounded corners.

If the hindquarters begin to drag, activity of the back slackens, positive contact with the bit is lost, or the steps become uneven and hasty, we know that we have asked for too much. We must return to the working rate in order to restore purity of gait and contact with the bit.

If we were to compel the horse to go at a middle trot notwithstanding, we would merely damage its feet and its dressage, since this gait is useful in training only if the horse's carriage is in harmony with its motion. When the co-operation of hindquarters and forehand is defective, without an elastically pulsating back as a connecting link, this gait ruins the legs and makes the horse peevish and ugly.

We must not overtax an animated horse with high mettle any more than we should allow a young horse to grow so tired that it loses the

27. Hand (medium) gallop. Compare the length of stride with picture number 26. Dan Marks on *Sultan* (Trakehnen) 1955.

28. Collected gallop. Michael Page on *Grasshopper* (Thoroughbred) 1959.

29. Typical of the effortless style of this exceptional Thoroughbred horse. Hugh Wiley on *Master William*. PHOTO L'ANNEE HIPPIQUE, LAUSANNE

30. Slide. Michael Page on *Grass-hopper* (Thoroughbred) winning three-day event, Pan-American Games, 1959.

as in a shoulder-in. The rider's weight follows the direction of motion forward and towards the outside, without abandoning the seat corresponding to the concave flexion.

Once the original circumference has been reached—preferably along the open side, before we reach the long wall—the outer leg, lying behind the girth, is applied to the side that is curved outward, corresponding to the flexion. This limits the lateral movements; it is sustained in this action by the outside rein, which is again touching the neck. At the same time, the outside leg acts in concert with the inside leg (which lies just behind the girth and exerts a stronger action) to drive the horse forward. The inside hand yields somewhat at the outset to facilitate the further extension of the corresponding foreleg.[39] The forward-driving controls may be reinforced by clicking the tongue and touching the inside shoulder with the riding crop.

Enlarging the circle in this manner has placed the horse under the outside controls, and the combination of these controls with the inside controls has put the horse in such a position that it cannot help departing at the correct gallop, provided it is responding pliantly to the forward-driving controls. To begin with, this makes the outside hind foot, which is held back somewhat by the restraining and hence sustaining outside rein, alight prematurely. Thus the diagonal footfall sequence—outside hind foot=inside forefoot—that has been operating up to now at the trot is broken up. The driving action of the inside leg now prepares for the powerful thrust of the outside hind leg, which is bearing more of the load and is still grounded (also see "Seat and Controls," p. 65ff.). Consequently its diagonal front hoof (the future inside one) is sustained as it reaches farther forward after a brief contact during the advance of the main diagonal (inner hind foot=outer forefoot), alighting as the inside forefoot after the main diagonal. Thus it automatically produces the phase element of the gallop.[40]

If we tried a gallop depart from a fast trot, it would be harder for the horse because the legs required for the initial thrust would not be immediately available, owing to the longer phase of suspension, especially as they are farther apart at an extended rate.

The more pliantly the rider, who places more load on his inner seat bone, adapts himself to the new movement and allows the leaps to occur

[39] This yielding, however, should never result in giving up an inner curvature of neck and head, no matter how slight, or an outward position of the neck and head, such as many rapid-dressage trainers demand, since the lifting of the inner front leg can be effectively supported by the contraction of the muscle connecting the base of the head with the respective foreleg only when this muscular contraction is assisted by the curvature towards the inside.

[40] I once heard a musically gifted riding instructor tell his equally musical pupil that a gallop depart could be compared to the start of the music for the dactyls of a melodic waltz.

by yielding, the smoother will be this changed phase sequence from the very outset, and the more constant will be the horse's contact with the bit. One or two turns about the hall will be quite enough at the start; then the driving controls should cease and the horse will itself fall into a trot. After a few strides at the trot the horse is walked and patted and praised with surrendered reins.

The transition to the gallop described above may not proceed so smoothly with all horses; some will immediately grow excited and want to bolt. One should not try to hold such horses back by restraining rein controls; this would merely increase their excitement. They would fight the rider's hands and learn how to stiffen their hindquarters and back against the compulsion of the restraining seat.

It is better for the rider to allow his seat to go along with the horse and to have his driving controls remain in contact as if he wished to increase the rate still more. If that is done, the suggestion of compulsion will soon vanish, even if the rider leaves the circle and rides straight ahead. This will give him an opportunity to take a better seat while following the horse's motion and to soothe the horse by stroking its mane, a procedure with which it is already familiar.

If lateral responsiveness is not sufficiently positive to enable the horse to develop the gallop from the enlargement of the circle, we can also exercise the gallop depart from the corner preceding a long wall—again from the shortened working trot. Here, too, the controls will have the desired effect: brief pressure with both legs, greater pressure being exercised by the inside leg, with an increased shift of the rider's load to the inner seat bone as is automatically effected by the seat in the turn, and the sustaining action of the outside rein. The rider should not use the same corner over and over again, for this will make lively horses grow restless ahead of time; they will become refractory and anticipate the controls.

If restlessness is detected between the individual gallops (which should be ridden on both leads, of course), it must be made a principle not to take a gallop depart until the horse has quieted down completely and has grown supple under the controls. A moderate working trot will do this best of all. Once the horse has been quieted down, shoulder-fore flexions, which also break up the gallop most easily during transitions to the trot, will distract it.

In work on the lunge we first drew the horse somewhat into the circle by pulling on the lunge in order to yield and drive it forward to develop its galloping leap. We can do the same thing now provided we do not employ the initial technique described above of enlarging the circle, which is based upon the same principle, and do not try a gallop depart from the corner, because the horse in question may exhibit a tendency to let its hindquarters evade towards the inside.

We place the horse in the trotting position (see p. 192, fn. 55) and after it has taken a few strides, we apply the controls required for a gallop depart, at the same time leading its forehand out on the circumference again. This procedure demands a fairly high degree of sensitivity from the horse, however, as returning the shoulders from the trotting position towards the outside to the circumference can involve a displacement of no more than a few centimetres.

This third type of exercising the gallop depart is particularly recommended for young horses because it is easy for the rider to maintain the even loading on all four legs by using his control of the inside hind leg. To be sure, like the first type of gallop depart described, it requires a fairly advanced lateral responsiveness combined with a certain degree of collection and sensitivity.

We mention the gallop depart from the preceding shoulder-in flexion at this point, however, because it is the best and most dependable way of correcting the fault of turning the hindquarters towards the inside in order to escape even loading on all four legs. This is a fault that creeps in unnoticed but is nonetheless very serious because it makes all further progress at the gallop impossible.[41]

If the horse's gallop depart is faulty, it should be quietly brought to a forward trot chiefly by the action of the inside leg and rein; then, only after complete suppleness has been achieved, is the gallop depart resumed. In general the more time we take in the initial introduction to galloping, the surer and more nearly correct will the galloping be later on. For this is the time when the foundations are laid for such faults as stiffness, crookedness, and the like, which are manifested later on. A horse exhibiting such fundamental defects must be restrained, starting with the ABCs, under much more difficult conditions.

The most rapid positive progress is made by the rider who is so psychologically balanced that he is prepared for a long period of training, governed solely by the progress made by the horse.

The natural leap displayed by the horse the first time it gallops in the riding hall should be retained for the moment, being modified or extended only after some days have passed. Driving or restraining controls develop an even rate, the working gallop, which can later—when the horse has acquired suppleness and poise—be raised now and then to the medium gallop, some 350 steps per minute, along straight lines. Though the first

---

[41] This fault usually develops as a result of the inner " positioning " rein exerting a backward pull. The horse tries to escape the faulty control by letting its inner hind leg turn out. Thus it turns the *travers*-like suggestion of the correct position into a faulty *travers*-like gait, in which the inside leg no longer tracks accurately, and if the neck is not firmly attached to its base, the horse falls upon its outside shoulder.

collection at the trot is best achieved with a young horse by gathering it from a smooth and spirited middle trot, the gait of the working gallop is shortened by means of frequent gallop departs from the walk. The transition from the walk to the gallop is made after about one year of training, when the horse's contact with the bit at the walk has become a positive one with slightly shortened reins. The horse, which is already familiar with gallop departs, will readily respond to the controls described above for the transition from the trot to the gallop, especially if it is allowed to take a few trotting strides at the beginning and if the gallop departs are taken from the corner or the volte for the first few times.

The natural limit to shortening the gait of the working gallop is preservation of the right gait and contact with the bit. Here are the infallible signs that too much has been asked of the horse for the time being:

(1) Its movements lose their lively springiness and become flat and dragging.

(2) The rider no longer is pulled forward in the saddle by the horse's elastically pulsating back. As a result, his inside leg no longer clings without effort to its place alongside the horse's ribs, which fall inward somewhat.

(3) The feel becomes dead or uneven in the rider's hands and jerky in his seat.

In principle the controls described above for the halt are utilized for the transition from the gallop to the walk [42] and for halting. The sole difference is that the outside rein exerts a somewhat greater sustaining action, corresponding to the slight longitudinal flexion automatically assumed by any horse galloping at a shortened gait and to the greater engagement and loading of the outside hind leg at this gait.

For a horse that has already completed its training, the procedure in slowing down from a walk and in the full halt, as well as when slowing down the gallop, will be approximately as follows: the rider exerts a driving-collecting seat control at the instant of complete suspension, when the head and neck of the horse are carried somewhat higher. Then the rider's hands, connected with his similarly extending upper body through his supple seat, withdraw. This control ensures compliance in the horse's back and neck, so that subsequent tugs on the reins in the rhythm of the horse's movements, which shorten the length of its leaps, are able to load its hindquarters without hindrance. Its hindquarters, in turn, are

---

[42] The test of an honestly executed slowing down from a gallop to a walk is the action of the foreleg immediately after the transition. If the horse fell to a walk " by itself ", so to speak, by planting its front legs and abandoning correct contact with the bit, thus deceiving its inexperienced rider, the first few strides of the front legs will be listless and flat, leaving the ground only reluctantly. The extension and advance of the forehand, which remains light, must be elevated after a correct transition executed with engaged hindquarters.

ready to flex, since the outside hind foot, which bears the entire load, always alights vertically below or in front of the hip joint after the movement of the horse's head and neck that causes the hands to withdraw. The inner hind foot cannot offer any resistance because it is swinging forward.

In slowing down, the rider's legs sustain the liveliness of the leap of the hind legs. The latter engage less forward, but are much more bent, while the hand continually releases the leap. The full halt is brought about, however, by the increased pressure of the seat bones, especially the inside one. This is produced by pushing the small of the back farther forward, with the legs stretched out so far (the inside heel kept particularly low) that the rider has the feeling that the stirrup leather might tear, and by the elastically sustaining hands, which restrict the horse's motion more and more.

The livelier the horse is during the last few leaps upon its bent haunches, which support the load, the finer and lighter the leg and rein controls can be. Consequently horses of good configuration will eventually require merely hints of the controls, allowing the seat control, consisting a mere tensing of the small of the back, to predominate.

Throughout this stage of training, however, departing at the working gallop from a short-gaited working trot should not be neglected as a loosening-up exercise and as the basis for a smooth gallop depart with the load evenly distributed on all four legs.

As we have frequently mentioned true *collection*, such as our young horse will be able to exhibit later on, let us say here and now that, from the purely theoretical standpoint, a horse can be absolutely straight at the trot when collected on a straight line. But in practice it will be found that when the neck that has come up to the bit in collection stretches upward, the ligamentum nuchae no longer lies directly above the first few cervical vertebrae. It slides off to the right or left in order not to have to participate in the extreme extension of the top of the neck, so that the horse displays flexion of the part of the lower jaw on the side in question. This is a hint to the rider to give the horse longitudinal flexion in the form of " position " at the collected trot to prevent it from assuming a false flexion of its own.[43]

A slight " position " in longitudinal flexion, with the inside hind foot always tracking on the same trace as the inside front foot, of course, will increase the suppleness of the inner side and with it the horse's readiness for closer turns even at medium rates of gait.

[43] It is all the more necessary that the rider adapt his seat and controls to the gallop, which exhibits a very slight, natural, concave flexion towards the inside—which will be discussed later on—even in its freer forms.

What is important is that our riding with longitudinal flexion, on a single track at first, produces a preliminary degree of flexion of the ribs, thus making the hind legs alight on as narrow a track as possible, both longitudinally and achieving greater engagement and the development of greater impulsion.

Apart from the advantage described above, the " position " should be adopted at the gallop if only because it is spontaneously offered to the rider as something quite natural, even without collection, by every horse moving without constraint. It must be supervised by the inside leg only to the extent of seeing that the loading of the horse's four legs remains even and that the inside hind leg keeps to the line from the inside ear to the inside shoulder or from the edge of the inside nostril to the inside shoulder (which amounts to the same thing if the horse does not twist its poll) when moving on a single track.

A horse that is moving correctly at a gallop requires this natural flexion of the ribs for locomotion reasons alone. It must be able to place the outside hind foot, which at times lifts the entire load and sustains it upon alighting after the suspension phase, vertically beneath the line passing through the centre of that load, thus supporting the latter under mechanical conditions that are best for thrust and load support.

Thus the sixth sense, the " sense of balance ", possessed by every living thing, causes the horse not to track with its outside hind foot exactly in the trace of the corresponding front foot. This is the exception to the rule of following in trace laid down at the beginning of this book.

The horse may insert a few trotting strides when effecting a transition from the gallop to the walk. If this is due to a lack of poise, it would be quite wrong to force it to a stop by using powerful controls. Such full halts with as few intervening strides as possible, and finally without any intervening strides, may be demanded only after the muscles of the hindquarters have been strengthened and their joints have grown more supple by work on the circle and transitions. But if failure is due only to lack of understanding, the horse's physique being adequate for the job—and this is something that the rider with equestrian tact must be able to feel —quiet repetitions of the exercise, which do not exceed its strength, will soon enable the horse to perform it smoothly.

After about one year of training the medium gallop can be increased to an ordinary gallop at a rate of about 500 steps per minute on suitable springy turf or meadow ground. The rider follows the horse's motion with shortened stirrups and his hands held low and quiet in order not to interfere with engagement of the hindquarters and the action of the back. He pushes his hips forward and remains in contact with the saddle in such a manner that he would not notice it if the rear end of the saddle were suddenly cut off. A corresponding following of the hands, yielding in the direction of the mouth on both sides of the neck, facilitates the balancing activity of the neck. This is particularly necessary at the free gallop and extends the leap. If the latter becomes too hurried and scratchy —an outward sign of this for the observer is the inadequate longitudinal spread between the hind legs—the rider's upper body, slightly bent forward with the small of the back pushed forward considerably, yields somewhat less to the motion. The legs, clinging to the horse with knee held low, maintain their firm position. The hands regulate and moderate the gait by means of brief tugs on the reins, but this is done only " within " the forward impulse and is constantly alternated with intervals of relaxation. Once the horse has calmed down completely, which may be the case only after it has changed to the working trot, a gallop depart can be taken again. Changing to the trot is very useful whenever highly nervous horses grow restless and begin to bolt. Other horses, however, calm down, say, on a large parade ground as soon as all the other riders present are travelling in the opposite direction, so that they see no horses running ahead of them which they think they have to overtake.

Temperamental horses should never be tired by being overridden. Long intervals at the walk under leg control (the leg must remain in supple, close contact under all circumstances once it has felt its way into proper position) and with as much freedom of the neck as possible are also a tested means of making the ensuing gallops quieter.[44]

The *extended trot*, like the middle trot, is a gait that serves gymnastic training of the horse.[45] It is also a touchstone that shows us how much impulsion and poise we have managed to develop in the horse.

Since it arises out of the middle trot described in the preceding section, we may discuss it here together with the extended gallop evolved from the medium gallop, although the time for both of these gaits actually falls within a later period of dressage.

The horse should not be called upon for the extended trot before the end of the second year of training or even later, for this gait, with its very long strides originating in a lowered hindquarters, is the end result and one of the culminating points of well-planned gymnastics, making extraordinarily high demands upon thrust, impulsion, and equestrian poise.

It is developed from the intensified middle trot by employing greater driving controls, though the extended movements caused by the particularly energetic thrusts should not become hastier than at the middle trot.

---

[44] If conditions permit, it is best to work particularly sensitive and shy horses, whose equestrian development has not reached the stage where they respond positively to the controls, during the early morning hours when they are still " sleepy "

[45] See p. 323 for the table of basic gaits.

The forehand operates high from the shoulder, and we must be able to distinguish clearly the bending, extending, and grounding of the different legs.

If the horse "falls apart," with neck extended, the accentuated precision of its steps is lost. It will overreach or the traces of its hind legs will grow wider, falling outside the track of the front hoofs instead of reaching beyond them, an indication that there is no longer any harmony between its carriage and its movement.

The extended trot, with its maximum degree of expression, should be ridden only along straight lines. We know of cases where born dressage horses, entirely devoted to the rider's control and to impulsion developed to the ultimate degree, collapsed as the result of a false step in the corner, putting a sudden end to their brilliant careers. See pp. 128-132, for the gait faults occurring in the trot.

As for the rider, we might add that "as he has made his bed, so will he sleep in it" at the extended trot. If he has managed to keep the back active, that is, pulsations elastic, during the entire course of dressage, he will find no difficulty in sitting out the powerful but regular and springy pulsations of the back in a correctly developed extended trot.

But if training was hastened too much, and the back has not become pliant, the posting trot must be resorted to for expediency. That is why every rider presenting his horse at the extended trot stays *in* the saddle in an effort to prove that his preparatory work was correct.

This should not be taken, however, as criticism of the posting trot as such; actually it is an indispensable aid to training. We have already mentioned its salutary effect upon horses that tighten up when they are mounted for the first time. It is also employed very successfully for sluggish horses or for those whose back and hindquarters are sensitive or for horses that have grown peevish for any reason whatsoever in order to secure vigorous engagement of their hind legs with more liking for the gait and, in general, to make forward movement pleasanter for them.

The *extended gallop* is developed from the medium gallop. As in the extended trot, the framework of the horse should be extended by a slight advance of neck and nose, though the timing of the shorter gait is retained. The leaps become flatter and cover more ground, corresponding to the greater driving action exerted by the rider and to the advance of the hands, which are in a lower position and afford a more positive contact with the bit as the neck is extended. The rider goes along with the greater speed and extension of the horse's body (without falling forward) in order not to disturb the action by remaining behind.

The horse responds energetically to the bit with long leaps, the triple beat and timing of which must remain the same as at the less extended gallop gait.[46]

Like the extended trot, the extended gallop should be ridden only along straight lines. The sides of a riding hall that is no more than 200 feet long are too short for fully developing this gait.

At the extended gallop, which is extremely important both for ordinary use as well as a training gait, responsiveness and poise will have to be manifested, especially in the turns. These turns are unavoidable when the horse is trained in a large rectangle and must be preceded by a half halt to the medium gallop.

Our comments on full halts during our discussion of the medium gallop apply equally well to full halts from the extended gallop.

No extended trot, which is only a training gait, is ever used in open country; the medium gallop (350 steps) and the ordinary gallop (400-500 steps) take its place whenever we have to exceed the speed of the ordinary trot (275 steps). The extended gallop, which can be taken at rates up to approximately 700 steps a minute when the horse's posture is freer than that used for training purposes, is the natural prolongation of the ordinary gallop and, together with the walk, the most important working gait for cavalry horses and hunters (see the Table of Basic Gaits and Their Gradations, p. 323).

These figures are merely standards of reference; they are the values employed in the standard military riding manuals, which must always consider the average horse or even the lower limits.

In the individual case, however, these limits will have to be exceeded somewhat without endangering legs and posture if the development of superlative natural machinery is not to be impeded or suffer because of being confined to a standard which conforms to a low average value.[47]

Securing even loading on all four legs really began the moment the horse responded to the controls. It did not exist in the lateral leg and rein controls, however; it consisted merely of compelling the horse to balance itself in the forward direction because the leg drove it forward and the yielding reins on the constrained side failed to provide the support the horse sought. This compelled the horse to abandon its crookedness, which was also less manifest as the horse's framework extended. We paid no attention, so to speak, to stiffness, allowing these difficulties to escape towards the front without dealing with them.

[46] The three-beat gait becomes a four-beat gait only in the racing gallop and the manège gallop. This is very clearly perceptible in the former and scarcely perceptible in the latter. In all other instances dissolution of the middle or principal diagonal (inner hind foot—outer front foot) is proof that the vigour and liveliness of the gallop have been lost, with the hindquarters dragging. (Also see Decarpentry, *Équitation Académique*, p. 229.)

[47] The entire locomotive equipment of such a horse would grow stiff because its joint would never be open to angles corresponding to its full natural radius of action.

But we cannot go on in this manner for ever; the response to the bit will not be the same on both sides. When we make greater demands upon the horse, its crookedness will make one hind foot or the other—usually the right hind foot—try to evade the uncomfortable burden and the influence of the rein on the same side by turning out laterally.

Once the horse has learned to pay attention to the rider's sideways-driving leg, and once we are able to emphasize the action of leg and reins by deliberate development of impulsion without making the horse hold back, the time has come for beginning the actual work of obtaining even loading on all four legs. This work will continue in greater or lesser degree throughout the period of training and will manifest itself in the continuous supervision of pure longitudinal flexion of even a perfectly trained horse (if there ever were such a horse), or, if necessary, in supervision of his straightening the horse out linearly.

For a horse to move in equestrian balance it is not enough for the fore-hand and hindquarters to take over the share of the total burden assigned to them by the lower or higher degree of collection demanded at any one time, with the major portion of the total weight of horse and rider falling upon the front legs except during schooled collection. The burden must also be uniformly shared by each pair of legs, each front leg carrying exactly half of the load on the forehand and each hind leg carrying exactly half of the load on the hindquarters, so that the horse is in complete lateral balance.[48]

Since the right and left sides of the body of a horse are unequally developed, as we have seen in the paragraphs of the " Definition and Explanation of Some of the Principal Concepts of Horsemanship " (p. 121f.) that deal with crookedness, one side—the constrained side—is always stiffer, and its shoulder always carries a heavier load.

Once we have realized that uniform distribution of weight, laterally as well as longitudinally, is the necessary prerequisite for equestrian balance and for enduring performances that do not ruin the legs prematurely, we must endeavour to find a way of achieving and ensuring such distribution.

As we have said, free riding forward has helped us overcome the initial difficulties caused by crookedness. But to combat these difficulties permanently, even when greater demands, such as those involved in all the different stages of collection, are made upon the horse, we require flexion work to achieve even loading. This enables us to attune the hindquarters

---

[48] The greater load on the lateral inside pair of legs when riding along curved lines, which we utilize to strengthen the inside hind leg and make it supple before we proceed to the more difficult problem of securing simultaneous flexion of both hind legs, is merely an apparent exception caused by the laws of centrifugal force.

to the forehand, and vice versa, on straight and curved lines, so that the thrust and impulsion of the hindquarters, the motor, act in the direction of motion without loss of power.

Horses that go sideways, with the hind feet failing to track the front feet, are not in equestrian balance, even though they maintain their natural balance, their natural poise, without support of the reins. Their suppleness will be incomplete because it is not based upon the even extension of the groups of muscles on the right and left halves of the horse's body.

We employ the indirect flexions or flexions of the first degree to loosen up any stiffness that may still be present and felt by the hands, say, as an increased pressure against the reins on one side or the other. After this the complete suppleness we have achieved is successfully employed to ensure even loading upon all four legs on a single track.

Before we discuss this in detail we should like to point out that the controls we use for a young horse that is stiff and commits the fault of going sideways (which we are employing here as a particularly bad case) will form the groundwork for successful flexion work only in this special case and only if their employment is adapted to the peculiarities of this case (also see pp. 63, 122, and the footnote on p. 161).

Here, for example, normal rein action in accordance with regulations for riding a well-trained horse would shorten the neck that is tight on one side even more and produce the opposite of what we aimed at with this control. Therefore, let us imagine a horse that is concave on its off side, hence is crooked from the outside rear to the inside front, so that its inside shoulder carries a heavier load than the outside one.

If we draw on the rein of the concave outside to begin a turn with such a horse, it will flex even more on that side and put even more load on the outside shoulder, but it will not obey, or will do so hesitantly.

The opposite will take place on the convex near inside. It will obey repeated tugs on the rein, in spite of the constraint, that is, the tense tightness of that side. But it will obey without flexing.

We deliberately chose the crass example of a horse in a fairly low stage of training, which does not respond positively to the outside rein as yet,[49] in order to emphasize the essentials of obtaining even loading on all four legs, with the co-operation of the reins and the laterally acting leg of the rider.

The underlying principle of all flexion work is this: making it possible for the horse to extend the outer side of its body to the same degree that the inner side becomes concave.

This principle must be followed in the turns even more so because the

[49] See footnote 13 on p. 122 and footnote 70 on p. 224.

horse does not yet respond to the outside rein, which is trying to prevent its falling upon its outside shoulder by setting up opposite pull. On the contrary, it would place an even greater load on that shoulder, thus making it harder to enter upon that turn. Moreover such rein action would also result in holding back because the horse has not yet learned how to yield with its mouth.

The outside rein, remaining quite passive and merely maintaining a light contact with the horse's mouth, must also enable the horse to stretch its convex side on lines other than curved one. On a straight line crookedness will also be manifested by the greater load placed on one shoulder, and it will demand appropriate action by the rider.

Since we have seen that balancing the weight between the two shoulders must never be produced at the beginning by an *active*[50] outside rein, the only rein we can use to achieve even loading is the inside rein.

On the assumption that the horse is crooked from right to left, the inside rein, shortened somewhat to provide steadier control, will turn the forehand far enough to the right and forward, with light " opening " tugs towards the side and away from the neck, for the outside hind foot to track the outside forefoot, so that a line connecting the two is parallel to the trace.

If the inside leg is not yet able to maintain even loading by its sustaining action, crookedness and the resultant tendency to put a greater load on the near shoulder will reappear once this lateral action of the opening rein ceases. At the next corner (provided we are riding on the right hand), it will result in an increased concave flexion on the right when the rider uses increased inside rein action in order to effect the turn. This is exactly what happened in the example discussed at the outset. This will result in even greater load on the near shoulder, so that the horse is actually flexed excessively by the drawing of the rein but is rendered unable to obey it because the overloaded shoulder has been forced outward.

If the rider should try to prevent this turning out of the shoulder and the excessive inside flexion of the neck by using an active outside rein, he would not achieve his purpose; he would merely hold back the horse, as we have seen.

Nor would driving the horse forward be of any use in countering this holding back. The horse, confined between collecting controls in such a fashion, would grow even tighter because it is unable to obey them as yet.

At this stage the rider's legs can operate successfully only if they are allowed to act in a forward-driving and directing manner on the straight lines, with the mere hint of an inside rein and a completely passive out-

[50] See footnote on p. 224.

side rein in the turns. What happens is this: the rider's inside leg behind the girth, acting laterally, will direct the outward-turning off hind leg against and in front of the outside hind leg, with the circumspect support of the inside rein.

The outside leg on the convex side, applied as far forward along the girth as possible, will take care of the forward drive (see the effect of the stimulating leg control in " Seat and Controls ", p. 64f.). Thus the inner hind leg, sustained by the inside leg of the rider, will come up to the rein on the same side and keep the gait fluid.

Now if I ride the same horse on the left hand, its tendency to be crooked from the outside rear to the inside front as it goes forward, a tendency which is the same on both hands, causes us to make some changes in our controls.

In the turn the horse, with its heavier load on the outside shoulder, will tend to turn inward. We must, therefore, no longer try, as we did on the right hand, to produce an even greater " turn " in the shoulder that is already turning out by employing an opening rein acting to the side. Thus the inside hand will remain alongside the neck and confine itself to giving the barest hint of the change of direction by an absorbing closing of the fingers. The right rein, which is now the outside rein, supports the stretching of the outer side of the neck as before by going forward, but it will also try to prevent a hasty turn by acting as an opening rein, this time from the inside towards the outside.

The left leg, which is now the inside leg, will exert lateral pressure just behind the girth in order to keep the horse from hurrying the turn, like the outside right rein, which acts outward from the neck.

Any driving action of the outside leg at this time would force the horse's body even more to the near shoulder and the near rein. Its spinal column—already crooked from the outside to the inside—is turned towards the inside of the riding hall.

The right leg, now on the outside, and behind the girth of the turning-out side as a restraining control, will therefore have the job (as it had on the right hand) of directing the turning-out off hind foot against the near hind foot, and thus endeavouring to achieve *even loading in a longitudinal flexion* corresponding to the curvature of the turn. Once longitudinal flexion is attained, the rider's outside leg, in addition to its restraining action that supervises the maintenance of longitudinal flexion, will drive forward (supported by the inside leg) as much as is required to maintain a uniform rate in the turn.

In work of this kind the rider will have to distribute his weight as symmetrically as possible on the two sides of the horse's body, using a light crotch seat. In this position he will be able to employ temporary lateral displacements of his weight to support the active rein that is producing an equalization of weight between the two forelegs. The active rein, however, follows the direction of motion except in the brief intervals in which these weight controls are exercised.

In our discussion of the first flexion effect we deliberately used the example of a badly crooked horse that had made little progress in its training.

Once the leg and rein actions on the same side but not at the same time (rather alternating with and supporting each other) have brought the horse to the point where it stretches the side that is to be arched and reaches forward to the bit on that side, the actual work of first-degree flexions begins.

The outside controls will only act to restrain, maintaining flexion of the ribs; they are not yet exerting a pronounced counteraction that flexes the horse directly about the rider's inside leg. This is done later on by second-degree flexions, the shoulder-in and the *travers* position.

The rib flexion sought for in initial flexion training enables us to straighten the horse, because it compels the horse's hindquarters to advance in the direction of the plumb line passing through its centre of gravity. Flexion of the ribs, however, also enables the horse to follow all curved lines, even making narrow turns smoothly and with even loading, that is, with hind legs that engage in the direction of the plumb line through the centre of gravity.

In *work on two tracks* the horse moves forward and to a side on double tracks[51] with the forehand and hindquarters attuned to each other in an even longitudinal flexion.

One objective of work on two tracks is increasing and perfecting the flexion of the ribs just described, thus making the horse nimbler and more supple.

But the degree of rib flexion can be increased only by work on two tracks, the forelegs of the horse crossing and its hind legs advancing in the direction of motion, passing each other as closely as possible. Its hind legs pass each other closely because the horse is flexed at the ribs, in contrast to a completely unnecessary lesson of "yielding to leg action", so

---

[51] The horse moves on a so-called double track as distinct from a single track when the path its travels, visible in its hoof prints, is broader (provided the longitudinal flexion is correct) than the distance between the outside edges of the hoof of its fore or hind pair of legs in the normal stance.

The single track leaves two hoof traces, or three in the first position and second position, whereas the double track leaves three hoof traces at the trot position and at the gallop position, or only two, parallel to the wall, in the *shoulder-in* and travers. Here engagement and forward reach become more and more pronounced owing to the increased flexion of the ribs, provided the responsiveness and collection are adequate.

that its hindquarters remain in the trace of a single track.[52] Hence this lateral movement is not the object but merely the consequence of work on two tracks.

Another objective of work on two tracks is improving the engagement of the hindquarters, that is, increasing the collection of the horse. But we can do this only when its spinal column has become so supple, as a result of the increased rib flexion—the essence of work on two tracks—that the hind legs, driven forward under the load, approach the forehand and can take over a larger part of the weight. The more the thrust, which is limited by this lateral position, is converted into increased ability to engage and carry the load, the more the hindquarters will be able to do so. The longitudinal axis of its base of support, shortened by the extent of rib flexion required, and its transverse axis, shortened by the crossing of the forefeet and the advance of the hind feet, also make the horse responsive and obedient to exceptionally fine controls, because of its resultant increased instability and decreased capacity to resist.

Longitudinal flexion on a single track, shoulder-fore, also called the first position, in which the horse's inside hind leg tracks between the two front feet, with the outside hind leg tracking the outside front foot, is the starting point and parent position of all movement on two tracks. This position of the hindquarters with respect to the forehand automatically produces flexion of the ribs, which is lost only when the hindquarters turn outward.

Correct riding on two tracks requires a certain degree of collection, which is advanced still further by two-track exercise. It is quite wrong, however, to assume that a horse that cannot be collected will learn collection by work on two tracks. Suuch a horse, which is not yet ready for work on two tracks, would merely throw more of its weight on its shoulders, and lose its carriage as well as the purity of its gait.

Therefore, work on two tracks will help rather than harm the young

[52] If the hind legs cross during work on two tracks, the horse partially avoids carrying the burden by no longer having its hind leg engaged forward towards the plumb line through the centre of gravity in the direction of motion, but by letting it run ahead to the side. Since the amount of collection and longitudinal flexion should be increased together with the amount of lateral deflection (*Abstellung*), such crossing of the insufficiently engaged hind legs indicates that collection and longitudinal flexion do not harmonize with the excessive lateral distance from the previous hoofprint. That is why such crossing may often be observed when the horse " yields to leg action ".

But when the hindquarters' joints retain a certain flexion, crossing is rendered impossible for purely technical reasons related to the structure of the horse.

In other words, if a hind leg engages forward towards the centre of gravity as it should, and laterally, instead of merely dragging with *short* steps, it is impossible for the other hind leg to cross, as its road is barred.

We might add that lateral displacements are easier for the horse at the gallop than at the trot. The reason is that the longer period of suspension at the gallop and the asymmetrical sequence of steps, which facilitate a lateral advance, make it easier to effect such displacements from the outside to the inside.

horse only after it has learned to increase the engagement of one hind leg and then has been prepared by full halts and backing for the increased loading of both hind legs, a requirement for two-track work. Engagement of one hind leg is increased by work on the circle and the volte which, with its diameter of six steps, represents the maximum pure longitudinal flexion of the horse's spinal column.

When a horse that has received this correct preparatory training is worked on two tracks (which will present no physical difficulties after a certain period of familiarization), its longitudinal flexion is improved, the carrying capacity and elastic impulsion of its hindquarters are increased, and the entire horse becomes more supple and responsive. The impulsion stored, so to speak, in the more greatly engaged haunches will be imparted to the freer gait and the result will be strides and leaps that are especially springy and ground-covering.

On the other hand, work on two tracks, when done after the medium gaits, should retain their freshness, vigour, and interest, together with the increased collection involved.

Before a two-track movement is begun, the horse must have assumed the posture that best prepares it for commencing the movement and continuing it. This posture is the " position " and it has a fourfold objective.

First, a " positioned " horse is already at a certain degree of collection, which cannot be produced during the work on two tracks itself.

Second, the longitudinal flexion of the " position " makes it easier for us to control and hold together the hind legs, which pass by each other closely, are better loaded by this movement on a narrow track, and hence can be called upon for greater efforts because of their flexibility.

Third, the longitudinal flexion that is the essential feature of the " position " also creates the conditions needed for the horse to enter the two-track movement smoothly and fluently, and with its forehand suitably prepared, that is, with even loading on all four legs.

Fourth, it is easier for us to maintain the correct pliability of the poll during the two-track movement when it is already established by the preceding " position ". But if flexion of the poll is incorrect in the " position ",[53] it makes it that much harder to establish contact from leg to mouth as by the lateral deflection the lateral distance from the previous hoofprint is increased.

---

[53] A twisted head (crooked forehead) with its corollary, one ear lower than the other, arises when the two parathyroid glands do not stand out equally between the back edge of the lower jaw and the muscles of the neck or are both located underneath these edges. It may also be due to impaired eyesight in one eye.

One-sided pressure of the chin-strap buckle of the halter, wrongly located, that is, not lying on the softer parts of the chin, results in crooked carriage of the head together with defacing excrescences on the rami.

31. (*Above*) "Italian" jumping seat. Following the motion and allowing the horse every opportunity for stretching and balancing itself. Italian cavalry officer, Palermo competition.

32. (*Right*) Exemplary descent. Captain C. Stoffel on *Tonio*.

33. High broad jump. The rider requires particularly good timing and suppleness in yielding and following over high broad jumps. William Steinkraus on *Riviera Wonder* (Thoroughbred) 1959. JUNE FALLAW

The lateral distance from the previous hoofprint depends upon the degree of collection and longitudinal flexion achieved, as stated above, but in ordinary or elementary field (cross-country) training it must not exceed the maximum of one step—32 inches. Then the centre of the forehand can be carried as much as one step to the side from the hoofprint of the outside hind foot in the shoulder-in, whereas, in the *travers* the centre of the hindquarters can be carried equally far to the side from the hoofprint of the outside forefoot. The purity and regularity of the gait suffer once this limit is exceeded.

An increased lateral distance can be demanded temporarily from the schooled horse in the lessons of the higher field (cross-country) school and the *haute école*, but these are outside the scope of this chapter.

Opinions still differ concerning the distribution of the rider's weight in work on two tracks. We often hear it said that the rider must sit on the inner side in all work on two tracks in order to have his weight act increasingly upon the inside hind foot for greater engagement, letting his weight follow the slope of the concave flexion.

The hindquarters' joints are equally engaged on both sides when travelling along a straight line, even in work on two tracks, so that the rider should get rid of the suggestion that he should or even could cause greater flexion of one hind leg when travelling along a straight line. Moreover any increased burden placed on the flexed side would in many cases violate a basic law of riding doctrine if carried out consistently. This law requires that the rider's weight go along in the direction of motion, remaining in harmony with the horse.

It is easy to find a way out of this dilemma, however, if we realize that the horse bends the haunch joints on both sides equally in all work on two tracks, because its hind legs, which are loose in all their joints, are set down close to each other.

Thus, the rider, using a " neutral " seat, need only let his weight follow the direction of motion, in our case, the direction of the two-track movement.

The rider must not bend from the hips when leaning to the side of the horse that is slightly flexed in the region of the ribs.[54]

The positions of the legs and of the hands are determined automatically in all work on two tracks for the rider who uses a supple seat, because his hips, parallel to the hips of the horse, determine the correct position and his shoulders, parallel to the shoulders of the horse, freely determine the most effective and natural position of the hands.

Turns on the forehand in motion, the narrowing and widening of the

[54] When one is riding a straight line, this leaning is caused not by a sinking of the inside hip of the horse, but by the flatter pulsations of the less thoroughly extended back muscles on the hollow side, which are crowded together.

circles, the shoulder-fore, and, lastly, riding in "position" have already prepared our horse for the diagonal co-operation of the controls and direct flexion in work on two tracks, with the opposing action of the outside controls. We now begin by teaching it what we require at the walk. But as soon as it has understood the new demands and has grown accustomed to them, we resume the work on two tracks at the shortened and then at the more collected trot.

Work on two tracks, strictly speaking, should be done only at the trot; it should be done at the collected gallop only in the secondary field school, the transition stage to the *haute école*.

Two-track work at the walk is feasible only if the horse can be completely collected at that gait, but this can hardly be done, even in the most favourable circumstances, much before the end of the second year of training.

We can begin work on two tracks when our horse has gained enough equestrian poise—as a result of shortening the working trot, riding on curved lines, closer turns, backing, and full halts—that it can be gathered from the supple and vigorous forward motion of the middle trot to a collected trot, while remaining in positive though soft contact with the bit.

The *shoulder-in* is best developed after riding through the first corner on a long side of the hall. Using *both* reins, we begin by leading the forehand only about one hoof-width away from the wall towards the inside.[55] The rider's outside leg, behind the girth, makes sure that the croup does not turn out towards the wall, while his inside leg, moving in time with the rising inside hind foot, drives that foot forward and sideways on the track of the outside foreleg, which is shifted towards the inside by one hoof-width. If the horse moves to the side, the rider's outside leg must keep it in place; if it holds back, that leg must drive it forward.[56]

The rider's upper body follows the movement.

[55] This lateral movement is the first stage of shoulder-in, the so-called *trotting position*, which is already work on two tracks, as the horse is moving along a double (broadened) track. We can distinguish three different hoof traces (outside hind foot, inside hind foot and outside forefoot on a straight line parallel to the wall, and inside forefoot).

The extent of longitudinal flexion, which is the same in both lessons, provides an analogy to the *gallop position* discussed later on. In the gallop position the hindquarters are turned away one hoof-width, like the forehand in the trotting position.

The trotting position is so called because the horse can be made to shift from the gallop to the trot by the use of controls that resemble those employed for its taking the trotting position, and also because it is made practically impossible for the horse to take a gallop depart from this position, so that it can be mechanically compelled to remain at the trot even against its will.

[56] Generally speaking, when riding in longitudinal flexion the rider's leg that is not principally concerned with lateral control or restraint takes care of the forward drive; his outside leg does this in the shoulder-in. The gallop depart is an example.

Each of the two reins that lead the forehand to the inside has a special job to do: the inside rein, held somewhat short, occasionally supplements the lateral action of the rider's inside leg, subsequently alternating with the action of that leg. The outside rein keeps the horse's shoulder on the line intended for the shoulder-in figure and supports the outside leg when required in order to prevent any turning out of the hindquarters towards the wall. At the same time, this rein, which lies close to the arched side because of the more powerful pulsations of the muscles on that side and for that very reason acts as a lever, must keep the horse's neck straight on its base and prevent excessive flexion.

This faulty flexion of the neck would involve the outside shoulder's turning out, which would be facilitated by the fact that it could occur in the direction of motion.

Such loosening of the neck in front of the withers, which the horse would soon exploit against the rider whenever it refused to obey, is best corrected by driving the horse energetically forward a few steps towards the centre of the hall in the direction of its lateral deflection. If enough impulsion is present, pressure exerted upon the horse's shoulder by the hand holding the outside rein lower, timed with the advance of the outside foreleg and acting as a restraining force directed inward, will prevent its turning out. This pressure must be exerted at the moment when the outside foreleg is raised, that is, when the outside, thrusting hind leg is grounded,[57] for only then is the horse able to obey immediately by stepping farther forward and sideways towards the inside with the outside foreleg.

The shoulder-in will be correct if the horse, slightly flexed at the ribs, assigns the rider's inside leg its position just behind the girth automatically, so to speak, where it clings effortlessly. The rider must also have the feeling that he can increase his leg pressure and yield his outside rein at any time to change to a volte on a single track in the direction of the lateral displacement or to make an about-face on the hindquarters, provided collection is complete.

Not only would it be useless to ride through the corners in this two-track movement at the present stage of training, but it would actually wipe out any collection we had achieved, for it would relieve the load on the hind legs, which cover a longer distance.[58] That is why the corner is handled as a quarter volte, as is often seen in the Spanish Riding School, the horse's forehand being allowed to reach almost the opposite wall in the shoulder-in. After that it is ridden through the corner on a single track, its longitudinal flexion being maintained. After the corner

[57] In this discussion we ignored the instant at which all four legs are in suspension at the trot. It is of no practical importance because of its brief duration (see the footnote on p. 67).

[58] It is harder to do a correct shoulder-in on curved lines in the corners or on a circle than a counter-shoulder-in, as the hindquarters travel a shorter distance in the latter figure and therefore find it easier to remain collected.

has been traversed, transition to the shoulder-in from the already existing longitudinal flexion can be effected by using the lateral controls.

If the horse can be halted at the shoulder-in without staggering and boring against the bit, its poise, impulsion, and even loading on all four legs are satisfactory. Then the full halt will consist chiefly of the horse accepting the somewhat stronger restraining outside controls and coming to a stop with even loading on its right and left legs. If the gait loses its expressive timing during the shoulder-in, becoming hurried or dragging, the work on two tracks must be abandoned. The horse's thrust, which no longer acts directly during lateral displacement, must then be re-awakened at a working rate in order to redevelop clean, long steps on a single track. Only then can the rider resume the collected trot, from which he shifts to work on two tracks.

To repeat, the reason why collection can be improved and perfected in lateral displacement on the foundation of already existing impulsion, but cannot be produced, is that the oblique position in work on two tracks limits the thrust. It is then impossible for this diminished thrust to develop impulsion and from the latter, collection.

But we can improve impulsion that is already present much better on two tracks than along a straight line, because work on two tracks enables us to drive the horse forward much more energetically. Since the sustaining action of the reins, especially of the outside rein, becomes a lever action and hence is intensified because of the arching of that side, owing to the lateral displacement, we can increase impulsion by greater driving without fearing our being unable to stand the impulsion imparted by the rider's legs and seat.

As in other work on two tracks, in the shoulder-in we must bear in mind that a few powerful and expressive strides with elevated crossing front legs and free shoulders are more than enough at the outset, and that the joints must again be allowed to stretch themselves by subsequently putting the horse through free gaits.

Riding the horse for too long a time at collected lateral flexion would achieve the opposite of what we intended. The overloaded joints, like springs under constant pressure, would lose their elasticity and liveliness and grow limp.

In the right shoulder-in most horses tend to twist their heads to the left with the right ear lower than the other, indicating that they have freed themselves of the action of the outside rein. It is inadvisable to try to restore the correct flexion of the lower jaw and contact with the bit by raising the right hand because this requires extraordinary sensitivity and considerable driving ability if the gait is not to suffer.

A more positive and better method is to keep the forehand and hind-quarters attuned to each other, chiefly by utilizing the driving and guiding action of the rider's legs. Then the horse will accept the outside rein as well, and its ears will automatically come back to the same level.

The rider must not be too hidebound in evening out the load on two tracks. For instance, if the forehand turns outward on the circle, it would be wrong to try to force it to follow exactly the track it is supposed to merely by acting upon the forehand alone. In such a case it is best to readjust the hindquarters to the forehand by driving them somewhat farther to the outside. The rider's inside leg should be applied somewhat farther to the rear to make it easier for the horse to understand, even at the expense of clean longitudinal flexion.

In the left shoulder-in horses often deceive us by seeming to yield willingly to the lateral pressure of the rider's inside leg. However, this yielding is nothing but escape from the leg, crookedness with a straight spinal column. Such crookedness appears only too easily on this hand if the rider's outside leg is not up to the job of supervising and maintaining longitudinal flexion. Counter-lessons are the best corrective measure for horses displaying this tendency to faulty evasion. In general it is often useful to begin shoulder-in training with its counter-lesson, because the horse will obey the lateral leg action more readily when its head is turned towards the wall.

Generally speaking, resorting to the counter-lesson for a few strides is very useful to correct faulty flexions in shoulder-in. A transition of this sort is the best way of eliminating a faulty flexion, such as a wrong flexion of the neck in front of the withers. The procedure would be about as follows: in the counter-lesson first flex the horse's head and neck in a direction opposite to that of the faulty flexion, then straighten the horse so that vertebrae and muscles fall into their proper places, and finally, carefully allow the horse to assume the flexion that was previously faulty.

To shift to the counter-shoulder-in when riding straight ahead, the rider first places the horse in the counter-position in order to make sure of the suppleness of the inner side turned towards the wall[59] and to be in better position to prevent the outside hind foot from falling out in the ensuing lateral movement of the hindquarters. This is of even greater importance than in the ordinary lessons, as the supporting wall is now lacking.

[59] It is always the flexion that determines which side is the inner side and which the outer. If we place and flex our horse to the left, for example, the left is its inner side even when we are using a counter-lesson, with this side facing the wall, while the horse moves to the right on the right hand. In this left counter-lesson the rider's seat and guidance must be placed as if he were riding in the same position to the left, that is, on the left hand.

Every lesson is a counter-lesson if the inner, flexed side is turned to the wall, and the horse is compelled to turn in a direction opposite to that of its flexion. This distinguishes it from the simple lessons, no matter what their names, when the horse turns in the direction of its flexion, corresponding to the hand on which one is riding.

The trace of the inside hind leg, which is provisionally shifted towards the centre of the riding hall by no more than one hoof-width in the counter-shoulder-in, will track the outside foreleg (counter-trot position).

A well-made horse requires no other active controls, so to speak, to keep it on two tracks. The supple seat, adapted to the flexion, easily leaning towards the concave side, and its weight going along in the direction of the two-track work, ought to suffice to maintain impulsion in the collected two-track position.

To return to the single track from the shoulder-in, both reins are used to turn the forehand out to the track of the hindquarters. This already constitutes a minor turn on the hindquarters.

The *travers* is actually closely related to the shoulder-in, from which it must evolve. But there are differences in the external picture: the hindquarters are on the inside lines in the travers, the outside feet advance ahead of the inside feet and partially cross them, and finally, the horse moves forward and to the side in the direction of its flexion.

To begin the *travers*, once the horse has been through the corner in " position ", the rider's outside leg presses the hindquarters towards the centre of the hall in time with the rising hind leg on the same side, just enough for that leg to track approximately on the line of the inside front leg.[60] Thus the initial lateral displacement will be about one hoof-width, just as in the shoulder-in.

Clean longitudinal flexion and collection are maintained chiefly by the rider's inside leg applied just behind the girth; this will take care of smoothness of the forward motion by driving ahead and prevent the hind foot on the same side from turning out. Its flexing action is supported by the inside rein, which maintains the position of the head and keeps the horse in the direction of motion. This rein must be adapted to the longitudinal flexion of the horse, i.e., it must be shortened somewhat.

The outside rein must control the longitudinal flexion of the neck so as to make it harmonize with that of the entire horse. Moreover, it has to support the lateral action of the rider's outside leg and maintain collection by very light, interrupted tugs on the rein.

What was stated at the outset concerning work on two tracks in general applies to the maximum degree of lateral displacement, which must be effected with pure longitudinal flexion (adapted to the degree of lateral displacement) at the *travers* as in all work on two tracks. The same holds true for the *renvers*, the counter-lesson of the *travers*. In the *travers* the outside hind foot goes forward, while the outside forefoot crosses in front of the corresponding inside leg. This crossing in the

[60] Also see the comments on p. 191 on increasing the amount of lateral displacement.

direction of flexion and movement is facilitated by the advance of the outside shoulder resulting from the *travers* position.

Since the inside hind leg must move along practically the same line as the outside one in a correct *travers*, with both legs in the same relation to the plumb line through the centre of gravity, it has to alternate with the latter in taking over the same load upon alighting and is thus subjected to the same loading action that bends its joints.

The inner hind leg can be subjected to greater load and greater bending only on a curved line, in consequence of the law of centrifugal force, even in the *travers*. This occurs as part of natural gymnastics, without participation of the rider. Hence, as we have often emphasized, this increased load and bending on a curved line are not the results of lateral flexion.

Both hind legs are bent to the same extent on two tracks along a straight line. They must be, for otherwise the impulsion and purity of the gait would suffer.

Thus what we have said concerning the distribution of the rider's weight in the shoulder-in also applies to the *travers* and its counter-lesson, the *renvers*. The sole *formal* difference is that in these two exercises the leaning towards the side of the horse that is slightly flexed at the ribs coincides with the direction of motion on two tracks, that is, the direction the rider's weight must follow, since the horse steps where it is "positioned".

Corresponding to the greater suppleness and carrying capacity acquired by the horse's hindquarters, work in the *travers* and the *renvers* can begin at the collected trot from the very outset.

The corners are traversed on a single track. Going through the corners in the *travers* greatly promotes the carrying capacity and engagement of haunches, as it constitutes a turn about the hindquarters, which are in step with the forehand but move on a narrower quarter circle than the forehand. Thus they cover less ground and represent preparation for the pirouette. It is an exercise that is part of the secondary field school. This school constitutes the preliminary stage of the *haute école*, since it requires a degree of collection, when performed correctly, that can be achieved only after many years of training and can be demanded only from horses of more than ordinary ability.

To determine whether the horse is fully responsive to the controls, it is useful to employ larger or smaller voltes on a single track to interrupt the *travers* exercises, which require more exertion than the shoulder-in because of the horse's stepping from its extended side to its bent side.

To shift from the *travers* to the single track, the rider's inside leg drives the horse forward in the direction of the forehand; the outside leg, which kept it sideways, grows more passive and merely provides support for the inside leg to keep the hindquarters from turning out. Thus the smooth forward depart on a single track, which should be executed with poise and good timing, is converted into a turn on the forehand. We should avoid such a turn in order to maintain the collection that has been improved in the work on two tracks.

Even in the *travers* and *renvers* horses tend to move their outside hind legs more to the inside than forward, with an unbent, turned-in spinal column, thus partially evading engagement and carrying of the load and destroying impulsion. In such cases, as well as where the inner hind leg turns inward, the rider's inner leg must exert more forward and lateral pressure, thus restoring the pure longitudinal flexion.

Resistance to the rider's outside leg, which sometimes occurs at the beginning of *travers* training, soon disappears if the horse is shifted from the *travers* to the counter-shoulder-in. When this happens we may assume that the shoulder-in work, which is the basic form and starting point of the other *travers* work on two tracks, was not thorough and conscientious enough. That is why difficulties arising in the *travers* two-track work are best overcome by work on the shoulder-in and its counter-lessons.

In general transitions from one two-track exercise to another are well adapted to increase the horse's suppleness and its attentiveness to the controls. Such transitions, which may be combined at will, must be developed smoothly towards the front, with turns about the forehand in motion carefully avoided. Changes from one two-track exercise to another are most natural and elegant when longitudinal flexion remains unchanged. The sole difference is that the other pair of legs becomes the advancing and crossing pair. Here the rider has the advantage of changing the exercising of an individual hind leg with every change of the two-track movement. As explained above, this work is intended to loosen up that leg and control it better rather than increasing its engagement and placing a heavier load on it, which can be done only on curved tracks.

One such transition, with a change in the sequence of steps, is the change from the shoulder-in to the travers, the corner being traversed on a single track as a quarter volte with shoulder-inflexion, after which the *travers* is started.

Another such exercise is the change from *travers* to shoulder-in, in which both legs press the horse forward into the shoulder-in after it has developed a volte on a single track from the *travers*. The same controls are employed to effect the transition to the shoulder-in after the horse has moved forward on a straight line, retaining its position on a single track. This has already been explained in discussing the transition from the *travers* to the single track. Flexion and sequence of steps remain unchanged in the transition from the *travers* to the *renvers* via a short about-face.

When the horse is brought to a full halt from the *travers*, principally by the outside rein and the inside leg, the leg must concentrate on supervising the inside hind foot to prevent its evading the load by remaining behind and stepping to one side.

Aesthetically speaking, the *travers* is particularly well suited to display a well-made collected horse in the most favourable light. The shorter path travelled by the hindquarter, say, on a circle, makes possible greater engagement of the haunches than in the shoulder-in, so that the forehand, placed in the direction of movement, gains in freedom and elevation of stride.

The transitions from one two-track movement to another are more than merely an excellent way of increasing the horse's attentiveness to the controls. Moreover, performing them perfectly is evidence of a high degree of impulsion and responsiveness. Over and above that, however, these changes of form and movement also provide an exceptionally harmonious picture of the unity of horse and rider when they are done without rigour or hesitation, evolving out of one another smoothly, evenly, fluently.

The rider deliberately lets the *travers* figures follow the shoulder-in, since the captivating charm of posture, gait, and action are most effectively displayed in the *travers* figures.

Crossing the whole hall or part of it at the *travers* is called a *traversal displacement* (or a *half pass*). If the rider imagines that the traversing line is replaced by a wall along which he must travel, and if he carefully keeps on the course for the end of the line at the opposite wall, it will be easier for him to avoid the fault of turning out the hindquarters excessively and thus making them lead the forehand. The horse's nose and inside shoulder must always be turned somewhat in the direction of motion, so that the horse moves sideways nearly parallel to the side of the hall.

The simplest and easiest form of traversal displacement, which is also called the half *traverse* when the lateral displacement totals only about one hoof-width, is done either along the diagonal from one corner to another or from the middle of the short wall to the middle of the long wall. The corner-to-corner diagonal is a simple traversing line through the entire hall, while the latter is a half *traverse* from the middle, a modified form of the half-turn (*demi-tour*) with traversal displacement. Because of the slight longitudinal flexion involved, both figures are best suited to get the young horse to step sideways without the " moral support" of the wall. But even with older horses that become listless and dragging in two-track work, whose impulsion we do not want to revive on a single track for one reason or another, nothing reinvigorates the trot as such traverses freely ridden, with slight lateral displacement, and freed from the soporific effects of the wall.

The traversal displacement requirements may be stepped up in the second and third year of training. For example, the traversal displacement may be started as soon as the horse has passed through the corner ahead of the long wall and continued to the middle of the opposite long wall. Then the exercise is continued on the other hand—a simple traversing line through half the hall. Or after the hall has been crossed, we may again depart from the opposite long wall, and return to the long wall from which the displacement started by employing another traversal displacement in the opposite direction. This *double traversal line* (also called a zigzag) will terminate just ahead of the far corner of the side on which the figure started.

If the riding hall is at least 70 by 140 feet in size, the rider can perform a *double half-traversal*, in which the change of position and direction of movement take place along the centre line of the hall. He can also perform triple whole or quadruple half-traversals, though only after suppleness and engagement of the hindquarters have been fully developed.

The full significance of traversing is realized when these preliminary conditions are satisfied and the traversing movements are actually obtained from the vigorously engaging and load-carrying hindquarters, so that the horse, becoming lighter on the forehand, develops impulsion and action.

The change of position and direction of motion must not degenerate into a stagger; the horse must be ridden at an expressive trot.

The *travers* affords an excellent opportunity of judging the gymnastic training of the horse as far as lateral motion is concerned. The rider will do well to have an observer posted farther out along the line followed by the horse to check longitudinal flexion and even loading on all four legs.

The still higher requirement of multiple traversals, involving changes of position, also exhibits the extent to which both halves of the horse's body are equally responsive. If the amount of longitudinal flexion and " position " is not the same on both sides, supple responsiveness has not yet been achieved and must be more firmly established by work on the circle at the working trot and by shoulder-in exercises with slight lateral displacement. Never forget that *all the other two-track exercises are the result of the shoulder-in* and are developed from it. That is why, whenever difficulties arise, we must return to this parent position with its many nuances, on which the evolution of all two-track exercises is based.

The tendency of older horses to exploit their crookedness against their riders by throwing their shoulders out to the left in a *travers* or a turn without waiting for the corresponding longitudinal flexion must be combated very vigorously. In some circumstances application of the spur on the left side will be more successful than the most careful guidance, for this impulse to the left cannot be eliminated by the reins alone.

The objective of changes of rate, work on two tracks, halts, and the like have resulted in an increasing positive control of the horse. One of the objectives of this rather limited control attainable in the ordinary or elementary field (cross-country) school is the turn (pirouette) on the haunches. This figure must always be done in motion. Even when it is performed following a full halt, the legs must first be set in forward motion before the turning controls are applied. If this is not done, the turn on the haunches has no value as dressage. Its practical usefulness also suffers, since the standing horse learns to look for support in the reins when the turning controls are applied at once, with its inner hind foot turning in place and its shoulder turning out. This reduces its manœuvrability instead of improving it, one of the objectives of ordinary horsemanship.

The young horse is ready for the turn on the haunches as soon as it can carry itself in the *travers*, easily taking a few steps on the circle in this two-track exercise without impairing its gait or contact with the bit. All it then needs is instruction to acquaint it with the new demands. This is best done by walking the horse and making several half-turns with successively shorter diameters and with the hindquarters turned in.

The turn on the haunches is performed in *walked steps* from the full halt, the walk, and the trot, though no fewer than three legs must always be grounded. The centre of the turn is underneath the inner hind foot, which must not turn in place but must remain in motion like the outside foot.

To perform the turn on the haunches, we begin by halting the horse, but this must not bring it to a complete standstill (three-quarters halt). The only purpose of this halt is to interrupt motion enough for the change of direction to take place with the hind legs stepping in place, guaranteeing the required degree of collection. The two reins lead the horse, already " positioned " towards the side of the turn before the halt occurs, step by step through a quarter circle or semicircle about the hindquarters that are treading in place. The rider's inside leg, chiefly driving forward and applied just behind the girth, as called for by the longitudinal flexion, sustains the motion of the hind legs. In this it is supported by the outside leg applied behind the girth to prevent turning out. The rider's upper body, with his outside shoulder well forward, follows the direction of the turn, the action of his pelvis complementing the driving leg aids that keep the horse in contact with the bit. Hands that pull back on the rein repress the elasticity of the hindquarters and throw them outside the turn.

At the beginning,[61] the young horse should also be allowed to step forward somewhat during the turn. What is essential is that the increased burden be willingly borne by the springy hindquarters and the horse remain responsive to the controls; it should make the turn smoothly though highly relaxed, without turning towards the inside and with the relieved forehand in contact with the bit. After the turn is complete, the position is changed in the riding hall unless the rider intends to put the horse through a counter-lesson.

If the timing of the gait, the carriage, and the loading on all four legs are better after the turn than before, the suppled hindquarters have been made more active by the turn. This proves that the turn was executed correctly, thus promoting the gymnastics of the haunches.

Analogously, the same controls are used for the turn on the haunches at the gallop, and for the quarter, half, and whole pirouettes, which are part of the secondary field school and the *haute école*. In the whole pirouette four to six equal gallop leaps are used to turn the horse about the outside hind leg, which is flexed more than the other and carries more of the load, besides taking the full initial load alone at each leap.

During all turns on the haunches the horse must respond to the controls in such a way that the rider is always able to interrupt the lateral movement and convert it smoothly and without hesitation into motion straight ahead.

If they have done preparatory dismounted work and have understood the unusual and not entirely natural co-ordination of trunk and leg movements required for stepping back with their legs, most horses will comply with a rider's demand and take a few steps backward, more or less straight, with feet dragging along the ground, provided the rider uses a relieving seat and employs the careful action of his hands placed low.

We who can effect displacement in close quarters by single or double turns on the forehand with our young horses will carefully avoid beginning backward motion—*backing*—as a gymnastic, collecting exercise before the horse has become fully responsive at the full halt. Restraining controls are stronger in backing than at the halt, backing being merely a continuation of the halt to the rear. Consequently the figure can be exercised to advantage only after the horse has attained so high a degree of responsiveness (including response to the forward-driving controls) that its constant readiness to move forward unconditionally is felt during the backward motion, while the rider's pelvis and leg can absorb every individual step at will.

[61] This stepping forward is a highly welcome imperfection (animation).

It is certain that the horse learns an entire pattern of tricks, dodges, and artifices (in fact, its attention is directly called to these tricks) by premature exercise of the backward step. It can easily use this step to escape the incomplete controls that summon it to perform movements that contradict its natural locomotion machinery.

The beneficial effect of backing upon the carriage and collection of a properly prepared and strengthened horse is quite different. Then it is no longer a backward creep, with front legs dragging along the ground because they carry a load and the hocks lifted high with the haunches stiff. Rather is it a schooling exercise, with the haunches bent at their major joints and the body of the horse, stretching out to the seat and reins from a lowered hindquarters and elastic back, tensed like a spring, ready to resume forward motion smoothly and fluently with unchanged posture at the whisper of a command and without the rider's having to bend his upper body back and forth. The latter condition is the test of whether the "rocker", the alternating stepping forward and back demanded in the Olympic tests, is successful.

Considered as a gait, backing is a recognizable diagonal, two-beat movement like the trot. But since there is no phase of suspension, the backward steps can never be of full length. The hind foot on one side steps backward only after the forefoot on that same side has alighted, so that the former has no time to make way for the latter hoof.

To back, the rider applies the same weight and leg controls to the horse, which is collected and in hand, that he uses to start forward motion, though the moment one hind leg leaves the ground the reins act as enough of a restraining force to make that leg and the diagonal front leg step backward rather than forward. As soon as that happens the reins must relax somewhat. This is repeated until the horse has taken the number of steps previously determined by the rider. Depending upon the degree of relaxation of the hands, an increase in the forward thrust of the pelvis must produce an immediate stop or a fluent forward motion that is not interrupted by any juxtaposition of the legs. The rider's upper body should be able to remain vertical.

A retracted forehand must not appear to be pushing back the hindquarters. When they are engaged correctly, they carry the forehand backward with the co-operation of the muscles of the back and neck. The bent hind leg lifts the corresponding diagonal foreleg.

The impression conveyed to an observer must be that the horse is going forward while backing.

Broadened steps of the hind legs, turning out to one side, creeping backward, and hurrying (the rider feeling that his seat is no longer filled out, as the horse's loins have grown thinner), weaving of the head, or raising or lowering it—all are symptoms indicating that the horse does not respond fully to the controls during backing or that the controls were falsely applied.

Like the full halt (though even more so), backing proves that previous training has made the hindquarters supple and flexible and that they are ready to accept an increased load at any time. The fluent execution of this exercise, controlled by the rider step by step, is also an infallible test of the harmony of the driving and restraining controls.

An increased degree of collection can be achieved only when the suppleness and carrying capacity of the hindquarters allow the rider to place a heavier burden upon them.

With normal development of the horse, such increased demands may perhaps be made during the second year of training or still later.

Collection is outwardly manifested by particularly vigorous, expressive, and positive strides coming from a lowered hindquarters and an elastic back, with the neck extended forward and upward. Let us now briefly review how it arises. This will also give us a chronological review of the work already done and still to be done with our young horse. This survey is needed because we have not always been able to discuss the individual exercises in their strictly chronological order. Some figures had to be explained to a degree of perfection that the young horse could not have achieved at that stage of training.

If *collection* is defined not merely as the bodily state in which the horse is best and most easily able to comply with the schooling requirements of its rider, it *signifies, when applied to all the branches of horsemanship, increased attentiveness and a readiness of execution that best corresponds to the particular object in view.*

In this sense collection is a relative term, comprising the readiness of the race horse at the start as well as that of the manège horse, flexing the springs of its hindquarters in the *levade* for the most difficult manège leap, the capriole. In both cases it involves the horse's positive control of its own body, as manifested by the fact that the time between command and execution of a movement is as brief as possible. The length of this "reaction time" will depend upon the precision of the controls, which do not assault the horse and confuse it but are clearly understood by it, upon the controlled activity of the trained nerves that command the movement, and upon the training and the strength of the muscles and their ability to execute what is required appropriately.

The best way of approaching the *origin and nature of collection* as it is sought for in the dressage meaning of the term—gymnastic training chiefly in the covered riding hall in contrast to education and familiarization—is to trace the evolution of these natural gymnastics. This will be followed by a summary of what the horse still would have to learn to achieve complete dressage, which is really the specialized area of the secondary field school.

When the young horse no longer resists the unaccustomed load by cramped tensions, it will swing along freely in its natural posture, in natural balance, and in pure but expressionless timing, its muscles pulsating regularly but without energy.

The dragging hind legs produce no more thrust than is absolutely necessary to maintain uniform motion. They share the common burden only slightly.

When the rider's leg begins to drive the horse forward actively after this initial stage of unconstraint, making its hind legs push off more forcefully and therefore also engage farther forward, the rhythm of the muscles will become more pronounced and more energetic, flexing and relaxing in time with the movement. One result of this and of the traction of the neck muscles that maintain the back in its correct arch is the extension of the entire spinal column from croup to poll. The horse stretches forward to reach the bit and fills out the rider's seat. Now the seat carefully burdens the hind legs brought forward by the rider's leg, in order to bend them and drive them forward, thus making them stretch even more energetically and leave the ground with even more spring.

This state, which we call suppleness, already contains the initial elements of collection, for the equestrian poise manifested in this extension requires that the hind legs make their contribution by bearing a larger share of the load. To do this their steps must become longer, livelier, and more elastic, and they must pass by each other much more closely. In a word, their steps must manifest impulsion.

The extension of the horse's spinal column and its stretching out to reach the bit (caused by the elastic flexing and relaxing of the motor muscles, with the hands now accepting and passively sustaining the weight placed on them) changes the hitherto " loose " posture. The horse comes to the bit and accepts it, the forehand growing out of the withers, because part of its excess load has been relieved by the co-operation of the hind-quarters and the back. Thus it advances with *relative lift* and with increased freedom of the shoulders.

Once this vigorous step is assured in a state of suppleness, the rider can begin to employ his forward-driving seat control to collect his horse, driving with the small of his back, passively sustaining with his hands the increased impulsion that the seat has contributed to them and—after the resultant yielding of the horse—making sure that this impulsion persists and can be converted into engagement and collection.

The line from hand to mouth has grown shorter as a result of the lifting of the neck and the yielding of the cervical spinal column, a condition that the rider must allow for by shortening the reins. The reins are basically passive, that is, they sustain what is laid upon them with unchanging pressure, always governed by the idea of yielding somewhat rather than exerting a backward pull. They must act only in brief accepting pulls whenever the horse wishes to abandon the engagement of the hindquarters acquired in this initial stage of collection, thus relieving the hindquarters of load at the expense of the forehand.

These backward pulls, which are sometimes needed, must cease as soon as they have achieved their aim; the forehand growing lighter while the hindquarters willingly resume their burden. If the rider's hands stick fast instead, the horse will unfailingly reply by employing a faulty gait; shortening the steps of the hind legs. Similarly the hind legs will hurry and take shorter strides if the rider's legs ruthlessly continue to drive during the brief tugs on the reins, mentioned above, as the horse will obtain relief from this position of constraint by shortening its steps.

Once these pulls have taken effect, the rider's legs cling gently to the horse's body, waiting to go into action whenever the hindquarters endeavour to evade energetic engagement and the stretching and bending involved by remaining behind. The rider's legs do this in concert with his weight, which follows the movement of the horse in the normal seat when there is no occasion to drive it forward.

The upper body of the rider, which is somewhat behind the horizontal when the horse is driven forward more intensively, should not remain in that position once the horse has obeyed any more than the reins should remain fixed. This continuing increased burden would interfere with the free activity of the back and result in stiffening the overloaded hindquarters or dragging. The gait defects would again be manifested in boring on the bit or uncertain contact with it.

But *maintaining collection* will require the rider's unflagging attention even if he makes no mistakes in his controls. Once the hands get the feeling that chewing has stopped, that the mouth is dead, action and impulsion have diminished. It is then the job of the rider's leg to make the horse's machinery fresh and vigorous again.

If the horse becomes violent and hurries, boring on the bit, the hands, sustaining the motion elastically or rejecting any excess by means of brief tugs on the reins, if necessary, must adjust gait and timing with the support of the small of the rider's back. They must make the hind legs, which again engage flexibly and smoothly, bear their proper share of the load unresistingly.

Dressage collection may be recognized by the expressive, positive, and nearly inaudible steps and by lowering of the hindquarters, which place more of the load on the springy hind legs in order to throw them forward and upward. The resultant lifting of the forehand is a consequence of its relief, owing to the increased engagement of the haunches and the extension of the muscles of the back and neck.

In this true engagement of the haunches the centre of gravity automatically shifts to the rear, so that the objective of engagement—support in the direction of the plumb line through the centre of gravity—is achieved with shorter steps.

The rider feels the evidence of collection unmistakably, just as the observer sees and hears it.

The supple play of the back muscles pulls the rider down into the saddle in the rhythm of the movement, so to speak, so that his buttocks and legs cling effortlessly. The entire horse is in such contact with the *rider's* elastic pelvis and legs that they can make its steps flatter and longer and give the neck a freer shape.

Responsiveness and freedom from constraint are now associated with the energy of impulsion, which places the horse in physical readiness (carriage) and psychological readiness (attentiveness).

In this state every command to change rate, direction, and carriage or to interrupt the movement—to come to a stop—is obeyed at once.

Depending upon its conformation and natural endowment, the ability of every horse to achieve collection should be developed with this ideal form in mind, to enable it to unite all the elements producing *collection in dressage posture* to the maximum extent in very brief exercises.

It will be easy for a horse that has obtained such a degree of gymnastic training in its dressage posture to maintain its acquired poise in *ordinary posture, which should be the standard in the riding hall*, its steps vigorous and long, coming from the active back in a freer and extended framework, thus sparing itself and the rider even in endurance runs.

Logically speaking, collection in dressage posture must be founded upon collection in the freer ordinary posture, which makes fewer demands on energetic impulsion of the gait and ability to carry a load.

On the other hand, temporarily increasing collection in ordinary posture to collection in dressage posture is needed as training proceeds to keep the horse in the easier form (ordinary posture) which guarantees the full development of the horse's power in practical use under control of the rider, especially in endurance runs.

Because of the differing endowments of horses and their conformation, usually far from the ideal form, the ordinary and dressage postures attainable for any given horse will always remain relative, as they will involve different degrees of collection in each case. The equestrian poise readily displayed by a balanced horse in the freer framework of its ordinary posture may represent the maximum in dressage posture for another horse less favoured by nature.

Certain peak achievements in long-distance rides have been achieved with horses running in their natural posture with very long reins under the lightest of weights, though the horse's health and strength left after the ride seem to have been ignored. But in ordinary use repeated endurance runs are feasible only at a certain degree of dressage which guarantees a certain amount of collection and with it an increased load upon the hindquarters and vigorous activity of the back.

As we have noticed in discussing the various exercises, the horse must have a certain prior ability to become collected in order that these exercises can improve and increase collection. If we try to teach the horse a lesson without first having collected it, the lesson will always be defective, besides being a source of faults such as stiffness, bends, and other evasions which would otherwise never have entered the horse's mind.

Once our young horse has acquired the necessary suppleness of the hindquarters' joints as a result of full halts and backing, we begin to try to make the shortened trot that we have developed from the working trot more expressive and loftier. Frequent transitions from the middle trot to a shortened rate, and vice versa, will increase the springiness of the hindquarters. This alternation between stretching in a somewhat lengthened framework and bending in greater collection will increase the impulsion and carrying capacity of the hindquarters so much that *the shortened trot will turn into the collected trot.*

No matter how lofty the horse's steps, their freshness and liveliness must remain unchanged in the collected trot to prevent any hovering (see p. 131).

The collected trot should be ridden only for short stretches and always alternated with freer gaits.

If the steps grow flat and lose expressiveness, the activity of the back and contact with the bit should first be adjusted by gait-improving forward riding, that is, riding the horse up to the bit. This will restore the lost gait automatically.[62]

If the horse leans on the bit at the collected trot, light tugs on the reins, as described above when discussing collection, followed by stimulating the hind legs, will restore correct posture.

When the horse passes from the full halt or the walk to the trot, the very first steps must be long, expressive, pure trotting steps, corresponding

[62] The more the horse is " made ", the better impulsion is preserved when the rate is shortened. Impulsion is necessarily extinguished in a raw, untrained horse, no matter how well-endowed, for engagement of the haunches and the resulting elasticity and suppleness are not yet present.

34.   Crouching, with the horse failing to follow the parabola of the jump and tightening its back downward. Major A. Mettler on *Exile* (Irish). (Compare with picture 31).

35.   The eyes of the horse, not interfered with by its rider, are already fixed on the next obstacle. William Steinkraus on *Magnify* 1954.

36. Resolutely yielding from the shoulders and elbows; the very short reins are therefore quite "fitting." The equally short stirrups promote the high lift of the buttocks, but they do not rise higher than the rider's shoulders. David Kelly on *Jack-o'-Lantern* 1955. BUDD STUDIOS

37. Winning time class. The rider's will to go forward coupled with positive control is essential in winning time class. Frank Chapot on *Diamant* (Holstein) 1959. IRISH TIMES, LTD.

to the gait desired. If they are not, the horse has not been responding to the controls.

The *collected gallop* greatly improves the posture of the horse and the suppleness of its hindquarters. This gallop is developed from a walk that has gained precision and expression by having been ridden in the ordinary position and in hand for a few steps after the horse has been slowed down from a trot.

The characteristics of the collected gallop and the halts at this gait were discussed in connection with galloping. Let us repeat for the sake of emphasis that what matters in collecting the gallop is not shortening the steps as such. The chief underlying principle in this work of collection must be maintenance of vigorous freshness, liveliness, and cleanness of the stride, with even loading on all four legs.

If the horse's hind legs stride instead of leap, the collected gallop turns into the so-called four-beat gait, an indication that the back is not properly co-ordinated with the hindquarters. The horse may be thoroughly ruined for the medium gait if it is allowed to travel at a four-beat *gathered gallop* without correcting this serious basic fault by departing immediately at a free gallop, which compels it to leap again at a vigorous three-beat gait. *Listless, dragging gaits, with lifeless haunches, violate the spirit of horsemanship.*

If the hindquarters engage pliantly, and the back is yielding and active, the rider will be carried along gently and evenly as if he were sitting in a motor-car, not only at the collected gallop but also at the freer gallop.

If the hindquarters fly upward when the hind legs leave the ground, so that the rider has to bend forward involuntarily with his upper body at every gallop leap, they are not yet fully loosened, but stiff in their principal joints.

This fault cannot be corrected by increasing seat control at the collected gait. The horse would defend itself against such attempted correction by increasing its stiffness and becoming crooked.

Smooth and gentle gallop departs for a short distance from a more positive *ordinary walk in hand,* followed by a halt after a few leaps before the haunches have had time to stiffen, will make the tendency towards this fault disappear, and the hindquarters will become more flexible. Stiffness of the haunches occurs very rapidly if the gallops are prolonged for too long a time, and the horse grows accustomed to gallop in the manner that is more comfortable for it, with haunches unengaged.

Once posture at the collected gallop has been firmly established by frequent gallop departs at this gait from the walk, the transition may be made from the medium gallop to the collected gait.

About this time we should let our horse traverse the corners, rounded off into arcs of a circle, at a slower *counter gallop*.[63]   In this exercise we must pay particular attention to maintaining the purity and smoothness of the strides and to distributing our weight correctly so as to follow the movement while disturbing the horse's back as little as possible.

The easiest way of changing to the counter gallop is to make a close half turn at the second corner of the long side of the hall without changing leads.

Once the horse knows that it should not change leads, the slight *renvers* position in the corners allowed it at the start must be eliminated, the horse being evenly loaded on a single track in proper " position ".

The counter gallop becomes especially valuable when the horse's shoulders are carefully guided, the forehand always being turned towards the wall ahead of the inside hind foot.   The inside hind leg near the wall can be better controlled and supervised in the false gallop than in the corresponding simple gallop.   This will naturally have a favourable effect on the activity of the outside hind foot and thus improve the horse's entire posture.

If the horse's steps are slower at the gallop left, say, than at the gallop right, it indicates that the two sides of its body are not equally developed. This defective lateral responsiveness can only be corrected at the freer gaits, which allow the horse to stretch again, followed by the simple lessons and counter-lessons on two tracks.

If the horse itself slows down when doing such figures as voltes, the steps becoming restrained and prancing, it indicates that impulsion is decreasing because the rider is no longer able to keep the hindquarters active in the closer turns.   When that happens, it is better not to try to re-establish vigorous and elastic steps in the lesson in question, which is already fairly difficult.   The rider will be more successful if he inserts vigorous transitions from the working gallop to the medium gallop, and vice versa, on a circle of large diameter until the horse has regained its impulsion.

Such a "conference" with the horse on the circle, the spur being employed for lazy disposition and stolidity, will restore the suppleness of the hind legs.   This can be tested by resuming the figure that caused the initial difficulty.   This should be enough for the day, so that the horse

---

[63] The best way of acquainting the horse with the false gallop for the first time is to ride very flat serpentines without change of leads on as large an exercise ground as possible.   The rider whose seat is soft and supple will regard any fault that may occur, such as change of lead or crossing, with sovereign composure.   Changing to a circle of large diameter, he lets the horse rediscover the original gallop itself.

Any sort of punishment for change of lead or, for that matter, even a rough slowing down before the next gallop depart would have disastrous results later on when teaching the flying change of lead, because it would establish a prejudice against changes of lead that would be very hard to eradicate.

can be returned to the stable with a pleasing impression after receiving its merited rewards.

We might add that, as our assurance at the gallop increases, we should get away from the wall from time to time and gallop without that imaginary support so as to accustom ourselves and the horse to precise even loading on all four legs.

It sometimes happens that an otherwise eager and animated horse suddenly loses its taste for its work and becomes listless and lifeless after making fairly regular progress for months.

We must look for the cause, which may be the development of some internal disorder, over-exertion, or shedding of hair. A change of feed and very careful observation, especially in the stable, are called for. If the rider believes the cause is excessive fatigue, interrupting work in the riding hall and allowing the horse to loaf in the open field may refresh its spirit in a surprisingly short time, so that a few capers and springy steps will reassure us concerning its psychological and physical condition. But if the melancholy and lack of interest persist despite our lessened demands upon the horse, it is best to call in a practical veterinarian who is also an experienced rider.[64]

There are horses, to be sure, that do their best only under the threat of the spur, because of their innate laziness and stolidity; only when spurred are they ready to move forward with energy.

Such horses have assumed an apparently complaisant attitude, but in reality they are not in hand; they hesitate and delay at every opportunity. Horses of this sort, which are well developed physically and could easily do what is asked of them but do not want to, and always carry a reserve of tension and refractoriness around with them, must be awakened quite energetically. They must be taught the ABCs all over again and unmistakably reminded of the dogma "leg means forward", with no ifs or buts. The following method has proved useful: Place the hands on the withers, with long reins, then apply a couple of energetic spurs, and shoot forward mercilessly. This is followed by a careful halt, without hurting the back or mouth. Only after the horse has learned the lesson of starting, a lesson that must be repeated whenever laziness set in again, can we resume exercises to remind the horse that "leg may also mean collection", with the reins playing their part.

Some older, knowing manège horses that are capable of much more than they wish to display require similar sharp warnings if an inexperi-

[64] Microscopic examination of the dung for worm eggs often explains previously inexplicable depressions in a young horse.

If the horse displays general fatigue of the legs (dull and inelastic gait), on the other hand, the experienced horseman will prescribe a return to nature for several weeks or months, depending upon the circumstances.

enced rider is not to break his heart trying to get them to perform.

Details of defects of disposition, character, and conformation are to be found in the section devoted to this subject (p. 247ff.). In general it may be said that we still have no standard disposition, despite all the efforts of the breeders who have been so successful otherwise. Moreover not all riders would be served by such standardization. *It is up to training to make the lazy horse industrious and the violent horse lazier, so that both extremes become workable and convenient in use.*

Once the carriage of the horse at the false gallop presents no difficulties, we can start exercising the simple change of lead at the gallop. To do this the rider changes to the walk, changes his seat and the horse's position, and departs at the gallop on the other lead after a few steps, depending upon the dexterity of the horse. This important transition, the smooth and fluent execution of which is a prerequisite for the flying change of lead that is an exercise of the secondary field school, can be readily performed at the stage of training now attained by our horse.

Animated horses of good conformation can be trained for the flying change of lead even earlier. They rapidly grow accustomed to the controls that restrain one side and invite the other to advance, soon meeting their riders half-way by changes of lead that are apparently faultless. We still believe, however, that a horse called upon to perform the flying change of lead only when it is completely responsive and in hand will be able to overcome the subsequent difficulties of several flying changes of lead in succession much more easily than a "prodigy", which has grown accustomed to idiosyncrasies and distortions because of changes of lead that were premature and hence not sufficiently precise.

We have deliberately delayed discussion of the walk until now because real workouts at the walk, using the collected gait, could not be done earlier.

The free walk with surrendered reins has been exercised ever since the first day the horse was mounted. Sometimes it was turned into a free walk with relaxed reins.[65] If the sequence of steps remained uniform and long-striding, we then tried for a temporary slight contact with the bit. This contact with the bit was automatically established when the young horse was halted after trotting. The faster gait's impulsion and posture kept the young horse in hand, with the rider's legs in supple contact. But we required this initial gathering at the walk for no more than very short stretches so as not to disturb the free and easy regular advance. We immediately gave the horse full freedom of the reins whenever its strides grew shorter and hastier.

[65] See the table of basic gaits, p. 323.

As posture and flexibility improved at the trot and the gallop, a some-what more positive bit contact, with shortened reins, developed auto-matically in these walking lessons after about a year's training. The horse's hind feet advanced more or less beyond the hoofprints of the fore-legs depending upon its natural locomotion machinery. This was the *ordinary walk*, a free walk under control, developed in free and uncon-strained equestrian poise from the walk with relaxed and surrendered reins.

If we proceeded moderately to secure this initial equestrian poise at the walk, we will now be able to gather this gait by means of *work at the* walk, properly speaking, as the last gait after the trot and the gallop.

Producing collection at the walk is no doubt one of the most difficult jobs a rider is called upon to do. We often see the so-called " well-made " horses, even those that have won high prizes in dressage tests, committing more basic faults at the walk than at any other gait.

A brief summary of some of the mistakes made by a rider in work at the walk will explain the numerous faults committed by the horse at this gait. All riders, except those possessing an enviable knowledge and ability, naturally tend to give the hands precedence when combining various controls. This is most serious in exercises at the walk. That is why the hands must be supervised with more rigorous self-discipline—to prevent them from interfering with the interplay of the horse's muscles—at the walk than at the other gaits, where mistakes of control are partly balanced out by impulsion. And many riders whose ambition is out of all propor-tion to their ability and who are incapable of shaping their horses to the bit from the croup forward to the mouth at the trot and gallop endeavour to do so at the walk, where there is least resistance to the hands.

The collected walk will also be defective because it is often ridden with the horse gathered for too long a time. Then the horse is not afforded an opportunity of stretching and relaxing at intervals in a free walk.

The *free walk* must always be controlled by the rider's driving legs, no matter whether it is ridden in its most extended form with relaxed or surrendered reins or as an ordinary walk. The extent of this supervisory action of the rider's legs must be carefully adapted to the peculiarities of the horse in question.

Violent, nervous horses, whose steps are short, hasty, or impure because of restlessness, must rediscover the calm and relaxation of free, ground-covering steps with a pliantly clinging rider's leg that drives them forward whenever necessary.[66]

Lazy and dissimulating horses are best stimulated to take lively steps by brief, alternating taps of the rider's legs in time with the gait. The riding

[66] See the passage on pushing leg control taking the place of brief pressure in " Seat and Controls " (pp. 63-64).

crop can reinforce this action when applied just behind the leg at the same moment.

But this stimulation must not be allowed to become a continuous alternating tapping of the legs on either side or a simultaneous tapping of both legs at once. Aside from the fact that the latter action disturbs the gait, any continuing leg control makes the horse dull, insensitive, and unresponsive to the leg. If this stimulation is insufficient, brief energetic pressure on one side or both, combined with use of the riding crop, must teach the horse to respect the driving leg control, so that in the future increased bracing of the small of the back and the threat of the calf muscles, tensed by the increased extension of the rider's legs, will suffice to keep the gait fluent.

The notion that at the walk the timing must be the same for all rates, as it is at the trot and the gallop, is largely responsible for the fact that some dressage horses walk with a hasty, broken, and hurried step, which has as much in common with active walking as cramped gnashing of the teeth has with correct chewing.

This general principle holds good for the collected walk of a well-trained horse, which walks smoothly with haunches that have been rendered completely supple. Following it blindly, however, may become dangerous if too much is demanded at the beginning of work at the collected walk. The horse would defend itself against the twofold requirement that it take lofty as well as very lively steps more successfully here than at the other gaits, in which impulsion and the briefer contact of the legs with the ground come to our assistance. It would take refuge in the hasty steps mentioned above, which often stiffen into a pace-like sequence.

Though soft hands have been mentioned so often, we must also mention softness of the rider's legs, which should be their normal state. Rough, sudden, and kicking leg actions should be avoided, especially at the collected walk. They cause disorder in the uniform phase sequence and produce stiffness of the hindquarters and back, thus interrupting the interplay of forehand and hindquarters, which in turn is manifested in nappy steps.

If movement grows hasty, a slight half halt with legs clinging to the horse's body (which is much harder to do in practice than it is to say) will first have to re-establish the pure four-beat sequence of steps. Only then can the rider's pushing legs endeavour to secure somewhat livelier steps, gradually and without surprising the horse, which is only too ready to react to impulsive action by tensing and tightening up.

As we know, the walk is the gait that is least improved by art (gymnastic training in the riding hall) or education (training on long lines and in broken country). The ability to take long steps at a free walk and to take lofty steps at the collected walk is largely a function of joint action and hence is inborn. It can be improved only up to a certain maximum by making the hindquarters and back more active, especially since we cannot employ the same development of impulsion that aids trotting and galloping so very much when training the horse at the walk.

But if bad conformation does not hamper us in developing this gait, the walk of a well-made horse affords us the possibility of riding an entire sequence of gaits—from the extended walk to the manège walk. This sequence is enough to demonstrate the responsiveness of the horse without trotting or making a single gallop stride.

We should not flatter ourselves that endlessly riding at a free walk with surrendered reins can ever improve that gait beyond a certain length of step, attainable by exercise, or that we can develop the *extended walk* in this manner.

This type of free walk raised to its highest form is by no means the result of letting the horse move rapidly; rather it requires thorough preparation and training. A hasty step is far from an active step or a long one. The latter must come from the hindquarters and will act correctly only when the back, neck, and cervical vertebrae are loosened by equestrian action.

This means that the extended walk is the result and fruit of previous engagement of the haunches, from which it must be "ridden out" in the truest sense of the word. *It can never be achieved by eternally toying with the surrendered reins.*

We will spare ourselves much disappointment if we reject a horse with a naturally bad walk, either for everyday use or for the special training of the dressage horse. The dressage horses that have grown famous in spite of this faulty basic gait can be counted on the fingers of one hand. What is more, these few exceptions that confirm the rule were trained by masters of the art.

The following are some of the lessons to be derived from the preceding discussion:

1. The hands should be used with even more discretion and self-restraint at the walk, if possible, than at the other gaits.
2. Never try to "shape" the muscles at the walk. After months of correct training at the trot and gallop, the horse will come to the bit by itself in more positive contact even at the walk. This means that one should not try for collection but should test again and again whether the horse is ready to stretch forward to reach the bit by frequently relaxing the reins and letting the horse chew on the bit.

3. Exercise the horse for short distances not only at the beginning of work at the collected walk but later on as well.

4. Do not give over-eager horses any opportunity to free themselves from leg control. If the rider's legs remain calm and in gentle contact, such horses calm down most quickly. They then find a more relaxed, clear, even, four-beat timing *at* the rider's legs, which they should respect, not fear or run away from.[67]

5. Do not expect to obtain the same lively timing in the phase sequence of the collected walk as in the freer types of walk. If the horse is in hand, and the sequence of steps is clean, we may be satisfied for the time being and wait for liveliness of phase sequence to improve as the haunches grow more flexible. If we were to try for this liveliness at the expense of purity of phase sequence, we would encourage the development of a serious fundamental fault in order to eliminate a temporary defect.

In conclusion, here is a brief *summary of the types of walk* as they appear to an observer (also see the table, p. 323).

The free walk with surrendered reins, with relaxed reins, and later on, with long reins is the type of walk used for the young horse during the first twelve months of its training. Its posture at that walk is a natural one, with the freedom of its neck practically unlimited. Its steps are regular, free, and vigorous, but they must be relaxed enough for the length of stride not to be shortened for the sake of excessive liveliness, with the hind feet advancing beyond the tracks of the forefeet.

In the course of exercise this develops into a second form of the free walk, the *ordinary walk*. In this walk contact with the bit has grown more positive, as the driving controls cause the horse to come forward to the bit by itself without any action of the reins. The active but quiet steps have grown more definite. The forward reach of the hind legs needs advance only slightly ahead of the tracks of the front hoofs because of the equestrian poise already achieved and the slight displacement of the centre of gravity towards the hindquarters. The neck, which was originally extended forward or forward and downward, stretches freely forward and upward as the hindquarters begin to take over the load.

The *collected walk* is developed from the ordinary walk as training progresses.

---

[67] The following is a general principle governing the work of the legs: Like the hands, the legs should begin with the gentlest indications, which by no means exclude positiveness and definiteness, when one rides an unknown horse for the first time. Start out with the assumption that the horse is receptive to finely graduated controls. That is, speak to it like a " gentleman " in the control language and endeavour to secure contact with it. One can always become energetic and emphatic later on; one must if the horse proves to be stolid or malicious.

The hindquarters are lowered in accordance with their increased engagement and the resultant narrowing of the angle of the hindquarters' joints. The relieved forehand steps out higher, and the neck rises upward almost vertically from the withers as it is extended. The driving action of the rider passes through the active back and the supple poll unhindered into the chewing mouth, where it is converted into correct head carriage by the gently supporting reins. The centre of gravity is displaced towards the rear, and all it now requires for firm support is a relatively pronounced engagement of the bent hind legs, so that their hoofprints alight behind the hoofprints of the forelegs.

Contact with the bit is positive but soft and elastic. The sequence of steps must remain that of the walk. In horses that are not completely trained, the observer's attention should be concentrated chiefly upon the uniformity of the elevated steps and then upon the animation of the movements. As the suppleness of the hindquarters increases, these movements will automatically obtain the action and timing of the other types of the walk.

At the collected walk the entire horse should give the impression of light mobility and inner liveliness. The physical and mental *readiness*, characteristic of the state of collection, technically *requires a shortened and narrowed base of support*. For mobility and manœuvrability in all directions are increased as a result of collection, because the forehand and hindquarters come closer together on the longitudinal axis, and the two hind legs come closer together on the transverse axis.

Once the horse has achieved the same lively timing in a pure four-beat gait as at the other type of walk, with its hindquarters lowered, all its joints loosened and flexed and its steps elevated, we have the manège walk. The hind legs swing off energetically, and the highly erect, steady neck stretches to come forward to the bit in certain and positive contact despite all gentleness. If we substitute the term " two-beat " for the term " four-beat " in the foregoing description, we have described the manège trot.

The third variety of the free walk, the *extended walk*, evolves out of the two preceding stages of the free walk described above and out of the increased ability of the hindquarters to engage, developed from exercise at the collected walk, which also must result in increased ability to extend.

The long steps from the haunches, loosened by flexion exercise, must be limited only by the horse's conformation and the regularity and purity of its steps, the hind feet alighting far ahead of the tracks of the forefeet. The horse must seek contact with the bit in free, natural carriage, its neck stretched forward and its nose seeking the hand, so to speak.

If the eagerness and action of the steps, covering as much ground as possible, turn into precipitate hurrying, if the tail does not swing *evenly* to both sides, in time with the gait, or if the horse in passing to the extended walk chews on the yielding bit tossing its head or produces jarring shocks downward, or if the expression of the horse's head is tortured and discontented, we know that the preceding work was done under constraint and was therefore defective and that the horse is not really loosened and compliant in all its muscles and joints.

IV. Leading With the Curb Bit and Mistakes to be Avoided

A. EVOLUTION OF LEVER-ACTING BITS FROM ANTIQUITY TO THE PRESENT

Excavations in what used to be called Pannonia, Noricum, and Gaul (Hungary, Austria, and France to-day) have brought to light curb-like bits as well as Byzantine coins, thus proving that bits of this type were in use in the late Roman Empire. If we are to believe Virgil (*Georgics*, III), the Lapithae used the curb bit, which they had invented as well as the figures of the *haute école*, long before the Sybarites and Thracian Cardiates of the sixth century. This is also attested by Athenaeus.

We do not know whether the horses of Julian the Apostate's heavy cavalry, which had to retreat before the Alamanni in the battle of Strasbourg (A.D. 357), were bridled with curb bits. But we have no reason not to suppose that Totila, the king of the Ostrogoths, used a curb bit, when he put his war horse " through the most graceful turns of the game of war " between the two armies lined up in battle array at Taginae in A.D. 52, moving the Byzantine historian Procopius to jubilant admiration.

The mounted single combat that was the favourite sport of the Goths evolved into the tourneys of chivalry, which in turn developed into the courtly festivals and pageantry of the Renaissance with their caracoles. This required the most positive control of the often violent horses with efficient bits, for they were quite unmanœuvrable unless they had some Spanish-Oriental blood.

The Neapolitan nobleman Federico Grisone, one of the first of the old masters, listed no less than fifty curb-shaped bits in his *Riding Rules*, published in the middle of the sixteenth century. Their long lever arms[68] and fantastically turned and ribbed bars—nearly all of them broken like

---

[68] Long lever arms act more slowly than shorter ones and thus automatically comply with a requirement that should be met by controls of all kinds.

This knowledge, together with the fact that the ancients began by training their horses thoroughly with a cavesson, puts their riding with chivalric and museum-piece curb bits in a much milder light.

Pelhams, however—can only make us sincerely hope that the pupils of his riding academy held " the reins in their left hand reasonably ", as the master recommended.

The old masters did not have any trouble in bridling with the curb bit because they used the cavesson for dressage. The cavesson lay directly upon the nasal bone of the upper jaw and affected the muscles of the poll directly, with the assistance of impulsion, so that the neck muscles could not stiffen. This stiffening can always occur if the lower jaw, faultily yielding to the action of the bit, turns out to the side when the mouth-piece lies across part of the lower jaw.

There are all sorts of curb bits, most of them invented to enable riders not yet ready for the curb bit to get along somehow on fully bridled horses or to feign a stage of training that has not yet been attained by horses still unready for the curb bit. The idea underlying the design of all these bits is always a loosening up of the mouth alone, the only result being false compliance. From the standpoint of the conscientious rider who wants to improve the handiness of his horse, these instruments afford no guarantee of actual progress. He will prefer to use the snaffle bit to achieve loosening from the rear to the front via the hindquarters, back, and neck. He will employ impulsion to shape his horse until it acquires an equestrian poise that makes it ready for the lever action of the curb bit, which differs from that of the snaffle.

B. USING THE FULL BRIDLE FOR THE FIRST TIME—GETTING THE HORSE ACCUSTOMED TO THE CURB BIT

If the training of our horse has reached the point where it can assume the degree of collection corresponding to its conformation, familiarizing it with the action of the bar bit will have no harmful effects.

But if there are no compelling reasons for riding the horse fully bridled, it will always be better to recondition it on the snaffle. One reason is that many faults of posture and contact with the bit manifested when riding with a curb bit will indicate how such reconditioning should be done. Even in the Spanish Riding School of Vienna the older horses are often ridden with snaffle bits except on official occasions.

Such reconditioning is feasible only because of the action of the jointed snaffle mouthpiece, as will be explained later. This reconditioning is facilitated when the pressure exerted upon the horse's mouth by the rider's hands is not multiplied. The rider is better able to test his controls, there-fore, than when he uses the curb bit, whose lever action multiplies the force of the hands many times before it reaches the load (mouth).

At the outset, however, it will be well to retain the thicker snaffle bit employed up to now instead of the usual thin snaffle, even for the fully bridled horse.

Once the gymnastic training of the horse has achieved a very high level, so that its suppleness and impulsion ensure perfect collection, using the curb bit—especially with the snaffle released—will enable us to refine and perfect our rein controls still further, and establish a steady, elastic connection between the rider's hands and the horse's mouth, such as can be achieved only with the lever action of the curb.

Familiarizing the young horse with the curb bit will have to be done principally at the ordinary gaits, on long lines in the open air, with the curb bit completely inoperative at the start.

At these lively, long-striding gaits we will extend the horse and very gradually let it reach the bar bit, to which is attached a very long curb chain or none at all for the present.

After a few easy-going rides in the open air, with the horse becoming supple as a result of its vigorous strides in contact with the passive hands, the curb chain is attached so as produce real lever action. Then the entire course of training described above, from the stage of suppleness onward, is repeated in the riding hall with the same free carriage. Collecting controls are applied only when the young horse has trustingly accepted the unusual bridle and is positively in hand. When this procedure is followed, all the faults described below (which arise only because the horse was not ready for the curb bit or defended itself against the constraint and pain that the new sharp bridling caused it by curling up, holding back and resisting) will be avoided.

If overhasty familiarization with the curb bit has frightened the horse away from the bit, long and patient work will be required to repair the mistakes committed and to regain the forward advance, i.e., the vigorous strides and supple extension towards the bit. Here too the apparently shorter path is not the quickest way to reach our goal.

We think the best way of indicating the nature of the curb bridle and its action is to discuss some of the mistakes that can be observed every day in the use of this bridle. Discussion of these mistakes and their consequences for gait and posture will automatically tell us how to avoid such difficulties in the training of our horse.

C. HORSES THAT ARE NOT READY FOR THE CURB BIT

If all the riders who gave their horses curb bits at too early a date were to take the trouble of reflecting somewhat on the horse's structure and the bit's lever action upon its skeleton in general and upon the joints of its haunches (hip and stifle joint) in particular, there would be fewer disagreements between horse and rider. The action of a horse is refined and perfected by the use of the curb bit, owing to its more positive and steadier action upon the horse's lower jaw, which does not allow any incipient stiffness to be manifested. The horse must be prepared for this bit, however, by work on the snaffle. But false gait and false contact with the bit are manifested much more clearly when we try to use a full bridle too soon than when we work the horse with a snaffle bit. Why?

The curb bit operates as a lever, which is intended to control the load (the evenly loaded horse in a state of acquired equilibrium) from the point at which this force is applied (the rings on the branches of the bit) through the neck, the spinal column, the pelvis, the haunches, and the hocks to the pastern joints. This force can be transmitted down to the tips of the hoofs of the hind legs without hindrance, however, only if the horse is supple, i.e., if the transmission line is not interrupted, so that the force cannot escape upward, downward, to the side, or in front or be blocked anywhere.

For this first condition to be satisfied the horse must be extended to the reins and be evenly loaded, that is, its spinal column must be adapted to the straight or curved line that it is following at the time. Moreover it must always be ready to assume the additional longitudinal flexion required for collection, work at the gallop, and work on two tracks.

The second condition is satisfied if prior work with the snaffle has already established an equestrian balance that provides the horse with such posture that the lever force of the branch of the curb bit is not blocked in the region of the pelvis but passes on to the haunches, which have been rendered able to carry the load and to bend as a result of flexion work. The haunches, reaching forward towards the centre of gravity ahead of the vertical line from hip joint to hoof, cannot resist the force, which is thus able to place a load on all the joints of the hindquarters.

The horse is ready for the curb bit if the foregoing two conditions are satisfied, but they can be satisfied only if the horse moves forward resolutely and vigorously, in steady contact with the bit and positively obedient.

The horse is not ready for the bit, however, if it opposes the lever action by active or passive resistance.

This recalcitrance is always due to faulty preparation, if we except feelings of pain produced by poorly fitting, wrong mounted curb bits[69]

---

[69] If the bar mouthpiece with its bit bars and port are not carefully fitted to the shape of the tongue and its channel, the tongue will endeavour to escape the irregular and excessively severe pressure. The horse will either lift its tongue above the bit or let it hang out to the side. This is proof that the tongue is the most sensitive part of the mouth, especially when it is large and fleshy. At any rate, it is more sensitive than the parts that are covered by the edges of the lower lip, as the horse allows the bars of the bit to lie upon them alone when it lets its tongue escape.

and curb chains and by the rider's generally defective seat and guidance. This recalcitrance will be manifested in evasion, stiffness, or distortion of the lower jaw, the neck, and the back, produced by impure, stiff, or dragging action of the hindquarters, which is always the principal source of resistance in the other parts of the horse's body. So if the horse is not one of the very, very rare specimens that combine perfect conformation and ideal harmony of weight and muscular force with a soul that wishes nothing better than to comply with the rider's desires as soon as it has understood them, we will do well to fit a curb bit only after two or more years of training, provided training began when the horse was four and a half years old.

If we do not obey this golden rule, and the reins are not in the hands of a real master but merely of someone who is self-appointed to that rank, premature use of the curb bit will merely achieve the contrary of what was intended.

The danger then arises that the gait, which was supposed to grow longer, more expressive, and nobler as a result of dressage, is lost. Contact with the bit becomes unsure and unsteady. The horse is leaning on, over, or behind the bit, for it no longer reaches forward to the bit willingly through its neck and poll.

But if it does not do so, the rider's control of its hindquarters is imperilled and obedience with it. The equestrian poise already achieved by work on the snaffle will be lost more and more, for once the hind legs no longer reach forward smoothly and fluently towards the centre of gravity, but oppose the lever action, staying behind or dragging sluggishly, the inadequately supported forehand will have to carry a greater share of the load. Then it hampers the free extension of the forelegs in equestrian balance, and the horse falls upon its shoulders in an expressionless gait.

D. RIDERS THAT ARE NOT READY FOR THE CURB BIT

We often see groups of young riders, accompanied by an instructor, taking their first cross-country rides on bridle paths and through fields in the outskirts of large cities. This picture loses something of its charm

If stretching out the tongue is not a congenital defect, checking the bit and fitting a noseband that allows enough play for the tongue to be able to regain its normal position without difficulty will gradually eliminate this vice. This requires, however, an active rider's leg with light guidance, the horse stretching to reach the bit and being allowed to chew on it, after which the tongue will return to its right place.

A horse that inveterately lets its tongue stick out will always be unreliable even under good riders and despite any number of " infallible " remedies and devices. No matter how rigorous the controls, it will entertain the judges and the public, particularly in dressage tests, with a shameless tongue shining in all the colours of the rainbow.

when we notice that some of them are riding their deserving, experienced livery horses with curb bits. Most of these ladies and gentlemen are not ready for the curb bit.

A prerequisite for learning how to ride a horse with a bar bit (a solid mouthpiece, therefore called "bar") is a supple, soft, and independent balanced seat plus the ability not only to use controls as signals but to apply them effectively.

Once the good seat has produced soft and steady hands, real "glass-of-water-fists", as Monteton calls them, which absorb all the shocks imparted by the movement in the elbow and shoulder joints, the time may be ripe for beginning to ride with the curb bit.

E. THEORETICAL KNOWLEDGE IS A FAR CRY FROM HORSEMANSHIP

We must, of course, be completely familiar with the nature, actions, and objectives of curb bits, which differ fundamentally from the snaffle. We must be familiar with the fit and position of the different parts of a curb bit and with the infinite variety in sizes of bars, ports, curb grooves, mouth angles, and the like. We must know that when we use a branched lever with the bar bearing on the lower jar and the tongue, which are directly connected to the entire nervous and muscular system, the horse feels many times the force applied by the rider's hands. We should always bear in mind this fundamental difference between the action of the curb bit and the milder action of the snaffle, in which there is a one-to-one ratio between power and load.

The second fundamental difference follows from the fact that the curb mouthpiece is not jointed, but is fixed in position by the opposing curb chain and acts upon both sides of the lower jaw at once, even though it may be made to act somewhat more strongly upon one side than the other if necessary. In this manner it flexes the joints of both hind legs.

Much can be learned from observing a master rider in order to see what contact with the curb bit looks like. The feathering of the bar should indicate that its reins are in light contact as a result of the horse's reaching for the bit, relaxed, yet vigorous and trusting.

Knowledge alone is merely a preparatory step to the conscious acquisition of practical ability, however. This takes place only when we ourselves sit in the saddle on a well-made horse and learn correct contact with the curb bit that is fitted according to regulations, for theoretical knowledge is a far cry from horsemanship.

There will always be moments when the horse will try to escape even loading on all four legs and try to render one of the curb reins inoperative by bending its body. That constitutes the best opportunity to learn in practice, under proper guidance, that uniform contact with the bit can be restored only by the corresponding reins of the bridoon,[70] since the curb bit, with its solid mouthpiece, makes no provision for purely one-sided action.

Important though it is for every horse to have a curb bit that fits and is placed so as to act correctly, let us state in conclusion that faultless riding with a curb bit depends less upon the form of the bit than upon the direction of the skeleton, which prepares the horse for accepting the bit.

It is, however, just as true that when a well-made horse of good conformation has a curb bit that does not fit it individually, it cannot move as well as when it is properly bridled.

V. Training in the Open Country and Over Obstacles by Means of Gymnastics, Education, and Habituation

A. ADVANTAGES OF CROSS-COUNTRY RIDING

The training the young horse is given in the ordinary or elementary field (cross-country) school has as its objective fitting the horse for many uses. Most horses will not go beyond the stage of training provided in this elementary field school, which requires only as much collection as is needed for the rider to control the horse's hind legs enough to achieve vigorous movement with a co-operating back and turns on the haunches—all with the reins gathered in one hand at times.

Once we have attained this objective by means of the exercises described in the preceding sections (which we have employed in a manner appropriate to the endowments of the horse), we can build upon it and develop any exceptional abilities displayed by the horse in the course of its fundamental training in order to turn it into a dressage horse or jumper.

Cross-country riding and jumping were employed as extremely valuable aids in all our previous training.

Natural dressage in the closed riding hall was regularly supplemented by riding outdoors, combined with exercises over *cavalletti* and later over obstacles, as soon as the horse began to move without constraint.

[70] If the horse has reached an advanced stage of dressage—and only on such a horse will the pupil learn how to feel correctly—the neck can be fixed and straightened out, if it should turn out, and the constrained side can be released from the tauter rein. The principal agent is the rider's leg on the same side, combined with elastic sustaining by the corresponding rein of the bridoon. (See footnote 14 on p. 122.)

Light, active pulls on the snaffle reins, alternating in time with the horse's movements, will be required to restore a horse that has thrown itself on the forehand to correct posture. But these pulls on the rein must not persist; they must cease as soon as their action has been effective.

On the one hand, cross-country rides and the shifts of the horse's centre of gravity that it must effect itself in covering rough terrain promote the flexibility of the hindquarters and the activity of the back. Thus the work in the riding hall is supplemented in a manner that is second nature to the horse. On the other hand, this easygoing sauntering in the open air, which reminds it of its early life in the pasture, rapidly gives the horse confidence in and contact with its rider. Psychological cramps, which result in tightening the body, are loosened more quickly in hour-long, easy rides through field and forest. The gait and the contact with the bit, which may become sluggish and blurry when the horse is constantly ridden around a confined rectangle, through no fault of the rider, automatically acquire impulsion and certainty on constantly changing paths in the open air. The danger of dulling the horse by having to drive it all the time disappears in the open air, where it naturally goes forward.

Riding with a great deal of neck freedom, often with the reins surrendered entirely (a feasible objective even with temperamental horses), maintains the horse's self-reliance and attentiveness and thus lays the foundations for the indispensable qualities of the hunter and jumper.

These rides, which should be taken with the young horse at least once a week, also keep it from losing its contact with the countryside and make unnecessary any subsequent "familiarization" for all sorts of uses.

If these cross-country rides are so arranged—in the company of a quiet older horse at the beginning, if possible—that motor-cars, steam rollers, railways, and other terrors are encountered only on the way home, our young horse, somewhat tired by now and no longer ready for high jinks, will get used to them. Another precaution is to let the teacher take the lead on the left the first few times the horse is taken out. If one happens to encounter a motor-car or the like when he is riding by himself, he should clearly signal the horse, without nervousness, to make a wide detour, because it will at once understand that the rider does not want to steer it right to the fear-inspiring object. Otherwise it would prepare to resist the rider by tensing its muscles in a cramped state, and an explosion occurs much more easily from such a state of tension than from trusting ease. A calm voice and hands are other important factors.

There are horses that do not mind the chaff of a thundering threshing machine that fills their nostrils, but lose their heads and grow desperate when they hear the rattle of a farm wagon behind them. With horses that are subject to such states of panic is it best to ride them on lonelier paths at first. Then the rider is able to make an about-face when a rattling wagon is heard approaching from behind in order to allow the horse to see the terror-inspiring object. At the encounter itself, the horse should be brought to a halt and fed delicacies from the saddle, accompanied by words that are always uttered in the same tone of voice. Once the association of ideas—rattle of wheel = bread—has been firmly anchored, the feeling of pleasure will predominate over the feeling of discomfort produced by the rattle even when the noise comes from the side or from behind. The rider will eventually have a hard time to prevent the horse from coming to a stop at the places where it formerly tried to bolt.

At the very beginning of this training in standing still we must try to allow the horse to stand in as unconstrained a posture as possible, with the longest possible reins, just as is done after the horse is mounted. Psychological cramps are also resolved much more easily and quickly when the horse does not have the feeling of being held tight.

These tests of disposition and character that occur naturally out in the open enable the rider to learn qualities of his horse which often are not manifested in the ordinary turns around the riding hall. Among them are tendencies to shying, nappiness, turning about, and the like. On such occasions riders who are convinced that they are in perfect control of their horse often make rather unpleasant discoveries.

Riding over rolling country is better than the flat terrain of the riding hall to teach us not to seek any new balance with the young horse, but to follow its motion so as to adapt to the balance it has chosen for itself. We must use a particularly supple seat in order to allow for the sudden changes in the centre of gravity dictated to the horse by the changes in the terrain. The action of the horse's back should be facilitated by the rider's upper body, which bends from elastic hip and knee joints to relieve it of some of the load. The rider's weight is shifted more to the inside of the thigh[71] and the fixed knee is in a low position. The elastically tensed small of the back, with the pelvis pushed forward, must always be ready to act during uphill and downhill riding, like the rider's legs, which lie just behind the girth with the heels depressed. The hands must be ready to allow the horse's neck full freedom of motion, yielding from both elbows in the direction of its mouth, since the neck takes over the role of a balancing rod in this freer posture and becomes the most important regulator of the horse's balance.[72]

[71] The buttocks must fit the saddle as if there were a thumbtack one-sixteenth of an inch high sticking out of the saddle or as if the rear end of the saddle were cut off. The upper body must not go along as a result of the buttocks being lifted out of the saddle, for contact with the saddle, which is needed in open country for unforeseen movements and which supplements balance, would then be lost.

[72] Only when the rider adapts himself to the rhythm of even the slightest movement of his horse will his seat and guidance or, putting it otherwise, his harmony, his balance, cooperate correctly. It is this that enables the horse to develop its gait and endurance to the utmost, combining the development of maximum power with the minimum of effort.

This rhythm is present from the very first day of training. No matter how the horse may move, it is manifested more or less perceptibly, depending upon the type of action. Racing and jumping riders assist the rhythm required for good performance by employing an appropriate seat. Since their buttocks are on the saddle or even above it at times, it does

This enables the horse's head and neck to do the job they are intended for by nature, harmonizing poise and movement at the free gait. Then they will become a "fifth foot" in the good sense of the term, a support in which the rider can place more confidence than in the crutch sought by a faultily moving horse—the reins. *The reins are there to maintain contact with the bit and obedience but not equilibrium.*

The support that the rider gives up in this relieving seat for the sake of freer action of the horse's back, with his buttocks no longer resting completely in the saddle, must be compensated by the support afforded by shortening the stirrups by two holes when jumping. The foot rests on the stirrup somewhat behind the widest part of the sole, the ankle is elastic, and the small of the rider's back is braced somewhat more.

Movement of the ankle is made easier when the ball of the foot rests on the stirrup, that is, somewhat farther forward, in the normal position, so that the entire width of the sole is in contact with the stirrup bar. But any endeavour to maintain this position during the shock of difficult jumps would produce stiffening of the rider's ankle. Literally placing the stirrup bar on the heel, however, interferes with the necessary mobility of the ankle and should be employed only when the horse is seriously disobedient (see p. 65).

The same groups of muscles are responsible for engagement of the haunches and for the development of thrust, which occurs chiefly when the ordinary gaits are ridden on long lines and across broken terrain. Therefore, a well-planned change from work in the riding hall to cross-country riding and vice versa, including climbing and jumping, affords the most dependable guarantee that the hindquarters, the horse's motor, will develop harmoniously (see footnote on p. 230). *Cross-country riding, which is the major objective in training the saddle horse,* thus becomes the practical application and complement of what it has learned in the riding hall.

B. LOW OBSTACLES—CLIMBING

We must prepare our young horse by work in the riding hall over *cavalletti* before we ride it over major obstacles in broken ground, such as

not matter so much whether their passive hands and arms hang on to the reins. Whenever the horse's movement requires an increased, perceptible rhythm, their buttocks rise higher on horses that are not fully trained, and the rider can never manage to disturb the horse with his unconsciously sustaining hands, for the arms move upward as well.

Although this greatest feat of horsemanship—always following the rhythm of the horse's movements, in fact, initiating and promoting it—may be achieved almost instinctively in other fields of horsemanship, the manège rider must acquire it by carefully planned, systematic exercises (riding without stirrups on a vigorously moving horse and later on—for the lucky horseman—riding on a piaffing horse).

low walls, dry, flat ditches, and the like. This teaches it to assume the "diving position" that the neck requires to overcome obstacles of all sorts, and to step and jump with a pulsating back, becoming conscious of these pulsations. *Cavalletti* are obstacles about five to seven feet wide and six to eight inches high, the crossed end pieces of which are supposed to make it impossible for them to fall. They must not be any wider or higher than the dimensions given. If they are wider, the horse cannot be compelled to follow the path exactly; if they are higher, the horse *jumps* over them instead of *stepping* over them in time, or it *fumbles*, tightening its back rather than yielding, which is just as bad.

Stepping over *cavelletti* teaches the horse to shift its centre of gravity quickly and surely, corresponding to its constantly changing balance, and thus prepares it for self-reliant travel over broken ground. Proper *cavalletti* work at the gallop also lays the foundation for correct behaviour before a jump. The neck is stretched to the "diving position" and the hindquarters reach forward to provide support.

As the horse is forced to adjust its steps at the walk and at the trot to the rigid bars, it gains considerable sure-footedness and handiness in its individual legs, because the phase sequence of its steps is made independent of the uniform sequence called for by the gait; on the other hand, it must make allowance for the necessity of providing support for its constantly shifting equilibrium and of keeping out of the way of the immovable *cavalletti* or logs.

Stretching the head and neck forward is a natural consequence of the freedom of the reins given the horse and of the correct, energetic steps of the hind legs with the resultant arched, that is, elastically pulsating, back.[73]

The stretching of the neck downward, which completes the diving position of the horse's head and neck, is a consequence of its endeavour to obtain a better view of the path to be followed over the *cavalletti*.

In all this work we must exercise strict self-discipline to keep from influencing the horse with the reins in any way. The reins must *hang*, except for directing hints at intervals, for even long reins held by the finest hands that follow all movements with the greatest sensitivity will keep the horse from letting its head and neck swing freely without psychological inhibition. The horse becomes completely free and independent, qualities which we wish to cultivate and develop, only when it feels the reins hanging loose on both sides of its neck.

Moreover in this work it is supposed to learn how to balance itself deliberately by its own efforts, without waiting for any controls or signals from the rider. The rider must lighten his weight by using the forward

[73] See "Relationship of the Rider's Weight and Controls to the Anatomical Mechanism of the Horse" (p. 259ff.).

38. The instant before landing. General Humberto Mariles winning the Prix des Nations of the 1948 Olympics on *Arete*.

39. A lady can compete successfully with the best masculine competitors in seat and control over an obstacle. Carol Gussenhoven (Mrs. David Kelly) on *Tourist Encore* (Genesee Valley).

40. Cutting across an obstacle to save time. Major John W. Russell on *Bally Bay*.

crotch seat, with the small of his back elastically braced to determine and regulate the extent to which his body follows the movements of the horse; this in turn, again, depends upon the changes in the horse's equilibrium, which occur with lightning rapidity. The rider's head is held high. His knee is the support, fulcrum, and shock absorber of the whole "rider" system. His heels are pressed so low, with elastic ankle joints, that they seem to be trying to touch the *cavalletti*. This work over the *cavalletti* offers the rider an opportunity of testing the position of his legs. Even with more experienced riders, the legs slip back when the horse's movements become irregular unless the knee's position is fixed as if it were screwed on. Or else they are thrown forward in turn with the toes pointed downward. All of these faults are doubly serious in jumping, where only the absolutely fixed, though bending, knee guarantees support and firmness for the seat and absorbs the shock produced when the horse lands.

Sliding forward and back in the saddle causes the rider to lose control of the horse, since the only way it can be driven correctly is in the normal leg position, with the heels depressed. The turned leg pinches more than it drives, and the toes, which are necessarily turned with the leg and are usually depressed, bring the spur dangerously close to the horse's side.

Work over *cavalletti* is begun and ended at the *walk*, no matter whether it is done on the lunge, with or without a rider, along a straight line, or to speed up the loosening process. This is also true of the initial familiarization of the young horse with individual bars or logs, no more than eight inches thick and fixed to the ground, which can serve as substitutes for *cavalletti*.

The *principal gait* in this training, however, *must be a vigorous working trot*: first over individual *cavalletti* and then over two or three of them spaced four to five feet apart. The spacing of the *cavalletti* depends upon the length of the stride of the horse at the working trot.

When working with *cavalletti,* the demands made upon the horse must be increased very slowly. It is especially difficult for horses with high natural muscle tone, which is characteristic of many highbred breeds. The exercise may be extended to a course of four *cavalletti* spaced five feet apart. If the horse takes additional steps between the *cavalletti*, the lesson must be made easier by diminishing the spaces.

The rider uses a *posting trot* at the beginning of *cavalletti* work at the trot in order to facilitate undisturbed oscillations of the relieved back as much as possible. Some riders would find it hard to follow the motion of the horse at the sitting trot without disturbing its back.

Cavalletti work at the gallop constitutes good preparation for work over obstacles, as the horse has to *jump* over the eight-inch bars if it is not to hit them. Hence it must assume the posture required for the higher jump as well.

The *cavalletti* are first set up individually, and then at intervals of 15½ and 36 feet, corresponding to the gallop leap.

If no gallop leap is desired between the *cavalletti*, two *cavalletti* can be spaced eight feet apart to prevent any intermediate leaps. This then becomes an excellent suppling exercise for more advanced horses.

The loosening, stretching, and free oscillation of the horse's spinal column that are developed by *cavalletti* work are advantageous as preparation for climbing—traversing slopes downhill and uphill—as well as for jumping with the rider in the saddle. *Cavalletti* should therefore be on hand wherever young horses are being trained, in the riding hall as well as in the outdoor rectangle and the cross-country training grounds.

The simple walk, trot, and gallop over *cavalletti* must be resumed whenever defects of carriage and other faults creep in during jump training, just as the ABCs of dressage training—the natural and working trot—are resorted to whenever irregularities of gait or contact with the bit develop.

We climb up slopes with our young horse at as slow a rate as possible, the rider's upper body leaning forward more or less, depending upon the gradient, the knee position fixed, and the reins completely relaxed. To begin with, we choose slopes with a slight gradient so that we can stop and let the horse graze (which calms the horse considerably) whenever it shows signs of restlessness during the climb. Long uphill stretches are taken at a zigzag in order to conserve the horse's strength.

Later on, we exercise the horse on short, steep slopes, allowing it to climb up in a series of short leaps. The work performed by the hind-quarters, back, and neck in such a climb is very considerable. We spare the horse as much effort as possible and allow it free disposition of its strength by standing in the stirrups and letting our upper body lean forward until it is parallel to the horse's neck, the hands gripping the middle of its mane or a throatstrap. The upward climb makes it impossible for us to keep our own balance or to keep in balance with the horse without seeking support in the stirrups and the horse's mane.

Downhill riding should always be done straight down the slope, for any zigzagging renders support by the horse's legs, which are unsuited to the purpose, more difficult, and results in loss of equilibrium laterally. The steeper the slope, the more this is so.[74] Basically the rider's upper

[74] Climbing paths must always have a natural appearance and blend into the surroundings. The paths often constructed artificially for this purpose, standing alone in the centre of barracks' yards and exercise grounds rather than blending into the landscape, are no good at all.

The old masters knew that climbing places the horse's instinct of self-preservation, and thus its poise, at the service of the gymnastic training. The outdoor riding grounds of the

body takes a position that is at least perpendicular to the back of the horse, that is, it leans forward more or less. The centre of gravity shifts forward, as must that of every object sliding down an inclined plane. Then it becomes stable and slides down along the shortest path. The rider's weight, shifted forward, also exerts a braking action (as in a toboggan). If the centre of gravity is too far back, equilibrium becomes unstable, but the centre of gravity may correct this fault automatically by shifting to the side, as indicated above. From the equestrian standpoint this means that the hindquarters slide off to the side, resulting in a fall. If the rider leans back, as was the practice a few decades ago, he can neither keep the guiding legs in place, with a fixed knee grip and deep heels, nor survey the road ahead. He would be riding blindfold, so to speak, and be unable to avoid holes, barbed wire, and the like, which are unfortunately often found at the foot of slopes. Moreover the saddle would slide forward to the withers.

In downhill riding the reins allow the horse to stretch and to lift or lower its neck as needed to act as a weight compensator. But they remain in contact in order to be able to prevent any departure from the desired direction, in co-operation with the legs, the heels being kept as low as in uphill riding. If the reins are not held in one hand, which finds support in the crest of the mane on steep slopes, the divided reins are kept on both sides of the neck, with the hands resting on it, even in fully bridled horses. The curb bit is rendered inoperative before downhill descent as a matter of course.

We might add that it is always a particularly good sign of the conformation and balancing ability of a saddle horse when our seat does not feel the descent of gradual slopes or is not disturbed by them.

Some authorities believe that on very steep slopes—to which we should not expose our young horse—the rider's upper body should vary in position from perpendicular to the horse's back to almost parallel to it, depending upon the gradient of the slope.

It is maintained by some that when the steepness of the slope exceeds a certain angle, the forward-leaning seat no longer makes it possible for the horse to avoid losing its balance forward and falling. Down slopes of more than 60 degrees, which are usually descended only for spectacular purposes, the rider would have to lean far backward in order to be able

sixteenth and seventeenth centuries were provided with artificial mounds called calades (from the French world *escalader*, " to scale "). Climbing up these mounds, sluggish horses developed better thrust because they had to shift their weight to their forehand, thus relieving the backhand. The activity of their backs was promoted by pronounced arching. It made them like extension forward and downward. Pacing horses automatically discovered the four-beat gait.

Going down the mound they instinctively learned how to engage their hind legs forward to provide support, how to shift their weight to the rear, and how to limit thrust.

to maintain equilibrium with his horse. Furthermore, they add, pictures of Caprilli while climbing and photographs of good riders descending steep slopes likewise prove that the only way for the rider to harmonize his own centre of gravity with that of the horse is to lean back.

We think this opinion is dictated solely by the situation prevailing in *static equilibrium*, which depends upon the relative position of the centre of gravity and the area of support. These theoreticians forget that the static equilibrium is replaced, wholly or in part, by a *dynamic equilibrium* during a slide or during motion in general, so that stability (keeping from falling) is assured even at times when the centre of gravity is not directly above the area of support (see "equilibrium", pp. 111-113).

This is true even in the case of a body sliding down an inclined plane; its centre of gravity must be well to the front, and it takes the shortest path downward, like water, in stable equilibrium.

That is why leaning back stiffly, even on steep descents, not only would interfere with the free activity of the horse's back and hindquarters, which is needed more than ever, but would also make the equilibrium of horse and rider unstable and uncertain.

The rider should therefore take descents, including those that are steeper than 60 degrees, with his body supple and leaning forward. In undisturbed harmony with his horse he should slide into the descent along with it. He should keep his thumbs crossed over the horse's crest in front of the withers. This may aid in supporting, if necessary, the upper body, and may also be useful in jumps involving drops on the far side (see p. 240).

C. JUMPING

(1.) ORIGIN OF THE CONTEMPORARY JUMPING SEAT

Until the end of the nineteenth century cavalry officers leaned backward in their saddles as they jumped their horses during hunts, regimental and army competitions, and the occasional *concours hippiques*. But jumping over high obstacles continued to be a hazard, and accidents, caused chiefly by a rider's backward-leaning seat interfering with the action of the horse's back, multiplied. These frequent falls, which incapacitated many Italian cavalry officers, led some Italian deputies to interpellate the government in the Chamber. They proposed to restrict the participation of officers in hunts and jumping contests "in order that the training and combat power of the army not suffer as a result of the large number of officers incapacitated by fractures"!

A genius in the history of horsemanship, Federico Caprilli, a lieutenant at the time, was stimulated by this public attack upon his beloved art, which had lost considerable prestige as a result of formalistic, unthinking application of traditional doctrines and of numerous contradictory " new " systems.

Caprilli saw the miserable impression all these falsely trained horses made in the hunting field, and he chose as the lesser evil a horse moving freely in more or less natural posture, subjected to no controls that contradicted the laws of motion and hampered it before, during, and after the jump.

Then he logically developed the seat designed only to enable the rider to adapt himself to the horse, the seat and his method both being called Italian. But he had to abandon any effort to control the hindquarters, to have leg and normal seat affect the activity of the horse's back, or to develop and improve the gait, all of which are part of the basic principles of our art. The suppleness of hindquarters, back, and neck that is undoubtedly developed by jumping exercises is not enough to develop these properties, which are inseparably linked with the concept of the correctly moving cavalry or saddle horse.

Though the method of training horses for riding use employed in Italy can hardly produce a dependable saddle horse that can be positively controlled in all situations and remain useful for a long time, it cannot be denied that successful jumping over obstacles is practically unthinkable to-day that without the advantages of the Italian method of jump training—the Italian style, which has been adopted by all equestrian nations.

But it is no less true that the greatest, most permanent, and most consistent successes in jumping have often been achieved on horses that were not absolutely tops in jumping ability, but were under better control by their rider, had become more manœuvrable, and allowed their rider to prescribe their rate as a result of correct riding-hall gymnastics. Anyone who thinks that jumping laurels are easily won should ask any jumping champion.

(2.) JUMPING THE YOUNG HORSE

Once the young horse has grown skilled and sure-footed as the result of work over *cavalletti*, we can begin jump training on our exercise grounds. They need not be large, but they must contain natural eminences, bits of forest, and climbing slopes, and (what is very important) opportunities for crossing small—not artificial—ditches through which water flows.

The best obstacles are small ones, solidly built, 2 to 2½ feet high. They should be narrow, naturally framed by bushes and trees or located in narrow passes and straight forest glades, and match their surroundings in material and colour so that they invite the horse rather than frighten it. They should slant in the direction of the jump and blend into the natural foliage of the surrounding ground. This is the best way of making the take-off easy.

Obstacles are provided with " wings " borrowed from the natural surroundings and are made unyielding and so narrow that the horse is not tempted to jump at an angle. They also keep the horse from hitting on the idea of running out, and train it not to expect the obstacles to yield easily, but to jump straight.

We begin by letting it inspect and sniff the new obstacles; then we trot over one obstacle or another, accompanied by a lead horse to give a good example.

After the jump the horse is allowed to slow down naturally. The rider braces his pelvis to bring it to a stop, his upper body leaning back no farther than the vertically upright position. Depending upon circumstances, the rider dismounts and lets the horse graze with a loosened girth, or while in the saddle he rewards it with dainties, letting it stand in free and easy carriage.

The approach is made at a walk, which is shifted to a trot just before the obstacle, though a very shy horse may be allowed to get over the obstacle at a walk a few times to begin with.

We choose the trot rather than the gallop because we wish to avoid all distracting complications during these first few jumps when the horse is carrying a rider. At a trot the additional difficulty of measuring its stride is automatically eliminated since the horse can always take off at this gait. At the start we jump only at the posting trot in order to interfere with the back as little as possible and to be able to follow irregular movements better. This lets the horse jump more quietly and comfortably and also diminishes the danger of the hands exerting a backward pull. During the approach and the take-off the hands must lie low in light contact with the bit, and the rider must be prepared to have them yield, if necessary, advancing on both sides of the horse's neck from the rider's shoulder and elbow joints.

If the horse shifts to a gallop by itself during the approach, the rider adapts his seat to the new rhythm without interfering, letting the horse approach the obstacle at the gait it has chosen.

As jump training progresses, each horse is allowed to find the galloping rate that suits it best. All the rider does is to intervene as a regulating and restraining force whenever headlong excess makes the necessary preparation for the take-off impossible. Or he drives the horse forward energetically whenever hesitant slowing down leads him to suppose that the horse's heart and impulsion will not suffice for the jump. But in neither case should the small of the back and the rider's legs abandon their role as supervisors.

Nowadays we have overcome the obsession that we must help the horse to surmount obstacles by applying various active " controls " and that we can help it maintain a wrongly understood balance by employing rein and weight controls. These controls are even more problematical, since all they do is to place a disturbing load on the horse's hindquarters and and prevent its neck from acting as a balancing rod.

The best assistance we can render a horse in jumping will always be to enable it to surmount obstacles suitably, but the only way in which we can do this is by means of our quiet, adapting, relieving *jumping seat.* The horse must always be the executing organ. It must place its own levers in such a position that the muscles have the best point of attack corresponding to the jump required. We can support it indirectly only by progressing systematically from the easy to the more difficult, strengthening its muscles, joints, and ligaments, and thus training its hindquarters, back, and neck for increasingly greater physical exertions. The slower the approach (walk, trot) and the greater the obstacle, the more the horse needs this intensive action of muscles and joints, called the *jumping mechanism*, that is required for any jump.

Second, we can also assist the horse by developing its *jumping technique.*

The more the working gallop and medium gallop take the place of the initial trot as jump training progresses, followed by even faster gaits that combine muscular take-off and lively speed to achieve as powerful a take-off as possible in order to produce the approach and vigorous take-off required for surmounting difficult obstacles, the harder will it be for the horse to judge the take-off correctly. This is the principal objective of jumping technique, which the horse can acquire only by considerable training over all sorts of jumps.

Estimating the take-off over a low obstacle is easy, as the horse can get over it in a low, flat trajectory even if it takes off rather early. This is not so, however, when a higher obstacle requires a higher trajectory, so that the horse has to choose the point from which a successful take-off is possible. The height of the obstacle also involves this difficulty for the horse: it must find the take-off point within a narrow zone from which alone a faultless jump is possible.

The best way for us to teach the horse to estimate its take-off correctly is to set up an auxiliary *cavalletto* about 24 feet before the obstacle. Since we know the length of a horse's gallop leaps—approximately 12, 24, and 36 feet—we will secure a proper take-off. The first gallop leap covers the auxiliary *cavelletto*, the second lies between that and the obstacle, and the third is the take-off proper. The observer can count one, two, three, and the horse takes off at three.[75]

If the rider counts along, he gets the habit (even if only subconsciously) of trying to help the horse over the obstacle, but this always turns out badly for the average rider. To be sure, the rider should help the horse by following its motions and giving it free play, but from the very start of galloping training over *cavalletti* he should never think of the word "jump". Man should not try to tamper with the marvellous mechanism that is a horse as far as execution in concerned; all he could do would be to interfere.

The **hardest** jumps to estimate are steep, high jumps, like those built up of **bare** rails. Such jumps should be attempted only after the horse has gained experience and assurance over slanting obstacles, which are easier to judge.

Jumping technique requires correct judgment, a quiet, uniform though smooth and vigorous approach, the proper diving position before the jump, and such co-operation of the horse's hindquarters, back and neck that the ascending branch of the trajectory and the phase of suspension over the obstacle follow the curve of a parabola to which hindquarters, back, and neck are fitted.

When the jump is taken at high speed, many horses are unable to do their best jumping with the prescribed *position of the neck* and the resultant location of the centre of gravity. They jump with their necks held high.

The riders must then be real acrobats, able to avoid all interference and to follow the horse's movements over the obstacle in a low crouch.

Over difficult jumps the rider can add a few highly valuable inches to the radius of yielding by holding the reins directly with the thumb and index finger (assuming that a simple snaffle bit is used). This makes it possible to re-establish contact without the assistance of the other hand.

[75] Double and multiple jumps should be exercised much later, only after the horse's jumping technique, with a supple, arched back and in diving position, has been considerably perfected. The diving position may be lost unless the smooth jump is always exercised over individual obstacles.

It is well to use jumping exercises over walls for a horse that does not arch its neck and back lines during jumping. Another aid is to set up auxiliary *cavalletti* just behind the obstacle so that the horse sees them only while in flight. It will then assume the diving position during the jump.

Auxiliary *cavalletti* set up just in front of the obstacle also produce proper take-off and extension.

It is a matter of course that the distances of 12, 24, and 36 feet are not absolutely binding distances for double or multiple obstacles; they must be dimensioned in accordance with the length of the gallop leap, since they depend upon the size and framework of the horse, its natural mechanism, and its more or less highly developed impulsion. The height and width of the obstacles, which involve landing at various distances from the base of the obstacle, must also be taken into consideration.

When the reins are held in one hand (using the whip) and are separated only by the index finger, the rider has the undeniable advantage of being able to let them slide through his fingers quickly and re-establish contact just as quickly. This cannot be done with crossed reins.

We might add that jumping style is subject to individual modification when peak performances like those displayed by a few exceptional jumping riders are required. Such riders, going beyond tested tradition, and developing a style of their own, remain isolated cases that one cannot and should not imitate.

The horse's jump at the gallop can be represented as an interruption of the four-beat locomotion of the racing gallop (off hind foot, near hind foot, off forefoot, near forefoot)[76] used by the horse before its take-off.

The jump over the obstacle is inserted between the alighting of the near hind leg, which touches the ground far underneath the horse's rump and takes care of the thrust together with the off hind leg, and the landing of the off foreleg, which absorbs the greatest impact.

A change of lead is frequently observed during this interruption of the sequence of footfalls in the jump. The horse does it instinctively in order to protect the principal diagonal (near hind foot—off forefoot), which is subjected to very great strain at the free gallop gait and in jumping in contrast to the collected gallop. The near hind leg and the off foreleg, though alighting at practically the same instant and supporting each other, are under greater stress at the free gallop than the off hind leg and the near foreleg, even though the latter two legs are merely single-leg supports at certain moments of the phase sequence.[77]

This is proved by the following: at the free gallop the outside hind leg does not have to carry all the load of the horse's trunk, though it may appear to do so and actually does so at the collected gallop. It takes over this load after the inside foreleg has alighted and the phase of suspension is terminated. But it acts merely as a temporary support in order to throw the entire weight of the horse, now moving forward and downward, to the principal diagonal, which has alighted in the interim. This weight may also be increased by the load of the rider (hitting the saddle), which has the greatest impact at this point of the phase sequence. The principal

---

[76] The suspension phase of the gallop is missing, however, since the near forefoot in the preceding phase sequence is still grounded when the alighting of the off hind foot, followed by the near hind foot, introduces the sequence of footfalls that was interrupted by the phase of suspension above the obstacle.

[77] *Phase sequence* is the interval of motion at any gait from one position of the horse's legs to the repetition of the same petition. Such a phase sequence consists of individual phases, which we shall call *constellations of support*, according to the groupings of the legs that are grounded at any one time.

diagonal has to lift the entire load forward and upward. Thus the last foot to alight, the inside front forefoot, which must allow the horse's trunk (already impelled forward and upward) to roll over it, has less work to do.

We have seen how we can provide indirect support for the executing organ, our horse, by developing the jumping mechanism and by training its jumping technique.

A third, and probably the most important way of providing indirect support for the horse in jumping, is the firmly rooted confidence of the horse and its rider. Much of the success of celebrated jump riders lies in this confidence, which has become mutual and must be supplemented by the horse's confidence in its own ability.

The forward jumping seat, which enables the horse to surmount the jump in the best way possible and thus is the only direct though passive control that we can apply to the horse during the jump itself and upon landing,[78] has been discussed in " Seat and Controls " and " Low Obstacles ".

The seat indicates the best approach to the obstacle, the rider using driving controls if necessary to maintain the even flow of forward motion or to increase the impulsion of the approach. The horse must be allowed to determine how to plan this approach in order to find the best point of take-off. The next job the seat has to do is to give the horse's neck, in light contact with the hands that follow the movement, the freedom it requires for extension and balancing. This constant readiness to provide more freedom of play must persist after the phase of suspension and landing; only then should the horse be given the opportunity of seeking firmer contact with the bit as it continues to gallop. The elbows advance slightly from the shoulders and follow the hands, which advance with the middle joints of the fingers *along* the neck, not along the crest of the mane. The hands are closed, opening slightly only if the take-off was premature (high and broad · jump) in order to let the reins slide through. It would be a serious mistake to set the elbows akimbo. This would cause the hands to move backward—butterfly style!

When the stirrup straps are shortened three or four holes, as is done for jumps more than a yard high, the position of our knees and legs would be wrong if we used the steeper pads of our working saddle. We therefore

---

[78] The rider can sometimes save the situation when the horse's hindquarters make mistakes going over steep, high, or broad jumps by throwing his upper body forward and sideways.

With this exception, the rule is that the jumping rider's hips must never reach an imaginary horizontal line drawn through his shoulder; his shoulders must always be " ahead " of his hips.

employ a jumping saddle,[79] with pads that are extended to conform to the length of our legs, a straight seat, and a low bolster.

Nor should we forget to use an over-girth and braided or rubber-covered reins (because of slipperiness when sweating).

Tugging on the reins of a stumbling horse is more than useless. It deprives the horse of its last resort of restoring its imperilled equilibrium—the freedom of movement of its neck, its "fifth foot"—thus making a fall unavoidable. That is why the rider should allow the reins to slide through his hands when mistakes occur during and after a jump. He must keep his upper body erect and his buttocks thrown forward so as not to interfere with the horse's hindquarters and back, which are engaged in the work of rescue.

Caprilli says, "It is a delusion to think that the horse can support itself when we tug on the reins. I have fallen four hundred times, and four hundred times I have found that my hand was never able to prevent a fall, but often facilitated the fall by depriving the animal of its natural freedom of movement."[80]

The characteristic example of how a horse uses its neck to maintain its endangered equilibrium and prevent a fall is seen in horse shows when a horse's forelegs begin to slip as it passes through a corner. It puts an extra load on its hindquarters and outside shoulder by sharply bending its neck down and towards the inside. The horse has combined the effect of vertical and horizontal movement of its neck "balancing rod", thus releasing its forehand from the dangerous slanting position. And if it does fall, the hindquarters are the first to hit the ground.

The cyclist who bends vigorously towards the left to throw his bicycle to the right when he tries to get around a stone observed at the last moment, leaving it on the left, also acts in accordance with the same principle.

When a horse stumbles, we see it try to re-establish its equilibrium by suddenly stretching its neck out forward and downward. The gestures of the neck instantly release the forehand, and prevent a fall. The same action occurs whenever the horse lands unsurely after a jump. The sudden

---

[79] The shortening of the stirrup straps and the shape of the jumping saddle (which is not the same as our working saddle or the hunting saddle that lies approximately half-way between these two extremes) automatically shift the position of the rider's leg somewhat forward—that is, not just behind the girth but at the girth—except when lateral and restraining controls are applied.

The jumping saddle in its present form was unknown to Caprilli.

[80] A well-intentioned sudden tug on the reins applied at the instant of stumbling sometimes seems to prevent the fall of a languid, sluggish, or very tired horse. But it was only the sudden pain that kept it from resigning itself to its fate and made it take the instinctive movements of self-preservation required to keep its footing. Nor can the so-called Joelson jerking method (fairly sharp, vertical tugs on the reins, directed against the horse's upper jaw) be considered wholly unjustified when used on horses that are not yet spent.

thrusting of its head and neck downward, as may be clearly seen in slow-motion pictures, takes the load off the forehand and brings up the hind legs for its support. If a horse concentrates all its energy in such a downward movement, the "free fall" produces a *lifting* force over and above the relieving force. Another instance is a horse that helps itself over an obstacle after the take-off in this manner or tries to avoid the bars.

If a major stumble is followed by a fall despite the rider's correct behaviour (that is, avoiding all movements that might further endanger the already imperilled equilibrium of the horse as well as letting the reins fly), the reins must be released at once, and the rider must utilize the free bound against his buttocks to let himself be thrown forward. He should draw in his head, pull up his knees, bend his arms and cross them, and close his fists before he reaches the ground. In this ball shape the human body is able to continue rolling to avoid getting underneath the horse.

The small of the back should, especially during the take-off, drastically braced and pushed forward to enter into the movement, while the low-positioned knee, firmly clinging, acts as a hinge to support the following action of the rider's upper body and base of support. His upper body actually follows the horse's movements during the jump and especially at the take-off, without remaining behind and interfering with the action of the horse's back. The rider's legs must remain fixed at the horse's side, with the widest part of the foot passing through the stirrup (see p. 227), so that the instep rests on the stirrup bar and the elastic, deep heel points downward.

The seat employed in steeplechase races over difficult jumps where the landing side is lower than the take-off—such as the Becher's Brook jump in the Grand National—with the upper body leaning back of the vertical and the leg pressed forward in the stirrup, has a certain advantage despite its interfering with the rider's following the motion of the horse. The shock of landing is so great that if the rider used a forward seat, he would fly over the head of the horse even if the horse did not stumble.

It is a matter of course that the hand is held low in the safety seat, letting the reins slide through as required, while the head is not raised.

Many instructors tend to confuse the forward jumping seat with the normal seat, so that they teach young riders both seats at once. This is quite wrong and harms his training in both types of seat.

The forward seat is developed organically from the normal seat (see "Seats and Controls" and "Advantages of Cross-country Riding", p. 6of. and p. 224f.), but the beginner can use this seat to advantage only after he has found his own balance in the normal seat and has grown soft and supple. Only then can instruction in both types of seat go hand in hand, the stirrups being shortened for the forward seat whenever jumps are to be made. The horse should not be trained to rush or pull, however, by exaggerated shortening of the stirrups, backward tugs on the reins, or abandonment of the customary weight and leg controls.

To repeat, the two complementary types of seat, one evolved from the other, must be taught separately. Only then will a future jump rider become truly supple in a thoroughly learned jumping seat, while presenting a good figure in the normal seat during dressage tests.

Training young horses to jump without riders is customary in the training of military remounts, where large riding halls, couloir, jumping pen, and enough attendants are always available. We, who may have to do without all this, will make a virtue of necessity and tell ourselves that our horse will get at least as good training in jumping without this equipment.

The jumps of a horse carrying a rider differ from those of an unmounted horse in the amount of power required and in their execution, though there may be no important differences visibly externally.

The horse that carries no rider finds it easy to approach quite close to the obstacle, cleanly and smoothly jumping over it at a fairly steep take-off angle, but when it carries a load it will have to revise all of its more comfortable take-off technique. It is probable that this will not be done without falls, which, like all other painful influences, such as an unfeeling hand, the rider falling upon its back, and hard landings, are not likely to increase the pleasure it derives from jumping.

We cannot tell you how to make your horse a champion jumper, but we should like to say that if it does show some ability—offering to jump, so to speak—too much should not be asked for at once. It is not enough for a horse, say, to jump a $4\frac{1}{2}$-foot obstacle without hitting it in order to be nominated for a competition in which the obstacles average $4\frac{1}{4}$ feet in height. Only after it is able to jump $4\frac{1}{2}$ feet high over all sorts of obstacles, including steep, high jumps and broad jumps, with the same sure technique and in the same fluent style as it jumps over the 2-foot obstacles with which its training began, are we justified in thinking that we have a real jumper in our stable with a briliant future ahead of it. Nor should we exploit its good will in subsequent training by consciously trying to find out how high our young horse can jump. This may have grave consequences.

If the horse refuses the jump, the obstacles have probably been raised too rapidly. Then jumps over similar obstacles that are lower, with a lead horse if necessary, must re-establish its lost self-confidence. This is particularly true when the horse stops, which usually happens because it has not found the proper take-off point.

If frequent, unmotivated stopping is caused by skulking or undependable behaviour, the rider energetically pushes his buttocks forward into the saddle, though they were just above it previously, and remains there until the take-off has actually occurred.

If a disobedient horse succeeds in coming to a stop, it should be punished by backing, followed by an energetic approach to the same obstacle.

A gallop of a mile or two once or twice a week, with the speed raised to the maximum towards the end of the run, is very good for skulking and uncertain horses.

Generally speaking, an extremely sensitive rider, who is in complete physical and mental contact with his horse, also possess a great advantage when approaching an obstacle. He feels exactly when the horse has *decided* to jump, as if he were a mind reader. His seat can then be concentrated upon facilitating and supporting the *take-off*, the second decisive moment in a jump.

On the other hand, a horse's fine sense of smell perceives a rider's " fear smell "—imperceptible to us—whenever he is irresolute. Then the horse becomes unsure and disobedient.

Whenever the horse knocks over the top bar because of stolidity or carelessness, good results are obtained by tying a square bar to the top edge of the obstacle. Rapping bars, which are wound with wire for insensitive horses, can work miracles when used carefully and at the right time. But since these bars must be used with considerable skill and understanding, they should not be entrusted to any stableman. More good horses have been ruined by their use than bad ones have been improved. We should therefore welcome the decree of the F.E.I. that horses may not be poled before the jumps in international tournaments.

In the event of runouts the rein on the constrained side, that is, the side to which the horse turns out and grows stiff, must yield completely, and the horse should be directed over the obstacle with the other rein, assisted by driving controls. However, if the horse succeeds in evading the obstacle, it is vigorously brought to a stop, turned about its forehand quietly towards the obstacle, thus making it more responsive to the control, and a new start made for the centre of the obstacle, somewhat from the side on which the runout occurred. Since the horse finds more support for its resistance in the stiffening right hind foot, which is less controlled by the rider because of its right-to-left crookedness, and therefore usually tries to run out towards the left, the new approach will have to be made somewhat to the right in this case.

It is easier for the horse to run out to the left when it is running at a right gallop, for example, because at this gait the right hind foot is farther advanced. It can then impart greater thrust to the opposite side, the side of the intended runout.

A rushing approach to an obstacle is not the same as a refusal; it should be treated by calming action as an expression of a violent temperament. Quiet gallops (no rushing) with long intermissions at a walk, work on a circle over *cavalletti*, a working trot on a circle alternated with trotting on a straightaway, going (incidentally) over an easy obstacle in the neighbourhood followed by several jumps in succession at different heights and different intervals—all will soon make impetuous horses jump more quietly and calmly.

This method, at any rate, is better than half halts, which cause pain when the horse's movement is irregular. They do not attack the faulty disposition at its root and completely eliminate judgment and understanding in a fearful horse, which may lead to serious consequences when jumping over an obstacle.

Rushing is often due solely to fear felt in advance by an otherwise none-too-eager horse anticipating the jerks on the reins and the impact of the blows on its back that it has learned to expect from its clumsy rider when going over a jump. Such horses soon abandon their misbehaviour once they have changed riders and gained confidence in the hands of their new and more supple rider. If changing riders is of no avail, we still have the ancient remedy of the " human manger ", the *homme mangeoire* of the French, who should be around during all initial jump training, if at all possible. In brief, do not try to hold back *before* the jump but always come to a stop after the low obstacle, surrender the reins, feed the horse, and then let it graze.

As a general rule: Never begin the jumping lesson before you are quite sure that you can " DRIVE " your horse!

VI. Hunting

Hunting is no doubt the severest test of what the horse has learned in the riding hall and cross-country, of its disposition, power, heart, and jumping ability. Better than any other kind of training, it develops bold approach to unknown obstacles, self-reliance, and animation.

Over and above these practical advantages, which complete the final training of a saddle horse, hunting is the crown and summit of equestrian activity in open country. It is the reward for the years of toil and effort involved in training the young horse. Finally it is the just compensation for disheartening reverses and disappointments that we could not have been spared during the long period of training. The classic equestrian authors have written so well and so thoroughly about hunting that I can really confine myself to mentioning only a few basic rules that are especially important if we want to take part in hunts with a young horse in order to train and exercise it.

We shall therefore discuss only easy hunts behind the master of the hunt (without live game at first and, if possible, without hounds) at a rate set by the latter and with the stretch to be covered at the gallop fixed in advance as well as obstacles suited to our pupil's ability.

The road to the rendezvous, even though it be long, makes the horse supple and responsive to the controls. Any defects that may have been noticed during this ride can be corrected during the last *examination of bridle and saddle packs* before the hunt begins. The stirrups should be heavy rather than light (so that it is easier to get them under your foot again if you should lose them) and by no means narrow, as the rider may be caught in them in case of a fall.

During the hunt itself we keep behind the rider of a steady jumper and somewhat off to the side so that the latter can act as a pilot for our inexperienced novice if necessary. The herd instinct will take care of the rest. This is why a horse that usually exhibits a tendency to hold back will move faster during a hunt and may even try to pull on the bit trying to overtake other riders.

We must try to keep our steady gait by employing equestrian controls, and we must not lean back in the saddle, legs spread far apart and pushing against the stirrups and our hands tugging at the reins.[81]

If we " ride " our horse using a forward seat, such as we have described for cross-country riding and jumping, and seek our principal support in the thigh and the knee, with the heel pressed down and the buttocks in contact with the saddle, any half halts that may be necessary—acting with the hands held low within the framework of the forward drive—will be more effective than using a toboggan seat that remains behind the movement of the horse. Such a seat would excite the horse still more, so that it would completely lose the timing of its gallop leaps that had already become unsteady. Another consequence would be continued interference with the rhythm of respiration and leap that determines·endurance at the gallop.

Considerable equestrian tact is required to determine the combination of freedom and control required for any given horse.

In open terrain the horse needs enough freedom to be able to develop

---

[81] See p. 73. The so-called " bridge " (having the end of the right snaffle rein pass through the left hand and vice versa) guarantees calm, steady control of pullers. The contact thus established between the two hands resting on the neck also prevents them from descending too low and provides support even when the horse stumbles.

all its mental and physical forces without feeling any disturbing tutelage so that it can concentrate upon its job. It also requires just enough bondage —response to the controls—for the latter to come through at all times, so that the rider's domination is never restricted or challenged when rate or direction need changing.

It is a matter of course that at the outset we will join only very easy hunts, say, hunts during which the horses gallop for two or three thousand yards, with a rest period. The master of the hunt, who has laid out the course, will gladly tell us about the obstacles. It is perfectly all right if they are no more than 3 to 3½ feet high provided they are solidly built. Ditches must be clearly visible, which means they must be mowed clean if necessary, and jumps across ditches in marshy terrain should be made in the neighbourhood of trees where the ground is firmer. If our horse was not quite sure of itself over these obstacles up to now, galloping with the field is the best opportunity to overcome this shyness. It will forget the inhibitions that deprived it of its ease on the exercise ground up to now and prevented it from discovering the right interplay of muscles for the broad jump. At the brisk hunting gallop even skulking horses will abandon their hesitancy and let themselves go without special summons. Many horses that hold back, displaying little heart or verve, become more animated after a few hunts, and secure confidence in themselves and increased assurance as their instinctive forces are awakened. They are then less sluggish in the riding hall and approach the bit vigorously in response to light controls. We will have reason to be grateful to the master of the hunt if he inserts the first few obstacles only after an introductory gallop that will have settled any initial restlessness. Jumping these obstacles with relaxed horses is of even more educational value.

Since we must try to arrive as fresh as possible at the kill, we will endeavour to spare our horse as we ride it, especially if we do not know the length of the stretch to be taken at a gallop. A hunt does not have the same purpose as jumping in a horse-show ring. We shall therefore look for the easiest places to get over the obstacles in order to economize our horse's strength, in so far as that is compatible with point-to-point riding without endangering other participants or ourselves by criss-cross riding, and provided we are not following a pilot. In many training hunts the obstacles are made somewhat lower at one side to allow for the inexperience of young horses and riders. In any event the rider should avoid approaching an obstacle alongside another horse that is half a length in front of him. His own horse would tend to take off this same half-length too soon.

In case of *falls*, which can occur sooner or later, the rider should roll away from the horse to one side, without surrendering the reins. If he does surrender the reins, there is nothing left for him to do but to start walking home, painfully conscious that his clumsiness and lack of presence of mind are interfering with the pleasure of the rest of the hunt. In fact, his riderless horse, galloping along wildly, may seriously endanger the field.

If the excessive restlessness and pressing of our horse makes it unmanageable in the field, and if we no longer have it under enough control to prevent its pressing ahead, we should take it off to one flank of the field, where it cannot bother anyone and where we can make a large bolt to the outside if we are no longer able to regulate its rate. Though the martingale should not be employed as an aid in dressage, it will be useful to us in hunting as well as jumping.

If our horse becomes too violent and tries to lift its head so high as to prevent the bit from acting properly, or if it throws its head around, the martingale will restrict these movements so that we do not lose entire control of the horse. It has another great advantage, too: it moderates the painful action of the hands whenever they rise involuntarily as a result of sudden movements or irregular jumps. It must be buckled in such a manner, of course, as to hang down in a loop when the head and neck are carried naturally and freely and the snaffle reins are in contact.

It is highly advisable to use double reins even when the horse is bridled with a snaffle, because of the possible breaking of one rein. Therefore it is unnecessary to take along a riding crop or a hunting whip, for the rider's hands have enough to do, especially on a horse that is still unsure of itself. The hunting whip with its crook bent at a right angle makes sense only when riding to hounds after actual game, but this is not the case now where we are merely practising easy gallops behind the master of the hunt. In actual hunts for live game, where no one knows whether the trail will pass over good terrain or bad or how long it will be, the rider's presence at the kill will largely depend on whether he has spared his horse. He will do well to spare it many unnecessary jumps by opening gates, using the crook of his hunting whip for the purpose.

Equestrian customs also prescribe that the loop sometimes attached to the crop not be worn. Only those handling the hounds have this privilege, the huntsman and his assistant. The other participants in the hunt must avoid approaching the hounds too closely for fear of disturbing them or possibly causing them injury from the horses' hoofs.

Once we arrive at the kill, our first thought must be for our horse. We dismount, loosen the girth, and walk it up and down where it is not exposed to the wind. We use the occasion to inspect its legs and the condition of the shoes, which may have been loosened while going over walls or in marshy terrain (see pp. 86-87).

The red coat, which is more or less prescribed attire in formal hunts and is favoured in all others, is not only sanctioned by tradition. Wearing

41. Note the infinitely fine gentleness of the rider over the bars. The open fingers remain in contact with the horse's mouth while allowing the balancing mechanism of the head and neck every opportunity to stretch. Colonel **H.** Llewellyn on *Foxhunter* 1948.

42. The moment before landing. William Steinkraus on *Ksar d'Esprit* (Thoroughbred) 1959. IRISH TIMES, LTD.

43. Fluid jump over parallel bars. Major John W. Russell on *Bally Bay*.

a red coat is of great practical value, since it is only the brilliant colours of the field disappearing in the distance that enable a rider left behind for some reason or other to catch up again.

The dark hunting cap (often provided with a steel liner) or the top hat protect the rider's head against serious injury from the horse's hoofs in the event of a fall better than any other headgear.

Before we leave the topic of hunting, with its rules and customs, let us say a word about handshakes in the saddle.

No matter how calm and good-natured our young horse may be when associating with its accustomed stablemates, never betraying offensive intentions, we never know what will happen when two riders approach each other to shake hands when mounted on horses that are strangers to each other. The horses may misunderstand the approach, and a battle may break out suddenly, especially as the two riders are distracted at such times by their social obligations, and their restraining legs are heaven only knows where.

No sensible rider of either sex will therefore object to our omitting the conventional handshake, for the horses' Emily Post is not the same as ours. While riders are exchanging greetings, introductions, and saying good-bye, many horses do the same by exchanging well-aimed kicks. Many a horseman has had a hunt thoroughly spoiled for him by this behaviour of another rider's hunter, his horse being lamed long before his first gallop.

VII. Defects of Conformation, Disposition, and Character —Making Allowance for Them During Training

Rarely will we have the good fortune of working with a horse that presents no difficulties in conformation and disposition. As training progresses, most horses sooner or later display difficulties of this sort.

Thanks to rigorous selection of stud lines, the breeders are meeting with increasing success in their endeavours to produce large-framed horses, well balanced and not too high, which possess a strong foundation and carry themselves well at their long-striding gaits, with the work of their trainers made as easy and as brief as possible by a minimum of conformation and disposition faults. Nevertheless, we must expect to find imperfections originating in inharmonious conformation and poor disposition, and not everyone can deal with the difficulties resulting from such defects. The successful horseman will be the one who combines tact, experience, and skill with a feeling of just how far he can go in any one case.

It is dangerous to give instructions or recipes for the procedures to be followed in certain cases. Although sensible observance of the principles governing the gymnastic training of every horse as set forth in the chapters dealing with the training of the young horse will solve practically any equestrian problems that may arise, their application to the individual case must be left to the rider's judgment. The true horseman must be able to diagnose every case, letting his experience and his tact dictate the measures that have proved successful in similar situations.

Diagnosis is made easier for the experienced horseman by the behaviour of a horse whose poor gait is due to defective conformation or poor disposition. The faults themselves point out the road to be followed in every individual case.

In the chapter dealing with the purchase of a young horse we were concerned with emphasizing the major difficulties occasioned by certain faults of conformation in later training. On the other hand, realizing that there are no absolutely perfect horses, we pointed out defects that can be compensated for by proper training and by other points of conformation that are particularly outstanding.

In this section we shall discuss faults of conformation and disposition. We shall try to provide some information on how to eliminate them by equestrian action or at least to lessen their effects.

Before we discuss some of the conformation faults of a horse, let us review the progress of gymnastic training and its underlying principles.

We all know that the two major requirements for the correct equestrian movement of a horse—I might say, the two cornerstones of any dressage —are (1) *poise*, which is based upon well-timed movement in a state of suppleness, and (2) *impulsion*.

The very first time we ride the young remount we get it to carry its own weight in natural equilibrium at an easy natural trot as soon as the horse no longer tenses against the unaccustomed weight of the rider and begins to swing along at its own rate without rushing. This first stage, *absence of constraint*, is reached when the horse has learned to balance its own weight plus the weight of the rider easily and unresistingly without the assistance of the reins. This is how it was able to maintain itself at any rate it desired in a congenital natural poise in the meadow, supported only by its own four legs and without any reins.

It is that natural equilibrium[82] in natural poise that enables us to con-

[82] The various degrees of equilibrium in the physical sense or of poise in the equestrian sense are two groups of concepts that are identical and mutually interdependent in so far as poise—from natural, inborn poise through all its intermediate stages to the poise of the schooled horse acquired through dressage—is a function of equilibrium and impossible without it.

Equilibrium, however, can be present only when the base of the plumb line through the centre of gravity of horse and rider lies within the area of support of the mounted horse, provided, of course, that the hindquarters do not evade but engage unresistingly in the direction of that plumb line to take their share of the load.

tinue training, acquainting the horse with the controls. We begin with the purely driving controls, the crop and the rider's legs, which make the hindquarters (dragging up to now) thrust and reach forward more energetically and with longer strides. This produces a more pronounced flexion and extension, or pulsation, of the same muscular ring that was active at the natural trot without constraint, but only sluggishly.

The immediate consequence of this fuller oscillation of the closely inter-related muscles of the croup, buttocks, back, ribs, neck, and belly—the activity of the back that is so important for the rider—is the extension of these groups of muscles. The actively pulsating back fills out the seat and carries it forward.

This extension, however, makes the horse, which has been moving along merely with constraint, i.e., without resistance, completely supple. We have achieved *suppleness*, a product of trusting absence of constraint and the energetic gait produced by driving, with its consequence: full of muscular pulsation.

Together with the initial driving controls the young remount learns another control. In fact it should seek out that control itself by stretching out to make contact with the reins, which up to now it has felt only as a guiding line from time to time.

To sum up, the horse moves without constraint even when it does not reach the bit, but it moves with suppleness only when it has extended itself as a result of the driving controls, has come to the bit, and has grown supple in contact with it.

The horse clearly feels that it is framed between the rider's legs and the reins in the state of suppleness; in other words, it is practically at the mercy of its rider's actions, so to speak—it has given him a blank cheque upon its body.[83] It is conceivable, therefore, that this trusting surrender to the rider may be delayed for lack of confidence. This is another reason why a friendly relationship between man and animal should be our aim from the very first time the horse is saddled and we put our foot in a stirrup.

Movement in natural poise, in equilibrium, with the plumb line through

It is equally necessary, however, that this predominantly static equilibrium be replaced by a dynamic equilibrium that develops from the vigorous motion at moments of suspension and at the faster gaits in general. This dynamic equilibrium participates in the maintenance of stability. Poise in motion is inconceivable without the co-operation of this dynamic equilibrium.

From the equestrian standpoint a horse moves in equilibrium when it does not increase its rate or its gait as soon as the reins are relaxed enough to break any connection between the rider's hands and the horse's mouth. Apart from special cases, the horse must not find any support in the reins (the stroking test).

[83] The readiness with which a horse still practically untrained reacts to shifts in the rider's weight along its longitudinal axis, and even more so along its transverse axis (which is a much shorter and therefore less stable basis), is really astonishing, provided it does not stiffen itself to resist the weight control.

the common centre of gravity shifted fairly far to the front towards the withers, must be achieved at the very outset as the foundation of uniform timing in the sequence of footfalls. In the course of dressage it turns into movement in acquired poise, in acquired equilibrium, as the ability of the hindquarters to engage and carry the load progresses.

We must constantly bear in mind the training course required for horses of approximately correct conformation and with no appreciable faults of character or temperament, and we must have gone through such a course of training repeatedly under the guidance of a good instructor before we can approach the infinitely more difficult job of turning horses with faulty conformation into usable saddle horses. This means getting the maximum out of these horses without damaging their bones or joints or ruining their character.

We may have the rare good fortune of training a naturally handy horse that willingly does what is asked of it, or we may wish to bring out the best there is in a horse of poor conformation without wearing it out prematurely. But in both cases we must always concentrate on poise— from natural poise to the schooled horse's acquired poise—and impulsion. These two cardinal requirements, which must be met from the very beginning of dressage to its completion, are the source and preliminary conditions of timing, suppleness, a pure, long-striding gait, longitudinal flexion, even loading on all four legs, and—the summit of all training— supple obedience and collection.

There are no faultless horses; the experienced rider and horseman must be able, however, to distinguish between the faults and defects in conformation that will present insurmountable difficulties in the training required to make the horse useful and those faults that can be eliminated or at least improved by understanding work adapted to the individual horse.

He must be able to recognize whether it is possible to compensate for temporary inadequacies of certain weak parts of the horse's body by calling upon parts of particularly good conformation for extra effort. He must know whether the defective parts of the horse's body can be gradually strengthened by relieving and sparing them at the start and deliberately reducing the load they have to carry, and what carefully graduated exercises this requires. Finally, he must be able to awaken latent or withdrawn forces for co-operative labour, his skill thus partially establishing or at least replacing the harmony that is naturally lacking in defective horses. The practical horseman is distinguished not by his obsession with faults, but by his skilful weighing of the good against what is not so good.

We do not intend to provide any cure-alls in our discussion of the most common conformation defects and ways to allow for them during training. At the outset we pointed out the problematical value of all such recipes. The cornerstones of a horse's gymnastic training, poise and impulsion, together with a feeling for the magnitude of the controls and an understanding of just how much can be asked for at any given time, must underlie every individual plan of work. Correct gait and contact with the bit will always be the visible and tangible proofs that this procedure was correct.

As we have said, the dressage of horses of poor conformation is much more difficult than that of horses of normal build. Faulty horses require much more allowance for their character, disposition, and nature during training, since they often feel pain and constraint that horses of more normal conformation never experience.

If the legs, hoofs, and digestion are healthy, the efficiency of our saddle horse will depend chiefly upon the supple activity of the extensor and flexor muscles that surround the back, ribs, and belly as a muscular ring. It is obvious that the shape and location of the back have the greatest influence upon the pulsation of the muscles.

The back of a saddle horse should be approximately horizontal from the depression just behind the withers to the slightly arched region of the loins and long enough to ensure the free interplay of its muscles with those of the forehand and hindquarters.

If the "fit" is perfect, and the long, well-developed withers extend to the rear, such a back will not present any special difficulties in gymnastic training, even though it may appear to be somewhat "long" to the observer. Indeed its suppleness will facilitate training, for the inherently slight flexibility of the spinal column, vertical as well as horizontal (this horizontal flexibility being called flexion of the ribs in practical use), becomes most effective in a back of such conformation.

A long back is a defect if its length makes it impossible for the hind legs to reach forward towards the plumb line in the centre of gravity. If a back of this sort is associated with weak loins, there is danger that the musculature will never swing adequately ("the rider sitting on two different horses"). The long-backed horse never fills out its seat because its hind steps are too short.[84]

[84] A characteristic of such horses is their "gallop", which resembles a four-beat gait without a suspension phase. As the abdominal muscles tend to persist in the stretched state when flexed and extended, they do not pull the hind legs forward far enough, so that the forefoot or hind foot of the principal diagonal (which no longer operates simultaneously) alights prematurely. The leap, which is the distinguishing characteristic of the gallop, is lacking.

On the other hand, the principal characteristic of the racing gallop is its four-beat timing (length of stride).

The rider's weight must be shifted to his crotch and the sides of the horse in order to restore the connection between the forehand and the hindquarters and produce relaxed, long-striding steps. After proper timing is achieved at the natural trot and a vigorous leap at the free gallop, the rider drives the horse. He uses his riding crop or legs, with the hands held low though not pressing downward, to make the hind legs take strides and leaps that are as long as possible, thus restoring harmony between forehand and hindquarters. Once the hind legs operate properly, the muscles of the " dead " back, which had been pressed downward and out of the way in a cramped manner, begin to pulsate elastically, flexing and extending regularly and uniformly and stretching the spinal column to reach the passive hand; now the horse becomes supple.[85]

Work of this sort strengthens the abdominal muscles, which make an important contribution to the correct action of the back, so that after a few weeks of training gait and pulsations of the back are no longer disturbed by the rider's sitting fully in the saddle. Special care must be taken at the halt to keep from bending the vertebrae of the horse's loins by sitting too low in the saddle. Clumsy use of the rider's weight hampers the free and easy forward reach of the hind legs, which cannot provide sufficient support, and the resultant pain produces unrest and struggle against the reins.

No endeavour should be made to go beyond ordinary carriage in such horses. But they can be turned into very pleasant saddle horses, as their excessively flexible backs absorb all the impact of the gait.

What we have just said about impact applies in the contrary sense to the short back. It is difficult for such a back to achieve the necessary flexibility to absorb and dissolve the movements of the foundation and of the rider. Consequently the rider grows very tired, and the joints and ligaments of the horse's legs take a beating.

Nor should the rider sit completely in the saddle on a short back at the start, but should endeavour to stretch the horse's back and deprive it of any opportunity to resist by employing a lively, free working rate at the trot and the gallop. Once the horse's back pulsates and the rider's buttocks no longer feel as if they were sitting on a humpback, he can employ very brief lifting tugs of the reins and a normal seat to promote sinking of the back. If he feels any stiffness, the horse's suppleness was incomplete, and this work must be done all over again.[86]

---

[85] Every thinking and sensitive rider has observed a regular interaction between the activity of the hindquarters and that of the back, which may be compared to some sort of feedback.

[86] In both of these cases the tensed muscles will be loosened up and poise achieved in surprisingly short time when the horse is worked over *cavalletti*. The posting trot should be

A short horse needs a great deal of neck freedom to feel sure of itself in open country. The less tightly the hands hold it, and the more opportunity the free reins give it to compensate for its short area of support by using the counterweight of its neck as a free balance, the quieter will be its gait.

But such " square " horses are usually incapable of long-striding movements. No endeavour should be made to turn them into future dressage horses or jumpers.

The cause of cramped tensions in backs that are otherwise normal is to be found in the itching or pain of the extensor muscles less frequently than one supposes. The flexor muscles of the back—the abdominal muscles—are often affected seriously by irregularities in the intestinal canal, so that they resist loosening. The cause, digestive disturbances, must first be eliminated by withholding feed before the working period.

If the horse's croup is higher than the top point of the withers, we have a downhill horse. This conformation defect is almost always combined with *long, obtuse-angled hind legs*. We shall therefore discuss both of these faults together.

The shape and position of this back and hindquarters give the inexperienced rider the unpleasant feeling of riding downhill, and he instinctively tries to balance out the elevation behind his saddle by pressing down with his weight and using his reins to lift the forehand actively. All he succeeds in doing, however, is to increase the stiffness of the hind legs and the back, which hold all the trumps in this struggle, including the open angles and their forward slope, so that they will successfully resist the small of the rider's back.

used until the horse grows supple; this should be followed by a supple sitting trot, which affords a better opportunity of using the seat to drive the horses.

In general it is easier to loosen up difficult horses that have not had any regular gymnastic training by using predominant lateral controls on the circle rather than on a straight line. The driving seat should be used and the horse's head turned inward somewhat; thus the outside rein applies delicate pressure for an instant and then yields completely in order to entice the horse's head and neck forward and down.

In this work, which should be done with the lightest sort of hand, and with the hands entering into the movement, the rider exploits the lesser counteraction of thrust on the circle and the greater leverage of the outer rein upon the horse's mouth. He also makes use of the predominant engagement of *one* hind leg (the inside one).

It is the rein on one side, acting vigorously and with lightning rapidity upon the more yielding side, that remedies the situation in the event of disobedience, such as shying, rearing, or bolting.

If an old, dyed-in-the-wool outlaw, which weak riders have often allowed to have its own way, shies and refuses to pass ccertain objects—standing rooted to a spot or turning about, for example—the following should be tried: have it perform successive voltes on the more supple side, growing wider towards the front and flatter towards the rear. In order to prevent any attempt at halting mechanically and to maintain uninterrupted movement, the rider may narrow these voltes until they become the so-called " mills ", like the " turns in motion ", the inside hand, holding a short rein, being given support behind the knee until the horses has passed the object that caused it to shy. To be sure, a horse's reputation is hardly improved by such performances in public.

The experienced rider, on the other hand, will shorten his stirrup straps by one or two holes and use the forward seat to drive the horse, making the steep hind legs engage far forward and not letting the horse bind his hands. Only after the horse's back yields does he think of increasing the load, followed by moderate flexion of the hocks as a result of lateral flexion work. Thrust will always remain the forte of such horses. The load thrown on the forelegs by the spinal column that slopes to the front will always involve increased strain on these legs, as well as hinder the development of horizontal equilibrium. Such horses are sometimes seen in thoroughbreds that are bred for the special purpose of winning sprints instead of improving the breed after being tested on the race track as well-balanced horses.

Horses whose *backs slope to the rear* and rest upon hind legs that are cow-hocked are said to have a " goose rump " or a " rainy-day croup ". The horses of poor conformation just discussed have too much thrust at the expense of carrying capacity, but here an opposite situation develops. If we don't want their hocks (which are already defenceless because of their narrow angles) to suffer, we must ride these horses at free gaits to develop thrust without dreaming of engagement of the hindquarters or lifting of the forehand in order not to force the hind carpal joints even closer together.

Like sway-backs, such horses are very comfortable to ride and are preferred for elderly gentlemen. Of course, none of these horses should be called upon for endurance runs.

If the horse is cow-hocked, and also has sickle hocks, the fetlocks suffer. Horses that have these defects and any tendency to bowed hocks, which lets the hocks "turn", thus evading any load, should be spared any attempts at manège collection.

As the preceding examples have shown, *correct action of the hind legs is the key to the pulsating activity of the back*. If they do their duty or can just manage to do so despite defective conformation, the back will stretch and the horse will seek contact with the bit, thus becoming supple.

The horse cannot move correctly unless its entire locomotive machinery co-operates by flexing and extending.

If the hindquarters and back are in order, defective conformations of the neck will also be corrected as far as the conformation of the horse permits.

Although we are familiar with this, we should always remember that the clockwork—hindquarters and back—governs the correct functioning of the clock's hands and that nothing is accomplished by tinkering with them. Translated into equestrian language this means: work on the hindquarters and back to secure good results on the neck. Only then will you obtain contact with the bit and a neck correctly shaped to the bit.

When the neck is long and muscular enough, we are sure of a good advance of the legs from the shoulders, since the muscle extending from the head to the neck and the humerus will be fully developed. The neck should grow out of the chest, neither too high nor too low.

A long, thin, strongly curved neck that is set on too high—a *swan-neck* —interferes seriously with contact with the bit.

The *ewe-neck* is in many ways the opposite of a swan-neck, though it, too, is usually set on too high. If an *upside-down* neck is associated with a short poll and lower jaws that are too wide or too sharp and not rounded off enough at their corners (inserted like pain-producing wedges between the muscles of the neck, the transverse processes of the second cervical vertebra, and the parathyroid glands, squeezing the latter and preventing them from falling into place above the edges of the lower jaw), the horse will always tend to get above the bit—to evade control. This is clearly manifested when the horse's mane is cut short.

The inexperienced rider always sees the horse's head and neck in front of him and tends to use his hands too much. Having heard that the neck is the horse's steering wheel and tie rod, he tends to " get hold " of the horse from front to rear, his hands interfering with the horse's muscular action in an endeavour to help out where they should remain passive.

Swan-necks as well as all thin and spindly necks, covered with thin, flabby muscles, involve many vices, and they require much effort to make them stretch until the rider gets the feeling of positive contact with the bit at vigorous gaits. These are the only ones that should be used and should be free gaits at the outset. Once this is achieved, the major problem is solved. But it may take years of patient work with a thick rubber snaffle before we reach that point. Time is needed because the base of the neck must be made broader, and the depressions between the sides of the neck and the shoulders must fill out with muscles in order to provide ·a steady support for the lower neck. The horse's neck must arise from a firm, broad foundation, like a fishing rod, whose lower end is almost unbending but whose upper end must be thin, elastic, and flexible. The principal factors in broadening the base of the neck are the scalenus muscles already referred to—an important pair of muscles running from the lower cervical vertebrae to the ribs, which pull the ribs, the abdominal muscles, and the hindquarters forward, and thus generate impulsion and advance.

Whenever a broad, heavy nape, attached to *a short, heavy, straight neck set on fairly low*, tempts the rider to simulate flexion of the poll by means of active alternating tugs on the reins—what we call " sawing "—before the horse has grown supple, the scalenus muscles are weakened, impulsion and thrust are not secured, and the horse, which already tends to use its forehand, falls on its shoulder and wears out its forelegs prematurely. But if our aims are more modest, and we train such a horse to carry itself in ordinary posture, it can be turned into a serviceable animal though never a good-looking one.

False articulation of the cervical vertebrae, with the muscles at the base of the neck standing out in a cramped fashion, makes the ewe-neck or upside-down neck a problem. The connection between the hindquarters and the mouth and vice versa is interrupted at the base of the neck, where this false lifting of the neck impedes transmission of controls (see "The Wrong Bend", p. 124). The only remedy for this is patient work to stretch the neck forward and downward and fix it in this position. Months later the lower muscles that now stick out like goitres will grow smaller because they have been extended by this stretching and can no longer be employed to hold the neck upright.

It is not only swan-necks that are unsteady and shaky. Saddle-horse necks of ideal conformation often become shorter, looser, and more curved as the result of the wrong kind of work. All of a sudden the rider's hands are empty, and the beautiful gait of the horse is lost.

Stretching such an arched neck and straightening it out, and steadying it, is one of the hardest jobs the trainer ever has to do. Gentle, forward-lifting pulls on the reins, with the rider's legs clinging to the horse's body, will not always be successful. It is better to use a feathery-light hand that follows the horse's mouth, remaining in the lightest contact with the bit. Pressing forward with the feet will result at first in nothing more than a hesitant endeavour to stretch. We are still far from letting the horse come to the bit. Such an inveterate " star-gazer " utilizes the slightest pressure on the bit, produced with the beginning of extension, to fall back again behind the vertical unless the hands follow the reins like a rubber band that refuses to let itself be stretched.

I therefore begin by yielding, letting the hands, and possibly the arms, advance without changing the length of the reins, allowing the neck to stretch still more, if possible, and trying to achieve very long strides *at the same time timing* by employing an adhering pressure of my legs.

My driving controls must maintain impulsion, but I must always be careful to drive gently to prevent any restlessness or rushing (see the comments on softness of the rider's legs at the walk, p. 214).

The rider's hands, remaining " rubbery ", must always " float ", and they must be employed only to keep the head and neck straight.

The horse's stretching to reach the bit will become more pronounced after a few lessons. Bringing up the hindquarters has also lifted the head and neck, and now the time has come for the hand, which has been merely "following", to become passive. Quietly sustaining, it fixes the extended mouth, that is, it ensures the sought-for contact with the bit.

But as soon as the horse relapses into its old faults, the pressure must cease, and the hands must again become "floating rubber-band hands", in order to make the horse stretch to reach the bit in impulsion and timing as described above.

This requires unremitting patience and the finest of feelings, but the objective is worth the labour.

"Defects of disposition are harder to correct than defects of conformation," as the old Austrian riding manual puts it. This is even truer of character defects.

The horse that defends itself against excessive "gathering" because of unresolved tension or pain does not have a bad disposition. The causes of a disposition and character that is hard to handle lie much deeper and are to be sought chiefly in the psychological field.

Sluggishly resisting dispositions are harder to bring to the point of joyful obedience—volunteering to meet the rider's demands. These are not always unblooded horses; they are often splendid specimens. All they lack is the *spark of animation, this most precious gift that a horse can present to its trainer*.

If the rider is unable to make this spark glow, all his work and efforts are in vain. Such horses will never do more than crawl around sluggishly. At the very outset they should be made to understand that they must jump forward *unconditionally* in response to the driving controls; the rider should use brief but vigorous spurring or, even better, strokes of the riding crop, just behind the girth. It is a matter of course that no compromise should be allowed nor any time for rearing or kicking. Once success has been attained, bring the horse to a stop very gently and praise it at once. Later on, a mere threat will suffice to make it prick up its ears and go forward to the bit. As a result the controls employed can grow progressively easier.

Such skulking sloths have latent reserves of power and energy that they display as soon as they feel they are carrying a weak rider who employs half-hearted measures. They buck and rear to free themselves of the controls, deliberately bolt, and prove that a phlegmatic temperament can well be combined with a choleric one.

If immediate results must be obtained with old, badly trained, fundamentally ruined horses that do not respond to the correct equestrian controls, and they must be prevented from rearing, kicking, turning about, refusing to move, or trying to bite the rider's legs, it is advisable to use "stiffened reins" (with a steel core); they enable the physically weakest rider to extend the horse's neck and head by advancing his hands. The forehand, thus pushed forward irresistibly like a wheelbarrow, pulls the hindquarters, the source of support, with it and prevents the horse from standing still. The only thing the horse can do now is to lunge out *forward*, so that the rider wins out.

Using the spurs too far behind the girth would merely intensify the recalcitrance of such inveterate, dissimulating outlaws, for they sunder the trunk in the region of the false ribs, thus hindering the hind-leg engagement that facilitates obedience and promoting dragging of the hind legs. Brief, vigorous spurring just behind or, even better, in front of the girth is the only possible support for the stiffened reins.

The horse is a peaceful vegetarian by nature, and, with the exception of stallions or mares defending their young, flight is its natural reaction to all kinds of fear and pain.

If the rider is rough or clumsy, if the horse is disturbed by strange sounds or unusual odours that we cannot even smell, or if it sees unknown objects, its first reaction is to run away. If this tendency is very pronounced and is further intensified by lack of confidence in the rider, it may turn into a habitual state of excited fear.

Many such horses that have had to carry a rider who was somewhat nervous and impatient, though otherwise a good rider, have been calmed down by a simple stableman who let them loaf around out of doors for hours on long reins. They later turned out to be exceptionally sturdy saddle horses. All that was needed was to restore their shaken confidence in man and then employ this regained confidence to establish the conviction that nothing can happen to them as long as they are in contact with a soft seat and gentle hand. The abatement of the psychological pressure produced by excitement will also diminish the excessive expenditure of nervous energy, which in turn will directly promote digestion and improve the horse's condition.

Fearful horses and *rushers* should first be allowed to find themselves by carrying a stableman of tried and tested steadiness at the walk, with no reins at all if possible, until they are bored. Then they should be worked on a very large circle, laid out in such a way that practically no guiding controls are necessary[87] (closed on three sides).

They are then allowed to move simply at the trot; the rider merely tries to follow their movements, using a supple seat without employing all his weight. He should avoid any idea of regulating the rate at the outset!

[87] Very light hints of opening rein action, forward and to the side, applied in time with the movement, may be employed to keep them on the large circumference, more or less, without any thought of equestrian longitudinal flexion, of course.

If the rider is sufficiently patient, the time will come when the horse will voluntarily slow down. He should then apply his legs gently and keep them in contact with the horse.

These moments of spontaneous gathering will recur more and more frequently, and as the horse quiets down, the rider will be able to *drive* it, though with infinite care. Once he is able to do so, the horse no longer rushes, for the steps taken by the hind legs are no longer too short. They also begin to engage farther forward, thus taking longer strides and having to slow down their timing. The horse receives better support from the hindquarters, is able to maintain itself, and no longer loses its equilibrium towards the front.

It will itself realize how much more pleasant this kind of motion is and will seek out the controls—legs and hands—from which it used to flee.

VIII. Relationship of the Rider's Weight and Controls to the Anatomical Mechanism of the Horse

The first objective in our training of the young horse is getting all the muscles required for locomotion and carrying the load to flex and contract freely. Later on, our driving influences produce longer and more energetic strides of the hind legs and hence more energetic pulsations of these groups of muscles, so that the whole spinal column is stretched towards the front, the horse is supple and in contact with the bit, and the flexing activity of the hindquarters counterbalances this stretching and maintains equilibrium. We strengthen these muscles by training and supple them by gymnastic exercise to enable them to do this job.

Some of the most important muscles involved are the croup (ischia) muscles linked to those of the back and reaching down to the stifle and hock joints; the gluteal muscles located around the hip joints, which also branch down to the stifle; the long dorsal muscles, whose action reaches from the dock of the tail to the occipital bone in the horse's head; the latissimus dorsi muscles that branch off from them and control the movements of the forelegs; the cervical muscles starting at the front thoracic vertebrae (the withers) and connecting them with the cervical vertebrae; and the spinal muscles, which transmit the forward pull of the cervical muscles upon the spinous processes to the vertebrae and act as a strong elastic suspensory band to prevent the back from sagging and to produce the free, elevated, and supple carriage of the tail when they function correctly.

The mastoidohumeralis muscles, which connect the head, the neck, and the humerus, are equally important, because they are necessary for the smooth co-operation of the forehand and the hindquarters. Then there are the scalenus muscles, which attach the ribs to the base of the neck, and lastly, the abdominal muscles which run along the belly and sides of the horse's body as a sort of truss, affecting respiration and acting as the bottom half of the muscular ring, in combination with the dorsal and scalenus muscles, to establish the connection between the forehand and the hindquarters.

Together with a few other muscles, these groups of muscles constitute a closed muscular ring, as may be seen in any atlas of anatomy.

A. ACTIVE AND PASSIVE FLEXION OF THE HINDQUARTERS

The strongest groups of muscles are those surrounding the thighs and the pelvis of the horse. These are the sources of the horse's locomotive power, and it is here—at the haunches—that equestrian action must set in.

Let us begin by observing the action of the two joints that constitute the haunches when the horse begins to move from a standstill at the vertical. When one hind leg is lifted to move forward, the stifle joint opens, whereas the hip joint closes. In the other hind leg, which is still grounded, however, both of the haunch joints remain open until the instant of push-off. At this moment both of them bend until the hind leg has reached the vertical as it swings forward. After it passes the vertical, the hip joint continues to bend, whereas the stifle joint opens, as described above for the start from a vertical standstill.

The bending of the hip joint and the stifle mentioned above is *active* bending and it has to take place, for the leg must be shortened to enable it to be lifted above the ground to advance. This active bending occurs in every horse that does not grow stiff or hold tight, whether it is moving in natural balance or a high degree of collection. The degree of bending depends only upon the irregularities of the terrain or the horse's endeavour to shorten its hind legs in order to facilitate their swinging back and forth. Examples of this are the pronounced shortening of the hind legs in stepping over *cavalletti* and at the racing trot[88] and the racing gallop.

Passive bending of the haunches, which is infinitely more important to us horsemen, takes place only as the result of the increased load on the

[88] This can be seen very clearly in the tremendous leaps taken by a trotter as it shifts from one diagonal to the other.

It should be added that the forelegs of almost all trotters, except those with very long legs, take off fractions of a second before their hind legs, so that their forehand remains off the ground for a longer time. This earlier take-off of the forelegs is what makes it possible for the trotter to compensate the shortness of its forelegs compared to the length of its hind legs, which is particularly prominent at maximum engagement. Secondly, its hind legs can now reach forward as far as possible without running the risk of hitting the forelegs or having to evade them by stepping forward and to the side, and thus losing speed.

hindquarters. This temporarily increased load may be observed even in the raw, riderless horse whenever it is excited, for example, and shifts its centre of gravity towards its hindquarters (putting a greater load upon them) by way of preparation for rapid changes of direction.

As a consequence of equestrian action, this passive bending of the haunches takes place during the supporting phase of the hind leg that is grounded. It reaches a maximum as the horse's body in motion moves over the vertical hind leg. If the hind leg evades this bending by growing stiff, the rider's upper body "see-saws" at the gallop and the buttocks jounce in the saddle.

The bending during the phase of support achieved by gymnastic training of the hindquarters is affected by the same groups of muscles that produce extension—the push-off in the phase of support. The extensor muscles, the muscles of the croup in our case, keep the hindquarters of the mounted horse in a state of appropriate engagement by preventing the haunch joints from opening completely during the extension movements. The more this phase of engagement is emphasized at the expense of pure extension, the more cradling and vigorous does the gait become and the less does the opening of the joint angles for thrust result in a gradual extension of the joints to their utmost, but rather in an elastic swing forward in the engaged state. As the horse's hind foot leaves the ground, it remains less and less behind the vertical, pushing off in time with springy action. The push-off, with a comparatively long period of time spent behind the vertical and the hindquarter joints open to their maximum extent, is turned more and more into a forward swing.

We notice that the muscles of the croup are practically never at rest, since they bend the stifle actively from the instant of take-off, including the first half of the hind legs' phase of suspension; they also stretch it somewhat during the entire phase of support following the second half of the forward swing, until the leg pushes off again. But the stifle is maintained in an appropriate state of passive bending even in this stretching action, depending on the extent to which the hindquarters are lowered.

In other words, the muscles of the croup are inactive only during one quarter of the entire phase sequence, which constitutes a complete cycle from a given position of the horse's legs to the repetition of the same position. During this period of inactivity—the second half of the forward advance of the hind leg until it alights again—their place is taken by two other muscles that extend the stifle.

This almost uninterrupted work that has to be done by the muscles of the croup, both as flexors and extensors, is another reason why young horses that are still not fully developed cease to engage their hindquarters during long periods at the trot, letting the tired hind legs drag flabbily or try to evade passive flexion by growing stiff or hurrying (taking shorter strides).

B. EFFECT OF HINDQUARTERS' FLEXION UPON THE BACK
AND THE FOREHAND

As in collection, the lowering of the hindquarters produced by the gait in passive engagement as a consequence of the activity of the muscles of the croup also results in a lowering of the spinal column from front to rear that can be seen and felt, depending upon the extent of this flexion. The relieved forehand is thus enabled to advance more freely and loftily (the so-called freedom of the shoulders) and grow out of the withers. The preceding forward carriage of the neck and head is replaced by a forward and upward carriage—the relative lifting of the forehand.

The abdominal muscles also participate in this activity of relieving the forehand. They contribute to the extension of all the muscles of the croup and buttocks, which have already been drawn backward and downward by the longer path they have to travel around the bent joints of the hindquarters. This effect, which is most pronounced at the gallop, is produced by the forward swing of the hind legs as the result of the rhythmic forward pull of the lower edge of the pelvis. Since the muscles of the croup and buttocks are connected to those of the back, their tensile action extends to the dorsal muscles, thus effecting the lifting of the spinal column in the chest and neck.

In a horse that is moving properly the back is extended in two ways: downward and to the rear, since the croup and buttocks muscles are stretched in this direction as a result of the closing of the angle of the hindquarters and of the abdominal muscles' forward pull upon the lower edge of the pelvis; and forward, as a result of the extension of the neck that is connected to it (see Section C below).

This double extension is the characteristic feature of correct collection, which is inconceivable without tension of the dorsal muscles produced by vigorous strides and the elastic interplay of the various muscular groups in the ring of muscles.

In this state the horse is also able to transmit brief backward tugs on the reins, which increase the lever action of the steady neck upon the hindquarters (active lifting of the forehand). In such a state of collection the rider clearly feels the hindquarters lowering and the back rising just behind the withers.

The double extension of the back owing to the stretching of the muscles of the hindquarters and the neck and the resulting tension that is required for collection, makes the topline of the horse—croup, back, crest of the

44. Exemplary manner. The horse given complete freedom by the rider is using himself in exemplary manner. Notice the position of the horse's knees. Al Fiore on *Riviera Wonder* (Thoroughbred).

45. A smooth jump with the rider "going with" the horse. David Kelly on *Andante* (Genesee Valley).

46. An excellent example of a straight line between the horse's mouth and the rider's elbow. William Steinkraus on *Baldoyle* (Thoroughbred) 1952.

neck—longer in collection than in any other posture of the horse. The term " gathered " is applicable to such a horse only in so far as the line from mouth to its ischium is naturally shorter than when its carriage is freer.

But the topline becomes longer in spite of the correct articulation of the hindquarters, the trunk, and the forehand, for, as has been stated repeatedly, the elevated neck and the bent joints of the hindquarters act like so many rollers, forcing the muscles to take detours, and thus stretching and lengthening them.

C. RESTORING CORRECT BACK ACTION BY USING THE ABDOMINAL AND CERVICAL MUSCLES

When the untrained horse is ridden for the first time, its reaction to the unaccustomed burden of the rider is a cramped contraction of its dorsal muscles, which is seen and felt as a cramped, arched back.

After the horse has calmed down and grown tired, this is followed by an equally cramped extension; the back sags, and the load is carried by the spinal column alone, with practically no co-operation from the muscles.

In both cases the functioning of the muscles is bad, since in the first they are hardly extended at all, while in the second they are hardly braced. Thus they function irregularly instead of pulsating elastically.

The rider's first job is to get the back to arch correctly, that is, to return it to the position—halfway between the two extremes described above—that it had in the free, natural run of the unmounted, untrained horse. As training continues, the rider employs riding controls to make the horse's natural, elastic pulsations even more elastic and expressive. He thus manages to make the back an indispensable co-operating factor in the sequence of motions. The back is naturally destined for this role by its connection to the locomotion muscles of the forehand and the hindquarters.

The more successful we are in relieving the dorsal muscles of the work of actual load-carrying, so that they are able to oscillate freely and elastically and are available for locomotion and the transmission of impulsion, the longer, springier, and better-timed will be the gaits. To achieve this, the rider must refrain from interference with the activity of the back, first, by using a relieving forward crotch seat (his seat in the saddle being particularly soft in the direction of the fibres of the dorsal muscles), so that his weight, feathering with the movements of the horse, does not interfere with their elastic oscillation.

Second, other muscle groups, the cervical and abdominal muscles, must be called upon to relieve the dorsal muscles, which are neither intended nor able to carry a load.

Let us first consider the cervical muscles with their ligamentum nuchae, which have to restore the loaded back to its natural position, that is, arch it correctly.

The spinous processes of the first thoracic vertebrae—the vertebrae of the withers—to which the cervical muscles are attached, are fairly long, slanting upwards from front to rear. Thus they are ideal lever arms for the tensile action that is exerted towards the front by the cervical muscles and transferred to the vertebrae of the back by the elastic supporting band of spinal muscles. This tensile action occurs whenever the neck is extended. The vertebrae associated with the spinous processes of the withers, pulled forward by the neck muscles and the ligamentum nuchae, are pressed together, as are the other back and lumbar vertebrae connected with them via the continuation of the ligamentum nuchae. As this thrust terminates at the practically immovable lumbosacral joint (not at the sacroiliac joint, as is often stated), the vertebrae of the back must deflect in the only direction possible—upward. They become arched, stretching from the defective sagging position into their normal one.

In young horses this tensile action of the cervical muscles must be allowed full play. This is done by allowing the neck to stretch forward as far as possible and to descend so that its not inconsiderable weight may instinctively reinforce the tensile action of the cervical muscles, which are still immature.

The further gymnastic training progresses, the less need is there for an *active* co-operation of the cervical muscles. Since the head and neck are passively suspended from the withers by the cervical muscles and the ligamentum nuchae, they balance the load of the rider's weight carried by the back (ordinary posture).

In well-trained horses the cervical muscles, which must have grown as hard as marble, are able to keep the back in its right position even when the forehand is lifted high.

The cervical and spinal muscles are supported by the abdominal muscles in arching the back, i.e., giving it the position in which it can swing most freely. The importance of the abdominal muscles as locomotion muscles must not be over-estimated, however, as they are subjected to stress by their major function of serving as a suspension for the viscera and cannot devote much force to pulling the pelvis and the hind legs forward.

The forward pull of the pelvis by the abdominal muscles in the state of collection is not a permanent state in the correctly moving horse, for this would seriously interfere with free respiration. It is a rhythmic forward pull of the pelvis and of the hind legs, in time with the gait, which is most clearly expressed when the hind leg swings forward in the suspension phase of the gallop and is felt by the rider as an elastic arching of the spinal column underneath his buttocks in time with the gait.

The fact that flabby " grass bellies " grow smaller and tauter after regular though brief work at the gallop, while hours of work at the walk and trot have no effect, is further proof that the abdominal muscles do more work at the gallop than in the other gaits.

D. CORRELATION OF BREATHING, TIMING, AND SUPPLENESS IN THE VARIOUS GAITS

The importance of free breathing during motion to the performance of a horse needs no special emphasis. But the horse can breathe freely only if the muscles that envelop the floating ribs, which expand with every inhalation, are supple in their functioning. If the muscles pulsate in a cramped fashion, i.e., irregularly, with tension predominating, so that they are held fast in the equestrian sense of the term, they interfere with the expansion of the chest and hence with breathing.

The long dorsal muscle and the external oblique muscle of the abdomen are the two muscles that chiefly envelop the floating ribs. If these two muscles pulsate elastically and are supple, the floating ribs can provide space for free breathing. The horse acknowledges this " dropping " of the hitherto raised ribs by snorting, thus telling our ear that it has achieved suppleness.

All the abdominal muscles, especially the one mentioned above, act to compress the lungs during exhalation. If their pulsations are supple, breathing in and out is regular and unimpeded; this is manifested by the horse's comfortable snorting. This breathing in and out occurs in time with the gait only at the gallop, where expiration coincides with the forward swing of the hind legs, while inspiration coincides with their push-off from the ground. Respiration is independent of the phase sequence at the trot and walk, however.

Another advantage of muscles that are supple is that the sensory and motor nerves, which actually set off the motion called for by the rider's legs, can now function along transmission lines that are free from interference.

The scalenus muscles, which run from the lower cervical vertebrae to the first rib, are no longer considered of much importance as supports for the first rib and hence for the entire thorax. They are too weak to hold the powerful chest all by themselves, with no support other than the movable base of the neck, and thus cannot provide a stable platform for the activity of the abdominal muscles that start at the ribs.

The scalenus muscles are important from the equestrian standpoint, however, because they may become the seat of local resistance to the longitudinal flexion of the neck in the event of one-sided stiffness (the horse going against the bit on the constrained side or twisting its neck). In the event of stiffness on both sides, they stand out as large muscular lumps, so that the lower edge of the neck becomes convex (horses that are over the bit, with a ewe-neck, see p. 255). When the flexion of the entire horse, including the neck, is correct, with the ligamentum nuchae snapping towards the bent side in collection, the scalenus muscles offer no resistance to lateral flexion. This is made visible by parallel transverse wrinkles of the skin on the concave side of the neck.

The scalenus muscles support the superficial locomotion muscles of the shoulders, which are strongly developed in powerful horses, like the cervical muscles, so that the hollow between the shoulder and the base of the neck disappears almost entirely.

If the rider weakens the scalenus muscles by see-sawing on the reins, the horse's compliance is false—its neck becomes short and loose and its gait is lost. The activity of the muscular ring is interrupted at this point.

The pulsations of the spinal column make the whole body of the horse pulsate, as we know. They are long or short, strong or weak, depending upon the energy and length of the hindquarters' strides, and they also produce pulsations of the cervical spinal column. When these pulsations flow like waves against the occipital bones and the rider's seat is correct, the poll grows supple, and the horse's head is carried with its nose somewhat to the front. The horse then offers itself to the action of the reins.

But if the rider's seat opposes the movement, the pulsations of the dorsal muscles and the other muscles are interfered with and become painful. The muscles begin to pulsate convulsively instead of elastically, stiffness sets in, and the horse will tighten its poll, the conversion point of the muscle ring, where the extensor muscular activity is supposed to be succeeded by the flexor activity.

CHAPTER THREE

THE SECONDARY FIELD SCHOOL

I. The Secondary Field School as a Natural Transition from the Elementary Field School to the Haute École

As a continuation of the ordinary or elementary field (cross-country) school, the secondary field school is both an elaboration of what the horse learned in the previous school and an organic evolution from the simpler to the more difficult, constituting the transition to the lessons of the *haute école*.

After completing the ordinary school, no experienced rider will have any doubts about whether he can make greater demands upon his horse, training it to be a secondary field horse with the correct schooled gaits—the prerequisite for all dressage horses of the higher classes. The principal requirement for all of these demands is a capacity for collection and a development of impulsion that is far above the average. The preceding training must have clearly told the rider whether this capacity for collection has reached its natural limits, fixed either by the horse's conformation or its disposition.

One thing is certain: among many thousands of horses only a few will qualify for the university of higher dressage science, and the horses that after long years of training merit the honorary title " manège horse of the *haute école* " are fewer still.

Aside from the dozen Lipizzan horses that have completed their training in the Spanish Riding School of Vienna and in the castle of Budapest (if we can ever speak of complete perfection in a manège horse) and are in a class of their own, there are hardly a dozen living works of art in all the equestrian nations of the world that fully deserve this title.[1]

One misconception is all too common among laymen. There are people who may never have seen a properly trained manège horse. They have, however, seen falsely trained " dressage horses ", broken down and robbed of their gait and impulsion, and believe that manège training stifles forward impulsion and the capacity for long-striding working gaits. Precisely the contrary is true. In intensified collection, for example, the muscles of the croup, which make the principal contribution to the bend-

---

[1] Written in 1941.

ing of the haunches and also act as extensor muscles, perform the greatest amount of work and are under extraordinary tension when the hindquarters are lowered. This exercise strengthens these muscles of the croup, which are equally important as flexors and extensors, to such a degree that the gait of a well-trained manège horse is more energetic, vigorous, and elastic in the extended gaits, where the fastest forward movement is required, than a general utility horse, whose locomotion machinery could not be improved by perfected and refined training.

The flexors and extensors must co-operate in smooth purity and fluid harmony if the changes of rate are to be faultless. Whether flexion or extension predominates at any instant will depend upon the degree of collection. Bracing the seat or opening and closing the fingers must suffice to make thrust predominate over carrying capacity, and vice versa, letting the horse fit into the changed framework with perfect poise. Such a horse adapts itself to any situation and is always under control. It has become " motion-pliant ", if I may coin the term, adopting the appropriate form for the given rate and degree of collection. It is just as ready for an extended gallop as it is to accept a half halt immediately thereafter, turning within the narrowest radius upon its lowered hindquarters. Rider and horse have been fused into a physical and mental unity; they are two hearts with a single thought—the miraculous alchemy of riding has truly made them one.

Such art is classic art, classic because form and content complement each other equally and synchronize, producing a perfect harmony!

Now, even if its rider had never tried to execute a passage with such a horse, it still would reserve the title of manège horse more than many, many other horses that display " perfect " manège gaits.

Impulsion is the reliable barometer as to whether the forward drive is threatened with extinction when carrying capacity is predominantly stressed. Seat and hands must always feel quite clearly how this most important aid of the manège rider merely waits, as it were, to accelerate the horse from its bent, energetic haunches elastically into the powerful extension of the freer gaits, fluidly and without the slightest hesitation.

II. Counter-gallop

The usefulness of brief rides at the counter-gallop to make the outside hind leg (which plays the principal part at the gallop) more supple was pointed out earlier in the discussion of galloping.

The counter-gallop is also an excellent remedy for crookedness, which will make its appearance more or less seriously whenever new demands are made upon the horse. We let the forehand gallop *into* the wall of the riding hall, so to speak, by leading with the shoulder, thus achieving more even loading on all four legs, since this bond prevents the inner hind leg from evading towards the inside and escaping our control.

The danger of such turning out is also slight in the corners, where the wall offers no support, since in the corners the inside hind leg cannot move sideways from the outside leg because equilibrium must be maintained. But we can and must pay all the more attention to maintaining a fluid, leaping three-beat gait in the counter-turns, which must not be taken on too small a radius. We must concentrate our attention on the development of impulsion, since the straightened, even-loaded hindquarters must also cover a somewhat longer arc and must gallop against the flexed position, which deprives the horse of impulsion. (This is also the case in races and turns in jumping competitions.) We must, therefore, maintain the impulsion and compactness of the gallop by tugging lightly on the outside rein to relieve the forehand and by employing a driving action that alternates regularly with the rein control. Otherwise the posture of the gallop would be lost in the turns and would break down into a sluggish, inexpressive, dragging four-beat gait.

The more the horse learns to balance itself with its strengthened and more pliant haunches in the counter-turns, made closer and closer, the more will the rider be able to do without the supervisory activity of his outside leg, often required at the beginning of his training, or an increased load applied by the outer seat bone (this seat bone must hold the outside leg[2] to prevent the horse from *changing the lead*) so that his weight can be distributed harmoniously. The rider then feels each individual hind hoof in his fingertips, as it were. His horse balances between his outside leg and his inside rein, which complement each other as diagonal controls, so interconnected that one never does anything without the co-operation of the other.

The inner leg and the outside rein, as regulators of even loading and poise, support the outside leg or the inside rein as required, seeing to it that the halts do not end at the outside shoulder.

Smooth and energetic riding of a figure of eight without change of lead along the short wall of the riding hall is proof of perfect gallop training. Counter-galloping on a circle is preparation for this exercise.

When done correctly, counter-galloping promotes the vigorous forward engagement of the hindquarters with perfect control of both hind legs. From this counter-gallop we can then develop the collected gallop in the gallop position[3]—the outside hind hoof tracking the inside front hoof, so

[2] See footnote on p. 164.

[3] The gallop position, the initial stage of the *travers*, is a two-track movement like the trot position, which has the same degree of longitudinal flexion (see footnote 55, p. 192). The outside hind foot and the inside forefoot track along a straight line parallel to the wall. The two track is bounded by the tracks of the outside forefoot and the inside hind foot.

that the lateral displacement is about one hoof-width, constituting a slight *travers*—and then the actual *travers* and *renvers* gallop with increased lateral distance up to the *redoppe*, which already constitutes a lesson of the *haute école*. The lateral deflection from the previous hoofprint in these two-track gaits must not exceed 45 degrees, as that is the outside limit beyond which longitudinal flexion is no longer pure. Then even loading is no longer present and impulsion is no longer effective.

The impulsion at increased collection that is required for trotting and galloping at this extreme lateral displacement without impairing the gait or even-loading can be developed, however, only by a horse that is ready for the *haute école*.

III. Pirouettes

The development of increased longitudinal flexion at the collected gallop, while maintaining impulsion, even loading, and responsiveness wholly unimpaired, enables the horse to make closer and closer turns on a single track, culminating in the voltes at the gallop. The diameter of this volte cannot be less than six steps for an anatomical reason, the maximum longitudinal flexion of which a horse is capable, and an equestrian reason, even loading on all four legs.

In contrast to the volte at the gallop, which is performed on a single track, in the *pirouette* the forelegs describe a larger circle than the hind legs. That is why it is laid out and taught from a preparatory *travers* (or *renvers*) position.

As the figure is perfected, the circle on which the hindquarters move in the pirouette is made smaller and smaller, so that the hind legs finally gallop in place in the *manège pirouette*. Qualified horses are able to pirouette correctly as early as the training stage of the secondary field (cross-country) school, although their posture and the flexion of their hindquarters are still unable to meet the requirements of the *haute école*.

In a pirouette that merits the honorary title of manège pirouette, we can differentiate and count each single gallop leap and turn, as they are clearly distinguishable at the instant the forehand is raised. It is a matter of course that the horse must not seem to be standing still after every partial turn; these partial turns, though clearly distinguishable, flow smoothly into one another.

The movements of the horse's legs during a pirouette are as follows: at

We therefore find three hoof tracks, as in the trot position and the two " positions ". The name " gallop position " is used because it resembles the " position " that is preparatory to the gallop, the only difference being that the longitudinal flexion is somewhat increased (one half a hoof-breadth). It is tolerated during the initial galloping exercises of a young horse to assist the remount's comprehension when training must be accelerated.

the instant the outside forefoot pushes off, it transfers the impulsion to the inside foreleg, which elastically transmits the load of the forehand upward and to the side. After the phase of suspension, the outside hind leg is the first to pick up the load, after which it whips the horse's body around for the turn. Then the inside hind foot moves forward to take over the load, immediately transferring it to the outside forefoot, that is, towards the front. As these two legs alight practically simultaneously, even at the manège gallop, no turning can occur at the instant the principal diagonal (inside hind foot—outside forefoot) is grounded, as is often stated, unless the pirouette is faulty. After every well-ridden pirouette the spectator must be able to see the horse coming out of the figure with complete impulsion and faultless position, resuming its path in a smooth gallopade on a straight line along the single track or two tracks from which the turn started. During the pirouette the rider must have the feeling of being able to stop the turning movement at any time and continue riding straight ahead. If he does not have this feeling, something is wrong. It may be that impulsion has vanished—the horse displays a "trampled-down" pirouette, in which the hind legs, which "are looking for something behind them", hesitatingly stick to the ground or even come to a complete rest without leaping. Or else suppleness has failed, so that the faulty longitudinal flexion makes the hindquarters turn out in some horses and turn in in others, depending on where the greater stiffness is located. Finally, if the flexibility of the haunches, and of the hocks that are directly dependent on them, is not up to the increased load, the three most important joints of the hindquarters grow stiff, and the rise of the forehand degenerates into prancing. The hind legs are spread very far apart, and the horse hesitates to advance its outside hind leg (in order not to have to place all the load on the inside hind foot). Thus it creates the impression that it grounds both hind legs simultaneously.

The widely held opinion that the centre of rotation in the pirouette lies " at " or " under " the inside hind foot is as erroneous as the compromise opinion that the pirouette is performed with equal distribution of weight upon both hind legs.

Since the pirouette is performed around the hindquarters, it is obvious that both hind legs participate and have to carry the load. But the outside hind foot is predominant, as is evident from the relationship of the two legs during alighting. We must not be deceived by the fact that the inside hind leg is engaged somewhat farther forward at the moment it takes up the load. What matters is the flexion[4] in the hindquarter joint

---

[4] See the passage on active and passive flexion of the hindquarters in Part Two, Chap. Two, Sec. VIII, " Relationship of the Rider's Weight and Controls to the Anatomical Mechanism of the Horse ", for the closing and opening of the angles in the joints of the hindquarters.

and the hock. But precisely during this phase, when the inside hind leg seems to carry most of the load, this flexion cannot be nearly so great (because of the greater extension forward) as it is in the outside hind leg during the preceding phase of the gait sequence, when the partial turn took place.

A correctly performed half or whole pirouette, in which—it cannot be repeated too often—the gallop leap must not differ from that of the manège *travers* or *renvers* gallop, i.e., the hind legs must not stick to the ground but must push off elastically, involves a sequence of two to four partial turns, 180 to 360 degrees.

Getting a horse to pirouette by gradually narrowing the volte at a *travers* gallop will be feasible only with a horse that is endowed with extraordinarily powerful hindquarters and considerable natural impulsion.

A more promising approach is to teach the pirouette from the counter-gallop, which is ridden five to eight steps away from the long wall and parallel to it. To do this we start from the far corner of the long wall and execute a *passade*, which is merely a wide or close half-turn in a more or less pronounced *travers* position, until we continue the counter-gallop at the given distance from the wall, keeping exactly parallel to the wall.

A few steps away from the corner we increase collection, so that the strides become shorter and higher, while maintaining impulsion and vigour, and go over to the *renvers* gallop, from which we perform a half-pirouette in the corner, the hindquarters galloping more or less in place. The corner into which the horse pirouettes, so to speak, makes it easier for it to understand what is required and provides additional moral support for its movements. This teaching procedure should be interrupted as soon as the horse displays good will and should be followed by an intermission at the walk.

As the hindquarters grow in strength and dexterity, we will be able to have the hindhand gallop more and more in place during the pirouette.

Later on we shall start the whole or half-pirouette at any point, starting either from the " position " on a single track—so that the *travers* is started only at the instant of the turn—or from a two-track movement.[5] But when this is done the rider must consistently proceed on a single track or two tracks after the figure is completed.

The smaller the circle described by the hindquarters, the more the horse's tendency to evade longitudinal flexion by turning out its hindquarters. This will require special vigilance of the rider's outside, restraining leg and the outside rein that assists it. The rider's inside leg is the

<hr />

[5] With horses that are still in their training period the *travers* or *renvers* should be performed before beginning the pirouette, because the rhythmical tugs on the outside rein, which are intended to put more load on the hindquarters and flex them further whenever necessary, are considerably more effective in a two-track movement, where thrust is naturally much less pronounced because of the lateral displacement.

one that does most of the driving, maintaining (in combination with the somewhat higher, positioning inside hand) the longitudinal flexion, which is controlled by his inside hand and outside leg.

If impulsion diminishes during the pirouette so that the movement becomes heavy and hesitant, the rider must break off the turn, using rigid self-discipline and avoiding all unnecessary disturbance of seat or hands. He must start out at a gallop straight ahead and secure new impulsion to get the resisting horse back in hand and thus get it to go forward correctly.

Over-eager horses try to abandon longitudinal flexion during the pirouette, throwing themselves upon their inside shoulder. They anticipate the controls and lose their even, elevated rhythm together with their longitudinal flexion. If the restraining action of the rider's inside leg applied just behind the girth and an inside rein kept somewhat higher are insufficient to prevent the independent turning of the horse in such cases, the rider must slow the horse down with his inside leg and outside rein (as when slowing down from the *travers*) and continue the pirouette quite calmly as a turn about the hindquarters at the walk. After the turn is completed the rider calmly strikes off at a gallop. Later, the transition to the gallop may be made from the pirouette after such a halt.

With well-schooled horses the pirouette will turn out smoothly and correctly when the rider assists the horse only by means of his seat and the position of his legs that are appropriate to the turn: deep inside knee, hips not pulled in, inner seat bone pushed forward, outside shoulder advanced, the whole combination supported by the elastically tensed back muscles, always ready for action. Anyone who has ever had the good fortune to work with the Lipizzan horses of the Spanish Riding School will agree with me!

The riding masters of the Renaissance were acquainted with the pirouette. Grisone (sixteenth century) rode it at the *travers* in several gallop leaps about the hindquarters, which remained at the centre of rotation. The pirouette, as one of the school figures, was of military importance as a means of defence for the rider.

With the development of firearms, however, manège horsemanship no longer was an end in itself. But the pliability of the hindquarters and the manoeuvrability achieved thereby still remained, alongside endurance, the most highly valued qualities of a cavalry horse.

A riding manual written in 1743 states: "A hussar must be able to exercise and turn his horse at will on a spot no larger than a plate."

IV. Single Flying Change of Lead While Galloping, and Changing Leads on Designated Strides

Before our horse has achieved the carrying capacity and suppleness of the hindquarters required for faultless execution of pirouettes, we can begin with teaching it the *single flying change of lead at the gallop*. We discuss this figure only after instruction in exercising the short half-turn at the gallop in order that it may be followed by a description of several successive changes in lead following a certain number of strides, which call for considerably more exertion on the part of the horse.

The flying change of lead must take place smoothly while advancing, without hesitation and on a single track.[6] Instruction in this movement, which is natural to the horse, can begin when it tells us, as it were, that it would like to start a new gallop by first inserting two unmistakable walking steps in simple changes in lead at the gallop, its contact with the bit remaining unchanged, with perfectly even loading on all four legs and gentle response to the controls.

As in all lessons, but particularly in the change of lead, we must not allow our animated, willing horse to become prejudiced against the new exercise. This would inevitably follow if we went at it without calm preparation and instruction, endeavouring to squeeze a flying change out of it as soon as possible by energetic use of the spurs and rein controls. A horse that has undergone such forcible exercising will never learn how to execute a change of lead with willing devotion to forward movement and an attentive, satisfied, concentrated expression—as if it wanted to do everything well. Such a horse will grow tense as soon as its rider *thinks* the words "change of lead", and it will execute the change with ears laid back, stumbling, holding back, and with a high croup, even if the phase sequence of its steps is correct.

Lymphatic and plump horses should be spared all instruction in the flying change, for they should not be tormented with the demands of higher dressage, since they lack the required congenital verve.

A brief summary of the movement of the horse's legs during the change of lead will show us the required controls, which naturally follow from the changed phase sequence.

Once the horse's inner forefoot has pushed off after the third beat of the gallop, the phase of suspension follows, during which it must change

---

[6] The flying change will be performed with complete assurance and regularity only by a truly supple horse; it must be physically able and psychologically ready to accept and respond to the controls. Its collection must not exceed a uniform load upon its fore- and hind-quarters so that the hind legs have enough freedom for the fluid execution of their " entrechats ".

its lead. To keep the outside hind foot from taking the load first, as it did up to now, greater load must be put on the leg that was formerly the inside leg, making it alight earlier. The other (now carrying a smaller load) swings forward for a longer time and alights later, so that the two hind legs have interchanged their roles.

The rider's controls must therefore act so as to facilitate this change, which of course involves also the horse's forelegs. Guidance and seat must "frame" the horse during this change in such a way that its only forward alternative is swinging into the new gallop.

Hence a load must be placed upon the legs that formerly were the inside legs and their stride must be shortened, while the hitherto outside legs must be relieved of load and caused to lengthen their stride and swing forward. If this change is carried out smoothly, it acts like a soft "interplay" of hindquarters, back, and poll. The preparation for these controls that produce the change is as follows: we get control of the future outside hind leg (which is most important for the smooth performance of the gallop) by forward drive, an increased load exerted by the seat bone on that side, and tugs on the reins, as well as by advancing the shoulder as in the shoulder-in. Once this has been done the rider shifts position and immediately changes his leg position. What was formerly his outside leg slides forward somewhat until it is just behind the girth, while his other leg moves somewhat farther back. The first leg must take care of flexion of the ribs, while the latter must adjust the horse's hindquarters so that its new outside hind leg alights after the change of lead occurring during suspension in the direction that lies between the two forefeet.

The controls for shifting and changing leg position must occur in this sequence (even though hardly distinguishable in point of time) at the instant the diagonal alights, for then the horse will change the lead at the instant of suspension that follows the push-off of the inside front leg, provided it is responsive and knows what is expected of it.

It is often said that the prescribed leg and rein controls should be exercised while the horse is in the phase of suspension. That is the most unproductive kind of theorizing. If we do that while training a young horse, we will always be too late. As we have said, the controls must be applied as soon as the principal diagonal is grounded!

During suspension, that is, at the instant of the change of lead, the small of the rider's back and his legs (the latter in the position described above, immovably clinging to the sides of the horse and stretched from the hip joints) drive the horse straight ahead, using pressure that is more or less pronounced. The rider's hand allows the new inner side to go forward, while the new outside seat bone exerts greater load in order to facilitate an earlier grounding of the hind leg, which formerly was the inside one.

The better the horse understands what it is expected to do, the more its rider will be able to apply the controls (which are not yet quite simultaneous) almost at the same instant, just before and during suspension.

Some riders torment themselves and their horses with uninterrupted " exercising " of the flying change and still fail to achieve absolute certainty. A clean change of lead is always an accident and a matter of luck for them. These are the riders who were unable to display enough patience and understanding during the preceding work at the gallop. They began flying changes before their horse was able to take gallop departs straight ahead on either lead and before it had achieved the necessary certainty and responsiveness in the simple change on a straight, free track. That is why we must not grow obstinate about difficulties that may arise in exercising the flying change and try to compel a change of lead. We reduce our demands for the time being. The fruit is not yet ripe. Once the horse really knows the gallop depart from the walk and the simple change, the flying change will no longer be a problem that the horse and its rider approach with hesitation and mixed feelings.

There are many " recipes " for making it easier to exercise the flying change of lead at the gallop. Transitions from one curved line to another, serpentines, or the counter-gallop in which we suddenly shift controls once we have reached the corner—all provide an opportunity for acquainting the horse with the new phase sequence. One rider swears by change of lead at the crossing of the figure of eight, while the other follows Fillis and makes the change in the corner. All this is a matter of temperament and disposition.

We who are in no hurry to exercise the flying change and begin it only when the horse lets us know that it is ready for it think that the straight road is the safest and best in the truest sense of the word.

Riding the horse across the hall, we increase its collection at an active gallop, with careful even loading on all four legs, which may become a shoulder-fore position under certain circumstances. If we begin to use the reins to effect the shift at approximately the middle of the hall and then change the position of our legs, our seat controls will have completed the change before the new change points have been reached without our having to call upon the horse for any greater flexion, such as is required when changing from one circle to another. If we made any such call, there would always be the danger that the horse would learn the trick of throwing its weight about. This would not only interfere with the correct execution of the single flying change but also result in insurmountable difficulties during later instruction in several successive changes of lead. Once this warped turning during the change of lead has become a habit, the greatest patience and a long period of time are required before we can correct this basic fault, which always results in the horse's being over-bent and holding back. At the beginning changing the lead along a straight line is easier for the horse than changing it on a half-circle, because on the latter the moment the rider changes seat must coincide exactly with the instant the horse enters upon the new turn. Besides, this figure requires a greater shift of seat.

The rider's change of seat must always occur in such a way that it is unnoticeable to a spectator. A mounted horse must convey the impression that horse and rider are cast in one piece and inspired by the same will.

At the outset it is well to execute the change several times at the same point on each hand. But once the horse has acquired some degree of assurance, the same line must be ridden across the ring without a change to keep the horse from anticipating the rider's controls and making a change automatically.

The more deliberately and methodically we proceed in this first lesson, the more rapid will progress be. We should arrange matters so that the exercises in the flying change of lead are scheduled at the end of the riding lesson; we dismount as soon as a successful change is made and lead the horse back to the stable.

We continue during the next few days and weeks in this rhythm of consistent reward after each indication of good will. Later still, rest pauses and gallop departs from the walk, as well as simple changes of lead on a free track, should be inserted between the individual exercises. Thus the horse will have no occasion to grow fearful and will remain attentive to the controls and responsive to them.

The change should never be executed if the horse manifests any uneasiness during preparatory collection. Calmly continuing to gallop as if nothing had happened is the best remedy for rushing, fearful pushing to the side, and anticipating. But if we are surprised by a premature change or by the horse's crossing its legs, we deliberately pass to the walk and resume the *original* schooled gallop (not a gallop offered spontaneously by the horse) only after the horse has calmed down completely. We should attempt another flying change from this gallop only after the horse remains calm after repeated simple changes and responds to the controls with its attention concentrated on his rider.

If the horse manifests no excitement during a single flying change, and its even loading on all four legs remains unimpaired, the only factors controlling its training in several successive changes after a certain number of strides are the degree of supple responsiveness achieved and the methodical training during exercise.

If difficulties arise in the change after two, three, four, or six strides, we must always return to the simpler exercise.

The following is a tested rule for executing several successive changes after a certain number of gallop strides: if the horse is able to slow down to a walk faultlessly after making five gallop strides, for example, changing after six leaps will involve no difficulty, since it has already mastered the single flying change of lead at the gallop.

A change after five gallop strides requires faultless slowing down to the walk after four leaps, and so on down to a change after two gallop strides.

Once the horse has mastered slowing down to a walk after one gallop stride, we can allow it to try a change of lead after every stride. In the gallop, near fore leading, for example, we call on the horse for two single changes of lead, after a few strides. The last strides would then occur as follows: first stride: gallop, near fore leading; second stride: gallop, off fore leading; third stride: gallop, near fore leading. Then the horse is rewarded. This is followed by the same exercise begun with the gallop, off fore leading.

Changes of lead after several successive gallops should be exercised only along a straight line, away from the wall, or along the line from one side of the riding hall to the other, so that the rider can clearly see how much of the horse's straightness is attributable to its obedience to the controls and be sure the horse is kept from growing accustomed to securing moral support from the wall.

A few horses will succeed in executing a faultless change of lead at every stride, responding to the controls, so that they move along fluid and straight as if drawn by a wire and still clearly change their lead at every gallop. The number of horses who can do this mechanically is much greater. Such horses often do more than is required—they change more often than is called for—and as they are not responding to their controls, their riders are unable to put a stop to this plethora of blessings.

We often see horses whose training is not quite complete executing fairly good changes of lead at every stride. All this confirms us in the belief that correctly executed changes of lead *à tempo* are far from the most convincing touchstone of complete gymnastic training despite the high factors assigned to them in the present Olympic dressage tests. They are, to be sure, a proof of dexterity, impulsion, and responsiveness, based on fairly advanced dressage. Nor can we reject the opinion out of hand that the changes of lead after four, three, and two gallops belong to the secondary field school and the *haute école*, because the natural gallop leap is expressed at least once between each change. We do reject, however, the change of lead at each stride as being artificiality rather than an art, in which the picture of the natural gallop is distorted.

Although we sometimes see unbroken horses executing passages, pirouettes, caprioles, and several successive changes of lead at the gallop down to two strides, flying changes at every stride will hardly be attempted by a foal no matter how pliant and enterprising it is.

In conclusion, we may add that any unnecessary tossing about of the rider's body, going beyond the controls described above (which operate within the narrowest limits and are imperceptible to an observer's eye), merely dulls the horse's responses to the rein and leg controls instead of making it easier for the horse to change the lead. This must impair the precision of the figure. An artist achieves his greatest effects by using the maximum economy of gesture.

V. Greater Demands in Halting During Collection, then Resuming at the Trot, and Preparing for the Collected Gallop

The increase in the horse's collection is paralleled by improvement of its full halts, so that the latter turn into a gentle forward engagement of the flexed hindquarters without any sign of tenseness. Our horse must now be able to stand still for a long period of time after being brought to a halt, in positive contact with the bit, with its forehand lifted and its load evenly distributed on all four legs. The position of its hind legs must be such that a plumb line dropped from the fulcrum of the hip joint, which constitutes the point of suspension or rotation of the load on the hindquarters, would meet the centre of the bottom surface of the hind hoofs—in the neighbourhood of the tip of the frog.

But when the horse is halted in a stage of even greater collection, its hind legs are grounded in a position somewhat farther forward—by one or two hoof-breadths. This further shortens the longitudinal axis of the horse's base of support, its hindquarters' joints fairly quivering with stored energy, and increases the horse's ability to obey the most delicate of controls still more.

At the halt the horse's forelegs are parallel and barely sloping backward, so that a plumb line dropped from the centre of the load on the forehand (which is located at the top of the shoulder blade) likewise strikes the centre of the area of support of the front hoofs. A light, invisible vibration of the rider's outstretched legs, combined with an imperceptible release of the reins, should suffice to advance the horse's front feet to the position described, if they should be grounded too far to the rear.

When a trot is started from a halt, the horse's initial movement must be a pure trot, just as it must take a gallop stride at once, without any intermediate steps, when departing at a gallop from a halt.

When executed with real precision these two transitions are an infallible test of whether the horse is collected and responsive to the controls and especially the positiveness of its contact with the bit. The latter exercise is extraordinarily difficult and, in our opinion, can be executed correctly only as follows, if it is not to be drilled into the horse as a mere stunt. The horse's collection must have been brought to a high stage of refinement by piaffe work dismounted and later in the saddle, and the rider must have been able to develop impulsion to such a degree that it is instantly and unquestionably available at the slightest signal from the rider's seat.

The major difficulty experienced in striking off at a gallop from a halt is that the horse must pass directly from a state of complete immobility to the spirited gait of the gallop without having taken a few steps at the walk or trot to get into stride, which would be more in accordance with its inherent nature.

The direct gallop depart, say, with the off fore leading, from the state of rest is executed as follows: When the highly collected horse, flexed in the direction of the future outside (left) hind leg, is called upon by the rider's leg and back controls to strike off at the gallop, it pushes off vigorously with its major diagonal (right hind leg—left foreleg). At the initial stage of its advance the inside (right) foreleg takes off. Only then does the outside hind leg take off, which up to now has remained grounded in elastic flexion, like a pole-vaulting bar for the entire system, carrying the load forward and upward. This completes the phase sequence of the gallop.

VI. Developing Collection with the Rider Dismounted and Holding the Reins

Developing collection with the rider dismounted and holding the reins is a useful exercise in the *haute école* as well as in its preparatory stage, the secondary field school.

Horses that are not ready for increased flexion of their haunches when carrying a rider run the risk of having their impulsion stifled by a load that they cannot handle elastically from the flexed haunches; but they readily respond to preparatory work in hand without a rider in the saddle. This eliminates stiffness and evasions to the side or the rear, which would be manifested if the horse were forced to throw its weight on its hindquarters while bearing a rider.

Similarly, nervous and fiery horses calm down much faster when framed

47.   Pirouette left. F. Lindenbauer, former Senior Rider of the Spanish Riding School on *Neapolitano Africa*.

48. Piaffe. Colonel A. Podhajsky, Chief of the Spanish Riding School, on *Neapolitano Africa*.

between the leading rein and the switch of the sympathetic trainer than when they have to carry the rider's weight, which still causes them pain when their haunches are severely flexed.

Let the reader execute a deep knee-bend himself, and then try to place two pounds of lead in the rucksack on his back while down in that position! Once he has made this harmless experiment, he will appreciate the situation of the incompletely trained horse, which finds the beginning of this work, with its demands upon the muscles of its hindquarters, rendered even harder by the additional load of even the lightest rider.

Another advantage of work in hand is that it affords the trainer the best opportunity for observing the horse as a whole, for which there is no substitute. He can compare what he feels when in the saddle with visual observation. The only disadvantage is the physical fatigue suffered by the trainer when handling big horses in soft ground.

It should be emphasized, however, that neither the supplementary training provided by dismounted work nor that of work in the pillars (to be discussed later on) can be fully successful unless the preparatory flexibility of the mounted horse has been developed to the stage described in the preceding sections.

We schedule dismounted work at the beginning of the riding lesson, when our horse is still fresh. We saddle it as if for lungeing and fit it with a cavesson, but not with a surcingle. It comes to the riding hall with light side reins, passed through the rings on the saddle.

We begin work on the left hand by first letting the horse walk along the long wall of the riding hall. We ourselves walk sideways, facing the horse's shoulder and try to secure light contact with the leading rein, held in the leading left hand two or three hand-breadths from the rings in the cavesson.

We halt before we reach the corner, move in front of the horse, and reward it. We take this opportunity to acquaint the horse with the long dressage switch, having an assistant feed the horse every time we touch it with the whip. Its previous work on the lunge has accustomed the horse to touches with the whip and to yielding without being startled.

The horse must reach the point where it can stand the touch of the switch on its back, thighs, and belly. It must allow itself to be stroked with it from the hips down to the hind pasterns without shrinking.

After a rest pause we make a wide half-turn from the corner and lead the horse to the other corner of the long wall, where we had started, accompanying it on the inside as described above. There we again come to a stop, reward the horse, acquaint it with the whip, and half-turn again.

Once the horse has grown completely familiar with these proceedings, we begin the actual dismounted work. The side reins are shortened just enough to provide the horse with a splint, so to speak, which makes it easier to maintain its own preferred form of collection. The hind legs can engage forward from the lowered hindquarters and the supple, swinging back, depending upon the degree of collection attained by the horse.

Developing collection by dismounted work is greatly aided by these side reins, whose length we had been able to "try out" previously and adapt them to the individual case. The horse must by no means be squeezed into a shape that hampers the rhythmic oscillations of its body. It will always seek an escape backward from such constraint. Its poll and mouth must always be able to give somewhat to the rear. But this will be the case only when the line of the nose is somewhat ahead of the vertical and the poll is the highest point along the crest of the neck.

We begin by letting our horse move forward surely and resolutely, with the whip first laid alongside the horse's belly, clicking our tongue and pulling on the leading rein if necessary. The leading hand must remain in contact, following the action to keep from interfering with the forward motion, even when pulling is no longer required.

The forward drive must become second nature to the horse during the development of collection by a dismounted trainer, as it must during the entire training of the horse. In fact, it must become its *idée fixe*, so that it spontaneously comes up to the bit through its neck, its trainer merely having to regulate its forward impulse. In our dismounted work training must culminate in the forward impulse being manifested automatically whenever the trainer is ahead of the surcingle.

About ten minutes of this training should be done daily. After a few days of this a couple of strides are taken at the trot, the horse is halted and rewarded, the trot resumed, and so forth. If the horse tends to rush, the rider's hand allows it to come up against the cavesson, bends it inward, drives it forward with greater force, and straightens it out again. Driving with the whip is now done by applying it to the hind leg below the hock, while the hand continues to demand collection. Driving at this point along the leg automatically produces an advance of the hind legs and is a control that is much more natural and more understandable to the horse than applying the whip just behind the normal position of the rider's legs, as we did when first mounting.

Later on, the rider's voice, tongue-clicking, or at most a threatening gesture with the whip should be enough to drive the horse forward and have it strike off at the trot directly from a halt or even from a backing position (diagonal phase sequence). If the whip should still be required, it should be applied gently and featheringly, with relaxed elbows and wrists.

We soon get a few more elevated forward strides, suspended in air and resembling a *piaffe*, when we apply the controls for trotting and allow our hand to advance only slowly. The first signs of elevated steps in the rhythm of the trot, with a somewhat longer phase of suspension, mark the decisive psychological moment (like the first willing flying changes at the gallop) when dismounted work should be ended for the day and the horse richly rewarded.

Many young horses lose their eagerness to jump because their riders want to find out "how high they can really jump". Similarly, reverses often occur in the development of collection by dismounted work because the initial periods of exercise, which are extremely tiring, are made too long; the trainer wants to "get something that looks like a piaffe". That is why this sort of work can easily be overdone—if we tried to put ourselves in a horse's place, we would be chary of demanding more and still more of a young horse as its reward for willingness and honest effort. That is why this exercise should last only a few seconds. We should and must be content with one to three lofty steps.[7]

The gently leading rein hand and the equally gently feathering whip frame the horse between driving and restraining controls. The driving controls predominate, for the horse must be in certain contact with the leading rein, but they must not degenerate into continual, repeated tapping with the whip. That would merely dull the horse. As training progresses, the rider's voice and the click of his tongue must be enough to make the horse take piaffe-like steps as it advances (about one hoof-breath at a time). That is, it must take independent steps as soon as it knows what is required. But it is the trainer's duty to break off the exercise before fatigue makes the horse display annoyance or hold back.

The brief exercises, which last only a few seconds and are alternated with very long rest periods, will produce a certain impatience towards the end of the rest period in every alert and high-spirited horse. It will offer a few new piaffe-like steps on its own even before we ask it to do so.

We allow this impatience to work its way out, since it produces the spontaneous steps of the horse, which is what we want. Later on, it will be easy for us to control this little bit of arbitrariness, which is wholly out of proportion to its inherent advantages.

There will be cases, however, where the training will not proceed so smoothly, and the horse's faults will be manifest.

If fatigue is not the cause for the horse's holding back and getting

---

[7] If a rider is one of the eternally dissatisfied type, he should turn his dissatisfaction inward, upon the mistakes that he—like all other riders—makes. This is particularly true in cases where final success depends on how we introduce a young horse to the initial requirements of a new and difficult exercise that demands all of its good will. One is never impatient enough of oneself!

behind the bit with a stiff back, it has been frightened of the rein controls by too severe handling of them or its freedom of movement has been constricted. Increased forward drive, with gentler and softer handling of the leading rein and an adjustment of the length of the side reins, must then be employed to bring the horse into contact with the reins and to make it engage its hindquarters and swing its back correctly.

If the hindquarters turn inward towards the whip, or if the horse holds back despite its being able to step out freely, we let it make a few volte-like turns about the supple forehand. Moving the leading rein forward and to the side, we use the whip to drive the inside hind leg at the instant it leaves the ground in the same direction under the load, and we keep it in that direction by making a transition from the turn around the forehand like a shoulder-in to movement on a single track along the wall.

As the horse gains strength and dexterity, training in the piaffe with a rider, which is part of the *haute école*, will evolve by itself from the training in collection without a rider described above. We begin by letting it carry a light rider, who is completely passive at first, his only job being to fit pliantly into the rhythm of the movement and to yield a bit with his seat when the horse offers piaffe-like steps. Later on, this load (which is far from " dead ", since it makes it easier for the horse to carry it by its supple use of the muscles of the small of the back to fit into the horse's movements) will be to brace the springs in the horse's haunches when its hindquarters must be flexed, thus achieving springier and more expressive piaffe steps than would be possible when working in hand.

With time, guidance and the driving controls will pass to the rider, and the trainer will then merely help along whenever necessary with his switch or whip.

In this phase of its training the horse still carries side reins. The reins, attached to the snaffle ring above the side reins, are now taken by the rider, who assumes control of the horse. The crop controls (chiefly applied with the switch for the time being), which are combined with the action of the rider's small of the back and legs in the saddle to call upon the horse for the piaffe-like movement, are the same as those used when working dismounted. Now they are supplemented by the simultaneous pressure of both of the rider's legs. Emphasized alternating stimulation to produce more elevated movements would favour the horse's tendency to shield his hind legs against complete loading by balancing from side to side. Here, too, the training should be broken off after no more than ten or twenty piaffe-like strides, whether or not the horse appears to be willing and fresh. In principle, these piaffe steps must follow directly upon a very brief but energetic trot. In this trot the trainer must face forward, for it would be hard for him to keep up with the horse if he continued moving sideways, and he would involuntarily hold the horse back (also see p. 300).

If this procedure is followed consistently and with understanding, the horse will develop piaffe steps that are increasingly more expressive, with its hind leg energetically drawn up forward and upward and with a pronounced prolongation of the phase of suspension.

As the horse's hindquarters grow stronger, work in hand becomes less and less necessary. The piaffe, which is a product of maximum impulsion and springy responsiveness, like the passage, can reach the acme of perfection only with a rider in the saddle. For only the rider who is intimately linked to the horse's body and to its most powerful spring, its back, and who adapts his seat and controls to the rhythm of the horse's movement, will be able to develop this rhythm to its maximum of expressiveness with certainty and precision.

Even in the hands of an expert, lifeless tools, such as side reins and pillars, will never be able to take the place of a rider. Not only can the rider, as a living and feeling organism, awaken the rhythm and follow it, but he can promote it by increasing the refinement of his controls so as to make the figure in question more spirited and perfected.

Part Three

THE *HAUTE ÉCOLE*

NATURE AND OBJECTIVES OF THE *HAUTE ÉCOLE*—THE BASIC GAITS IN SCHOOLED COLLECTION

I. The Haute École *as the Highest Form of Gymnastic Training*

THERE still are riding authorities who prefer to make a sharp distinction between the training of the general utility horse and that given in the *haute école*. They say that the manège horse that is brought to the highest expression of its flexibility and carrying capacity does not have to pass through the same initial stages of gymnastic training as any other saddle horse that deserves the name.

In reality, if we presuppose ideal training conditions, it is only the fully trained general utility horse that is able to become a manège horse, provided its spirit, machinery of locomotion, conformation, and industriousness qualify it for the high degrees of impulsion, responsiveness, and collection that are prerequisites for the *haute école*.

Training in the *haute école* has been right, and a horse so trained will be able to execute its lessons cleanly and perfectly, only if its rider is always able to expand or contract the horse's framework, its posture, without causing its gait or contact with the bit to suffer.

Gustav Rau says in this connection that " the *haute école* should not be a stunt school but rather the last link in a chain whose initial stages produce the general utility horse that is properly prepared for any kind of employment."

One out of ten thousand saddle horses must reach this higher stage. The average rider should always be able to see what specially qualified horses can do when we develop and refine the ordinary gaits by employing the same principles and controls that were taught him.

It can never be said too often that all the gaits and leaps of the *haute école* are latent within the young horse, which manifests them at moments of excitement. Anything else that has been exhibited by self-styled masters in the way of artificial distortions of the natural gaits (which are nothing but a parody of classic form and a grotesque distortion of their content; in others words, poor circus performances) has nothing in common with the academic *haute école* founded on the teachings of the old masters. If these ideas are borne in mind and put into practice, manège riding cannot help fertilizing and refining general utility riding.

The standard by which the art of to-day is measured is the art that flourished yesterday and the day before, the exercises and lessons of which are cultivated in their classic purity and full brilliancy in the Spanish Riding School of Vienna. This art is firmly anchored in the present and is officially recognized in the Olympic dressage test, which requires figures than can be satisfactorily performed only by a horse that is able *temporarily* to maintain the high degree of collection that is a permanent characteristic of the true manège horse throughout the entire equestrian programme.

The ability of a horse to allow itself to be collected to a posture in which the fore and hind pairs of legs each carry half the load, a posture that may go so far in certain figures as to make the hind hand willingly and elastically carry most if not all of this load, makes it superior to all other horses. The action of the relieved forehand makes it seem to be free of the force of gravity and enables it to perform rapid, though smooth and pliant, transitions and turns. It will therefore satisfy all the requirements of daily use while conserving its own strength and its rider's. It will be superior to the horse that has received less training in every respect but one: the production of absolute racing speed, which can be achieved only as a result of systematic training concentrated on the forehand.

II. The Manège Walk, the Manège Trot, and the Manège Gallop. The Manège Halt, Two Tracks

The shortened, collected rate of the three basic gaits reaches its climax in the manège walk, the manège trot, and the manège gallop.

Work at the walk and stepping up collection at the trot and gallop were discussed in detail in Part Two, Chapter Two, Section 3 B (pp. 208-218). We refer the reader to that passage, adding merely that the only difference between the collected rates of a well-schooled general utility horse and those of a manège horse is the degree of collection and hence the increased vigour and loftiness with which it executes these gaits. The phase sequence and the timing remain the same.[1]

To be sure, this is precisely the difference that matters, for very few horses among ten of thousands are able to develop to a maximum such

[1] See the Table of Basic Gaits and Their Gradations, p. 323.

49. Piaffe. R. Waetjen on *Burgsdorff* (East Prussian).

50. Passage. R. Waetjen on *Burgsdorff* (East Prussian).

51. Energetic passage. Jessica Newberry on *Forstrat* (Trakehnen) 1959.
VEDEL'S REKLAME-FOTO

52. The instant before the diagonal thrust in the passage. Major de Mestral on *Bajum* (Hungarian).

springy impulsion and carrying capacity in their hindquarters in direct proportion to the degree of collection.

As we stated in our discussion of training at the walk, the trainer's major attention should be concentrated upon the evenness of the lofty steps when practising the *manège walk*, and only secondarily upon the liveliness of the horse's movements. The reason for this is the effort that such steps cost the horse; and that is why they should be demanded for only very brief periods at a time. The liveliness of the horse's movements in the manège walk will automatically develop energy and timing in the other gaits as its hindquarters develop greater suppleness.

The bases upon which the supporting legs advance, which grow smaller as collection is intensified, increase the horse's mobility and manœuvrability, thus ensuring instantaneous response to the slightest intimations of control. In this stage of training the horse will come up to the bit unquestioningly with its forehand lifted high and its poll supple, even when its hindquarters are lowered. The timing of the elevated legs, which are pliantly bent in all their joints and alight in a pure four-beat gait, will have attained the intensity that makes the schooled collected walk an actual manège walk—one of the most difficult lessons for the horse to learn.

The degree of collection that is feasible at the *manège trot* depends upon the impulsion developed, the purity of the gait, and the gentleness of the horse's contact with the bit. As all two-track movements are also ridden at this gait, it is extremely important that impulsion be maintained and ensured at the manège trot. Without it the freshness, lightness, and brilliancy of the gait cannot be maintained during rides and figures executed on a single or double track.

A horse whose forehand is lifted high has a lighter contact with the bit at the manège trot than at the collected trot, though positive contact must always be maintained between the rider's hand and the horse's mouth. These steps are lofty and do not cover much ground. The hind legs pass by each other very closely because of the high degree of collection. The horse's readiness for changes of tempo or of direction, as well as for instantaneous obedience, is at a peak for the same reasons that it is at a manège walk. Its expressively cadenced, though powerful and vigorous, strides indicate that its back is completely supple and oscillates elastically. Endeavours of the horse to execute hovering steps are indications of false tensions, which are best prevented by developing the manège trot via a collected, shortened trot from a supple, lively middle trot.

If the hovering referred to is tolerated at the manège trot or if inexperienced riders welcome and therefore favour it as an alleged preliminary stage and a special endowment for the execution of the passage, the horse will repeatedly exploit this defence and thus escape the total surrender of its back. The subsequent transition from the passage or the piaffe to the manège trot and vice versa, one of the clearest and most important marks of the responsiveness of a manège horse, then will never be able to take place purely, clearly, and with fluid transition from one timing to another.

The *manège gallop* is the culminating form of the collected gallop. The latter was discussed in the section on galloping, and all we need add is that the manège gallop evolved from it is distinguished particularly by the freshness and fluidity of the springy, lofty leaps taken by the vigorous hindquarters. The even hoof beats are barely audible owing to the horse's springy advancing and alighting with its leg joints bent. The outside hind leg plays the principal part, as it has to take the load gently and transfer it elastically. The increased weight supported by the hindquarters produces a highly elevated position of the neck, together with lofty, unimpeded action of the forehand.

Here too, the shortening of the gallop leaps still available to the rider depends upon his maintaining the freshness and liveliness of the leaping movement and on the uniform loading of the horse's legs.

In the highly developed manège gallop the three-beat gait becomes a four-beat gait because the load rests for an instant only upon the hindquarters, even after the grounding of the inside hind leg. The outside foreleg alights only an instant *after* the inside hind leg (the forehand is carried higher), the difference being hardly perceptible to the observer's senses, as in the pirouette. This statement, however, is merely theoretical. In practice, whenever we clearly hear and see the four-beat gait, we also observe that the gallop loses its distinguishing characteristic—the powerful and lively forward engagement of the hindquarters. Its movements lose their fluidity and roundness and became dragging and dull, stiff and choppy. We have frequently commented on the immediate consequences of this false gait of the horse for the seat and especially the upper body of the rider, who is then compelled to follow the up-and-down movements of the horse's hips and back, which are pounded by its unbent joints.

All that need be added to the comments on the full halt made in Section 5 of the chapter on the secondary field (cross-country) school (pp. 279-280) is that the greater the proportion of the load borne by the engaged hindquarters of the horse and the longer it is able to remain motionless in this collected posture with positive, light contact with the bit, complete lifting of the forehand, and correct head carriage, the closer will the manège halt be to perfection.

The control exerted for this manège halt consists of tensing the muscles of the rider's seat (provided the horse has developed enough impulsion). At the same time the rider's legs, acting on both sides, keep the forward-engaged hindquarters beneath the load. The simultaneous rein tension, acting on both hind legs, must be accepted by them unresistingly.

The levade—a schooled rearing of the horse with a tendency to advance —is the culmination of the manège halt in the sense of its extension to the ultimate limit of carrying capacity, though the forward drive is fully maintained.

The two-track movements are ridden in the *haute école* at the manège walk, manège trot, and the manège gallop, and in a deflection from the straight line that may go as high as 45 degrees.

All the more stress should be laid upon maintaining the impulsion, liveliness, and purity of the gait. If difficulties should arise, the collection, the lateral distance on two tracks, and the length of the ride should be reduced, and simpler demands should be made upon the horse at the working trot, the collected trot, or the manège trot on a single track. Defects in the execution of the *travers* and the *renvers* are best remedied in the manner described above or by employing the simple and the counter-lessons of the shoulder-in, which is the parent position and starting point of all other two-track movements.

The advantages of galloping at the shoulder-in—promoting the flexibility and suppleness of the entire horse and especially the springy action of its inner hind leg—will be manifested to great advantage in this stage of dressage, where lateral responsiveness is brought to a high state of perfection.

The sequence of steps at the gallop permits only a slight lateral distance at the shoulder-in. The limiting point is the so-called trotting position, in which the inner hind leg and the outer foreleg track along the same line, so that the forehand is deflected one hoof-breadth, like the hindquarters in the gallop position. But we should endeavour to develop even this comparatively insignificant lateral distance by gradually increasing the longitudinal flexion from the vigorous, well-collected manège gallop. We should keep the exercises very short, often changing from the shoulder-in position to riding a circle on a single track. We likewise traverse the corners on a single track.

If the *travers* gallop is preceded by training in the shoulder-in gallop, it will be easier for the horse to execute it because the shoulder-in gallop has placed the horse's inner hind leg entirely within the rider's power, and it is this leg that is particularly hard to control in the *travers*.

If we try to ride the shoulder-in gallop without having perfect longitudinal flexion and hence even loading on all legs, all the advantages inherent in this lesson will be lost. Moreover, the horse will suffer as the result of irregular crossing of its legs. Hence the shoulder-in gallop should be ridden only when the rider is able to keep the horse's outside shoulder and outside hind leg in their correct position, corresponding to pure longitudinal flexion.

The riding of half-pass movements (discussed in full detail in Part Two, pp. 199-201) should not be omitted from any demonstration of a manège horse. They should also be part of every programme of free figures, as they exhibit the seemingly easy response to forward and lateral controls and are a convincing expression of the over-all picture of the unity of rider and horse. In the *haute école* the half pass is executed, like the other two-track movements, by increasing the horse's degree of collection until it reaches the manège walk, the manège trot, or the manège gallop.

CHAPTER TWO

FIGURES ON THE GROUND—HISTORICAL COMMENTARY

I. Dividing the Haute École *into "Figures on the Ground" and "Figures Above the Ground"*

IN the lessons of the *haute école* most or all of the entire load rests upon the hindquarters. In the trot-like figures, the piaffe and the passage, the very high demands made upon the carrying capacity of the hind legs are modified in so far as they alternate in taking up and transferring the load. They also are assisted by the forelegs, which alight simultaneously with them, even though the load they carry is light. But in the levade and the leaping figures or manège leaps (in the initial stage of the latter and to some extent during their entire execution), the elasticity and the carrying capacity of the hind legs are called upon exclusively and simultaneously, since the forehand is permanently or temporarily off the ground during these figures. The classification into "figures on the ground", such as the piaffe and the passage, and those "above the ground", such as the *mézair*, the courbette, the croupade, the ballotade, and the capriole, is based upon this criterion: whether the horse's hindquarters do not leave the ground during the execution of the figures or are off the ground throughout their execution or at least at certain times during the figure.

The levade is the transition from the "figures on the ground" to those "above the ground", since it is the starting point for the latter figures. That is why we shall discuss it only in the chapter devoted to these figures.

II. Work Between Pillars

The first authentic mention of pillars in the history of equitation is found in Pluvinel's posthumous work (published in 1620), *Manège du Roi.*[1]

[1] The Greeks had had the idea of having horses exercise while held in place. It is reported that Eumenes, one of Alexander's generals, kept his horses healthy and active while his cavalry was besieged in a small mountain fortress by tying them up in their stalls and having them pricked with pointed sticks, for want of a riding ground.

The idea behind the invention of pillars was to use mechanical means for opposing the thrust of the horse, which was tied up with a cavesson and a rope between two pillars or to a single pillar. This was done to subjugate the primitive, still disordered and uncontrolled forces of the horse. Pluvinel himself says that this invention of his cut in half the time required for training man and horse. One thing is certain: Pignatelli, Pluvinel's teacher, knew nothing of pillars.

The Duke of Newcastle (who died in 1675) rejects Pluvinel's invention because, as he says, many horses have been ruined by unskilful work between the pillars. And we must agree with him whole-heartedly. Nonetheless he did not hesitate to adopt some of Pluvinel's ideas by letting the young horse work on a circle around the pillar as its fixed point.

Despite the opposition of the greatest riding master of his time work between two pillars was adopted in all equestrian countries of the Continent, and it is still cultivated in the Spanish Riding School of Vienna. But in that school it is employed chiefly to give pupils a feeling for timing and harmony in the piaffe and to determine the individual talent for certain manège leaps of horses whose training is already rather far advanced.

Work between pillars requires considerable understanding and experience as well as a high degree of tact on the part of the trainer. The firmly hooked pillar reins do not allow the horse to move forward, which would make its work easier, while direct contact with the hand, as in collection when the horse moves forward, is no longer present.

Mistakes made in work between pillars may frighten the horse away from them forever and give rise to serious defects of character.

The comments at the end of the section on developing collection when dismounted (Part Two, Chapter Three, Section 6) apply to the general value of pillars as in aid in higher training.

It would be a serious mistake to put a young horse between pillars before it has offered well-timed, piaffe-like steps as it moves forward during training in dismounted collection. On the other hand, understanding work between pillars can contribute to further lowering the hindquarters of a horse that has been prepared for it by dismounted collection training and can refine the rhythm of its timing in the piaffe to a certain extent and make it more expressive. Moreover, as we have already said, it is between the pillars that we have the best opportunity of learning whether a certain horse has a latent ability for certain figures "above the ground".

At the beginning of work between pillars it is best to proceed extremely slowly and easily; we should start out as if the horse had never been called upon for dismounted collection.

It is best to set up the pillars in the centre of the riding hall, though not along the diagonals or circles. They are round logs about ten feet long and eight inches in diameter, set into the ground about three feet and spaced about five feet apart. On the sides that face each other they are provided with five or six recessed rings about two and a half inches in diameter. The lowest ring—for small horses—is attached four feet above the ground, with the others spaced at four-inch intervals above it. Other necessary items are a strong pillar halter with a double leather lining, but without a brow-band. The nose-band and the crown-piece should be lined with felt or buckskin. The equipment includes two strong pillar reins (pillar halter straps) with snap hooks or lever locks. A padded caves-son which is fitted over the snaffle (as used for lungeing) completes the equipment, the buckle of its nose-band being looped beneath the snaffle bit without pulling it upward.

After our horse has been lunged or given a workout in the saddle, followed by a few minutes' work in side reins along the long wall with the rider dismounted, we lead it around and between the pillars a few times, allow it to sniff them, and finally bring it to halt between the pillars with its head facing the exit. We then feed it. This is repeated frequently until the association of ideas—standing between the pillars= reward—has taken root. During one of these feeding periods we place the halter on the horse and hook the straps in so that the buckles point downward. Horses that are approximately sixteen and three-quarters hands high are buckled to the second rings from the bottom—about half-way up to their shoulders. A leading rein was previously attached to the cavesson ring for the preceding work dismounted.

Now, while facing the horse, we take the pillar reins in both hands and allow it to advance carefully against the halter, remaining in contact with the latter for a few seconds. Then we push it back. This procedure is repeated often, and we feed the horse every time it comes to a standstill in contact with the halter. By doing this we accustom the horse to the pressure of the halter without exciting it, and second, we strengthen its conviction that it is futile to rush up against this apparently insuperable barrier. The pillars must reach up to the horse's shoulder. When more than its head, neck and the point of its shoulder projects above the pillars, one hind leg or another may tangle with a pillar if the horse should turn crosswise. This has been the cause of fatal accidents.

We then stand alongside the horse's head, holding the leading rein in our left hand and the switch used for dismounted work in our right hand, and try to make the horse's hindquarters move out towards the right by applying the switch to the left (near) side of its body until the hindquarters reach the pillar. If the horse hesitates to step to the right, the rider's left hand flexes the horse to the left, thus assisting the lateral whip control. The horse should be rewarded as soon as it manifests good will. We proceed similarly on the other side of the horse. Once these initial demands have been met, we call it a day and lead the horse back to the stable.

After we have practised nothing but moving away from the switch applied from the front for a few days, an assistant (whose presence at the horse's head is a calming factor in itself) takes over the leading rein. We take a stand-off to the left behind the horse and make it turn towards the right by calling out " Turn! " and applying the switch to the left side of its body. If necessary, the assistant comes to our aid by taking a step to the right or by flexing the horse to the left with the left snaffle ring. If the horse kicks out with its hind legs, it should be ignored; this releases its tension and should be regarded as a natural reaction rather than a vice.

In any event it is advisable to bandage the hind legs for this work and provide them with over-reach boots. The shoes on the hind hoofs should also be removed, if possible, since the horse may injure itself in its state of excitement as a result of its initially clumsy steps to the side.

Once our horse has obeyed the command that it move to the right, a halt should be called at the right-hand pillar, and the horse should be caressed and fed bread or oats. The same procedure is then followed at the left side, the assistant stepping out towards the left if necessary. The slight resulting pull on the leading rein should never be allowed to degenerate into tugging. It is always the assistant's major job to employ the leading rein so as to prevent the horse from stepping backward and thus abandoning contact with the halter. Once the horse has understood this sidewise motion in response to a control applied from the rear, we again call it a day and reward it by leading it back to the stable.

It does not matter *how* the horse executes this sidewise movement of its hindquarters at the outset. All it has to do is to take a few steps to the side away from the switch, for now the trainer has a switch in each hand. The better it understands what we want it to do, the more will a mere signal control suffice to make it step to one side and then the other by itself. We stop for a pause only after ten or twenty of these exercises.

Now that the horse is beginning to work independently, the switches are employed mainly to regulate and stimulate the positioning of its feet. It is important that it no longer merely cross its legs laterally, but rather forward and to the side as well. This means that the hind leg in question initiates the new movement by one step forward and across the outside leg. This lateral advance and crossing makes the horse respond to the controls, and results in a certain degree of collection which involves a bending of the haunches and of the hock.

Once the horse begins to advance and cross its legs laterally with the very first step of the near hind leg, it will move back to the rear with its second and third steps in order to escape approaching the halter and the increased load produced thereby. We must then be ready to apply the switch below the hock of the near hind leg that is moving to the rear to force the horse to take the second step forward.

If the off hind leg steps merely to the side instead of advancing at the same time, that leg must be impelled forward by applying the switch held in the other hand to the outside fetlock. After the third double step, as well as at every rest pause, the trainer should place the second switch below both hocks to prevent the horse from sliding backward.

Once these demands are met by the horse after a few days' training, we begin to work for a livelier, more collected sequence of steps, henceforth permitting only two double steps to each side, so that finally we get an uninterrupted and lively stepping from one side to the other between whips that regulate and limit the movement, the horse remaining in positive and definite contact with the halter. The corresponding diagonal movement of the front legs develops automatically as the hindquarters' steps become more rhythmic.

The horse—framed more and more tightly—will soon make only one double step to each side, and the legs will alight closer and closer together, so that their lateral movement is no longer manifest. Now the horse has achieved the pure, diagonal, lofty, trotting motion in place with marked suspension—the piaffe.

An understanding trainer will never let the horse reach the point where it shows signs of fatigue, when its vigorous, spirited steps become dull and degenerate into a dragging motion. One of the proofs of his skill is never demanding too much and knowing when to stop.

If apparent fatigue, with uneven lifting of the individual legs, sets in only because of the horse's wilfulness, we may resort to a trick borrowed from circus art that is not truly academic; it does not affect the horse as a whole but merely locally. We touch the foreleg or hind leg that seems to be sticking to the ground, rising less than the other leg, just above the knee or on the front side of the hind cannon at the instant it leaves the ground.

It should be added that a horse that is otherwise responsive and fresh always exhibits uneven steps when the trainer's carelessness allows it to be positioned obliquely between the pillars; the leg that is too close to a pillar will be instinctively paralysed, as it were.

Now we can place a rider on the horse and proceed as we did with our work of collection while dismounted.

At the start the rider should remain entirely passive, acting merely as living ballast that does not disturb the rhythmic timing but pliantly follows the horse's movements. Once the horse has grown accustomed to carrying this load between the pillars (the fact that it had been accustomed to carrying a load after completion of collection training while dismounted will speed this up), it will be wise to mount the horse ourselves and continue further piaffe training in the saddle.

Whenever there are any indications of the horse's holding back in any of this subsequent training (this also applies to the passage), we must immediately shift to a brief but energetic forward ride at the trot as a continuation of the piaffe steps. Only then should the horse be granted a rest period by way of reward. Otherwise horses that are not perfectly animated look forward to the moment of reward while performing the piaffe and slow down prematurely, their movement growing duller instead of more spirited (also see pp. 284-285).

It should be added that in work between pillars the assistant's leading rein serves merely to correct contact with the halter at the outset and to assist the driving control of the trainer from time to time. Any such action, however, must be completely eliminated later on. If this rein were always tight, the horse would grow accustomed to offering resistance to it, and all our work would be spoiled.

The pillar reins (halter strap) must take the place of the rider's reins or of the leading reins for a horse collected while dismounted. That is why the contact of a horse doing the piaffe with its halter corresponds to its contact with the trainer's rein during collection training or with the reins of its rider. And that is why, when the rider takes over the reins later on, the horse's contact must never exceed the contact taken by a horse that is performing correctly between the pillars.

There are fearful horses that may be frightened of pillars if we proceed too rapidly when we first tie them up there. These horses will calm down considerably if we tie them to only one pillar rein at first, replacing the other by a leading rein that passes through the corresponding ring on the other pillar and is held loosely by an assistant. In even more difficult cases two such leading reins may replace the pillar reins, the horse being held between the pillars by two assistants.

III. Piaffe—Passage—Transitions

It is not easy to find a brief definition of the piaffe or of the passage that is evolved from it. The characterizations of these two classical figures as "the highest collection and perfection of trotting[2] in place"

[2] Neither the piaffe nor the passage is a trot such as we require of the general utility horse or of the manège horse, because every trot, whether it be a working trot, a utility trot, or a manège trot, must be ridden without hovering, with lively, active timing, and covering some ground. Otherwise it would be neither a faultless working trot nor a perfect manège trot. The highest degree of perfection that the trot may display as the result of schooling is found in the extended trot and the manège trot. That is why it is preferable not to define the movement of the horse in the piaffe and the passage as a trot, but as " trot-like " or, still better, as " executed in the phase sequence of the trot ".

and as "the culmination of the manège trot" that we often hear cannot be accepted without contradiction, for though they are captivatingly brief, they fail to exhaust the essence of these two figures or to define them unambiguously.

PIAFFE

In our opinion the following definition of an ideal *piaffe* executed in place is closer to the truth:

"The piaffe is a movement executed in the phase sequence of the trot, in which all the thrust is converted into elasticity and carrying capacity evenly distributed between both hind legs. With perfect responsiveness, this yields a lofty and sustained trotting action in place that corresponds to the maximum flexion and powerful springiness of the hindquarters."

All the requirements that must be met by a perfect piaffe can be derived from this definition. It also make it possible to distinguish clearly between the minor defects that nearly every piaffe exhibits in practice and fundamental faults.

First the requirements: The bending of the hindquarters makes it possible for the forelegs, which carry hardly any support and are grounded lightly, to step loftily from the shoulder and to prolong their steps, the horse's forearm being raised to the horizontal position. Because the hindquarters are thus bent and carry a greater load, each hind leg can raise its hoof only somewhat above the pastern of the grounded hind foot, but it will sustain this step in harmony with the motion of the diagonal foreleg once it reaches its maximum elevation.

The lowering of the hindquarters, animated by impulsion, then produces the correct action of the horse's back, the most powerful spring in the horse's body, which depends upon the hindquarters directly. The elastic tension of the back supports the lifting and sustaining of the legs, which push off and alight vertically in a completely uniform diagonal sequence of steps. Another result of the increased load placed upon the hindquarters is the high carriage of the horse's neck, which is raised with a supple poll. The completely uniform carrying of the load and the rhythmic, springy advancing of the hind legs produce an even, light, but positive contact with the bit, giving the rider the feeling that the horse is always ready to shoot forward in a fraction of a second, passing into the passage or the trot. It must also be ready to change to a schooled rearing up—the levade—when the controls are intensified.

In practice, the action and cadence described above will be hard to achieve in place, especially with a horse that is still undergoing training. It is therefore advisable to allow it to advance one to two hoof-breadths at each step and not try to accentuate the sustained cadence of the figure at the expense of the purity of the diagonal, vertical positioning of its feet.

Other fundamental faults are lateral evasion of the forehand and hind-quarters; dull alighting of the legs, which stick to the ground; excessive rapid rising of the stiffening hindquarters, usually combined with a cramped arched back; excessively low and loose neck; indefinite and irregular contact with the bit; and inadequate activity of the front legs, which are grounded behind the vertical with the forehand projecting in front of them. Generally speaking, all hasty, uneven steps are faulty; so is a pressed-down back with excessive elevation of the forehand. This means faulty harmony between the forehand and the hindquarters, as in the case of cramped arching,[3] with all the resulting defects of gait and contact with the bit.

The final fault is advancing the stretched, unbent hind legs too far forward; they are no more able to take off elastically from this position than they are when they do not engage far enough forward. In other words, lowering the hindquarters must not be the result of an excessive forward engagement of hind legs, which are then opened too much at the stifle and hock joints.

All these faults and defects of execution cannot and should not be corrected in the piaffe itself. We must first correct action of the hind legs and the back by energetically pressing the horse forward to make contact with the bit at the collected trot or the middle trot. Then we employ the resultant pure movement to restore the collection required for the piaffe while maintaining the horse's powerful strides and positive contact with the bit.

In brief, we believe that the principal underlying requirement for a correct piaffe is the rhythmic and perfectly simultaneous grounding and advancing of the legs in a diagonal sequence of steps. Any grounding or pushing off that is too early or too late constitutes an imperfection in the pure gait.

Almost as important is the requirement that the legs alight exactly upon a straight line. A rocking, sideways balancing enables the horse's hind

[3] If the piaffe is executed faultily, with a cramped arched back, that is, in cramped tension, the forelegs alight in a position slanted to the rear, that is, behind the plumb line from the elbow joint to the ground (see the footnote on p. 108), so that the overhanging forehand carries too much of the load. When the back sags and is cramped, i.e., is pressed downward, the front hoofs alight ahead of the vertical. In both cases the horse is not making honest contact through its poll, because the false activity of the back results in an unsteady, curled (crisped) neck in the first case and in a stiff neck in the second.

It is peculiar that both of these faulty forms of the piaffe have proved particularly attractive to sculptors and painters. Equestrian monuments and the pictures of generals in battle paintings of past centuries are ample evidence of this.

53.   Grand Quadrille of the Spanish Riding School in training at Kenilworth Riding Club, Rye, New York 1950.

54.   Levade.

55. Levade in hand.

legs to evade carrying the load, bending, and dividing the load evenly between the two legs.

If the bending of the hind legs is insufficient, the hindquarters, which are not lowered enough, will make the croup shoot up every time the horse rises. Consequently the sequence of steps becomes irregular, nappy, mincing and jerky because the haunches no longer carry their share of the load. Since the horse can take off springily only from bent hind-quarters, which in turn enable its legs to sustain themselves when they reach their position of maximum elevation, this will interrupt the cadenced, rhythmic gait. The impression conveyed to the observer will be that the legs are lifted from the ground hesitantly, appearing to stick to it, or that they take off in a cramped fashion rather than elastically.

As indicated above, the pure phase sequence of the legs taking off vigorously along an absolutely straight line is the prerequisite for a cor-rect piaffe. With this straight position of the horse at the highest degree of collection, striving forward at every stride, the ideal piaffe in place with highly cadenced sustained steps can be developed in specially qualified horses after adequate training.

The cadence, the sustained timing of the horse's steps, can be regulated by the rider with a well-schooled horse in the piaffe as well as in the passage. He can accelerate or slow down the horse's steps by imperceptibly opening and closing his fingers.

Once when a visitor to the Spanish Riding School doubted that the cadence could be fixed precisely in the piaffe and the passage, Matthaüs Niedermeyer (1865-1887), senior instructor at the time, had an attendant bring a metronome from the adjacent Burg Theatre and asked the visitor to set it for any rate he chose, fast or slow. Niedermeyer's stallion (Pluto Betalka) piaffed exactly in time. After this proof of maximum obedience had been proffered, the visitor thought he would compliment the senior instructor by exclaiming: " Sir, that was as good as the circus! " Nieder-meyer, who was hardly pleased with this praise, then had an attendant place a glass nearly full of water on the croup of his grey horse and executed the piaffe without spilling a single drop. He then said: "You see, that is elasticity and smoothness! See if they can do that in the circus! "

This stillness of the horse's body, which we have illustrated in the fore-going example, can be achieved, however, only if the horse's feet do not hop. The rising and grounding of the horse's hind legs must be soft and gentle; their push-off must be springy, rather than abrupt, from the bent haunches, notwithstanding all their energy and positiveness. In a movement of this sort, which is based upon complete suppleness at maximum collection, the buttocks of a pliant rider cannot leave the saddle.

On the other hand, a correct piaffe can be executed by the horse only when its rider is able to adapt his seat and guidance to the rhythm of this ingenious gait. As we have said, such a rider will not only initiate and maintain the rhythm but also assist and activate. There must be nothing hard or crampedly tense, i.e., produced by over-exertion, in his seat. The horse's movements themselves, its swinging legs, its oscillating back, and the swinging spinal column of the rider, will inspire the rider's pliant leg, which hangs down alongside the horse's body, completely relaxed from his hips down, so that the movement is sustained and can be made even more vigorous if necessary by the rhythmic alternating swinging of his legs in time with the gait.

This rhythm also governs the guiding hand which, as a component part of the seat, surrendered to the movement and breathing with it, unconsciously provides the correct controls that maintain and invigorate the piaffe.

What we have said about the piaffe also holds for the passage. Perfection can be achieved in the passage only if the rider's legs abandon all tension (even though the tension be elastic), swinging in an arc that is invisible to the naked eye. If the horse is not yet sensitive enough, the spur must be resorted to, barely touching the horse's side as the leg swings. More positive controls might be able to squeeze out a gait that resembles a piaffe or a passage, but they would never be able to create the perfected work of art represented by these classic figures, which conceal their extraordinary difficulty by the winged lightness of their execution.

PASSAGE

Though it may be said that the *passage* is the equivalent of a piaffe while advancing, there is a great difference between a passage and a piaffe, in which we allow the horse to advance somewhat in order not to put too great a burden upon its carrying capacity, which is not yet equal to working in place. In the piaffe only that part of the thrust that is not completely converted into elasticity and carrying power in order to spare the hindquarters produces the forward movement. In the passage we deliberately make the thrust—governed and regulated by our controls— a part of the movement in order to produce correctly timed, floating forward steps. The foregoing remarks on the passage yield the following definition:

"The passage is a floating forward movement executed in the phase sequence of the trot. The elasticity and carrying power evenly divided between the two hind legs, combined with the thrust that is partially converted into energetic forward and upward impulsion and with the elastic flexing of the pulsating back muscles, produce a powerful push-off of the diagonal pairs of legs, which are sustained for a longer period in lofty flexion and extension."

All the requirements of a perfect passage can be derived from this definition, if they are not already included in it. In the passage, again, the horse's forearm is raised as closely as possible to the horizontal, as an indication that the hindquarters are lowered and sustained in that flexed position. As in the piaffe and for the same reasons, the hind legs, which, deeply bent, cannot be raised much above the fetlock. The lifting of the forehand and contact with the bit are the same as in the piaffe.

It should be added that, as in the piaffe, the expression and the impression produced cannot be the same in all horses. With thoroughbreds and Lipizzans, we see ideally executed passages, whose manner and gesture cannot be stamped into any universal pattern—the action, conformation, and temperament of various individuals and races differ. We would be equally justified in demanding that all horses execute the basic gaits—the walk, the trot, and the gallop—identically. But any passage can fairly claim to be perfect when it advances spiritedly and energetically from flexed haunches in a pure, well-timed sequence of steps along a straight line, with perfect responsiveness, an elastically flexed, active back, and lofty, prolonged suspension. Making full allowance for individual differences, therefore, every passage is correct and must be evaluated as such if the fundamental conditions, impulsion, timing, and straightness, are satisfied.

As the foregoing indicates, the passage is governed by the same rules as the piaffe. If it is not ridden in spirited collection and straightness, it will exhibit the same fundamental defects and faults. They are corrected in essentially the same way as in the piaffe.

To make matters somewhat clearer let us add a few words about suspension, which is a characteristic feature of the passage. The maximized springy push-off of the hind legs from their position of elastic flexion produces persistence in the piaffe and persistence and suspension in the passage, where the horse moves forward. Whenever the elastic flexing of the back muscles (made possible by this vigorous springy push-off) ceases, the piaffe becomes an expressionless mincing in place, and the passage a plain trot.

Let us emphasize again that the false hovering at the trot, which was discussed in detail in a previous section of this book (Part Two, Chapter Two, Section 1, p. 131), is caused by stiffness in the hindquarters[4] and in

[4] In nine cases out of ten the source of all difficulties lies in the hindquarters. Their physical weakness or insufficient pliancy (usually caused by the former factor) is felt by the rider as faulty activity of the horse's back. The back as such would have to be very faulty or weak to be the direct cause of faulty gait. The trouble almost always lies farther back.

the back. In contrast to correct suspension in the passage, it is always a symptom of inadequate suppleness of the back, which is held cramped in false tension, and of the horse's holding back.

In a well-ridden passage all the horse's muscles, pulsating energetically, are working in perfect responsiveness, so that impulsion can flow forward without hindrance from pasterns through the hindquarters, the back, the neck, and the poll into the rider's hand and can be regulated by his hand and seat so that the rider, mounted on a manège horse, can regulate and determine the rhythm of the cadence, the loftiness of the steps, and the ground covered as he likes—within natural limits, of course.

At the opposite extreme we have badly trained horses, so-called manège horses, whose stunts are not " ridden out " by academically correct controls and which therefore require special warning signals that are principally aimed at their memory—depending upon their agreement with their riders —to perform their figures, rides, and airs.

In horses that possess considerable verve, animation, and temperament, the passage may be developed from the piaffe by gradually letting the horse move forward while carefully maintaining a cadenced timing.

In the great majority of horses, however, it is advisable to follow the contrary procedure. We slow down the tempo from a spirited middle trot to a manège trot by gradually increasing collection, and from this trot we use half halts, which are adapted to the slower cadence of the passage, to pass smoothly to this more sustained gait.

The rider's seat must be particularly steady and quiet in the passage as in the piaffe. This so-called academic seat is not a special kind of seat, but merely the ideal form of the normal seat. Upright and unconstrained, its pliancy must conform to the horse's balance on the longitudinal and transverse axes of its shortened and narrowed base of support, a balance that is intensified and refined still further in the manège gaits. It must do so notwithstanding the elastic and pliant firmness of the rider's spinal column, corresponding to the higher degree of collection.

Utterly economical in its movements and controls, which seem to melt into the rhythm of the swinging body of the horse, such a seat achieves a maximum of spirited responsiveness with a minimum of physical effort. Its action is confined to a more or less pronouncecd shift of the rider's weight in complete harmony with the rhythm of the motion, which not only initiates but also maintains and stimulates this rhythm; an alternating swinging of the rider's legs, hardly perceptible to the eye, and " breathing " of his hand.

Like a seismograph it records the rhythm of the gaits, and like an equally fine instrument it transmits the expressions of the rider's will to the sensory nerves of the horse, whose body becomes the sounding board for each of its movements. A horse will spontaneously accept the controls required to maintain the vigorous though smooth and fluid movements from such a seat.

The finely adjusted balance of this seat makes all physical effort super-fluous, in fact harmful, for sudden and hard actions, or those that do not fit into the rhythm of motion, would inescapably throw the finely tuned mechanism of the horse, floating in schooled collection, into disorder.

The rider's upper body rests upright upon the horse's spinal column. As this column slopes somewhat to the rear at times because of the increased flexion of the hindquarters, his upper body is not quite vertical with respect to the ground at such moments, but almost imperceptibly tilted backward.

In a truly well-schooled horse it is no longer the rider who has to seek harmony with his horse. The contrary is true. The lightest weight controls cause the responsive horse to bring its centre of gravity into harmony with that of its rider. The harmony between the two is so far-reaching that it is sought and found by the horse, so to speak. It is a matter of course that sensitive riders will never allow this shaping of the horse to the seat that requires increased collection to degenerate into disturbance of the harmony between the two bodies. The rider adapts himself to the swinging rhythm of the timed movements even when he increases collection (and all the more so when he maintains it), so that harmony is constantly maintained, a harmony that could only be adequately described if a writer were able to clothe music in words.

As we stated when discussing the initial piaffe-like steps while carrying a rider, the leg control that produces the gait should be exercised by simultaneous pressure on both sides. This pressure must not last too long, since it could result in unnatural movement and an unsteady or constrained carriage of the horse's tail. On the contrary, the brief leg pressure, more energetic when necessary, must suffice to make the horse start the passage and the piaffe spiritedly and willingly. Then it auto-matically secures the controls required to maintain the gait from the rider's gently hanging, swinging legs.

A piaffe or a passage squeezed out of a horse by laborious leg and weight controls will always be faulty.[5] The rider's domination is most complete and the school figures are purest when the observer obtains the impression that the movement costs neither horse nor rider any appreciable effort.

[5] When we have occasion to observe the visible efforts made by many riders to squeeze a few modest steps from their ill-humoured horses, we are reminded of the biting comment made by a senior instructor of the Spanish Riding School on such an occasion: " Everything moves except the horse's feet ! "

A horse going through its figures correctly should work spontaneously. The passage and piaffe should not " exhaust " themselves.

In such a pair fused into one the most difficult exercise will look like free play.

Once we have laid the correct foundation for the piaffe and the passage we cannot remain content with these lessons as they are required for dressage tests. Bending of the haunches and flexibility will become better and better when we repeat all the gymnastic exercises that we used in the elementary and secondary field (cross-country) schools to anchor the foundation: even loading in spirited posture. These exercises are repeated in the stage of collection required for the *haute école*. That means that we should exercise the passage on two tracks, especially half-pass movements, and the piaffe in the turn about the centre, where the centre of the turn lies beneath the rider's seat.

TRANSITIONS

The *transition* from the piaffe to the passage, which is practised only with highly temperamental horses, as we have said, must take place without any disturbance of timing, exactly like the opposite transition. The difficulty is that impulsion dies down only too easily during this transition, the horse changing its carriage against its rider's will, so that the cadence of the timing is lost.

As any endeavour to improve impulsion during the transition would doubtless disturb the horse's carriage and hence the uniformity of the timing, the impulsion required for the transition to the passage must be developed earlier, in the piaffe.

The same principle applies to the transition from the passage to the piaffe. It we do not carry enough impulsion with us from the passage, the transition will not be smooth and the uniformity of the horse's steps cannot be maintained. But interruptions in timing are just as much faults in a manège horse as if a field horse were to change timing and rate spontaneously during various figures.

Smooth transitions from the passage to the free or collected trot, from the trot to the passage, are a touchstone of complete schooling. They are also the best proof that the elastic tension of the active back is the result of equestrian action.

A horse that piaffes positively and well should be able to make the transition from the trot to the piaffe without the slightest disturbance in its phase sequence. If the rider wishes to pass from the piaffe to the trot, the purity of the steps must be maintained exactly as before.

Whereas the timing of the steps must remain the same during the transitions from the passage to the piaffe and back, the horse must adapt itself to the new gait without hesitation and "stickiness" during transition from these figures to the trot and vice versa; that is, it must shift smoothly from the sustained rhythm to the more lively one, and vice versa. The rider and the observer must involuntarily have the feeling that the rhythm dies down or speeds up gradually and continuously. The passage, the swinging step, was known to the ancient Greeks as a "parade step". As we know from Xenophon's book *The Art of Horsemanship*, which was influenced by the hippologist and veterinarian Cimon, as well as numerous ancient coins and gems, this parade step was not much worse than the passages that we see nowadays. In the representations that have come down to us we clearly see the bending of the haunches, the lofty step, and the high carriage of the forehand. The lower edges of the horses' necks, which are often convex, are probably due less to false equitation than to anatomical peculiarities of racial origin, as in many Lipizzan stallions of the present day. The ancients were also acquainted with a piaffe-like, dancing step in place.

During Roman times equitation did not flourish quite as it had in ancient Greece, but it was not completely forgotten, as the few relics that have come down to us indicate. These include the monument to the Emperor Marcus Aurelius, whose horse exhibits the unmistakable characteristics of a proud parade step. The fact that the Roman cavalry employed covered riding halls and that the Emperor Aurelius took a daily ride along the gallery of his palace likewise indicates that riding was cultivated among the Romans.

The Italian riding masters of the Renaissance called the swinging step *passeggio*, from *spassegio*, a "promenade".[6] The French turned this into *passage*, an expression that has persisted to the present day.

The word *piaffe* comes from the French *piaffer*, "a stately marking time"; it, too, has been retained as the universal expression for the stately step in place.

The first wholly clear descriptions of the passage and the piaffe and of the work between pillars required to secure the latter (with a third post in front of the horse's head taking the place of the assistant, if necessary) are found in Guérinière's *École de cavalerie* (1751).

In the Spanish Riding School of Vienna the term "Spanish step"[7] is

[6] As in music to-day, Italian was the equestrian language at the time the Italian school flourished. Then France became the centre of academic writing, with Pluvinel and his disciples, and the epoch-making works of that time were written in French.

[7] The Spanish walk (also called the *pas espagnol* or marching step), a trot-like movement at the walk which a horse can easily learn, in which the hindquarters develop no impulsion but are pulled along by the forehand, and the outstretched forelegs are raised in cramped fashion up to the horizontal if possible, is an unnatural, inharmonious parody of academic form that captivates the layman's eye by its swaggering movement. Like the exaggerated steps of the Spanish trot—euphemistically called an extended passage—the Spanish step is part of the foundations of the circus school.

also employed instead of passage. This term was originally used to describe the natural gait of horses of Andalusian-Neapolitan origin, whose gravely proud and elevated steps provided the basis for a particularly effective piaffe and passage. Pliny (in his *Natural History*) is the first to speak of the "proud or Spanish step" of the small Iberian horses (*asturcones*), the ancestors of the Lipizzans, which were very popular among the Roman *equisones* (trainers).

The Spanish trot is nothing but a floating trot with unbent haunches, the extended phase being prolonged as much as possible. The transition from this faulty gait cannot be effected by fluid conversion of the timing but only by means of a sudden interruption.

Whereas these stunts, which also include rearing with unbent haunches, the piaffe with forehand and hindquarters balancing by swinging from side to side, curtsies, and the like, impress the expert as more or less faulty lessons of the *haute école* and as a caricature that makes them ridiculous, such fantastic gaits as galloping on three legs or galloping backward (even with change of lead!) are no longer harmless, shoddy parodies but grotesques that distort the idea of classical art.

FIGURES ABOVE THE GROUND

As we said in Part Three, Chapter Two, Section 1, the levade is a transition from the "figures on the ground" to those "above the ground". These latter figures, the manège leaps, are organically interrelated, since one leap is developed from the other, is already contained in the germ in the other. It should be stressed, however, that in practice the ascent from the "easier" to the "more difficult" does not always take place in the sequence we set up, which is dependent largely if not exclusively upon the psychological and physical talents of the horse in question. Its trainer will give it an opportunity to display any such talent between the pillars, by work when dismounted or with a rider in the saddle (courbette). In other words, it will hardly ever be possible to predict in advance the manège leap that we are going to teach our horse. In general only an infinitesimal proportion of horses have any talent for learning more than one of these jumps.

The individual manège jumps, the *mézair*, the croupade, the courbette, the ballotade, and the capriole, will be described and characterized only briefly in this book, for we could consider it presumptuous to lecture on systematic training in these leaps without ever having trained a horse ourselves in such leaps in the academic sense and with the methods of the classical school.

Before we proceed with the difficult task of teaching our horse one manège leap or another, it is best to begin by mounting an old jumper and learning how to "feel" and follow such a leap under the watchful eye of a master. Then we learn how to remain in the saddle during the release of the tremendous stored-up energy, which takes place with lightning speed, as in the capriole, for example. This is even more necessary than in other phases of riding.

Anyone who wants to study the manège leaps as taught in the academic school in all their purity must make a pilgrimage to the Castalian source of classical equitation, the Spanish Riding School of Vienna. There his own eyes and, if he is lucky, his own riding, will make many things clear to him that neither a writer's pen nor an aritist's brush could convey.

As we have said, we propose to confine our description of the work required to achieve a well-schooled rise—the levade—and the resulting *mézair* to the essentials, merely summarizing and giving a comparative description of the leaps themselves: the croupade, the courbette, the ballotade, and the capriole. For, aside from the fact that only the gentlemen of the Spanish Riding School with their decades of experience are qualified to give detailed instruction on this subject, a rider who has brought his horse to so high a stage of gymnastic training that its schooling and natural talent indicate its readiness to attain the highest stage of the art—the manège leap—can really do without an instruction manual on the subject. The harmony between him and his horse will have reached such a state of perfection that the mutual feeling, refined to the uttermost, will be the best guide and counsellor for further training.

I. Levade—Mézair

The *levade* is practised between the pillars or with the rider dismounted after collection has progressed rather far.

It requires vigorous steps in the piaffe, from which the horse is called upon to make a manège halt by driving with the whip together with simultaneous reining-in. If the trainer's hand does not give way, the responsive horse will rear up in front, provided the hindquarters are strong enough to carry their load, to which the load of the rider must later be added.

Uniform contact is needed, with the leading rein during dismounted work along the wall and with the pillar reins during work between pillars, for this enables the horse (aided by appropriate side reins) to draw up its forelegs energetically, so that the hoofs appear to lie almost against its elbows. Only when its forelegs are sharply bent can a horse " sit " on its hindquarters in perfect equilibrium.

Once it is familiar with the levade in hand or between the pillars, we place a rider on its back as we did when introducing it to the piaffe. The rider remains wholly passive at first, the trainer exercising the control for the lift as before. All the rider has to do is to remain seated in the saddle gently during the levade, with the muscles of his small of the back braced and at right angles to the ground. Later on, the trainer will get into the saddle himself.

In the levade the whole load is borne by the deeply bent hindquarters. The deeper this bending, or "sitting", and the longer the horse can balance its body on its hind legs in this position, its spinal column making an angle of about 45 degrees with the ground, the more perfect the levade. The impression conveyed must be one of freezing into complete immobility, like a statue. The horseman endeavours to prolong this position by sitting quietly in the saddle, the small of his back braced and the reins held low. The horse must maintain positive contact with the bit just as it did in the preceding piaffe.

The levade should end with a gradual descent. Once the forehand touches the ground again, the horse should go into a piaffe at once. This piaffe, following directly upon the levade proper, proves that the horse was always under control. Moreover, this sequel frames the entire figure and gives it a classical stamp.

If the hindquarters are not bent as much as set forth above, the figure is called a *pesade*, which is merely a levade that failed. If the hindquarters are stiff and the forelegs are not drawn up, but thrash about as they hang down, we no longer see a classical figure, but merely a rearing horse.

The farther back the unbent hind legs are and, hence, the farther they are from the centre of gravity, the closer this rearing must approach the vertical and, therefore, the greater the danger of a backward somersault. For the hind legs can carry the load in equilibrium only if the *load* is balanced almost vertically above the point of support.

The *mézair*, also called *terre à terre,* is a levade combined with a forward advance. The smoothly successive jumps are produced by having the forehand alight briefly, followed by the leap-like alighting of the hindquarters.

The *mézair* is performed by having the horse fall back on its haunches after a gallopade, then rising on its hind legs after this full stop, descending again, impelled forward to another gallop leap, followed by another levade, and so forth. All these movements take place with the longitudinal bending required for galloping.

This figure, too, is first exercised with the rider dismounted and holding the reins. Later on, the rider must carefully attune his forward-impelling controls, which make the hindquarters jump after the forehand touches the ground, to the checking controls, which cause the forehand to rise.

This figure is particularly effective when changing lead while galloping in the ring on two tracks.

II. Courbette, Croupade, Ballotade, and Capriole

The *courbette* is one of the most difficult manège leaps. It is discussed here ahead of the other three, which differ only in their third phase,[1] because it is rarely exercised between pillars but usually with the rider in the saddle.

The procedure is approximately as follows: a piaffe, a manège halt, the lift. At the moment the horse rises, the trainer, who is standing below, applies his whip or switch to the horse's hocks. The rider assists by exerting vigorous pressure with his legs or using his spurs, while he holds the reins taut. The horse will then leap forward and upward[2] with deeply bent hindquarters and land again on the springy hindquarters, to leap again without letting its forehand touch the ground. A horse that is well trained in the courbette will be able to make four or five and even more such leaps in succession.

At the outset we will be satisfied with a single leap, of course. In this case, once the horse has landed on its hind legs in the same position from which it started its leap, we will exercise no further driving controls and will allow the forehand to alight by relieving the load on the hindquarters.

If several leaps in succession are demanded as training progresses, the sensitive rider must be able to distinguish clearly the final instant of the first leap, which almost seems to coincide with the initial moment of the next leap, in order to exercise his controls correctly and at the right time. At the last moment of the first leap, when the hindquarters are deeply engaged forward, the forward thrust is also partially effective; whereas only the elasticity and carrying power are manifested at the initial moment

---

[1] In the croupade the horse draws its hind legs completely underneath its body; it does the same in the ballotade, but in this figure the horseshoes are displayed as if for a kick. In the capriole it actually executes the movement suggested in the ballotade and kicks out as hard as it can.

The forelegs cannot remain drawn up when the horse lashes out, as we sometimes see in fanciful paintings. A pupil of Guérinière's, Montfaucon de Rogles, who was the only *écuyer* of Versailles to leave any writings (1778), gives definitions for the four manège leaps treated in this section that agree exactly with the notions prevailing today in the Spanish Riding School. Saumur, on the other hand, understands by the term "courbette" a pesade, that is (as now defined) rising on hindquarters that are previously unbent or inadequately bent; whereas it uses the term "croupade" for a non-academic lashing out of the hind legs with the horse resting on its forelegs. For the "capriole" the deputy chief of the *Cadre Noir* has the horse lash out only after its hindquarters have been raised so that its alighting resembles a steep landing after a low jump (also see General Decarpentry's *L'Ecole Espagnole de Vienne*, Compiègne, 1946).

[2] Applying the whip before the horse rises, while its forelegs are still grounded, would merely cause the horse to kick out, with its foreleg providing its support, instead of leaping as it should. If this exercise is done between pillars, only a single leap is possible, since the hindquarters advance as much as twelve to twenty inches in the courbette.

of the next leap: the rise forward and upward from the bent position of the haunches. That is why the opposing action of the reins should be so adjusted when performing a series of courbettes that the horse is prevented from grounding its forehand, though it is still able to perform the next leap when the leg control calls upon it to do as the hind legs alight.

The croupade is a preliminary stage of the courbette. It is a leap in place in the posture of the courbette; whereas the courbette is a croupade combined with a forward advance; in other words, it is a repeated forward leap in the posture of the croupade, the horse letting its elevated forehand touch the ground only after the series of leaps has been completed.

The croupade, like the ballotade and the capriole, is taught mainly by the dismounted rider or between pillars. The procedure is approximately as follows: from the piaffe the horse is called upon to perform a levade, and an energetic leg control is applied at the instant the horse begins to alight. Depending upon the horse's disposition and talents, it will either leap in a croupade or lash out energetically with its hind legs (a capriole) or perform a ballotade. In the latter figure it draws up its hind legs as soon as it leaves the ground, as in the croupade, but shows the soles of the hind hoofs, so that the horseshoes flash and we get the impression that it is ready to kick.

As training progresses with a rider in the saddle, he will make the hindquarters shoot out at the instant when the haunches give way slightly by employing a leg control supported by a click of the tongue. The reins give the horse the necessary freedom, but immediately resume their role as reins of opposition to prevent the forehand from alighting before the hindquarters.

As we have said, the leap becomes a croupade or a ballotade, depending upon whether or not the hind legs, which are drawn up immediately after they leave the ground, show their soles. In both leaps the horse's back approaches the horizontal, so that its forehand does not alight before its hindquarters.

Once the horse has managed to do the *capriole* without a rider or between the pillars, its rider employs the same controls as for the croupade or the ballotade. The sole difference is that just before the horse reaches a horizontal position in the air, a stroke of the crop on its croup, combined with clicking of the tongue, causes it to lash out with its hind legs.[3]

[3] Use of the crop, which has grown somewhat unfashionable in recent years as a result of its rejection by the Fédération Equestre Internationale, nevertheless remains a completely valid tool of the *haute école*. The crop promotes the horse's understanding when applied to

The more temperamental the horse and the more it naturally tends to respond to any use of the whip by lashing out, the better will its capriole be. Well-schooled execution of this most difficult of all the leaps also requires the greatest bending of the haunches at maximum collection; in other words, perfect responsiveness and compact conformation, with the extraordinary power in the hindquarters and the back helping to satisfy the demands made on the horse when it lashes out in the air, giving the impression of trying to tear itself in two.

Even among talented manège jumpers it is very rarely that we find a horse whose courage and confidence in its own strength embolden it to perform this most violent, highest, and most perfect of all manège leaps, and enable it to do so cleanly. Most horses will be able to perform only the ballotade.

Horses whose natural talents for the capriole have been carefully cultivated and whose pleasure in their skill has not been spoiled by over-exertion during exercise will soon look forward with a certain passion and impatience to the moment when their rider calls upon them to make a manège leap from a somewhat higher levade than usual after a preliminary piaffe along the diagonal.

A capriole in which the forehand rises somewhat at the instant the horse lashes out is more desirable, since the hind legs, which must have been drawn under the horse's body again to synchronize with the landing of the forelegs, then alight together with the forelegs, and the somewhat flexed, springy joints of the hindquarters help to take the impact and the weight.

If the horse does not lash out before it reaches the horizontal position, it cannot alight on all fours simultaneously. In this case the forelegs, which are grounded first, have to bear a heavy impact load.

It is a fault, though not unnatural, for the lashing out to take place with the hindquarters higher than the forehand (also see Footnote 2 on p. 314). This makes the premature landing of the forelegs, which constitutes an excessive strain for them, so much more unavoidable. It is also difficult for the rider to keep his seat during such an "upside-down" bouncing capriole.

One capriole that is high and performed correctly contains within it the germ of the next capriole, so to speak. The springs of the horse's

the shoulder for the levade, and to the croup for lashing out. Pressure of the rider's legs or a touch of the spurs, combined with and partially replaced by clicking of the tongue, should suffice to get the horse to spring up from the levade position in all leaps, since it is one of the principles of the classical school that no control should be visible. But the crop is indispensable to get it to lash out, at least at the outset, since it is better suited than the leg control to produce the natural reaction that lashing out represents.

On the other hand, since a horse executes only one of the manège leaps as a rule, the use of the crop may be dispensed with later on in the capriole, because the horse will always perform the manège leap for which it is adapted.

56. Capriole. Painting by Alexander Pock.

57. Capriole in hand.

58. Courbette.

haunches and hocks, which are highly compressed after a correct landing, will develop tremendous elasticity in the same direction from which the load produced the compression. That is why powerful jumpers are able to perform several successive caprioles almost on the same spot, continuing immediately thereafter with a piaffe or a passage.

The value of the manège leaps, especially the capriole, in training and perfecting the rider's "feel" in his seat should not be under-estimated. The rider must advance the small of his back and his hips gently in order not to land painfully upon the horse's back at the instant it lashes out. At the same time, however, his knees and legs must cling firmly to the horse; otherwise the extraordinarily deep breathing of the horse when it leaps would literally hurl the rider's knees and legs away.

The capriole is regarded as the top achievement of dressage because in it the two principal forces governing motion, carrying and thrust, are expressed to the utmost: the carrying capacity developed to the ultimate limit of physiological feasibility throws the entire weight of horse and rider upward, while the lashing out of the hind legs, as the release of concentrated thrust, restores the balance between these two dominant forces.

The ground covered in several successive caprioles should be as little as possible. If the rider does allow the horse to advance, it will be unable to keep its forehand in suspension long enough (as when it lashes out from the horizontal position), so that its centre of gravity is no longer close to the hind legs, and the forefeet will be grounded prematurely.

III. Summary of the Historical Evolution of Figures

Above the Ground

Like the parade step, to-day's passage, the Greek *haute école* also had a "rearing under control", the levade. Xenophon considered the passage to be academically correct only when the horse floated along, its hindquarters bent, and its steps supple, springy, well-timed, spirited, and lofty; he expressly rejected all movements forced out of the horse by false tensions. He insists that only when a horse rises upon its hindquarters freely, as it were, in response to the rider's control, is the lift of the forehand the most beautiful position a horse can take. Such a position is, he says, a splendid and marvellous thing, suited for the representation of gods and heroes, for it is then that the horse displays all its glory.

A collected gallop, as well as a sort of courbette, is shown in the Parthenon frieze. Apparently the Greeks tried to have an assistant on foot get the horse to leap by making its hocks react.

Most of the source material fell victim to the invasion of the Huns and other catastrophes of war, and academic equitation was completely forgotten after the Romans. It was reborn, like the other arts, only in the Renaissance. That is why we have to wait more than fifteen hundred years for authentic descriptions of the "newly discovered" academic rises and leaps in the *Ordini di Cavalcare*, published in 1552 by the Neapolitan Grisone.

The horse was supposed to raise its forehand to protect the rider against bullets aimed at him, while the capriole (from the Italian *capra*, goat, or *capriolo*, roebuck) was intended to wound a pursuing enemy. Pirouettes, passades, and counter-gallops were employed to seize the enemy's rear and flanks. We see that the *haute école* served a useful purpose at the time firearms were invented and hand-to-hand combat was still the rule.

In his book, dedicated to Cardinal d'Este, Grisone recommends that the lift (*posata* from *posare*, "to sit down", whence later *pesade* from *pesare*, "to weigh") should be taught after bringing the horse to a halt downhill. For we know that the pillars were first invented by Pluvinel, Louis XIII's riding instructor and Master of the Horse. Prior to that time the manège leaps (Grisone was familiar with the capriole and the courbette) were taught to horses tied up in the stalls. Later on, an assistant on foot drove the horse forward in the riding hall.

The German Löhneysen (about 1600) handles the material more systematically and understandably than his predecessors. He adopts Grisone's methods for achieving lifts and school leaps and draws a precise distinction between the vice of rearing and the *posata*.

According to Löhneysen, rising from bent haunches is the foundation for perfection in the *haute école*, as a horse's manœuvrability in hand-to-hand combat and its ability to show itself and its rider off to best advantage on state occasions are both based upon the lowering of its hindquarters.

Löhneysen also mentions the courbette, the rudiments of which he calls "sliding". He states that it evolves as a perfection of the lift, when spirited and powerful horses make a short leap forward from the levade on their hind legs.

Löhneysen calls Grisone's capriole a "curvet with lashing out". At that time landing on the forehand was considered desirable. Löhneysen was acquainted with the *mézair*, which we know as a figure halfway between a manège gallop and a courbette, subsequently called *terre à terre*, consisting of a rise and a forward advance, as the combination of two rises with an intervening leap.

Pluvinel, who died in 1620, stresses the tendency of certain horses to make the leaps for which they are particularly qualified by nature. He speaks of the mézair (which he calls "rocking"), courbettes, and caprioles, and states that ballotades and croupades are variations of the capriole at lower intensity.   He writes that he knew only four horses in France that could really do good caprioles; one of them was a prodigy of strength and endurance—it was able to leap twenty-four caprioles in succession.

Pluvinel reminds one of Xenophon when he warns against degrading horses to instruments without wills of their own.   Like the Greek, he looks for models in the horse's natural movements, which he proposes to refine without robbing them of their fluidity and natural charm.   He considers his best ally the good will of the horse.   He is superior to his predecessors and contemporaries, with their Cartesian denial that an animal has a soul, in his humane spirit that permeates all his doctrines and makes allowance for the psyche of the horse.   His methods, which are based on psychological factors and insights, are far ahead of his age.

The Duke of Newcastle exercised courbettes and *mézairs* (which he called "rocking", like Pluvinel) at a single pillar, while he practised "high leaps" by ruthlessly driving the horse against the wall.

Steinbrecht may have his own reasons for calling the duke one of the greatest masters and admirers of the horse that any country has ever known.   It is certain, however, that his methods, like those of the Neapolitans, were often designed to bend or break a horse, and thus suffer by comparison with those of Pluvinel.

Guérinière, who died in 1751, also made his contribution to the evolution of academic rises and leaps, though the greatest of his many achievements is undoubtedly the fact that he clearly realized the fundamental importance of responsiveness in general and in longitudinal flexion in particular and based a system of training on it (shoulder-in).   In his *École de cavalerie* he explains the levade as a preparation for the manège leaps; the *mézair*, "*moitié air*", as a figure intermediate between the manège gallop and the courbette (which it actually is as an advancing levade); and the capriole as a leap that resembles the tying of a knot.   Like Pluvinel, he knew of horses that could repeat the capriole without interruption as long as their strength held out.   He calls such a treatment of caprioles "leaps *à tempo*".

Seeger, a pupil of the celebrated Max von Weyrother at the Spanish Riding School, emphasizes the immediate usefulness of exercising trainers of utility horses in making academic leaps, using a manège saddle without stirrups.

Oeynhausen (about 1850) and Fillis (died 1913) differ with Seeger. Though both of them often advocated exactly opposite equestrian theories, neither was a friend of academic leaps.

Heydebreck (died 1935) and Josipovich (died 1945), the last representatives of classical equitation and the most authoritative interpreters of Steinbrecht's *Gymnasium*, warmly advocated the cultivation of academic lifts and leaps.   They regarded them as peak achievements, developed in accordance with a uniform plan of instruction and based upon a common foundation with the elementary field (cross-country) school, that are of gymnastic and plastic value in the education of highly qualified instructors.

To-day we still do not have complete agreement on the definitions of the various figures. This was recently demonstrated during the guest performances given by the Saumur *Cadre Noir* in various European capitals.

Many so-called " airs " are nothing but incorrectly performed distortions of classic lessons that have originated by accident. The often involuntary departures from the academic model were then given high-sounding names by their "inventors" and were eagerly booked as new achievement by industrious chroniclers. As a result we have a plethora of names for the same movement, depending upon the more or less typical irregularities that distinguish it from correct execution. For example, the conceited and high-sounding *piaffer balancé* with a literally broad-gauge and rocking evasion of the forehand or hindquarters to the side, wherein it differs from the academically correct piaffe, is nothing but a virtue made of necessity, though it is dear to many a circus rider as a display piece.

EPILOGUE

I SHOULD like to add a few words about the accumulated experience behind this book and how it was secured.

Many of the methods employed at the former Vienna Riding Instructors' Institute before 1914 were not accepted by me at the time without a certain inner resistance. I urgently wanted to observe the outstanding representatives of horsemanship in other countries doing their daily work in the saddle before reaching definite conclusions about the value of what I had learned at the Institute.

The years 1921-22, which I spent at Saumur, the citadel of French horsemanship, were a welcome opportunity to learn other methods which differed considerably from those I had used up to that time. They involved the application of principles that stemmed from the same roots, but had been interpreted and understood differently in Germany and France ever since the time of Guérinière.

I was captivated by the prospect of making an unprejudiced analysis of these differences between Teutonic and Latin equestrianship, weighing their practical effects in the light of the goal that was common to both schools. I wanted to reach a wholly independent judgment, uninfluenced by any other considerations, discarding any of the methods I had hitherto employed that could not meet the challenge of this new knowledge.

In spite of the many new and good things that I saw in Saumur, which expanded my equestrian horizon and kept me from becoming narrow-minded, I grew firmly convinced that the course of instruction that I had followed until then was the better one.

My stay in Saumur, followed by many voyages to foreign training centres and international horse shows, was extremely useful for my future activity as a horseman. After contrasting what I had seen abroad and tested there in the saddle, I was convinced of the superiority of the Teutonic school; after long years of wandering I returned to my father's house, that is to say, to the principles of my apprentice years as a horseman.

As the reader will no doubt have realized, the ideas set forth in this book are the result of careful weighing of the good as against the less good, and the author has not hesitated to reproduce tried and tested material in almost the same unexcelled form in which he was taught it. Some of these ideas, however, are inferences from newly won knowledge, which he largely owes to his unforgettable teacher, General von Josipovich.

Some concepts, which may perhaps make a slight contribution to the further development of our art, are the fruit of my own efforts and experience. The author publishes them as such, always ready to do justice to a differing opinion that is free from bias. For it really doesn't matter who has the last word. What does matter is that new truths and knowledge crystallize out of the clash of opinion, widen our horizons and supply fresh, healthy impulses to horsemanship. That is how we can best serve the cause so dear to all of us—our beloved art!

TABLE OF BASIC GAITS AND THEIR GRADATIONS[1]

WALK

Free Walk			Collected Walk
Free Walk with wholly surrendered reins (held by the buckle) *or with loose reins*, and later on with long reins. Used as a matter of principle during at least the entire first year of training. Later used to loosen the horse after mounting, in difficult terrain, and as a rest.	*Medium or Ordinary Walk* with reins adjusted to the framework of the individual ordinary posture.	*Extended Walk with wholly surrendered reins* (held by the buckle) *or with loosened reins*, the steps being as long as the horse's conformation permits without hurrying. The end result of all the basic training of the horse.	Like the extended walk, the end result of all the basic training of the horse. Can be developed to a manège walk, with increased engagement of the haunches and loftier steps of the forehand.

TROT[2]

Natural Trot	Working Trot	Middle Trot	Gathered Trot	Ordinary Trot	Extended Trot	Collected Trot
		Dressage gait.		End result of the posture, responsiveness, and impulsion secured at the three foregoing trots, and possibly at the collected trot. For practical use and use in the riding hall.	End result of gymnastic training. Only a dressage gait.	End result of gymnastic training. If the horse displays special talent, it may be increased to the manège trot.

GALLOP[2]

Natural Gallop	Working Gallop	Medium Gallop	Gathered Gallop	Ordinary Gallop	Extended Gallop	Collected Gallop
				End result of the posture, responsiveness and impulsion achieved at the three foregoing gallops, and possibly at the collected gallop. For practical use.	End result of gymnastic training. Ordinary and dressage gait. A freer carriage used oftener in cross-country riding than in training.	End result of gymnastic training. If the horse displays special talent it may be increased to the manège gallop.

[1] Described in greater detail in the text (also see number of steps per minute on p. 183).
[2] The various gaits are arranged from left to right in the chronological order of their employment in dressage training.

INDEX AND GLOSSARY

This Index and Glossary makes no claim to completeness, but it will often spare the reader the time-consuming job of wading through the Table of Contents. Some explanatory comments have been placed here to avoid weighing down the text too heavily.

The Index has thus turned into a minor lexicon, a *dictionnaire équestre*, which can often supply the answers to the reader's questions without reference to the text.

Higher, positioning inside hand (pirouette), 273

" Higher in front ", 152. *See also* Spinal column, Hindquarters, Bending of haunches

Hind feet, advancing beyond track of fore-feet, 216

Hind leg, coming up to the rein on the same side, 188; counter-gallop increasing suppleness of outer, 269; crossing outer—a fault, 196; evasion (crossing) of inner or outer—a fault, 196; greater load on inner (curved tracks) 167, 169, 193; inner, at the counter-gallop, 269; outer, in pirouette, 271; turning out, 207

Hind legs, automatic advance (dismounted training), 282; cow-hocked, 254; crossed—a fault, 30, 189n., 198; dragging-in young horses, 150, 261 (*See also* Hind-quarters *and* Strides); evade—a fault, 121, 157, 198, 261; evade to one side—a fault, 121; evade to rear—a fault, 121, 128, 157; evading the lead—a fault, 125, 184, 198-9, 303; extension, 129, 175; falling behind—a fault, 153; key to back action, 254; long and obtuse-angled—a fault, 253; rushing (taking shorter steps)—a fault, 206, 262; sickle-hocked, 254; spread (at the gallop), 182; springy, not abrupt, push-off in piaffe, 303; stiffened—a fault, 129-30, 161, 209; sustained in the piaffe, 301, 303; track very close together, 108, 118, 171, 180, 190, 291; tread far apart—a fault, 108, 182, 203; vigorous engagement, 182

Hindquarters, 26 et seq.; attuned to fore-hand, 117, 132, 151, 153, 172, 185, 188, 194; dragging—a fault, 32, 125, 130, 162, 183n., 206, 222, 263 (*see also* Hind legs); dragging—in natural posture, 205; engagement, 121, 124, 126-7, 129-31, 149-50, 152-3, 180, 189, 206, 269, 292; evade—a fault, 120, 170, 206, 248n., 320; evading toward the inside on a circle—a fault, 177; flexion, 129, 179, 270; flying upward at gallop—a fault, 209; forward reach, 127-9, 133, 157, 189, 274; interaction with back, 252n.; lowered, 110, 113, 125, 172, 181, 203, 206, 217, 261, 268, 282, 291, 305; pulled along by forehand (Spanish walk)—a fault, 257, 309; " remaining behind "—a fault, 31, 206; rising too fast in piaffe—a fault, 301; source of resistance and evasion, 122n., 222; stiffened—a fault, 176, 302, 305, 313; turning out—a fault, 104, 193, 198, 199, 271, 272;

turning out to a side—a fault, 86, 177; turning out towards centre—a fault, 177

Hip joint, horse's, bending, 171, 221, 260; point of suspension of hindquarters' load, 279

Hock, 31, 32, 97, 119; " turns " in bow-legged horses—a fault, 32, 254. *See also* Cow hocks, Sickle hocks

" Hog-backs ", 30

Holleuffer loop reins, 93. The reins help to keep the horse in the framework it has already assumed as the result of equestrian action. Otherwise they are an asses' bridge or a razor wielded by a monkey.

Hollowed inner side, 123

Hollowed rider's back—a fault, 57

Hoof, leaving the ground, 28, 66, 67, 139; cramped (piaffe)—a fault, 302; sluggish (piaffe)—a fault, 302

Hoofs, 28, 29, 37, 85-7, 118; breathing, 29, 86; care, 85-7

Horse avoiding a fall as it slips in a corner, 239

Horse dealer and his staff, 23, 25, 27n., 36, 39

Horse holding back, 131, 214, 244-5, 274, 277, 283, 300, 306

Horseman, born, 25

Horsemanship, definitions, 106; evolution, 105; natural, 106, 267-8, 309, 317

Horses for elderly gentlemen, 254

Horse shifting its weight when climbing, 231n.

Horseshoeing, 29, 74. *See also* Childeric

Horseshow judges, 36, 76, 106

Horse's legs, 28-9 et seq.; sticking to the ground in the piaffe—a fault, 302

Horses not ready for curb bit, 211-12

Horse's thigh, position, 31

Horse's willingness to let itself be driven, 115, 116, 117, 153, 156, 249, 283

Horse throwing its weight about in change of lead, 276

Horse throwing its weight on its inner shoulder in the pirouette—a fault, 273

Horse throwing its weight on its shoulder—a fault, 189

Horse thrown on its forehand—a fault, 224n.

Hounds, 244, 246

Hovering—a fault, 208, 291, 305

Hunting, 23, 60n., 73, 75, 243-7; test of constitution and temperament, 23

Hunting classics: Stonehenge, " Nimrod ", Whyte-Melville, Dincklage, Dale, Crich-ton-Hamilton, Comminges, Sassoon,